Macroeconomics
A NEOCLASSICAL INTRODUCTION

Macroeconomics
A NEOCLASSICAL INTRODUCTION

MERTON H. MILLER
CHARLES W. UPTON

THE UNIVERSITY OF CHICAGO PRESS
Chicago & London

The University of Chicago Press, Chicago 60637
The University of Chicago Press, Ltd., London

© 1974, 1986 by Merton H. Miller and Charles W. Upton
All rights reserved. Published 1974
University of Chicago Press edition 1986
Printed in the United States of America

95 94 93 92 91 90   5 4 3 2

Library of Congress Cataloging in Publication Data

Miller, Merton H.
  Macroeconomics : a neoclassical introduction.

  Includes index.
  1. Macroeconomics.   I. Upton, Charles W.   II. Title.
HB172.5.M48   1986   339   86–16028
ISBN 0-226-52623-2 (pbk.)

Contents

Preface, 1986

WE BEGAN this book in 1970 because we could no longer bring much enthusiasm or conviction to teaching macroeconomics along the then standard Keynesian lines. The largely ad hoc Keynesian consumption, investment and money demand macrofunctions were often in conflict with the better-motivated treatments of those same subjects that our students were seeing in their courses in price theory, labor economics, and finance. The Keynesian policy emphasis on 1930s style unemployment was becoming increasingly irrelevant to students coming of age in the booming 1960s. And even the academic true believers were finding a model built mainly for depressions hard to adapt to the growing concerns over inflation. Rather than try to patch up a creaking model, we proposed to start afresh.

As it turned out, our dissatisfaction with the Keynesian macromodel came to be shared widely throughout the profession by the end of the decade. The Keynesian hegemony was shattered in the 1970s.

Our then radically different approach to teaching macroeconomics is now much closer to the standard. The general theme described in our original preface—that macroeconomics should focus first on the determinants of aggregate supply under conditions of product and resource market equilibrium—is widely accepted these days, although our emphasis on neoclassical growth theory as a way of modeling the basic, full-employment economy may still strike some as idiosyncratic. In the section on public finance (chaps. 7 and 8) our focus on the allocative effects of tax and spending policies, rather than on their demand effects, anticipated much of the "supply side" thrust of public policy discussions in recent years. Our section on money (chaps. 9–15) went beyond the usual 1960s Keynesian treatment of liquidity preference by bringing in many matters now routinely covered, such as real vs. nominal interest rates, Fisher's law, the payment of interest on demand deposits, the dynamic form of the Quantity Theory, inflation as a tax, and the budgetary impact of open market operations. So too for our section on household consumption (chaps. 4–6), with its emphasis on consumption functions derived from structured Fisherian models of intertemporal resource allocation (notably the Modigliani-Brumberg life-cycle model).

To be sure, we would make further changes if we were preparing a new edition rather than a reprinting of the old. The '70s, after all, were a period of great construction as well as destruction in macroeconomic theory. It is clear now, for example, that if macrotheory is to be presented from its microfoundations, consideration must be given to the work-leisure choice as well as to the consumption-saving decision we emphasized. The basics of the work-leisure choice have long been familiar to economists (though much new material has been developed on human capital and on the economics of the household with important implications for macrotheory). Indeed, our computer simulation model had—and has—an endogenous labor supply function constructed in the same spirit as our consumption and money demand functions. For fear of putting too many balls into the air at once, however, we treated labor supply as exogenous in the text. For similar reasons, we decided against explicit treatment of the bequest motive in the text and the simulation model. This topic, which has come to figure so heavily in recent discussions of deficit financing, was relegated to an appendix to the chapter on the burden of a national debt.

A strong case can also be made for quickly dropping our assumption of a closed economy, as soon as the basic model has been presented. Even in our one-commodity world, it would be easy to connect economies to analyze some kinds of international capital flows of current concern as well as to introduce the monetary theory of exchange rates and interest rate differentials. The role of comparative advantage as the basis for international trade and exchange which is the focus of "real" international economics cannot be discussed, of course, in such single commodity models. Multiple commodity models, however, quickly become very complex. Our judgment then, as now, was that this complexity would be incompatible with a "broad brush" macroview of how an economy works and was best deferred to more specialized advanced courses.

Other concerns underlay the relatively brief allotment of space we made to issues of short-term labor market dynamics. In the early '70s, the short-run analysis of labor markets was in a state of flux which still persists despite the explosion of research in labor economics on contracting, both optimal and implicit, imperfect information theory, incentives, search, efficiency wages and the like. We tried to give some flavor of this newer line of research in our chapter 16 on the microfoundations of unemployment. But for the macrotheory of short-run unemployment in chapter 17, our treatment was closer to the older standard Keynesian formulation. We did manage to introduce an expectation-augmented Phillips curve, however; and we did warn of the stagflation nightmares it portended for policymakers.

We had hoped originally to do more with rational expectations than just our frequent references at critical points to Lincoln's law. We found, however, that a thoroughgoing treatment would have required more background in formal statistics than we could then reasonably expect from most students. Hence we settled instead on a mixture of certainty models with occasional unanticipated "surprises" which led to adjustment paths that we tried to make sure were at least not grossly inconsistent with rational expectations. Adjustment paths that would be in no way inconsistent with rational expectations paths might conceivably have been brought in without explicit use of stochastic terms by models with iterative convergence to the perfect-foresight adjustment path after each shock. Models of that kind are now routinely used in simulations of major tax regime changes. Computational limits ruled that out in the 1970s, and probably still do, despite the emormous recent increases in computational power.

These increases, however, and especially the widespread availability of personal computers, make access to a "hands-on" model of the kind underlying the text now much easier. A version suitable for IBM-compatible personal computers has been prepared and is available at a nominal charge from the authors.

Preface

THIS BOOK is offered as an alternative to the standard approach to teaching macroeconomics. That approach, all too often, leaves students with the impression that an economy, left to its own devices, settles into an equilibrium with substantial amounts of unemployment. Stagnation can be avoided if the government stimulates private spending or, more reliably, if it acts as the spender of last resort. Care must be taken not to overdo it, however. For then effective demand will exceed full employment supply and cause inflation. Macroeconomics, in sum, comes through essentially as a course in economic therapy stressing how the government can keep an inherently dysfunctional economy alive by a nicely timed sequence of transfusions and bleedings.

We believe that the course in macroeconomics should emphasize rather that a market economy left to its own devices will settle into a full employment equilibrium. External shocks, of a variety of kinds, will dislodge it from equilibrium from time to time, but the economy's internal defenses will speedily return it to equilibrium barring new shocks or actively destabilizing policies by the government. In special circumstances, government policies may speed the return to full employment equilibrium, but the scope for such policies is limited and temporary. Once the public catches on, fiscal and monetary stimuli lose their potency, though, not always, alas, their unpleasant long-run side effects.

Changing the emphasis dictates a corresponding change in the order of topics and the space allotted as compared with the standard texts. We begin with the neoclassical growth model that is usually relegated to the end of the standard course, if it is covered at all. The neoclassical model developed in Section One describes the full-employment equilibrium path of a growing economy with flexible wages and interest rates and serves as the backdrop for all subsequent discussion. The model is then extended successively in four subsequent sections entitled: Consumption and Saving (Two), Government Finance (Three), Money and the Price Level (Four), and Unemployment (Five). Some idea of the coverage can be gained from the brief overviews provided at the start of each of these major sections as well as the short annotated bibliography at its end.

Despite our use of the neoclassical model as the organizing principle, this book is and is intended to be a text in macroeconomics and not in growth theory, as both those terms are understood. We make no attempt to deepen the analysis of the simple growth model by incorporating such refinements as embodied technical change and vintage capital, nonneutral technical change, production functions other than the Cobb-Douglas or multi-sector models. We provide no discussion of the determinants of technological change or population growth, nor do we take up such esoterica as the reswitching problem, turnpike theorems or Von Neumann growth models. Instead, we work throughout with the simple one-commodity, two-factor model of moving, full-employment equilibrium in a closed economy, merely widening it, as it were, to bring it to bear on the particular class of problems that have come to be called macroeconomics — the effects of tax and debt financing, money and the price level, and unemployment.

The emphasis on growth does not mean that our concern is only with the long run. The short-run responses of the system and the immediate effects of government policies receive a considerable share of the attention throughout. Our heavy reliance on the Modigliani-Brumberg life-cycle model of consumption is in part an attempt to provide some of the detail about short-run behavior that gets suppressed in the basic neoclassical model. The same is true of our treatment of recently developed "search" theories of unemployment. But we have not attempted to provide a complete catalog of the adjustment lags often associated with discussions of short-run behavior.

We have managed to treat most of the standard topics in macroeconomics (including even some of the rudiments of national income accounting) within this widened neoclassical framework, but we have not always treated them in the standard way or with the standard vocabulary of macroeconomics. In particular, we have found no need in telling the story to bring in the marginal efficiency of investment, liquidity preference (though we do discuss the famous liquidity trap), the speculative demand for money, the interaction of the multiplier and the accelerator, the relative income hypothesis, built-in flexibility, or even effective demand; and we have given only passing reference to many other concepts such as the IS-LM apparatus (for which we have what we believe to be a more versatile substitute), permanent income, and the velocity of money. Our hope was that by pruning away unnecessary concepts and by treating macroeconomics as an extension of microeconomics the central core of the subject would come through more easily to the students for whom this book is intended — essentially undergraduate and MBA students taking a one-quarter or one-semester course in intermediate macroeconomics.

Although the neoclassical growth model is usually regarded as an advanced topic — which is perhaps one reason why it has so far had little effect on the teaching of macroeconomics — we have taken pains to present the model and its extensions in ways accessible to those with only very limited mathematical preparation. We make no use of the calculus, for example, except in certain appendixes which can be safely skipped without loss of continuity. We try to substitute explicit functional forms for implicit functional representation wherever possible (with due warnings about their special properties). And, instead of merely listing the system of simultaneous equations and relying on implicit differentiation for tracing out the interactions, we have developed a computer model of an imaginary economy built up from the underlying micro components described in the text. Simulation experiments based on the model are described in some detail at two critical points (Chapters 6 and 12). Knowledge of computer programming is not essential for following those experiments.

Insofar as possible, we have tried to set the basic parameters of the experimental models to produce numbers for the capital/labor ratio, the capital/output ratio, the saving/income ratio, the real rate of interest, the share of wages in national income, and so on that are of the same order of magnitude and yield the same "stylized facts" as those found in modern economies. We have, however, made no attempt to fit the models or their components to empirical data nor, with a few exceptions, to relate the experiments to particular real-world episodes or events. In the belief that the law of comparative advantage holds for textbooks of economics we have chosen to specialize this book to the task of expounding the neoclassical theory of macroeconomics in as clear and coherent a way as we could. In our classes, we do, of course, try to flesh out the bare bones of the theory by issuing a supplementary packet of assorted empirical readings, polemics, and "current events" material. And we would imagine that most instructors would want to do the same.

Any text by authors currently at the University of Chicago will inevitably be labeled (and in some quarters dismissed) as "monetarist." The basis of distinction between the "monetarists" and the "fiscalists" has never been entirely clear to us, but if an operational definition of monetarism is work that has been strongly influenced by the writings of Milton Friedman, then ours is certainly in that class. In fairness to him, however, we should emphasize that his contribution has been that of a capital input through his writings and not a labor input. We have not had the chance to discuss the material with him and none of our sins should be laid at his door.

The *cognoscenti* will also detect the strong influence of that rapidly growing body of work in the field of finance under the heading of the "efficient markets hypothesis." We have tried to purge basic macroeconomics of all results that would seem to leave opportunities for individuals to earn above-normal returns from mechanical trading rules or chart-reading (including charts of the money supply or of the National Bureau's leading indicators). We regret that we have not been as successful in this purging as we had hoped, but at least we have tried. Our colleague, Fischer Black, has been particularly helpful in keeping our attention focused on this class of problems and in suggesting ways out of the difficulties when we stumbled into them.

Michael McPherson and Charles R. Nelson gave us a detailed critical reading of the entire manuscript and we have incorporated many of their suggestions in the final version. Robert Clower, Lloyd Reynolds, B. F. Roberts, and Joseph Stiglitz, who also read the manuscript, were extremely perceptive in their comments and we greatly appreciate their advice.

A number of our colleagues have read and commented on individual chapters. In particular, we wish to thank Paul Breck, Walter Fackler, John P. Gould, Katherine D. Miller, and Jeremy Siegel. J. Phillip Cooper provided invaluable help in the early stages of devising the solution algorithm for the computer model of Chapters 6 and 12, and Gary Curtis did much of the programming for those models and for the conversational-mode version that we have used in our courses. Of course, we assume responsibility for any remaining errors.

A special word of thanks also to Mrs. Julius Schuster who did her usual outstanding job of shepherding the manuscript through the preparation stage, to Steven Manaster who prepared the index and to Mrs. Lowell Nelson who assisted in the proofreading.

February 1974

M. H. MILLER
C. W. UPTON

section one

The neoclassical theory of economic growth and production

MACROECONOMIC THEORY is abstract in its approach to economic questions, as indeed is economic theory generally. One cannot walk along a street and point to a "unit of capital" or to an "effective labor unit," to name two terms used throughout this book. But abstraction does not mean irrelevance; the issues to which macroeconomics addresses itself, such as the determinants of the standard of living, the effects of government monetary and fiscal policies, and the causes of unemployment, to name only a few, are real and important. The emphasis on abstraction represents rather a belief that much can be learned about important economic problems by stripping them of institutional detail and clutter, which often serve merely to confuse the main issues.

Chapter 1 takes up an early application of macroeconomic analysis to important social and economic issues, the Malthusian analysis of the relationship between population growth and the standard of living. Although the discussion has been restated in modern terms, this restatement primarily reflects changing tastes for exposition. The basic model is that of Malthus. This chapter shows how abstract models can be applied to various policy questions.

Despite its impressive historical background, most economists today regard the Malthusian model as of limited importance, partly because Malthus made too little allowance for technological change and partly because he overlooked the role of capital as a means of production. Chapter 2, therefore, turns to developing the more general model which is the basis of this book. This model, called the *neoclassical model,* emphasizes the role of capital accumulation and technological improvement in determining the standard of living. The development is continued in Chapter 3, which shows how wages and capital rental rates are determined in a neoclassical economy and how both are affected by technological change.

1

An introduction to macroeconomic reasoning: The Malthusian model

ALTHOUGH the phrase "war on poverty" dates from the middle 1960s, the concern of economists with the causes and cures of mass poverty is by no means so recent. In fact, from its very beginnings with the writings of Adam Smith, Thomas Malthus, David Ricardo and other "classical" economists of the late 18th and early 19th centuries, economics has focused on the forces governing the average standard of living and its growth or decay over time. The steps that a wise government might take to increase that average standard of living or to accelerate its rise have been a major preoccupation throughout.

A good case in point is the controversy over the Poor Laws in England in the late 18th and early 19th centuries. Like some more recent welfare programs in the United States, the English Poor Law of 1601 provided direct grants to the local poor to be financed by local property taxes. As distress rose throughout Great Britain in the wake of the Napoleonic wars, proposals were made to have these local grants and income supplements taken over by the central government and extended on a national scale. Proposals were also made for what today in many countries would be called "family allowances," or in the United States AFDC programs (aid to families with dependent children), with the motivation partly humanitarian and partly to encourage the production of future soldiery. Malthus believed these proposals, however well-intentioned, to be completely unsound and counter-

3

productive; and his justly celebrated essay on *The Principle of Population, As It Affects the Future Improvement of Society* was his attempt to explain why.

THE MALTHUSIAN MODEL

To make his point, Malthus constructed what economists would today call a *macroeconomic model*. In keeping with the standard practice of his day, of course, he presented his model entirely in discursive, verbal fashion, supplemented with occasional illustrative numerical examples, rather than as the explicit system of equations that the term model usually connotes today. But that is a matter of style rather than substance, and the main lines of his argument translate readily into the more convenient and compact modern way of presentation. As we shall see, economists no longer accept Malthus's analysis of the limits to economic growth. Nevertheless, his model has left an indelible mark on all subsequent modeling of economic growth; and its essential structure so typifies the macroeconomic approach that it remains the logical place to begin any study of modern macroeconomic theory.

The aggregate production function

Central to the Malthusian model is an *aggregate production function* of the kind pictured in Figure 1–1. The vertical axis measures what Malthus would call the total "means of subsistence" available to a particular country, measured in bushels or pounds or some other appropriate units. The horizontal axis measures the size of the country's population. The curve labeled $Y(N)$ is the aggregate production function and shows the maximum amount of means of subsistence that can be produced by any specified population, given the amount of arable land and other natural resources in the economy, and given the current state of the technological arts. Thus, when the population consists of N_1 individuals, the maximum total output for the economy is Y_1 units of subsistence per year.

What is critical about $Y(N)$ to Malthus's argument is not the actual numerical value of Y that goes with any given value of N, but the qualitative property of the direction of its curvature. As drawn, the curvature of $Y(N)$ reflects Malthus's assumption that

FIGURE 1–1
The Malthusian aggregate production function

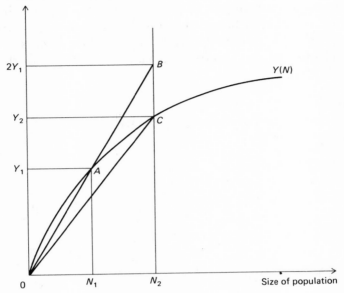

the production process in an economy with a fixed stock of arable land would be characterized by *diminishing average returns* to labor inputs. When the population is N_1, the total output will be Y_1, implying an average output per capita of Y_1/N_1, or equivalently, of AN_1/ON_1, the slope of the line OA. Let the population double to $N_2 = 2N_1$. If output per capita remained unchanged, Y would rise to a total of $2Y_1$ bushels per year. $Y(N)$ tells us, however, that output will only rise to Y_2 bushels, leading to a fall in the average output per capita (i.e., to a fall in the slope of the line through the origin from AN_1/ON_1 to CN_2/ON_2). The relation between average output per capita and total population implied by the aggregate production function $Y(N)$ is graphed in Figure 1–2 as the curve $y(N)$, where y equals output per capita. (Obviously, $y(N) = Y(N) \div N$.)[1]

---

[1] Here, and throughout, we shall adopt the convention of using capital letters to indicate aggregate quantities and lowercase letters to represent per capita variables. Thus, Y represents total output and y output per capita.

The Malthusian population growth function

The function $Y(N)$ of Figure 1–1 shows the relation between the means of subsistence and population with population as the independent variable. More population leads to more output, though at a diminishing average rate. Malthus argued, however, that another relation between Y and N also existed, in which the roles of the two variables were reversed. The means of subsistence became the independent variable and the size of the population the dependent one.

FIGURE 1–2

Average output per capita in relation to population size

Output of means of
subsistence per capita

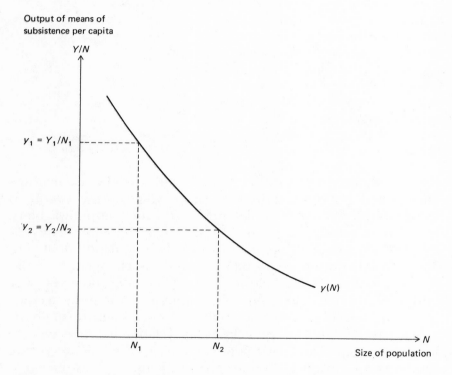

The relation between standard of living and size of population assumed by Malthus for this second function is shown in Figure 1–3A. The vertical axis now measures the rate of growth of the population in percent per year denoted by $n = \Delta N/N$, and the horizontal axis measures the average standard of living, y. As before, Malthus's argument hinges on qualitative properties of the function relating the two, rather than on the precise numerical values involved. What is critical is that the curve cuts the horizontal axis in only one place, that it cuts from below and that it has a positive but finite slope at the crossing point.

The forces that act on population to produce these properties are summarized in Figure 1–3B which shows birth and death rates per year in any given population as a function of the standard of living. The curve representing birth rates $b(y)$ is drawn to reflect the belief of Malthus and his contemporaries that birth rates were relatively insensitive to economic conditions. They were assumed to be governed mainly by what was quaintly referred to as the "passion between the sexes," which was taken as one of nature's constants, plus such deep-rooted and slowly changing customs as the normal age for marriage. Death rates, however, were regarded as much more directly related to the standard of living. At low average standards of living, such as y_L, famine, pestilence and related natural disasters take a heavy toll of the undernourished and weakened population. The death rate function $d(y)$ in Figure 1–3B lies above the birth rate $b(y)$ at that point, implying that the net change in population, shown in Figure 1–3A, is actually negative. Population is declining. At higher values of the standard of living, death rates are successively lower,

FIGURE 1–3A
Rate of population growth and the average standard of living

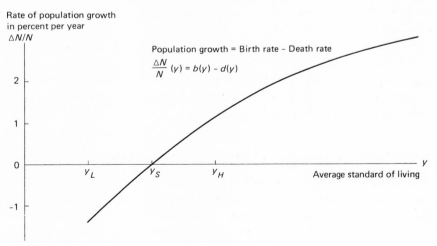

Rate of population growth
in percent per year
$\Delta N/N$

Population growth = Birth rate – Death rate

$\dfrac{\Delta N}{N}(y) = b(y) - d(y)$

y

Average standard of living

FIGURE 1–3B
Birth rates, death rates and the average standard of living

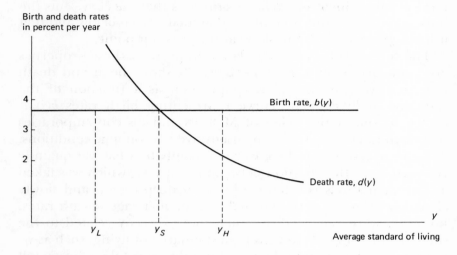

and at high levels such as y_H, death rates are less than birth rates. Population is increasing.

The curve $n(y)$, representing the net population growth rate, $b(y) - d(y)$, has been drawn to be asymptotic to the particular growth rate of 2.8 percent per year in recognition of Malthus's famous dictum that population, if unchecked, might double every 25 years. Growth rates of this magnitude have in fact been observed in some Latin American and Asian countries, but, as noted earlier, the force of the argument does not depend on the numerical magnitudes used.

Somewhere between y_L and y_H is a standard of living, y_S, in which the birth and death processes are just in balance. The standard of living is high enough to stave off starvation and to maintain the population at its then given size, but not high enough to permit further growth.

THE EQUILIBRIUM POPULATION SIZE AND STANDARD OF LIVING

Figure 1–4 portrays the interaction between the two Malthusian functions connecting population and the standard of living—the production function in which population enters as "hands," and the population growth function in which population enters as "mouths." The key to the evolution of the system is in the line *OS* which has been drawn with slope equal to the level y_S of Figure 1–3A. The line thus measures the total amount of means of subsistence per year needed to maintain any given population. If, for example, the population of a country were at size N_0, then the total amount of food and other means of subsistence necessary to keep population at this same size N_0 would be precisely $Y_{S,0} = y_S \cdot N_0$.

While the line *OS* (which is just the relation $Y_S = y_S \cdot N$) shows the minimum total amount of subsistence needed for zero population growth (ZPG, for short) for any size of population, the *actual* amount of the means of subsistence that would be produced by any population is given by the production function

FIGURE 1–4
The equilibrium solution of the Malthusian model

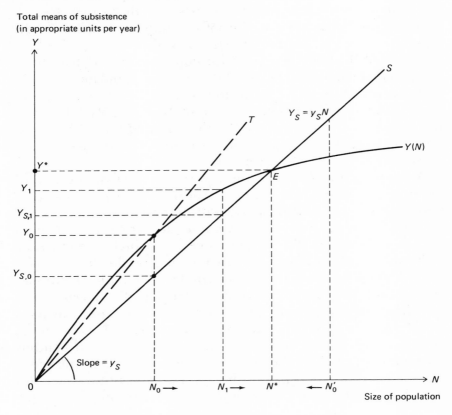

$Y(N)$. Thus when population is N_0, total output of means of subsistence is Y_0, which is greater than the level needed for ZPG. The average standard of living is Y_0/N_0, the slope of the line OT, which is clearly greater than (Y_0/N_0), the slope of the line OS. But by virtue of the mechanism summarized in Figures 1–3A and 1–3B, this excess of the actual standard of living over the critical value y_s implies an increase in population. Hence, N moves along the horizontal axis of Figure 1–4, away from the initial value N_0 in the direction indicated by the arrow. After some time has passed, population may have reached some higher value such as N_1. At that value for N, total subsistence requirements are now at the higher level $Y_{S,1}$. Actual total output has increased, thanks to the larger labor force, but less than proportionately. The margin of the means of subsistence per capita over the ZPG standard of living is smaller than before, but still positive. Again population grows, and keeps on growing in this fashion until a population of N^* is reached. At that size the actual average standard of living produced is just enough to maintain the population, and no further growth takes place.

Note that the same *final* value for population would have been reached no matter what its initial value. If the population had initially been N'_0, for example, to the right of N^*, then the movement of N would have been from right to left. At N'_0, actual output of means of subsistence is less than needed for ZPG. Starvation and disease cut population back, and that dreary process must continue until N^* is reached.

A point such as E, where the two functions cross and toward which the N values and Y values tend to return if displaced, is said to define the *equilibrium* values of the variables of the system. That word, here and throughout, is intended strictly as a technical term to indicate that the various contending forces are in a state of balance, and not to convey any notion of well-being, or goals toward which to strive. In fact, the equilibrium in the Malthusian model, as should be clear from the discussion of its mechanisms, is a wretched one indeed. The equilibrium standard of living is Y^*/N^*, just the bare ZPG standard of living level. This is a bleak enough prognosis of mankind's future to have earned Malthus the sobriquet of the "gloomy parson" even if he had pushed it no further. But when he and his successors went on to use his model to analyze various policy proposals for improving the condition of the poor, economics quickly earned the sobriquet bestowed on it by Thomas Carlyle of the "dismal science."

THE POLICY PRESCRIPTIONS OF THE MALTHUSIAN MODEL

Consider, for example, a proposal to improve the condition of the poor by better public health services such as, say, purer water supplies. To the extent that the purer water reduced the incidence of such water-borne diseases as typhoid fever, cholera, or dysentery, no one would deny that, in the immediate short run at least, such a program would serve to prevent much personal pain and tragedy. But a Malthusian would point out that a general lowering of the death rate has longer-run consequences as well. In terms of Figure 1–5A, the program amounts to shifting the death-rate curve from its original position to the new position indicated by the dotted curve. This shift in turn implies a corresponding shift of the population growth function in Figure 1–5B and, most critically, a shift to the left of the ZPG standard of living from the original level y_s to a new lower level, y_{s_1}. With less subsistence now required to maintain the population at any

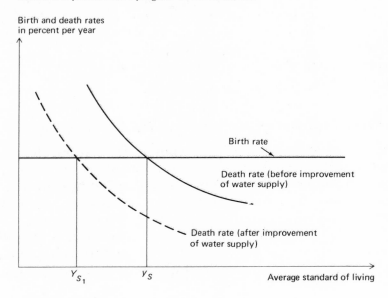

FIGURE 1–5A

Effects of a public health program on the death rate

Birth and death rates
in percent per year

Birth rate

Death rate (before improvement
of water supply)

Death rate (after improvement
of water supply)

y_{s_1} y_s Average standard of living

FIGURE 1–5B
Effects of lowering the death rate on the rate of population growth

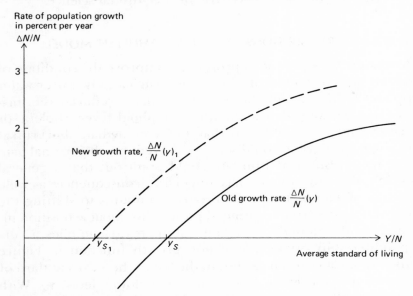

given size, the ZPG line in Figure 1–6 shifts downward from *OS* to *OS₁*. Population now begins to increase from its equilibrium value at *N** and the process continues until a new equilibrium is reached at *N₁**. Thus all that the public health program has accomplished has been to increase the total number of the poor. The standard of living, moreover, is actually lower and the conditions of life even more wretched than before the well-meaning but too short-sighted venture in health improvement was undertaken.

The effects of income redistribution in a Malthusian world

It was not lost on Malthus's contemporaries that not all members of society seemed to be suffering equally from the cruel mechanisms of his model. Side by side with grinding poverty for the masses was enormous opulence for a favored few, especially among the nobility and the landholding class generally. Observers in the late 18th century believed that the gap between rich and poor was not only wide, but steadily widening. Small wonder then that the air was filled with proposals for the redis-

FIGURE 1–6

Effects of an increase in the rate of population growth on the equilibrium size of population and standard of living

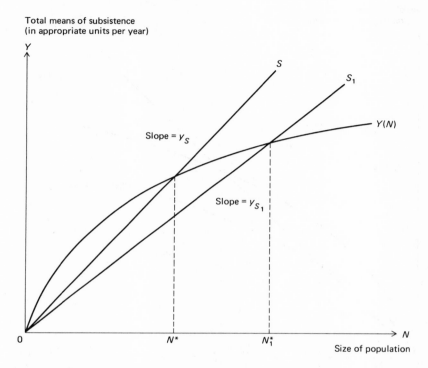

Total means of subsistence
(in appropriate units per year)

tribution of wealth from rich to poor, ranging from such relatively mild schemes as reforming the Poor Law to drastic calls to "expropriate the expropriators" along the lines of the then recent French Revolution.

The Malthusian model, with a slight extension, could be brought to bear on proposals of this kind as well. Figure 1–7 presents the extended version of the model. Below the production function $Y(N)$ is another curve $C(N)$ showing that part of the total production of means of subsistence that would be made available to the "laboring classes" under the workings of unfettered competition. Precisely how that share would be determined in a free market economy will be deferred to a later chapter. For the moment, the important point is simply that a distribution mechanism of some determinate kind is in operation and that it gives the poor less than the total output being produced. For

FIGURE 1-7
Effects of a revolution on the equilibrium size of population and standard of living

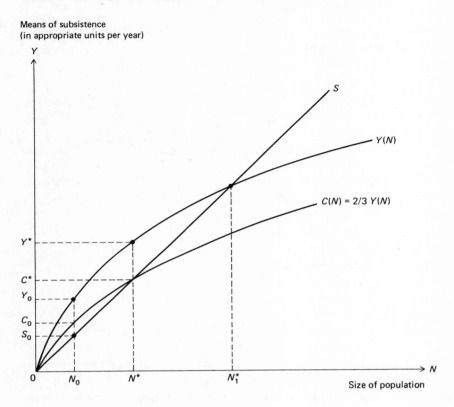

simplicity, the share of the workers has been set at two thirds of $Y(N)$ with the remaining third accruing to the landowners. Note that as N increases, the average output available per member of the working force declines (i.e., $C(N)/N$ falls with increasing N). At the same time, the *absolute* size of the share accruing to the landowners rises (because they are still getting one third of a larger absolute total output). Hence if their numbers, which are small relative to N in any event, do not increase as fast as those of the laboring poor—a proposition that Malthus and his contemporaries accepted—the per capita income of the landed will actually increase. Thus as population increases from N_0 to N^*, the rich get richer and the poor get poorer.

Suppose now that in the interest of social justice steps are taken to transfer output from the rich to the poor. For simplicity, suppose that the landowning class is wiped out completely so that labor's share rises from two thirds $Y(N)$ to 100 percent of $Y(N)$. Initially, such a redistribution clearly results in a substantial betterment in the condition of the working classes. The standard of living per worker rises from C^*/N^* per person to Y^*/N^*. Travellers would bring back glowing accounts of the success of the revolution in raising the standard of living of the common people. To a Malthusian, however, such tributes are premature. The initial improvement will simply lead to a more rapid rate of increase of population. Eventually the economy will return to a steady-state equilibrium at N_1^* where the standard of living is once again at the prerevolutionary level. Nothing lasting has been accomplished — except to extend the misery of a minimum subsistence existence to a larger number of people.

Was there then to be no escape from this cycle of misery for mankind? The best hope that Malthus could hold out was that population growth might some day come to be held in check through the exercise of "moral restraint" on the part of those in the procreative age groups. (By moral restraint he meant voluntary abstinence from procreation, not the sort of mechanical birth control or sterilization programs that present-day Malthusians tend to stress. Malthus, after all, was an ordained Anglican priest!) How such reductions in birth rates might affect the evolution of the economic system and the standard of living in an otherwise Malthusian model is the subject of some of the exercises at the end of this chapter.

WHERE DOES THE MALTHUSIAN MODEL STAND TODAY?

Although modern macroeconomics, as we shall see, uses an apparatus very similar in outward appearance to the Malthusian model just studied — which is, of course, precisely one of the reasons for starting with the Malthusian model — no leading present-day economist would claim to be a Malthusian as that term is currently understood. The Malthusians of today are found mainly among the biologists or ecologists. Nor is this interest on the part of the biologists entirely surprising, since Malthus's essay had a profound effect on his countryman, Charles Darwin.

What has led economists to reject Malthus's model as a description of the way an economy works is not merely that it is "too simple" or that the assumptions underlying it are "unrealistic." The accepted major theories in economics or any other field of scientific inquiry are always based on a drastic pruning away of surface "realistic" detail. There is no other way to get at the really crucial essentials.

What has led economists to reject Malthus's model is rather that they have developed a better model that explains more of the observed facts of economic evolution. Just as in astronomy the Ptolemaic, earth-centered model of the solar system was displaced by the Copernican, sun-centered model, so in economics has the Malthusian model been displaced by what has come to be called the *neoclassical model of economic growth*.

The neoclassical model accounts for two general classes of facts better than does the simple Malthusian model: those relating to differences in the standard of living of different countries today, and those concerning the evolution of the standard of living of particular countries over time. As to the former—or *cross-sectional* differences, as they would be called in economist's jargon—the Malthusian model predicts that high densities of population will be associated with low standards of living. (Remember that the population in Figure 1–4 was assumed to be put to work on a given total acreage of land, so that as N increases, so does population per acre). Certainly one can readily point to countries today in which these two properties do coexist. The Malthusian model may have been supplanted by a better one, but no one would claim that it is totally lacking in explanatory power. But one can also readily point to countries (such as Holland, Belgium, Switzerland or Japan) with higher than average densities of population and higher than average standards of living. In the other direction, cases abound in which an extremely low standard of living is found even without an exceptionally high population density. Mainland China, for example, has more than three times as much total land per capita and more than twice as much cultivated land per capita as Great Britain or Germany.

The Malthusian model also had a very gloomy prognosis, as we saw, for the evolution of the standard of living over time unless mankind somehow learned to curb its procreative instincts. Yet in the 170 years since Malthus's essay, the population of an even then seemingly crowded Britain has increased about fourfold. The increase in the average standard of living over the same interval is harder to quantify, partly because the component items in the standard of living have changed so drastically, and partly because we still have few reliable ways of measuring changes in those components of the standard of living (in the broad sense) that are provided outside the market economy. But such direct and indirect evidence as we have about rates of economic growth in Great Britain would suggest an improvement in the average standard of living of fivefold at the very least since 1798, and almost certainly more. (The basis for believing that a fivefold increase in the average standard of living is likely to err on the low side will become clearer in the chapters to come.) Nor has the experience of Great Britain been unique in this respect. Many countries in all parts of the world have grown as fast as Great Britain over the last 170 years, and not a few considerably faster.

To a convinced neo-Malthusian, these past examples of rapidly rising living standards despite substantial rates of population growth would be regarded as merely temporary deviations from the fundamental downward trend (just as the revolution pictured in Figure 1–7 led to a temporary rise in the standard of living). To economists, however, such an alibi for the failures of prediction of the Malthusian model would not be acceptable. It is not simply that they regard 170 years as a bit too long to be considered a temporary departure from trend in human affairs. It is rather that, as noted earlier, they can account for the discrepancies by specific processes not allowed for in the simple Malthusian version (which processes, incidentally, also hold out very different and far less gloomy prospects for further improvement in worldwide living standards over the foreseeable future even in the face of continuing worldwide population growth). The processes are those of *capital accumulation* and *technological improvement*. Britain may have less land in cultivation per capita than China, but it has considerably more railroads, refineries, factories and machines. Furthermore, the machines available to British workers today are many times more effective than those used by their counterparts in Malthus's day.

How these processes work to increase a society's productive

power and how they interact with population growth to determine the standard of living and its evolution is what the modern
neoclassical model seeks to explain. The development of that
model and its major implications is the task of the next two chapters.

PROBLEMS FOR CHAPTER 1

1. What effect would a lowering of the birth rate have on the equilib-
    rium standard of living in the Malthusian model?

2. At the time Malthus wrote, the amount of land under cultivation
    around the world was increasing; indeed, there was land in England
    not under cultivation. Yet Malthus believed that bringing this land
    under cultivation could at best only temporarily stave off the di-
    lemma. Using Figures 1-3 and 1-4, show the effects of a one-shot
    increase in the amount of land under cultivation — for example, by
    building a dam, and irrigating a desert — on the standard of living,
    and on population growth and population size both in the short run
    and in the long run.

3. One factor not included in the Malthusian model is technological
    innovation, an increase in the amount of output that can be ob-
    tained from any given inputs of land and labor. Using Figures 1-3
    and 1-4, show the effects of a once-for-all "Green Revolution"
    doubling output per acre on the standard of living and on popula-
    tion growth and population size both in the short run and in the
    long run.

4. A final factor overlooked in this chapter is the role of capital equip-
    ment. Again, using Figures 1-3 and 1-4, show the effects of a single
    increase in the number of tractors on the standard of living and
    population growth and population size both in the short run and in
    the long.

2

The neoclassical model
of economic growth

THE TERM "NEOCLASSICAL" is used in economics in a variety of
different, though related, ways. It sometimes refers to a particular
school of late 19th and early 20th century economists, mainly
British, but including also the French economist Léon Walras
and the Swedish economist Knut Wicksell. More generally, it has
come to be applied to models that take full employment of all
resources to be the natural state of an economy when its prices
and wage rates are flexible. That is the principal sense in which we
shall be using the term throughout the book. A particular case of
a neoclassical model is the neoclassical growth model discussed
in this chapter—a model whose precise formulation dates from
the 1950s in the work of the American economist Robert Solow
and the Australian economist Trevor Swan.

CAPITAL AS A FACTOR OF PRODUCTION

THE neoclassical growth model, like the Malthusian model from
which it is descended, takes human labor as one of two inputs or
factors of production in the aggregate production function. The
second factor of production, however, is no longer land but
capital, defined as productive resources whose supply can be increased by production. Thus capital differs from labor whose
supply is presumably governed to a considerable extent by biological and social mechanisms rather than by strict economic cal-

culations of profit and loss. And capital differs also from land and other so-called natural resources whose supply is presumably fixed, or, at best, subject to expansion in irregular bursts as a result of chance discoveries.

Clearly these distinctions between land, labor and capital are not airtight. In a slave society, labor is bred and sold in a process no different in any essential economic respect from that involved in producing buildings or machinery. In nonslave economies, the substantial investments that individuals (and their parents) make in education with a view to enhancing future earning power could well be considered capital. Land, too, can be augmented systematically by draining swamps, cutting terraces and the like.

In short, *all* productive resources are, in a fundamental sense, capital. The use of a two-factor, labor-capital dichotomy in the neoclassical model instead of a single all-capital model is not to be taken as a denial of this important insight — due, along with much else, to the great American economist and philosopher Frank H. Knight. The distinction reflects rather the view that the process by which the labor supply expands over time (or, at least, our understanding of that process) is sufficiently different in degree from that of most capital goods so that it is simpler and more revealing to pretend that they are different in kind. Recent research results have considerably illuminated the economic underpinnings of marriage and birth rates and thereby brought closer the day when a single unified model of economic growth will be available. That day, however, is still to come.

Since it involves two factors growing over time, the neoclassical model is inevitably more difficult to describe than the simple Malthusian model of the previous chapter. Our strategy will therefore be to proceed in a series of stages starting with simple cases and adding further details and extensions one step at a time. This chapter will show why an economy with a growing population and a growing capital stock will eventually reach an equilibrium and how that equilibrium differs from the Malthusian equilibrium. The route that we shall take to the equilibrium conditions will be somewhat longer and more circuitous than strictly necessary; but the equilibrium conditions are so fundamental to an understanding of subsequent chapters in which the same basic model and its extensions are applied in more complicated settings, that spending the extra time at this point should prove a worthwhile investment.

The productivity of capital

That the combination of capital with labor in a productive process can be profitable to the owners of the capital will hardly seem remarkable to present-day readers. To economists of the 19th century, however, the source of this profit was a puzzle, and elaborate explanations were offered to account for it. Karl Marx, for example, gave the title *Capital* to his three-volume tome, much of it an attempt to prove that the gain to the owners of the capital came from the "exploitation" of labor; that is, from paying labor less than the value of labor's contribution to the productive process. Later writers, notably the so-called Austrian School that flourished in Vienna in the years before the First World War, tried to counter the Marxian exploitation charge by locating the source of the productivity of capital in the supposedly greater efficiency of time-consuming or, as they put it, "roundabout" methods of production.

The great British economists of the period, notably Alfred Marshall—whose *Principles of Economics* provided much of the intellectual underpinnings of the neoclassical tradition—were content to leave to their continental confreres the philosophical speculations and the polemical battles over the reasons for the productivity of capital. They simply took the productivity of capital as one of the technological facts of life, no more requiring an explanation by economists than the fact that putting one kernel of corn into the ground can return a whole ear of kernels at harvest time. And that is essentially the position taken by economists today.

Consumption now vs. consumption later

More interesting than the question of why capital is productive is why the countries of the world have not long since taken advantage of this productivity to banish poverty once and for all. The answer is that just as population in the Malthusian model had two sides, "hands" and "mouths," so capital has two sides which might be called "consumption now" and "consumption later." A country can obtain more capital equipment to raise its future productive power generally only by diverting resources that would otherwise have been used to produce food, clothing and other items making up the current standard of living.

Sometimes a country may be able to postpone for a while this hard choice between consumption now and consumption later. It may, for example, have unemployed labor or capital resources that could be put to work; it may be able to dismantle monopolistic practices that hold down the amount of output obtainable from the current resources; it may be able to beat its swords into plowshares. But however desirable eliminating these wastes might be on economic and social grounds, it cannot be expected by itself to provide enough additional capital to avoid the problem of choice. The overwhelming bulk of any increase in a society's stock of capital and hence of its possible future consumption must come from a sacrifice of possible consumption today.[1]

The trade-off between consumption today and consumption tomorrow is so fundamental to the process of economic growth that it is worthwhile to consider an illustrative example of how the trade-off works before attempting to develop a formal model of growth.

The natural framework in which to construct such an example is that of the national income accounts. These accounts are essentially the counterparts at the aggregate level of the familiar income statements and balance sheets of standard business accounting. In fact, the aggregate national accounts are built up from the underlying standard accounts. This means, among other things, that the national accounts have the same "double entry" properties as ordinary accounting, a fact that will help to illuminate the two sides of capital in economic growth.

PRODUCTION, INCOME AND THE ACCUMULATION OF CAPITAL

The national balance sheet

Table 2–1 presents the opening balance sheets of an imaginary and highly simplified economy composed of three types of economic entities: firms, banks and households. In this economy the banks hold title to all productive capital equipment. The firms (or perhaps better, the entrepreneurs running the firms) lease

---

[1] Here and throughout we ignore the possibility of obtaining resources from abroad, whether by transactions between governments (foreign aid, reparations and the like) or between private individuals and firms. These complications regretfully must be deferred to more advanced courses.

capital equipment from the banks and hire labor services from the households. The households, in turn, buy consumer goods from the firms and hold deposits in the banks. Needless to say, these distinctions between the functions of the various sectors are much sharper than those in real-world economies—where, for example, firms typically own some or all of their capital equipment and where banks have to use labor and capital to service their deposit accounts. But the sharp distinctions simplify the posting of the accounting entries without sacrificing anything essential to the story.

These assumptions about the functions of each group are directly reflected in the pattern of assets and liabilities shown in the top three T-accounts in the table. Thus, firms, being pure producers and not owners, have no assets (or liabilities). The stock of productive capital is entered as an asset on the banking sector's balance sheet. The liabilities of the banks are in turn the assets of the household sector.

The accounts of each of the three sectors are *consolidated* accounts. They are obtained by adding up the assets and liabilities of each individual member of the group and cancelling out from both sides any claims of one member on another member of the

TABLE 2-1
Initial balance sheets (in dollars)

Households

Assets		Liabilities	
Deposits in bank	5,700,000	Net worth	5,700,000

Banks

Assets		Liabilities	
Capital goods	5,700,000	Deposits	5,700,000

Firms

Assets		Liabilities	
	0		0

The National Balance Sheet

Assets		Liabilities	
Capital goods	5,700,000	Household net worth	5,700,000

same group. Thus if household B borrows from household L, B's debt is L's asset and the two items will not appear in the final consolidated accounts. The same principles of consolidation can be extended to groups of sectors. Some interest may perhaps attach to the accounts of a "business sector" consisting of the combined banks plus the firms, or to those of a "nonfinancial sector" consisting of the firms plus the households. When the consolidation ·is made over *all* sectors, the result is the National Balance Sheet shown as the last set of accounts in Table 2–1. Note carefully what the entries consist of: the capital stock on the asset side and household net worth on the other. The asset entry is clearly the "consumption later" side of capital. The relation between the liability entry and the "consumption now" side of capital will become clearer after we trace out the records from a year's productive activity in the economy.

National income and national product

Table 2–2 shows the statements of receipts and expenditure during the year as well as the closing balance sheets at the end of the year for each of the sectors and for the nation as a whole. Thus we see that households purchased $1,600,000 worth of consumer goods from firms (entries 1 and 1′) and banks purchased $700,000 worth of new capital equipment (entries 2 and 2′). To produce this combined output of $2,300,000, the entrepreneurs running the firms used capital equipment for which they paid $570,000 in rentals to the banks (entries 3 and 3′). They hired labor services worth $1,530,000 (entries 4 and 4′); and they received the remainder of $200,000 as the return for their own entrepreneurial services (entries 5 and 5′). Meanwhile, the banks were paying interest to their depositors of $570,000 (entries 6 and 6′) and receiving new deposits of $700,000 (entries 7 and 7′) equal to the difference between total household receipts from all sources and total household expenditures. The receipts and expenditure accounts of all the sectors are now in balance.[2]

---

[2] The dotted lines in the accounts of the household sector and the bank sector separate transactions that national income accountants would call "income account" transactions from "capital account" transactions (those below the dotted line). The latter are transactions that change the ending balance-sheet value of some asset or liability item. The significance of the distinction will become apparent shortly.

The term *national product* is economists' shorthand for the total value of the national output. In the example of Table 2–2, national product so defined can be obtained directly by adding up the receipts side of the consolidated firm accounts, giving a figure of $1,600,000 plus $700,000, or $2,300,000. Note that we could have obtained the same figure in more roundabout fashion by going to the expenditure side of the accounts of the other two sectors and adding up the value of their purchases from the producing firms. Real-world national income accountants, who rarely have the complete coverage of the economy that we can build into our examples, have ingeniously exploited this double-entry property in the construction of their published series.[3]

The term *national income* is economists' shorthand for the "value of total factor inputs to the production process." The simplest way to measure it is to go directly to the consolidated firm accounts and add up the entries on the expenditure side giving $570,000 plus $1,530,000 plus $200,000, or $2,300,000 in total. It can also be picked up from the receipts side of the household accounts—a property of the accounts long a major tool of the taxing authorities.

It will surely not have escaped notice that the national product and the national income have the same value. The value of total output must equal the value of total input, just as total assets must equal total liabilities or total receipts equal total expenditures. In real-world tabulations of the accounts, however, this fundamental identity between national income and national product is not immediately apparent. The differences between national income and national product in the reported series, however, exist mainly because of complications that arise when a government sector enters the picture. Some of these complications will be touched on in due course in subsequent chapters. For the present, the important point, and the one that we shall be making use of re-

---

[3] You may be wondering whether this equivalence of the two approaches for measuring national product holds up when we allow for the production of raw materials and also for the production of goods that are not sold, but wind up in inventory. The answer is that it does hold up. You can see this immediately in the case of raw materials if you keep in mind that the accounts of the firms shown in Table 2–2 are the consolidated accounts for the sector. Production by one firm that is sold to another firm gets cancelled in the consolidation. Inventory is perhaps harder to see, but the essential clue is that inventory is merely a kind of capital. Some exercises on national income and product accounting with inventories and other complications are presented at the end of the chapter.

TABLE 2-2
Receipts, expenditures, and closing balance sheets (in dollars)

Households

Receipts		Expenditures		Assets		Liabilities	
Wages (4)	1,530,000	Purchases of consumer goods(1)	1,600,000	Initial deposits	5,700,000	Initial net worth	5,700,000
Entrepreneurial returns (5)	200,000			New deposits during year (7)	700,000	Net saving during year	700,000
Interest received (6)	570,000	Deposited in bank (7)	700,000				
Total Receipts from other Sectors	2,300,000	Total Payments to Other Sectors on Income and Capital Account	2,300,000	Final Total Assets	6,400,000	Final Net Worth	6,400,000

Banks

Receipts		Expenditures		Assets		Liabilities	
Rents received (3)	570,000	Interest payments to depositors (6')	570,000	Initial capital goods	5,700,000	Initial deposits	5,700,000
		Purchases of capital goods (2)	700,000	Purchase of capital goods during year (2)	700,000	New deposits during year (7)	700,000
New deposits by households (7')	700,000						
Total Receipts on Income and Capital Account	1,270,000	Total Payments on Income and Capital Account	1,270,000	Final Capital Goods	6,400,000	Final Deposits	6,400,000

Firms

Receipts		Expenditures	
Sales of consumer goods (1')	1,600,000	Rental payments for capital equipment leased (3')	570,000
		Wage payments for labor services (4')	1,530,000
Sales of capital goods (2')	700,000	Returns to entrepreneurs (5')	200,000
Total Receipts from Sale of Output	2,300,000	Total Payments for Productive Services Used	2,300,000

The National Balance Sheet

Assets		Liabilities	
Initial capital stock	5,700,000	Initial net worth	5,700,000
Net investment	700,000	Net saving	700,000
Final Capital Stock	6,400,000	Final Net Worth	6,400,000

peatedly in this and the next few chapters, is that the value of national output is equal to the value of national input.

Investment, saving and the accumulation of capital

The asset side of the national balance sheet in Table 2–2 shows that the economy's stock of capital grew during the year. The total capital stock at the end of the year is $6,400,000, which is equal to the beginning total of $5,700,000, plus the $700,000 of net new production of capital goods during the year. In the language of economics, such an increase in the capital stock during the year is said to constitute the economy's *net investment* for the year.[4] It measures the increase in the ability to produce and consume in the future.

The national balance sheet also shows that during the year the combined net worth of the households in the economy increased by $700,000. Such an increase in net worth is said to constitute the society's *net saving* for the year. It measures the consumption foregone this year. Note that we now have another fundamental identity, namely, that of saving and investment, to go along with our earlier identity of national income and national product. In fact, we can readily derive the saving-investment identity from the income-product identity, since

Saving ≡ Change in Household Net Worth = National Income minus Consumption

and

Investment ≡ Change in Capital Stock = National Product minus Consumption.

To say that saving equals investment tells us nothing, of course, about what the level of saving/investment will be. That will depend on the solution to the choice between consumption now and consumption later. As long as some part of current national in-

---

[4] The word net in this context means after allowance for any depreciation or wearing out of the capital stock that has occurred in the course of the year. The terms *gross investment, gross national product* and *gross rentals* are used for the corresponding totals before any allowance for depreciation. For simplicity, we shall work with the concepts in net form throughout the text of this chapter. Some exercises covering how the accounts are modified when depreciation is introduced explicitly are given at the end of the chapter.

come is being saved by households there is room to raise the immediate standard of living. But a reduction in saving means a reduction in investment and hence a reduction in the productive power available for generating consumable output in the future. And similarly in the other direction. As long as some part of current national product is being devoted to the satisfaction of current consumer wants, there is room to expand the capital stock and hence potential consumable output in the future. What conditions must be met if this process of capital accumulation via higher saving/investment is to be able to stave off the Malthusian nightmare? Under what conditions can the process lead to steadily rising standards of living? What is the maximum level and rate of increase of its standard of living that an economy can achieve? To answer questions of this kind we turn now to the more formal theoretical framework provided by the neoclassical growth model.

THE NEOCLASSICAL MODEL OF ECONOMIC GROWTH[5]

Like the Malthusian model, the neoclassical growth model starts with certain essentially qualitative assumptions about the production possibilities available to an economy at any point in time, given the state of the technical arts. They are assumptions about how national product would change if more manpower and/or capital equipment were available to the firms in the productive sector. Rather than simply listing these assumptions at this point, we shall adopt a tactic that we will be using repeatedly throughout the book, namely, that of introducing a specific mathematical function with the properties desired. Having a specific function will make it easier for you to test your understanding as you go along and to check the statements in the text by constructing simple numerical examples of your own where needed. The danger in the approach, of course, is that it may not always be apparent which conclusions are truly general and which are mere artifacts of the particular function being used. We shall try to alert you to these dangers in cases where they are likely to arise.

Many types of mathematical expressions have the desired

---

[5] A statement of the model and the main results in mathematical form is given in the appendix to chapter 3.

properties, and hence could serve as production functions for our exposition of the neoclassical model. The simplest one, however, and the one most frequently encountered in the neoclassical literature, is the so-called *Cobb-Douglas function,* named for the American economist (and U. S. Senator) Paul A. Douglas, and his mathematician collaborator C. W. Cobb.

The Cobb-Douglas function and its properties

The Cobb-Douglas production function is

$$(1) \qquad\qquad Y_t = A\, K_t^{\alpha}\, N_t^{1-\alpha}, \qquad\qquad 0 < \alpha < 1,$$

where $Y_t =$ total national product during year t,
$\quad K_t =$ the capital stock at the beginning of the year,
$\quad N_t =$ the size of the productive labor force available during the year,
and
$\quad A =$ a scaling constant to convert the physical labor and capital units on the right to the units in which national product is measured (e.g., from man-hours and from machine-hours to dollars of national product).

In principle, we might have put a time subscript on the scaling constant A as well, to allow for technological improvements that permit more output to be derived from any given level of inputs. For the moment, however, we want to consider only the simpler, special case in which the technology, such as it is, is constant and unchanging.

Note that while (1) is now a *two-factor production function,* unlike that of the previous chapter, it is still a *one-sector production function.* It assumes, in effect that a single "average" production function can be used to describe the production conditions for all the many different kinds of consumer goods and capital goods that make up the national product. Clearly, this is a heroic assumption. It should be taken rather as another instance of the strategy of suppressing the details (in this case the "product mix") so as to highlight the behavior of a few critical aggregates.[6]

---

[6] Multisector extensions of the neoclassical model have been developed as well as extensions with capital of differing types and vintages, but their mathematical foundations are too complex to be treated in this book.

Returns to scale.   A Cobb-Douglas production function of the form (1) implies, among other things, that a given percentage increase in capital and labor inputs simultaneously will lead to the same percentage increase in national product. Thus, if the inputs of capital and labor were to be doubled in any period t the total output would be

$$A \cdot (2K_t)^\alpha \ (2N_t)^{1-\alpha} = 2^{\alpha+1-\alpha} \ A \cdot K_t^\alpha \ N_t^{1-\alpha} = 2Y_t.$$

Production functions with this property are said to display *constant returns to scale* (or, equivalently, to be functions homogeneous of degree 1 in the inputs). If we had made the exponents on capital and labor α and α', respectively, with $\alpha + \alpha' > 1$, then a doubling of the inputs would have led to an output more than twice as large. Such a function would display *increasing returns to scale*. And, in the other direction, the case of $\alpha + \alpha' < 1$ would represent *decreasing returns to scale*.

The case of constant returns to scale is the natural place to begin any theoretical investigation of growth. Such direct and indirect evidence as we have on returns to scale at the level of the economy suggests that it is certainly reasonable as a first approximation. (We shall have a bit more to say on this point in the next chapter.) It also permits, as we shall soon see, some extremely helpful further simplifications of the model.

Returns to proportions.   In assuming constant returns to scale for our production function we are not abandoning the kind of diminishing average returns to labor that Malthus made central to his model. Recall that Malthus was considering a case where increasing numbers of workers were applied to a fixed amount of the other factor (in his case, land), whereas returns to scale tell us what happens when *both* factors increase. To distinguish the two situations, economists refer to the former as *diminishing returns to proportions* – the point of the word "proportions" being to emphasize that applying more labor to a given quantity of land raises the proportion of manpower to acreage, whereas no such change in proportions occurs when the process is simply scaled up or down.

That our Cobb-Douglas production function displays both constant returns to scale and diminishing returns to proportions is easily seen. Suppose, for example, that we take the opening capital stock K_t as fixed and ask what happens to average returns per worker as the number of workers increases. Dividing equation (1) through by N to get output per capita gives

(2) $$\frac{Y_t}{N_t} = y_t = (AK_t^\alpha)\frac{N_t^{1-\alpha}}{N_t} = (AK_t^\alpha)N_t^{-\alpha},$$

which is clearly a decreasing function of N.[7] The larger the work force applied to the given capital stock, the lower the average return per worker, exactly as in Figure 1–2 of Chapter 1.[8]

That what matters for diminishing returns is the proportion of capital to labor in the input mix and not simply that one or the other is taken as fixed, can be seen by rewriting the Cobb-Douglas function in per capita terms as

$$\frac{Y_t}{N_t} = y_t = A \frac{K_t^\alpha}{N_t} \cdot N_t^{1-\alpha} = Ak_t^\alpha.$$

Thus, even if both labor and capital are increased, but capital is increased by a smaller proportion than labor, the capital/labor ratio k_t will fall, and so will average output per worker. And conversely. If the capital stock available for the production process is increased proportionately more than the labor force, the capital/labor ratio will rise and output per man will rise. (Output per unit of *capital*, on the other hand, will fall when the capital/labor ratio rises. If it is not immediately apparent to you why, turn to exercise 4 at the end of the chapter before going ahead.) A relation between output per worker and capital per worker is pictured in Figure 2–1 as the curve $y(k)$.[9]

Population growth, investment and the capital/labor ratio

Granting that an increase in the capital/labor ratio raises output per worker, and hence also the potential average standard of living, how might an economy raise its capital/labor ratio? From the strictly arithmetic point of view, of course, the answer is easy:

---

[7] Again, recall that we are using lower-case variables to represent per capita variables. Hence y_t represents output per capita and k_t (below) the per capita capital stock or capital-labor ratio.

[8] Mathematically, $dy_t/dN_t = -\alpha AK_t^\alpha N_t^{-\alpha-1} = -\alpha\frac{y_t}{N_t} < 0$.

[9] It is the property of constant returns to scale that permits the production function relating the three aggregate variables Y_t, K_t and N_t to be rewritten in simpler form in terms of the two per capita variables y_t and k_t and not that the function (1) happens to be of the Cobb-Douglas form.

make the capital stock grow through investment at a rate faster than the rate of growth of population. For, if population should be growing at a rate of $\frac{\Delta N}{N} \equiv n$ per year and if the capital stock were also to grow only at that rate, we would have

$$(3) \qquad k_{t+1} = \frac{K_{t+1}}{N_{t+1}} = \frac{K_t(1 + n)}{N_t(1 + n)} = \frac{K_t}{N_t} = k_t,$$

and the capital/labor ratio would be unchanged. Alternatively, we could say that if a country can achieve an investment rate of only

$$I_t = n\,K_t,$$

or in per-capita terms, of only

$$(4) \qquad \frac{I_t}{N_t} \equiv i_t = n\frac{K_t}{N_t} = n\,k_t,$$

then it will be unable to raise its capital/labor ratio and hence unable to raise its output/labor ratio.

The particular value of i_t, to be denoted as i_t^*, that solves equation (4) for any given value of k_t is sometimes called the *capital widening* level of investment. The word widening is intended to convey in this context the notion of a capital stock that may be growing in absolute size, but only just rapidly enough to equip any new workers entering the labor force with the same amount of capital equipment per worker as available to the existing work force. By contrast, *capital deepening* requires a level of investment sufficiently large to permit an increase in the capital/labor ratio. The relation between k_t and the capital widening level i_t^* given by (4) is shown in Figure 2–1 as the line through the origin OA with slope equal to the population growth rate, n.

The line OA tells us only how much investment per capita is *needed* to maintain any given capital/labor ratio, not how much investment will actually be forthcoming. That will depend on the decisions made as to how much of the available output is to be consumed currently and how much is to be saved and invested. Precisely who makes these saving decisions in any country, and on what basis, will depend on the country's political and social institutions. The fraction of current output allocated to immediate consumption in centrally-managed economies is presumably

determined mainly by government directives of one kind or another. In countries that organize their economic activities mainly
through voluntary market transactions, the critical saving decisions are made separately by the millions of private individuals
who receive incomes (though, of course, actions by the government such as its tax policies often have a considerable indirect
influence on the decisions). At the present stage of the analysis,
however, there is no need for us to specify the process underlying
the saving decision. (The micro foundations of saving decisions
will be discussed at length in Chapters 4 and 5.) In fact, there
may even be some advantage in leaving the process unspecified
at this point. This will serve to emphasize that some of the important limitations on the standard of living and the rate of economic
growth are entirely independent of whether an economy happens to be organized according to "socialist" or "capitalist" principles. Let us therefore simply assume at this juncture that, by
whatever process, a certain fraction of current per-capita income,
say βy_t, is devoted to immediate consumption and that the remainder $(1 - \beta)y_t$ is allocated to saving and investment.

The equilibrium conditions of the basic neoclassical model

To trace out the evolution of the system from any starting value
for k_t we need only add to Figure 2–1 the saving/investment
function $(1 - \beta)y_t = s_t \, (= i_t)$ as in the curve OB. Suppose, for
example, that the initial capital/labor ratio is k_0 so that the initial
output per capita is y_0, the initial level of saving and investment
per capita is s_0 and the initial standard of living is $y_0 - s_0 \, (= c_0)$ per
capita. The capital-widening level of investment is i_0^*, which is
less than the actual level of investment i_0. The capital stock is
thus growing at a rate faster than the rate of labor force growth
n. The capital/labor ratio must therefore be increasing as indicated by the directional arrow to the right of k_0. (That is, capital
deepening is taking place.) Clearly, movement of the capital/
labor ratio in this direction must continue as long as $k_t < k_e$, since
the saving/investment function $s_t = (1 - \beta)y_t$ lies above the i_t^* line
over that range. Conversely, if the initial value of the capital stock
had been k_0' lying to the right of k_e, the saving and investment at
that point would have been insufficient to equip the newly entering workers with the same amount of capital as employed by the

FIGURE 2–1
The neoclassical model of economic growth

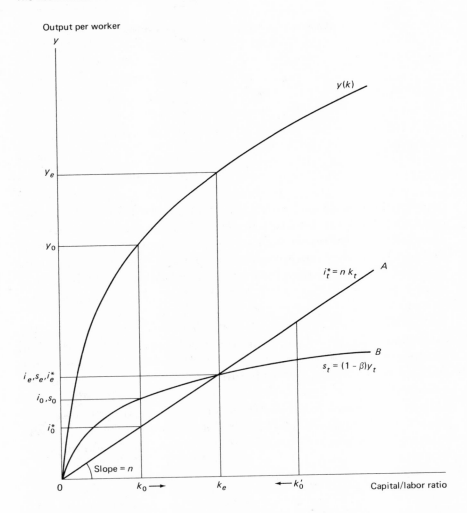

current labor force. The average amount of capital per worker will decline and must continue to decline as long as $k_t > k_e$. (Capital is "shallowing," as it were.) Thus k_e is the equilibrium capital/labor ratio and y_e, s_e and $c_e(= y_e - s_e)$ are the corresponding equilibrium values of output (and income) per capita, of saving (and investment) per capita and of consumption per capita.

An economy that has reached an equilibrium such as that pic-

TABLE 2–3

A numerical illustration of growth and equilibrium

| (1) | | (2) Capital stock | | (3) National product | | (4) |
| Year | Population | Level | Rate of growth | Level | Rate of growth | Saving and investment |
	$(N_t = N_{t-1}(1.05))$	$K_t = K_{t-1} + I_{t-1}$	$K_t/K_{t-1} - 1$	$Y_t = \sqrt{K_t} \cdot \sqrt{N_t}$	$Y_t/Y_{t-1} - 1$	$(S_t = I_t = .25Y_t)$
0........	1,000	16,000		4,000		
1........	1,050	17,000	0.625	4,225	.0562	1,000
2.:......	1,103	18,056	.0621	4,462	.0561	1,056
3........	1,158	19,172	.0618	4,711	.0559	1,115
4........	1,216	20,349	.0614	4,973	.0557	1,178
5........	1,276	21,593	.0611	5,250	.0555	1,243
25 :......	3,386	67,113	.0563	15,075	.0532	1,312
0........	11,467	253,280	.0533	53,893	.0516	3,769
quilibrium			.05		.05	13,473

tured in Figure 2–1 in which the capital/labor ratio and all other per capita magnitudes are constant—and in which, therefore, all absolute magnitudes such as the total capital stock, total national product or total consumption are growing at exactly the same rate as population—is sometimes said to be in a *Golden Age.* That poetic phrase is a way of emphasizing the harmony among the elements that such a nicely balanced growth path represents.

A numerical illustration. A numerical illustration showing the essential properties of the equilibrium solution and the path taken in reaching it is presented in Table 2–3. The population (column 1) is assumed to be 1,000 individuals in year 0 and to be growing at a steady rate of 5 percent per year thereafter. The initial value of the capital stock is $16,000 (column 2) so that the initial capital/labor ratio (column 6) is $16.00.[10] Total national product (column 3) is obtained from a Cobb-Douglas production function of the

---

[10] For simplicity, we shall continue to express K, Y, C and all other components of the income and balance-sheet accounts in dollar units as we did in Tables 2–1 and 2–2. In making comparisons between dollar totals at different points in time, we assume that corrections have been made wherever necessary for any changes in (1) the relative dollar prices of the component elements of any of the aggregates or their relative weighting and (2) the overall dollar price level itself. The problems involved in making the corrections of the former kind are those considered in microeconomics and statistics under the heading "index numbers." They will not be discussed further in this book except for occasional reminders that such problems do exist. Corrections for the price *level,* however, fall very definitely in the province of macroeconomics and will be discussed at some length in later chapters.

(5) Capital widening level of investment $I_t^* = .05K_t$	(6) Capital/Labor Ratio		(7) Output per worker		(8) Average standard of living	
	Level $k_t = K_t/N_t$	Rate of growth $k_t/k_{t-1} - 1$	Level $y_t = Y_t/N_t = \sqrt{k_t}$	Rate of growth $y_t/y_{t-1} - 1$	Level $c_t = .75y_t$	Rate of growth $c_t/c_{t-1} - 1$
800	16.00		4		3	
850	16.19	.0119	4.02	.0059	3.02	.0059
903	16.38	.0116	4.05	.0058	3.04	.0058
959	16.56	.0112	4.07	.0056	3.05	.0056
1,017	16.74	.0109	4.09	.0054	3.07	.0054
1,080	16.92	.0106	4.11	.0053	3.08	.0053
3,356	19.82	.0060	4.45	.0030	3.34	.0030
12,664	22.09	.0031	4.70	.0016	3.52	.0016
	25.00	.0	5.00	0	3.75	0

form of equation (1) above with the specific values of $\alpha = 1 - \alpha = 1/2$ and $A = 1$. Output per worker, which may be computed either as Y_t/N_t or as $y_t = \sqrt{k_t}$, is shown in column 7. The ratio of saving and investment to income, $(1 - \beta)$, has been set at .25 so that total saving and investment in year 0 (column 4) is 1,000, greater than the capital-widening level I_t^* (column 5), which is equal to the opening capital stock times the rate of population growth. Thus the capital/labor ratio rises in year 1 to 16.19. The higher capital/labor ratio in year 1 implies in turn a rise in output per worker (and, by the same token, a rate of increase in the total national product greater than the rate of population growth). The behavior of the average standard of living is shown in the last column. Note that it, too, increases as the capital/labor ratio increases, but that its rate of increase is always less than that of total national product because the level of the latter reflects the population growth rate of 5 percent per year, as well as the growth in output per capita.

The last row of the table shows the equilibrium values for all the growth rates and for all the per capita values. Since equilibrium in the neoclassical model involves an unchanging ratio of capital to labor and of all other per capita magnitudes, we know that the values of K_t, Y_t and C_t in the numerators of those ratios must be increasing at exactly the same rate as the population figure N_t in the denominator, namely, 5 percent per year. The actual per capita values themselves are easily computed from the equilibrium condition $s_e = i_e^*$, since we have

$$s_e = (1 - \beta)y_e = .25 \sqrt{k_e}$$

and

$$i_e^* = .05 \, k_e,$$

which together imply $.05 \, k_e = .25 \sqrt{k_e}$, and hence $k_e = 25$. Given k_e, we then have $y_e = \sqrt{k_e} = 5$, and $c_e = .75. \, y_e = 3.75$.

Note that the time required to reach equilibrium may be substantial. By year 25, for example, the capital/labor ratio has reached only 19.82 or about 80 percent of its ultimate value; and even by year 50 it has reached only 88 percent of the equilibrium value. The time path by which the capital/labor ratio rises from its initial value at period 0 is pictured in Figure 2–2.

FIGURE 2–2

Time path of the capital/labor ratio

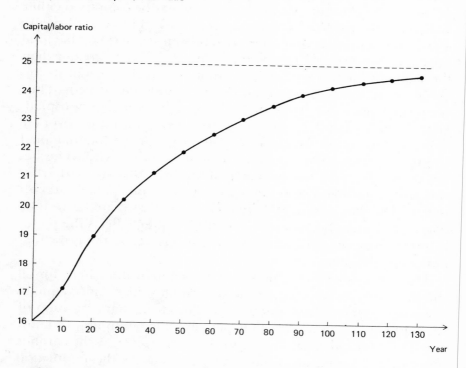

Comparison with the Malthusian equilibrium. Comparison and contrast of the neoclassical equilibrium with the Malthusian one can be instructive. The main similarity between the two models, of course, is that they both reach a steady state with an unchanging level of output and standard of living per capita. The neoclassical equilibrium, however, is reached even though population still continues to grow. The additional saving and investment each year provide the new workers with just enough new equipment to keep the law of diminishing returns to proportions from coming into play. The steady-state consumption level of the neoclassical model, moreover, is not a bare ZPG level. As can be seen from Table 2–3, the equilibrium standard of living under the assumptions given turned out to be nearly 25 percent higher than in the initial year 0, thanks to the considerable increase in the capital/labor ratio over the interval.

As with the Malthusian model, the fact that a steady state is reached eventually in neoclassical economies does not rule out the possibility of observing substantial differences in standards of living and growth rates of output between countries or in the same country over time. Citizens of the U.S., Canada, and western European countries generally, with high capital/labor ratios, need not be dismayed to find that growth rates are sometimes higher in countries less well-supplied with capital. And, by the same token, the citizens of these now rapidly-growing countries need not lament the deterioration of the national character when their growth rates taper off as their capital/labor ratios catch up with those of countries closer to equilibrium. (This tendency of differences between countries to narrow with the passage of time is a theme to which we shall be returning in later chapters.)

The neoclassical model predicts that countries with the same saving rate and same rate of population growth will ultimately have the same growth rate of national product and the same levels of income and consumption per capita. At the same time, however, it also provides, like the Malthusian model, apparatus for exploring whether and to what extent the eventual equilibrium can be affected by deliberate national policy. One such class of policies is that relating to population growth. The analysis of these, though interesting and important, holds few surprises and will be relegated to the exercises at the end of the chapter. Another class is policies relating to the saving/income ratio $(1 - \beta)$. Here some of the key results are sufficiently counter-intuitive to warrant some discussion at this point, before considering further extensions of the basic model.

The effects of differences in the saving rate

Consider two neoclassical economies similar in every respect except that one has a considerably higher saving rate. Which of the two economies will be growing faster in the long run? It is natural to suppose that the economy with the higher saving rate will be the one with the higher growth rate.

Figure 2–3, however, which presents the equilibrium conditions for both economies, shows that this supposition about saving rates and growth rates is false. The country with the lower saving rate has an equilibrium capital/labor ratio at the point k_e where its saving/investment function $s_t = (1 - \beta)y_t$ crosses the capital-widening line $i_t^* = nk_t$. At an equilibrium value of the capital stock such as k_e, the growth rate of all the *per capita* magnitudes is zero, and the growth rate for total national product Y_t, total consumption C_t, and the total capital stock K_t, is precisely n per year. But exactly the same growth rates will be found in the economy with the higher saving rate $s_t = (1 - \beta')y_t$ whose equilibrium capital/labor ratio is at k_e'. Its per-capita magnitudes are all constant at that point and its aggregate magnitudes are all growing at the rate of n per year. Thus we have the first of what might be called the neoclassical paradoxes of thrift: in the long run, a country's rate of economic growth, whether of per capita or absolute magnitudes, is independent of the fraction of its national income that it chooses to devote to saving and investment as opposed to current consumption.[11]

Efficient and inefficient saving rates. To say that the long-run growth rate is independent of the saving rate is not to say, of course, that the saving rate is a matter of no economic consequence. Though income per capita, for example, may be constant in equilibrium in both countries, it is higher in the country with the higher equilibrium capital/labor ratio. And this, in turn, must

---

[11] Note the necessity of the qualification "in the long run." An increase in saving function from OB to OB' in Figure 2–3 would shift the country's equilibrium value of k from k_e to k_e'. And, as we saw earlier, the growth rates of the per-capita magnitudes must be greater than zero and the absolute magnitudes greater than n while the economy is on its path to the new equilibrium (cf. Table 2–3). Furthermore, as we saw in the example, the length of the interval over which the growth rates exceed their equilibrium values can be a substantial one in terms of real time even though only a "short-run" phenomenon from the analytical point of view.

necessarily be the country with the higher saving rate. Is the same true for consumption per capita? Does the country with the highest rate of saving and investment and hence the highest equilibrium capital/labor ratio always have the highest standard of living in the long run? The answer is no, and here we encounter a second neoclassical paradox of thrift: sometimes a country may be able to raise its long-run standard of living by saving less, rather than more.

To convince yourself that such cases are indeed possible, consider the extreme situation in which a country saved all but a tiny

FIGURE 2–3
The effects of differences in the saving/income ratio

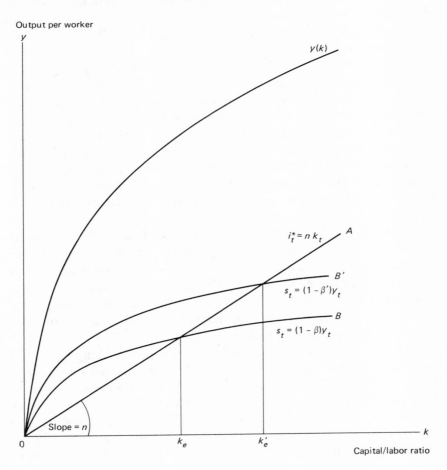

fraction ϵ of its income. In terms of Figure 2–3, its saving function would lie so close to the production function $y(k)$ that the two curves could not be distinguished from one another. The equilibrium capital/labor ratio for such a high-saving economy would be very far to the right, approximately where $y(k)$ eventually intersects the extended capital-widening line. The average standard of living would be represented by the tiny distance (equal to only ϵy) between the production function and the saving function at that value of k. Yet at the lower saving rate of $s_t = (1 - \beta')y_t$, the standard of living in equilibrium will be represented by the far from insubstantial distance $y_e' - s_e'$. Nor would it be necessary for the citizens of this country to wait until the new equilibrium at k_e' is reached to enjoy a higher level of consumption per capita. Cutting the saving rate back to $(1 - \beta')$ leads to an immediate increase in consumption as well as a long-run improvement.

Economists use the term *inefficiency* to refer to any situation in which a gain can be made at no cost. The self-defeating high-saving rates we have been considering clearly fall in this category since a reduction of the rates permits more consumption later without the cost of less consumption now (in fact, it even permits an increase in consumption now, as well). Are any of the world's economies currently in this unenviable position, or have any been in the past? For the nonsocialist economies, at least, we can be pretty sure that the answer is no, but the basis for this belief will have to wait until the next chapter.

Maximum consumption per capita and the Golden Rule. A more general picture of the conditions under which the equilibrium standard of living would benefit from a change in the saving rate is given in Figure 2–4. To keep the graph as uncluttered as possible, only the portions of the saving functions in the neighborhood of equilibrium have been drawn in, but the other functions are the same as in Figures 2–3 and 2–4.

Consider first the country whose saving rate brings it to the low equilibrium capital stock of $k_e^{(1)}$. Its equilibrium standard of living will be the vertical distance between the production function and the capital-widening line at that value of k (the line between the points labelled $y_e^{(1)}$ and $i^{*(1)}$). Through the point $y_e^{(1)}$ on the production function, the line IJ has been drawn parallel to the capital-widening line (i.e., with slope equal to n, the rate of population growth). The line IJ will thus indicate how much of any increase in equilibrium output per man beyond $y_e^{(1)}$ must be devoted to maintaining the larger capital stock per man required to produce the increase. Thus, if the saving function were somehow raised so as to lead to a new equilibrium capital/labor ratio at $k_e^{(2)}$, output per man would rise by the vertical distance $y_e^{(2)}F$ and the capital-widening level of investment per worker would rise by the amount JF ($= J'F'$ on the original capital-widening line). The remainder of the increase in production, $y_e^{(2)}J$, can then

FIGURE 2–4

The saving rate and consumption per capita

Output per worker

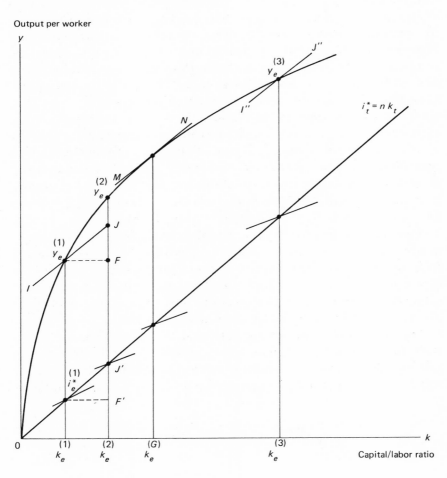

be devoted to increasing the equilibrium standard of living above the level attained when the saving rate permitted an equilibrium output of only $y_e^{(1)}$.

We know, of course, that increasing the saving rate will not always have so beneficial an effect on the long-run standard of living. An example of an inefficient saving rate of the kind discussed in the previous section is that leading to the equilibrium capital stock of $k_e^{(3)}$. Here increasing the saving rate would raise equilibrium output by less than the capital-widening requirements and consumption per capita would actually have to fall to maintain a higher equilibrium capital/labor ratio. Only by moving in the other direction and cutting the saving rate could the standard of living be raised.

Having seen that a movement from $k_e^{(1)}$ to $k_e^{(2)}$ would increase the equilibrium standard of living, we could start afresh at $k_e^{(2)}$ and repeat the reasoning, continuing in this fashion successively until we had found the value $k_e^{(G)}$. At that value, the auxiliary line *MN* with slope n is exactly tangent to the production function. Changing the saving rate in either direction will cause the standard of living to fall: increasing the saving rate raises capital requirements by more than the output increase and cutting the saving rate reduces output by more than the cutback in capital requirements. The capital/labor ratio $k_e^{(G)}$, where the slope of the production function exactly equals that of the capital widening line, thus provides the maximum long-run standard of living attainable under the conditions of the problem.[12]

The particular value of the saving rate that leads to the maximum equilibrium standard of living is often called the *Golden Rule* value because it succeeds in doing unto each generation as it would be done by. Once the Golden Rule level has been achieved, there is no higher level of consumption per capita that can be enjoyed equally by all generations.

To characterize the saving rate that leads to $k_e^{(G)}$ as a Golden Rule policy is not to suggest that a country with a lower saving rate should always try to raise it to the Golden Rule level. There will be more consumption later if the level of consumption today

---

[12] Mathematically, the standard of living will be equal to $y(k) - nk$, and this is maximized by choosing $k_e^{(G)}$, where $y'(k) - n = 0$.

can somehow be cut back (and cut back in such a way as to avoid damage to the incentives to work and to produce). But a cutback in current consumption will have to be made, and it is by no means clear that the generations adversely affected would feel the sacrifice worth making. We shall return to these issues of intergenerational equity in later chapters after we have described in more detail the main kinds of policy tools available for changing the saving rate in societies that rely on voluntary individual decisions with respect to saving and investment.

An extension to include capital depreciation

The discussion in this section has proceeded without any explicit allowance for the fact that capital wears out. However, it is an easy matter to remove that omission. For this purpose return to the distinction between *Gross National Product*, the total output of an economy and *Net National Product*, output net of the investment required to replace worn-out capital. We will suppose that annual capital depreciation equals a constant fraction δ of the capital stock. This assumption, the so-called capital evaporation model, is not the only one that could be made. Other assumptions, such as the "one-hoss shay" model,[13] make annual capital depreciation a function of the age of the capital stock. But the available evidence is consistent with the capital evaporation model and, since it drastically simplifies the analysis, we shall employ it.

In Figure 2–5, $y(k)$ represents gross output per worker and the dotted line labeled $y(k) - \delta k$ output net of depreciation. Gross saving/investment is $s = (1 - \beta)y$ and net saving/investment is $s'_n = s - \delta k$. The amount of gross investment required for capital widening is now $(n + \delta)k$, to allow both for population growth and capital depreciation. Hence the equilibrium capital/labor ratio is k_e where gross saving/investment equals the level required for capital widening. Gross output per worker is y_G and net output is y_N.

You will note that the equilibrium occurs where net saving

---

[13] See Oliver Wendell Holmes's poem, "The Deacon's Masterpiece; or, The Wonderful 'One–Hoss Shay.'"

FIGURE 2-5

Equilibrium with capital depreciation

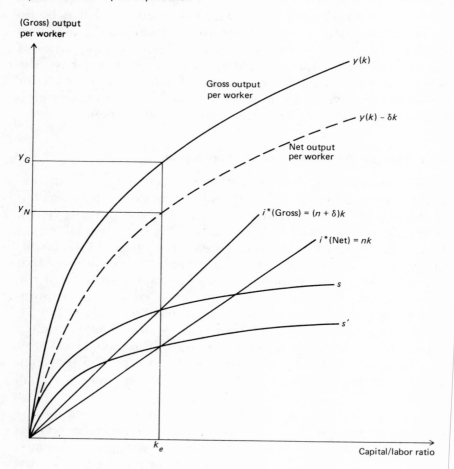

s'_n is also equal to nk. This is no coincidence, but we will leave the proof as an exercise.

PROBLEMS FOR CHAPTER 2

1. Recompute the entries in Table 2–2 if
    a. $50,000 of the "capital" purchased that year represents investment in inventory.
    b. $100,000 of the capital purchased that year was required to replace capital which wore out during the course of the year.

2. Using your numbers from part (b) of question 1, show that net saving and net investment are equal.

3. What will be the effect of a rise in the birth rate on the equilibrium capital/labor ratio?

4. Show, by rewriting the Cobb-Douglas production function in terms of output per unit of capital, that output per unit of capital falls when the capital/labor ratio rises.

5. Using the assumptions of the example of Table 2–3 (that the production function is $y = \sqrt{k}$), calculate the equilibrium capital/labor ratio if
   a. the population growth rate rises to 10 percent,
   b. the saving rate rises to 30 percent.

6. What will be the effect of a reduction in the capital depreciation rate δ on the equilibrium capital/labor ratio if
   a. net saving as a percent of net output remains constant?
   b. gross saving as a percent of gross output remains constant?

7. Show that when the neoclassical model is extended to include capital depreciation (as in Figure 2–5), the equilibrium occurs where net saving s_n' is also equal to nk.

3

Some further properties
of the neoclassical model

In the previous chapter we saw a number of quite remarkable properties of the basic neoclassical model of economic growth. First, we saw that even with constant population growth the capital stock per capita, output per capita, and consumption per capita reach an equilibrium level. Second, though the per capita values reach a stationary equilibrium, aggregate national product, aggregate capital stock and aggregate consumption will continue to grow indefinitely and at precisely the same rate as population. Third, the rate of growth of aggregate national product may differ in the short run from the rate of population growth. If the capital/labor ratio is below its equilibrium value, national product will grow for a time at a rate faster than that of population; but as the capital/labor ratio approaches its equilibrium value, the growth rate of total output will slow down until it eventually reaches that of population. And, of course, exactly the opposite happens when the capital/labor ratio is above its long-run equilibrium level. Finally, we saw that a cut in the fraction of national product devoted to immediate consumption, and hence a rise in the fraction devoted to expanding the capital stock by investment, will have no effect on the equilibrium growth rate of aggregate national product. That growth rate remains the same as that of population. The sacrifice of immediate consumption, however, will lead to a rise in the equilibrium value of per capita output in the future. It may or may not lead to a rise in the equilibrium value of per capita consumption. There is a maximum sustainable level of the standard of living, called the Golden Rule level, and once it has been reached further sacrifice of current consumption would actually be self defeating.

The key to these results lies, of course, in the capital/labor ratio. The denominator grows at the rate n; if current saving were large enough to permit the capital stock in the numerator to grow at a faster rate than n, then the ratio would rise and, with it, output per worker. In discussing this process, we have so far simply assumed that the available labor force and the available capital stock would both somehow always be utilized to the fullest by entrepreneurs. Hence to compute the effective capital/labor ratio in any period we need take only last period's starting labor force updated by any population growth and last period's capital stock updated by any net investment. In this chapter, we shall begin by taking a closer look at the mechanism that justifies such an assumption. Careful study of this mechanism not only yields additional insights to previous results, but sets the stage for further extensions of the basic neoclassical model. Some of these, such as allowing for new inventions and related improvements in the state of the technological art, are direct enough to be taken up in this chapter. Others require still further probing into the underlying mechanisms and are deferred to later chapters.

THE DEMAND FOR AND THE PRICE OF CAPITAL SERVICES

The mechanism that brings about the employment of the available capital resources is, in principle, a relatively straightforward one, at least in market economies. People go into the business of production with a view to making profits. They will keep hiring additional capital services as long (but only as long) as it pays them to do so.

Marginal productivity and the demand for capital services

Figure 3–1 shows the problem of deciding how much capital it pays to employ as it might appear to a potential entrepreneur. For simplicity, suppose that the only labor inputs required for the particular production process are those of the entrepreneur (whose labor thus constitutes the "fixed factor" in the problem), and that the production function is of our standard Cobb-Douglas form. Without loss of generality, we can regard our entrepreneur as contributing exactly one unit of labor (say, one person-year). Hence, we will be able to use the same symbol k to represent both the capital/labor ratio and the absolute number of units of capital. Suppose further that the capital goods needed by the entrepreneur are owned by a bank, as in Table 2–1 of the previous chapter, and that the bank charges a rental of r_0 units of the entrepreneur's output for each unit of capital rented.[1] The total payments to the bank for any given quantity of capital rented are shown by the straight line OA_0 with slope equal to r_0. The distance between the production function $y(k)$ and the rental bill OA_0 at any value of k thus measures the return to the entrepreneur. For example, when the number of units of capital rented is k_0, total output is $y(k_0)$, total rental payments are $r_0 k_0$ and the difference $y(k_0) - r_0 k_0$ is left to compensate the entrepreneur.[2]

In the case pictured, the entrepreneur can increase his return by renting more capital and producing a larger output. We can see that the entrepreneur's return is higher when k_1 units are rented by drawing the line ST with slope r_0 through the original output value at $y(k_0)$. The distance between $y(k_1)$ and V will then measure the increase in output. Of this increase, the amount VT $(= V'T')$ is required to pay the rent on the additional capital so the difference between T and $y(k_1)$ accrues to the entrepreneur. We can repeat the procedure for the new capital level k_1 to see whether a still larger capital stock would be profitable and con-

---

[1] For concreteness, it may be helpful to think of a unit of capital as a piece in an Erector set (or Meccano set, Tinkertoy, Lego, etc., depending on the country in which you spent your childhood). Having more capital units means that you can put together more machines of the same type or more complicated machines using more parts. This ingenious interpretation of the "malleable capital" assumption of the neoclassical model is due to the Australian economist Trevor Swan.

[2] We are here and throughout using the terms "entrepreneur" and "profit" somewhat loosely. In price and distribution theory profit is the reward to the entrepreneur for accepting the residual share of the earnings of the enterprise, and the uncertainties attaching thereto, in a world in which future demands and supplies cannot be forecasted perfectly. In our illustrations, profit is merely a hypothetical residual serving to illuminate the nature of the eventual equilibrium. Once that equilibrium is reached we shall see that there is no longer any profit residual; the entrepreneurs receive the same reward that they would receive if they had chosen to work for someone else.

FIGURE 3–1
The profit-maximizing level of *k* for a given value of *r*

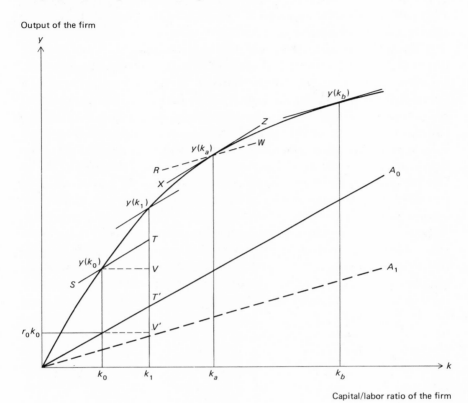

Output of the firm

Capital/labor ratio of the firm

tinue in this fashion until we finally reach the level k_a. At k_a the line XZ with slope r drawn through the output level $y(k_a)$ is exactly tangent to the production function, and it is no longer possible for the entrepreneur to raise his profit by a move in either direction. k_a, in sum, is the *optimal* or profit-maximizing value of *k*.

Suppose, however, that the bank had announced the lower rental rate of r_1 units of output per unit of capital rather than r_0 units. The new rental bill line becomes OA_1 and k_a is no longer the profit-maximizing level of capital for the entrepreneur. To see this, we need merely draw through the point $y(k_a)$ a new auxiliary line RW with slope equal to r_1. By reasoning now familiar, it follows that it would be profitable for the entrepreneur to increase the amount of capital used, and to continue to do so until the level k_b is reached. At that level the auxiliary line through $y(k_b)$ is again exactly tangent to the production function and the new optimum has been achieved.

An equivalent, but somewhat more compact way of showing how the optimal amount of capital for the entrepreneur varies with the rental charged by the bank is shown in Figure 3–2. The x-axis in Figure 3–2, as in Figure 3–1, measures the amount of capital used. The y-axis measures the slope of the production function at the particular value for k. Thus in Figure 3–3 — which is simply Figure 3–1 redrawn without some of the clutter — the slope of the production function at k_0 is $y'(k_0)$, the slope of the line tangent to the production function at $y(k_0)$. At k_1, the value of the slope is $y'(k_1)$ and so on, in principle, for every other value of k, such as k_a or k_b.

Economists frequently use the term *marginal* as a shorthand expression for the slopes of functions (because the slope measures the change in the y-axis variable due to an incremental or "marginal" unit of the x-axis variable). In the present case, with y

FIGURE 3–2
The marginal product of capital as a function of k

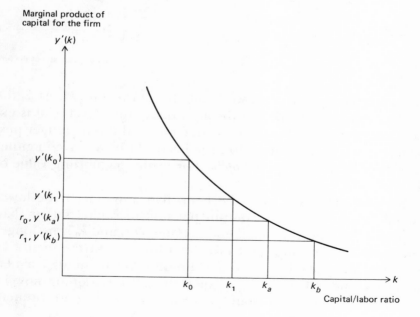

measuring production and k standing for varying levels of capital input, the slope $y'(k)$ would be called the *marginal product of capital*. The decision rule for the entrepreneur in Figure 3-2 could thus be summarized as the dictum: keep adding to the capital stock as long as the marginal product of capital exceeds its rental rate. If the rental rate is r_0, for example, move from k_0 through k_1 to k_a. If it is r_1, move on to k_b.

FIGURE 3-3
Marginal product and the slope of the production function

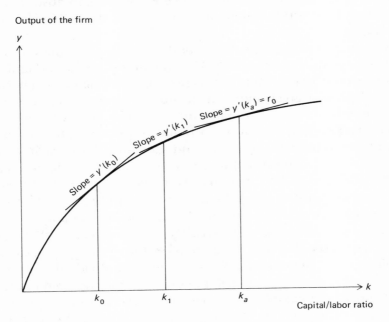

Output of the firm

The capital/labor ratio

The capital stock and the price of capital services

For the individual entrepreneur the decision problem, as we have seen, is how much capital to use at any given rental rate. For society as a whole, the roles of given and unknown in the problem are reversed. The total amount of capital available at any point in time is the given; the rental rate to be charged is the unknown.

In market economies, the processes that determine the rental price of capital services and the allocation of the given capital stock to particular firms are the same, in essence, as those governing the prices and quantities of any other commodity or service.

The prices adjust until the quantity demanded equals the quantity supplied. In practice, of course, these adjustments involve thousands of individual transactions in many separate markets, sometimes over a considerable period of time. In the particular case of capital goods, moreover, there are many quite complicated kinds of contractual arrangements by which the users of the capital compensate the ultimate owners. These details are often of considerable interest and are studied in courses in finance. For macroeconomics, however, the concern is mainly with the behavior of the aggregates, and hence we may again abstract away much of the institutional detail so as to focus more sharply on the essentials.

One expository device, frequently used in economics to bring out the essentials of the process governing prices and quantities, is to assume that all the transactions in a particular commodity take place at a given moment in time in a single central market presided over by an all-knowing specialist or *auctioneer.* The auctioneer's job is to call out a tentative price and to record the quantities tentatively offered and demanded by each of the market participants at that price. If the quantities demanded and supplied are not equal, he is to call out another price and to repeat the process until supply and demand are in balance. The price that equates supply and demand is the *equilibrium price,* and it is assumed that all transactions actually made are made at that price.[3]

In the particular case of the market for the aggregate stock of capital goods, the demand schedules of the individual traders will be marginal productivity schedules of the kind pictured in Figure 3–2. Strictly speaking, of course, no entrepreneur could enter bids for capital goods directly from the marginal productivity

---

[3] The tradition of substituting an ethereal auctioneer for an explicit description of how a market reaches equilibrium dates back to the latter part of the 19th century in the writings of the French economist Léon Walras. Walras referred to the successive tentative prices called out by the auctioneer as *tâtonnements* and the name has stuck, even in the English literature. Because the tâtonnement process is so vivid and because we shall be making such heavy use of it in subsequent chapters, it may be worthwhile to emphasize once again that any particular tâtonnement steps along the way to equilibrium that come into the discussion are to be thought of merely as figures of speech and *not* as attempts to describe the actual dynamics of price adjustment in a real world market. Some of the kinds of phenomena that can arise when we eliminate the auctioneer or at least severely curtail his ability to find the market clearing price are considered in Chapters 16 and 17.

schedule without some prior assurance that the output produced with that capital could in fact be sold. We shall therefore assume at this point that the appropriate assurances have been given and leave to a later chapter the story of how the auctioneer can deliver on these assurances.

We shall assume further that in our hypothetical economy all N members of the labor force are entrepreneurs, in business for themselves, and with production functions and marginal productivity schedules identical in every case to those pictured in Figures 3-2 and 3-3. We shall see later in this chapter that this assumption of an "artisan" economy, is much stronger than is necessary, but it simplifies the telling of the tale. It permits us, among other things, to represent in Figure 3-4A the aggregate bids for capital in response to any rental rate called out by the auctioneer by multiplying the corresponding quantities in Figure 3-2 by N.[4] The aggregate stock of capital is K_a, all of which,

FIGURE 3-4
The aggregate demand and supply of capital

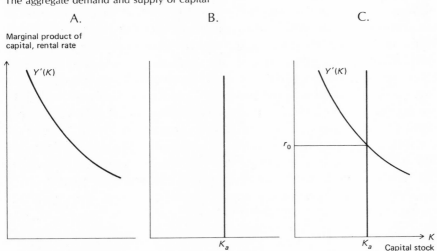

[4] Under the assumptions of the neoclassical model (constant returns to scale, diminishing returns to proportions and malleable capital), the demand curve for capital is necessarily a downward-sloping function of the rental rate throughout. In models with heterogeneous capital, however, cases can be constructed in which the demand curve for capital is backward bending, implying that lower rentals would actually be associated with less capital-intensive techniques. Such perverse cases (usually discussed under the heading of the "reswitching problem") have not so far been shown to be of any empirical relevance and are best deferred to more advanced treatments of growth theory.

it will be recalled, is assumed to be owned by banks and available for rental by entrepreneurs. The vertical line at the value K_a in Figure 3–4B is the supply function for capital. As drawn, it signifies the banks' intention to have their entire stock of capital out earning rental income at whatever rate the traffic will bear. Figure 3–4C, which brings together the demand and supply curves of Figures 4A and 4B, shows the equilibrium rental rate, under the conditions assumed, to be r_0 units of output for each unit of capital rented.[5]

The effect of capital growth and population growth on the equilibrium rental rate.   Figure 3–5 shows how the equilibrium rental rate would change in response to changes in the stock of capital, and in the number of worker/entrepreneurs. Panel A shows the effect of increasing the capital stock from K_a to K'_a while holding the number of worker/entrepreneurs constant at N. As can be seen, the additional capital all gets put to work, but it now takes a lower rental rate, r'_0, to clear the market. Panel B shows what would happen if the number of worker/entrepreneurs should increase from N to N_1, while the stock of capital remained unchanged. With more individual marginal productivity functions now making up the aggregate demand, the aggregate demand function shifts to the right. A higher equilibrium rental, r''_0, is now needed to get the original N entrepreneurs each to use less, and allow the newcomers to equip themselves. Panel C shows the results of a simultaneous expansion of both labor and capital. As drawn, it is a balanced expansion, with labor and capital increasing in the same proportion. (We know that the expansion must be a balanced one because the equilibrium rental rate is the same before and after, which implies that the marginal product of capital is the same and which, in turn, implies that the capital/labor ratio must also be the same in the two cases.)

---

[5] The scenario presented assumes that entrepreneurs incur no costs in adjusting their capital stocks up or down at the start of any period. If such adjustment costs exist, it may become economic for entrepreneurs to spread the adjustment of the actual stock to the desired stock over several periods rather than to make all the adjustments at once. Whether such costs are or are not assumed to be present at the *micro* level, however, will have no effect on the steady-state properties of the neoclassical model. The *path* of adjustment to steady-state equilibrium following a shock may well be somewhat different in the two cases. But there is no reason to believe that the differences are large enough to justify basing the macro analysis of investment on the considerably more complex model involving adjustment costs.

FIGURE 3-5
Effects of changes in K and N on the equilibrium rental rate

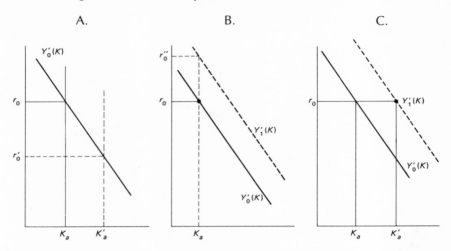

Marginal product, the rental rate and the neoclassical model.
How such changes in K, N and r tie in with our earlier analysis
of the neoclassical model can be seen with the help of Figure
3-6, which is essentially the same as the neoclassical model of
Figure 2-1 of Chapter 2. In that chapter, we could say only that
a per capita production function such as $y(k)$ described the production process for an "average" or "typical" firm. If, however,
we continue a bit longer with our assumption of this chapter of
an economy with N identical worker/entrepreneurs, we can also
identify $y(k)$, when the need arises, as the production function
of any (and every) particular firm.[6]

Consider first the situation when the economy has K_a units of
capital, N_a worker/entrepreneurs and hence a capital/labor ratio
of $k_a = K_a/N_a$. We know from the reasoning underlying Figure
3-4 that the auctioneer will be able to find a rental rate for capital,
call it r_a, at which all the capital stock will in fact be utilized. We
also know from the reasoning underlying Figures 3-1, 3-2 and
3-3 that the marginal productivity of capital in every firm will

---

[6] This is an assumption of convenience, not of substance. Even if every firm in
the economy faced a different production function, the principle of marginal
productivity would still govern the employment and remuneration of every
factor of production. It would no longer be possible, however, to represent the
full general equilibrium in a simple, two-dimensional graph.

FIGURE 3–6
Marginal product, the rental rate and the neoclassical equilibrium

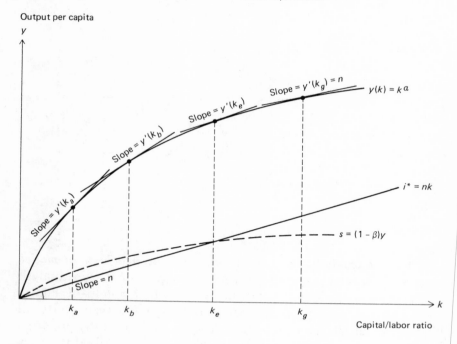

also equal r_a. Hence, in Figure 3–6, we can represent both r_a and the marginal productivity of capital in the economy as the slope of the tangent to the production function at the point $y(k_a)$.

At a capital/labor ratio of k_a, the saving function lies above the capital-widening line. The capital stock will therefore be growing faster than the labor force. From the reasoning underlying Figure 3–5 we know that the auctioneer will be able to get the new and old entrepreneurs to utilize the additional capital fully, but only by inducing them to do so with a lower rental rate. And indeed, as can be seen, the slope of the tangent to the production function at k_b is flatter than that at k_a. The rise in k and the fall in r will continue until k reaches its neoclassical equilibrium value at k_e. At k_e, K and N are both increasing at the same rate, n. Hence we would have a balanced growth in the supply and demand for the capital stock, of the kind pictured in Figure 3–5C, and r as well as k and all other per capita values would be constant and unchanging.[7]

FACTOR PROPORTIONS AND THE RELATIVE COMPENSATION OF THE FACTORS

Our discussion of the mechanism underlying the neoclassical equilibrium was carried out in terms of the convenient fiction of an "artisan" economy in which worker/entrepreneurs rented capital equipment. Suppose, however, we had considered an economy in which the roles were reversed; in which, for example, the labor was hired by the "banks" that owned the capital. In what respects would the story have been different?

Wage rates and the marginal productivity of labor

The answer is that, for the most part, the differences would be in wording, not substance. Figure 3–1, for example, instead of showing a typical worker/entrepreneur's profit-maximizing level of the capital/labor ratio for a given value of r, would show a typical bank's profit-maximizing level of the labor/capital ratio for a given wage-rate w. The production function would be of the same general shape—that is, it would be

$$Y(N/K) = A(N/K)^{1-\alpha} \text{ instead of } Y(K/N) = A(K/N)^{\alpha}$$

and the various auxiliary lines used to find the maximum would all have corresponding interpretations. Figures 3–2 and 3–3 would now show the marginal product of *labor* as a function of the labor/capital ratio, and Figure 3–4 would show the aggregate demand and supply of labor as seen by the auctioneer (whose task would now be to call out the equilibrium wage rate). Figure 3–5

---

[7] Figure 3–6 also provides additional insight into the so-called Golden Rule case that we were describing at the close of the previous chapter. The Golden Rule level of k, it will be recalled, is the one yielding the maximum equilibrium level of consumption per capita and is found at the point where the slope of the production function is the same as the slope of the capital-widening line (as at k_g in Figure 3–6). Using the terminology and results just developed in the previous section of this chapter, we can thus also characterize the Golden Rule solution as the case in which the marginal product of capital and the rental price of capital are exactly equal to the rate of population growth.

would then show how that equilibrium wage rate would change in response to changes in N and K.

Not only does the analysis proceed exactly in parallel in the two cases, but the conditions in Figure 3–5 are mirror images of each other. The labor/capital ratio of our second scenario, after all, is just the reciprocal of the capital/labor ratio of our first scenario. Hence, whenever capital increases faster than labor so that the capital/labor ratio rises (as, e.g., from k_a to k_e in Figure 6), the rental rate (and the marginal product) of capital must fall. But the rise in the capital/labor ratio is a fall in the labor/capital ratio so that the equilibrium wage rate (and the marginal product of labor) rises as the economy moves from k_a to its equilibrium at k_e.

The assumption of constant returns

Although the qualitative picture of the movement to equilibrium is thus unaffected by our choice of scenario, what of the quantititive magnitudes? Will the equilibrium values of w and r (and hence of the shares of labor and capital in the national income) be different in the two cases? The answer is that under our assumption of constant returns to scale, the equilibrium values of w and r will be exactly the same whether labor hires capital or capital hires labor or whether both types of industrial organization exist side by side. A rigorous proof of this proposition, unfortunately, requires sufficient mathematics that we have deferred it to the mathematical appendix following this chapter.

The assumption of constant returns to scale thus once again permits a drastic simplification of the analysis. Keep in mind, however, that it is necessary to assume only that constant returns be an acceptable approximation at the level of the economy as a whole and not for every (or any) particular firm. It may well be the case that if a particular firm, already of substantial size, were to increase in scale still further the consequent problems of internal communication and coordination might prevent a rise in output in proportion to the increase in the labor and capital inputs. Or, in the other direction, the firm may be operating at output levels so low that the greater specialization possible at a larger scale would permit a more than proportional increase in output. But there are ways of expanding output other than by expanding the output of firms already in existence. Industries can expand in scale by bringing in new firms of the same average size as those in place. And economies can expand in scale by bringing in whole new industries!

TECHNOLOGICAL CHANGE AND THE NEOCLASSICAL MODEL

Up to this point, all our discussions of the neoclassical model have proceeded on the assumption that the state of the technological art was given and unchanging. Differences in the specific *techniques* of production were allowed, of course, in the form of differences in the capital/labor ratio. A country with a high capital/labor ratio would build a road with a small crew running power shovels, dump trucks, steam rollers, and similar heavy equipment; a capital-poor country would have to employ an army of men and women with shovels and wicker baskets. But the only differences allowed were in the capital/labor ratio so that a given endowment of capital and labor would always yield the same total output no matter when that endowment was achieved.

The process of technological change

Despite the folklore surrounding particular inventions and inventors, the process of technological change in modern societies is mainly one of slow but steady improvement rather than a series of convulsive lurches following some particular "breakthrough." American schoolchildren are taught that Robert Fulton invented the steamboat in 1809 and often assume from that fact (or supposed fact) that sailing thereafter was confined to regattas. But it was only gradually that steam displaced sail, first in areas where sail was least effective such as on inland waterways, then in areas where speed was worth a premium such as mail and passenger traffic, and finally, but not until the end of the century, in general ocean cargo carriage.

A process of steady diffusion of new technology of this kind is similar in many respects to the steady growth of population, and economists often find it useful to model the two in a very similar way. That is, technological change is treated in much of the elementary discussion of economic growth as essentially a trend, governed by forces *exogenous* to (i.e., coming from outside) the model. And a trend, moreover, that serves to increase the *effective* labor supply in much the same way that population growth increases the actual labor supply.

The neoclassical equilibrium with technological change

Figure 3–7 shows the neoclassical equilibrium in the presence of technological change of this kind. The capital/labor ratio and all other per capita variables are now to be interpreted as *per effective labor unit* rather than as per worker, but in all other respects, the variables and functions have the same meanings as before. The only difference, though it is an important one, from all the previous graphs of the neoclassical model, is the value of the slope of the capital-widening line. To keep the ratio of capital to *effective* labor units constant in the face of the continuing technological growth requires more investment than needed simply to maintain a constant level of capital per worker.

FIGURE 3–7
The neoclassical equilibrium with technological change

Output per effective labor unit

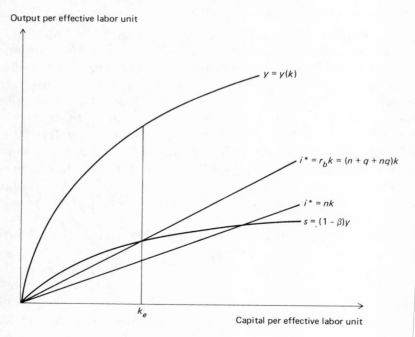

$y = y(k)$

$i^* = r_b k = (n + q + nq)k$

$i^* = nk$

$s = (1 - \beta)y$

k_e

Capital per effective labor unit

In particular, suppose that the rate of technological improvement, denoted hereafter by q, was 10 percent per annum at a time when the rate of population growth n was, say, 5 percent per annum. Then the number of effective labor units in the economy in any year, N_t^*, would be growing at the rate $(1 + n)(1 + q) - 1 = n + q + nq = 15.5$ percent per year. This rate, the equilibrium growth rate, is often called the *biological interest rate*. We shall denote it hereafter with the symbol r_b.

The equilibrium pictured in Figure 3–7 is similar to that considered for the basic model in that k_e, y_e, s_e, i_e and c_e are all constant and unchanging. But since the constancy is now in terms of *effective* labor units, which grow at the biological interest rate of $r_b = n + q + nq$ per year rather than in terms of *actual* labor units which grow at the rate of only n per year, we know that income, saving and consumption per actual worker must actually be *increasing* over time at the rate of q per year. That is, in equilibrium we will have

$$\frac{C_t}{N_t^*} = \frac{C_{t-1}}{N_{t-1}^*}, \text{ but } \frac{C_t}{N_t} = \frac{C_{t-1}(1 + r_b)}{N_{t-1}(1 + n)} = \frac{C_{t-1}}{N_{t-1}}(1 + q).$$

Technological change, in sum, makes it possible to more than merely stave off Malthus. It also can lead to a steadily rising level of income and consumption per capita. Indeed, in any society in which population is growing, it is the *only* force, in the long run, that can sustain a continually increasing standard of living.

APPENDIX TO CHAPTER 3
MATHEMATICAL PROPERTIES OF THE NEOCLASSICAL MODEL

It is useful to restate some of the results of Chapters 2 and 3 in simple mathematics. We will again use the Cobb-Douglas production function,

$$Y = K^\alpha (N^*)^{1-\alpha},$$

where $Y =$ output, $K =$ capital stock, and $N^* =$ effective labor units.

Equilibrium growth rate

The first property is the equilibrium growth rate. Taking the total differential of the production function, we find

$$dY = \alpha \frac{Y}{K} dK + (1 - \alpha) \frac{Y}{N*} dN*,$$

and with respect to time,

$$\frac{dY}{dt} \frac{1}{Y} = +\alpha \frac{dK}{dt} \frac{1}{K} + (1 - \alpha) \frac{dN*}{dt} \frac{1}{N*}.$$

Now, $\frac{dN*}{dt} \frac{1}{N*}$ is simply the rate of growth of the effective labor force, both from population growth and technological change; we will let it be given by $n + q$,[8] where n represents the growth from population and q from technological change. The term $\frac{dK}{dt} \frac{1}{K}$ is the rate of growth of the capital stock. As we have already seen graphically (and will show mathematically in a moment), in equilibrium the growth rate of the capital stock must be equal to that of output. If we let r_b, the biological interest rate, represent the equilibrium growth rate of the capital stock and output, we can see that this rate is given by

$$r_b = \alpha r_b + (1 - \alpha) (n + q),$$

or simplifying,

$$r_b = n + q.$$

Note that the equilibrium rate does not depend on the saving rate. Investment equals $\frac{dK}{dt} = (1 - \beta)Y$. The growth rate of the capital stock is given by

$$\frac{dK}{dt} \frac{1}{K} = (1 - \beta) \left(\frac{Y}{K}\right)$$

This rate is constant over time if

$$\frac{d}{dt} \left(\frac{dK}{dt} \frac{1}{K}\right) = 0$$

and this is true only if

$$(1 - \beta) \left(\frac{dY}{dt} \frac{1}{K} - \frac{Y}{K^2} \frac{dK}{dt}\right) = 0.$$

If we multiply through by K/Y, we get

---

[8] In the appendix we are working with continuous time, not discrete time as used in the text.

$$(1 - \beta) \left(\frac{dY}{dt} \frac{1}{Y} - \frac{dK}{dt} \frac{1}{K} \right) = 0$$

implying that equilibrium growth rates for capital and output must be the same.

Wage and rental rates

Now what about wage and rental rates? The Cobb-Douglas production function can be rewritten in terms of output per effective labor unit by dividing through by N^*:

$$y = \frac{Y}{N^*} = \frac{K^\alpha (N^*)^{1-\alpha}}{N^*} = \left(\frac{K}{N^*} \right)^\alpha = k^\alpha,$$

where y = output/effective labor unit and k = capital/effective labor unit ratio.

This elementary function has all the properties we require of our production function. Since

$$y' = \alpha k^{\alpha-1} > 0,$$

and

$$y'' = \alpha(\alpha - 1)k^{\alpha-2} < 0,$$

the marginal physical product of capital is both positive and diminishing. If it can be rented at a rental rate r, then our typical worker/entrepreneur will maximize his net proceeds,

$$k^\alpha - rk$$

by renting capital to the point where

$$\alpha k^{\alpha-1} = r.$$

The only way the market for capital can be cleared with demand and supply equal is if $r = \alpha k_1^{\alpha-1}$, where k_1 represents the average amount of capital per effective labor unit. Each worker/entrepreneur will then demand exactly his share of the total amount of capital.

If the rental price of capital is equal to this, then the total payments to the owners of capital are given by $rk = \alpha k^\alpha$, and the return to the worker/entrepreneurs,

$$w = k^\alpha - rk$$

is given by $(1 - \alpha) k^\alpha$.

One very interesting property of our production function is that the share of total output which goes to the worker/entrepreneurs and to capital owners is completely independent of the size of the labor force. That is, the capitalist's share of each worker/entrepreneur's output is given by

$$\frac{rk_1}{k_1^\alpha} = \frac{\alpha k_1^\alpha}{k_1^\alpha} = \alpha$$

and the worker's share of his output is given by

$$\frac{w}{k_1^\alpha} = \frac{(1-\alpha)\,k_1^\alpha}{k_1^\alpha} = 1 - \alpha.$$

Note the obvious result that the worker and the capitalist share all the output. More importantly, the shares α and $1 - \alpha$ are completely independent of the amount of capital available for each worker, a property known as *constant factor shares* and specific to this representation of the production function.

So far we have done all of our analysis under the assumption that the workers hire the capital and place themselves in the role of entrepreneurs. It is, of course, possible that the real world does not work this way and that the entrepreneurs in the system are the capitalists who hire workers to tend their machines. Now that we have our aggregate production function, we can show that this case does not make any difference and that all of our results are still true in this case.

If the total output is given by $Y = K^\alpha (N^*)^{1-\alpha}$, then the amount of output per unit of capital is given by

$$z = Y/K = K^{\alpha-1}(N^*)^{1-\alpha} = (N^*/K)^{1-\alpha} = x^{1-\alpha},$$

where x is equal to the number of effective labor units per unit of capital. As we can see, the amount of output per unit of capital obtainable by a capitalist is completely independent of how many units of capital he owns, due to our assumption of constant returns to scale. The capitalist's problem is to maximize the profit per machine, given by

$$x^{1-\alpha} - wx,$$

where w is the wage rate paid workers. This is maximized when

$$(1-\alpha)\,x^{-\alpha} - w = 0.$$

However, the supply and demand for workers must be equated, and this will happen only when each capitalist wants to hire N^*/K labor units per unit of capital $= x_1 \equiv 1/k_1$.

But this, of course, means that

$$w = (1 - \alpha) \left(\frac{1}{k_1}\right)^{-\alpha}$$
$$w = (1 - \alpha)k_1^\alpha.$$

Thus the wage rate is exactly the same as before.

The capitalist's profits are equal to

$$\left(\frac{1}{k}\right)^{1-\alpha} - (1 - \alpha)k^\alpha\left(\frac{1}{k}\right) = \alpha k^{\alpha-1}.$$

The total profits are again equal to $\alpha(K/N^*)^{\alpha-1} K = \alpha K^\alpha(N^*)^{1-\alpha}$. That is, factor rewards are independent of who plays the role of entrepreneur.

A more general proof

We can also show more generally that it doesn't matter whether capitalists or workers manage the economy for *any* production function with constant returns to scale.

Both capital K and labor N^* are factors of production. That is, output Y is given by

$$Y = Y(K, N^*).$$

If this function is homogeneous of degree one (has constant returns to scale) then the function can be written as

$$Y = KY(1, N^*/K)$$

or

$$z \equiv Y/K = Z(x),$$

where z is the output per unit of capital and x is the number of effective labor units per unit of capital. If the economy is managed by the capitalists and workers are paid a wage rate w, then profits per unit of capital are given by

$$z - wx,$$

and maximized by setting $z' = w$. The wage bill will be $wx = z'x$;

the total amount of wages paid to all workers by all capitalists will be $z'xK = z'N*$.

Now the partial derivative of Y with respect to $N*$ is

$$\frac{\partial Y}{\partial N*} = z'(x),$$

so the total wage payments can be rewritten as

$$z'(x)N* = \frac{\partial Y}{\partial N*}.$$

Let us see what the worker's proceeds would be if the workers organize the production. The production function can again be rewritten as

$$Y = Y(K/N*, 1)N*$$

or

$$y \equiv Y/N* = y(k),$$

where y is the amount of output per effective labor unit, and k is the capital/effective labor ratio. Workers maximize

$$y - rk,$$

(where r is the rental price they pay for capital). The condition for maximization is, of course, that $y' = r$. Then the rent bill will be $y'k$ and the worker's profit will be $y - y'k$. Total receipts by all workers will be given by $(y - y'k)N* = yN* - y'K$. Now since the partial derivative of Y with respect to K is defined by

$$\frac{\partial Y}{\partial K} = y'(k),$$

the total worker receipts under worker-organized production are given by

$$Y - \frac{\partial Y}{\partial K} K.$$

If the production function really is homogeneous of degree one, Euler's Theorem states that

$$Y = \frac{\partial Y}{\partial K} K + \frac{\partial Y}{\partial N*} N*.$$

So

$$Y - \frac{\partial Y}{\partial K} K = \frac{\partial Y}{\partial N*} N*.$$

That is, the worker's proceeds are the same regardless of who organizes the system.

PROBLEMS FOR CHAPTER 3

1. Figure 2 represents the output per unit of labor as a function of the capital/labor ratio. Draw a graph which represents output per unit of capital as a function of the labor/capital ratio and which also has diminishing returns. Using this graph, show that a rise in the capital/labor ratio causes the wage rate to rise and the capital rental rate to fall.

2. What will be the effect of a reduction in the capital depreciation rate δ on the wage rate and the capital rental rate
    a. if net saving as a percent of gross output remains constant?
    b. if gross saving as a percent of gross output remains constant?

3. What will be the effect of a rise in the birth rate on the equilibrium wage rate? The equilibrium capital rental rate?

4. Does an increase in the rate of technological change raise or lower
    a. capital rental rates?
    b. wage rates?
    c. wage rates per effective labor unit?

5. Show that an economy's saving rate is efficient if saving is less than the share of output paid to owners of capital.

6. Show that when capital depreciation is included in the model, the Golden Rule of Chapter 2 requires the capital rental rate (net of depreciation) to be equal to the biological interest rate.

Bibliography for Section One

Perhaps the most readily accessible version of Malthus is

Malthus, Thomas. *On Population*. New York: Modern Library, 1960.

It reprints several editions of the essay; we personally find the first edition the best.

The seminal work on calculating the national income is

Kuznets, Simon. *National Income and its Composition 1919–1938*. 2 vol. New York: National Bureau of Economic Research, 1941.

The national income accounts of the U.S. are now reported periodically in the *Survey of Current Business*. For a detailed discussion see

United States Department of Commerce. "National Income Account Revisions." *Survey of Current Business*, August 1965.

Summary data for other countries are reported in the *Statistical Yearbook* of the United Nations.

The literature on the neoclassical growth model is enormous and we can mention only part of it. Our graphical exposition owes much to

Johnson, Harry G. "The Neoclassical One-Sector Growth Model: A Geometrical Exposition and Extension to a Monetary Economy." *Economica*, August 1966.

Also see the exchange between Johnson and James Tobin in *Economica* in February 1967.

The first proofs that the equilibrium growth rate is independent of the saving rate are found in

Solow, Robert M. "A Contribution to the Theory of Economic Growth." *Quarterly Journal of Economics*, February 1957.

Swan, Trevor W. "Economic Growth and Capital Accumulation." *Economic Record,* November 1956.

The introductory chapter of

Solow, Robert M. *Growth Theory.* Oxford University Press, 1970.

is an excellent nontechnical discussion of the so-called "stylized facts" of growth theory; subsequent technical chapters describe a variety of extensions of the simple model.

The Golden Rule and Golden Age are discussed in

Phelps, Edmund S. "The Golden Rule of Accumulation: A Fable for Growth Men." *American Economic Review,* September 1961.

———. "Second Essay on the Golden Rule of Accumulation." *American Economic Review,* September 1965.

Empirical estimates of the sources of growth are contained in

Solow, Robert M. "Technical Change and the Aggregate Production Function." *Review of Economics and Statistics,* August 1957.

Denison, Edward. *Sources of Economic Growth in the United States and the Alternatives Before Us.* New York: Committee for Economic Development, 1962.

We shall provide no specific references on the factor-pricing material in Chapter 3. Any standard book in price theory will suffice for those in need of a review.

The foundations of the neoclassical demand function for capital are reviewed in

Jorgenson, Dale W. "Capital Theory and Investment Behavior." *American Economic Review,* May 1963.

For some extensions, see

Gould, John P. "Adjustment Costs in the Theory of Investment of the Firm." *Review of Economic Studies,* January 1968.

Lucas, Robert E. "Adjustment Cost and the Theory of Supply." *Journal of Political Economy,* August 1967.

Uzawa, Hirofumi. "Time Preference and the Penrose Effect in a Two-Class Model of Economic Growth." *Journal of Political Economy,* July/August 1969.

A survey of empirical estimates of production functions is contained in

Walters, A. A. "Production and Cost Functions: An Econometric Survey." *Econometrica,* January 1963.

For a discussion of a three-factor model with land, labor and capital, see

Nichols, Donald A. "Land and Economic Growth." *American Economic Review,* June 1970.

Our discussion is limited to a one-sector growth model. For an introduction to multi-sector models, see

Johnson, Harry G.   *The Two Sector Model of General Equilibrium.* Chicago: Aldine Atherton, 1971.

Some of the difficult problems of aggregation, glossed over here, are discussed in

Fisher, Franklin M. "Embodied Technology and the Existence of Labor and Output Aggregates." *Review of Economic Studies,* October 1968.

For a view critical of the neoclassical approach, see

Robinson, Joan.   *The Accumulation of Capital.* Homewood, Ill.: Irwin, 1956.

Further references along this line are provided by

Harcourt, G. C.   "Some Cambridge Controversies in the Theory of Capital." *Journal of Economic Literature,* June 1969.

section two

Consumption and saving

SECTION ONE emphasized the critical role of the saving rate in determining the equilibrium capital/effective labor ratio and the long-run standard of living. No explanation was given, however, as to how the saving rate itself is determined. The determinants of saving and consumption are the subject of this section.

Chapter 4 analyzes the consumption-saving decision at the microeconomic level. Using standard simplifying assumptions we derive an expression for the individual's desired consumption level in any year as a function of the individual's age and wealth. The important properties of this consumption function are then illustrated in Chapter 5, and the time pattern of consumption over the life cycle it implies is calculated for a hypothetical individual decision-maker. These calculations are then repeated to show how the individual consumption and savings patterns would differ with different lifetime earnings profiles and different rates of interest.

Chapter 6 then performs the crucial step of marrying the individual life cycle consumption functions to the neoclassical model of economic growth and production of Section One. The discussion in Chapter 6 shows how the equilibrium aggregate saving rate is determined and how the saving rate responds in the short run and in the long run to a variety of external shocks.

73

4

The microeconomic foundations of aggregate saving and consumption functions

THE NEOCLASSICAL MODEL, whether in its simple or extended forms, implies that an economy's long-run growth rate is independent of its saving rate. The equilibrium growth rate depends only on the rate of population growth and the rate of technological change. The saving rate is far from unimportant, however. It has a very direct effect on the *levels* of income and consumption per capita in the long run as well as the short.

To complete the picture of the forces governing the long-run standard of living we must, therefore, be able to explain how the saving rate is determined. For market economies, at least, this means that we must understand the main influences on the saving behavior of the individual households whose separate decisions each year combine to make up the total flow of saving into productive capital. The exploration of these saving decisions at the micro level, and, in particular, the presentation of the so-called *life-cycle model* of individual saving will be the main task in this chapter and the next. In Chapter 6, we will then extend the neoclassical model further by incorporating the key features of the life-cycle approach. Some of the main properties of the new model will be illustrated by a computer simulation.

INTRODUCTION: SOME HISTORICAL BACKGROUND

Macroeconomics received much of its present-day form and vocabulary with the publication in 1936 of *The General Theory of*

Employment, Interest and Money, by J. M. Keynes. Keynes, who was even then perhaps the leading figure in economics, meant his title, with its overtones of Einstein, to be quite descriptive of the contents of the book. He argued that the previous main stream of economic theory — essentially the kind of analysis we have been working with up to this point — was seriously deficient because it considered full employment of all resources as the only possible position of stable equilibrium for the economy. All questions of unemployment and of fluctuations in the level of economic activity and prices were relegated to another and quite separate body of economic theory known as "monetary theory." His new work, by contrast, would attempt to unify the treatment of employment so that full employment and less-than-full employment would each be seen as special cases in a single, more general theory.

A major new concept in this supposedly more general theory was *the propensity to consume* which Keynes defined as "the functional relationship χ between Y_w, a given level of income . . . and C_w, the expenditure on consumption out of that level of income, so that $C_w = \chi(Y_w)$." As to the properties of this function, perhaps, in view of subsequent controversies, we should let Keynes speak for himself.

> The fundamental psychological law, upon which we are entitled to depend with great confidence both *a priori* from our knowledge of human nature and from the detailed facts of experience, is that men are disposed, as a rule and on the average, to increase their consumption as their income increases, but not by as much as the increase in their income.
>
> This is especially the case where we have short periods in view, as in the case of the so-called cyclical fluctuations of employment during which habits, as distinct from more permanent psychological propensities, are not given time enough to adapt themselves to changed objective circumstances. For a man's habitual standard of life usually has the first claim on his income, and he is apt to save the difference which discovers itself between his actual income and the expense of his habitual standard; or, if he does adjust his expenditure to changes in his income, he will, over short periods, do so imperfectly. Thus a rising income will often be accompanied by increased saving, and a falling income by decreased saving, on a greater scale at first than subsequently.
>
> But, apart from short-period *changes* in the level of income, it

is also obvious that a higher absolute level of income will tend, as a rule, to widen the gap between income and consumption. For the satisfaction of the immediate primary needs of a man and his family is usually a stronger motive than the motives towards accumulation, which only acquire effective sway when a margin of comfort has been attained. These reasons will lead, as a rule, to a greater *proportion* of income being saved as real income increases. But whether or not a greater proportion is saved, we take it as a fundamental psychological rule of any modern community that, when its real income is increased, it will not increase its consumption by an equal *absolute* amount, so that a greater absolute amount must be saved, unless a large and unusual change is occurring at the same time in other factors [pp. 96–97].

The properties Keynes assumed for his propensity to consume are pictured as the line C_0F in Figure 4–1. To guide the eye, the figure also has a line OA drawn through the origin with a slope of $+1$. The slope of the Keynesian consumption function is flatter

FIGURE 4–1
The Keynesian propensity to consume

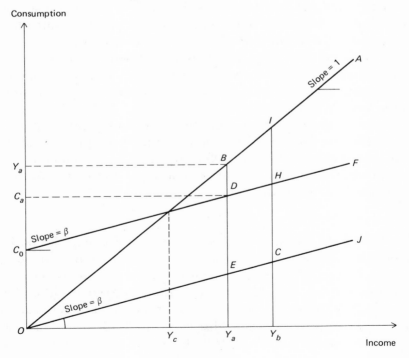

Consumption

Income

than that of this auxiliary line (or, to use the standard technical jargon, the *marginal propensity to consume* of the Keynesian function is less than unity). This is a reflection of Keynes's "fundamental psychological law."

With the help of the auxiliary line *OA* we can also directly read off the level of saving implied by Keynes's function at any level of *Y*. When income is Y_a, the distance BY_a is equal, by construction, to the distance OY_a. Hence, the distance DY_a will measure that part of Y_a that is consumed, and the distance *BD* that part of Y_a that is saved. Note that if income were higher, say Y_b, then it would also be the case, as Keynes asserts in the last sentence of the passage quoted, that the *absolute* amount of saving would also rise (i.e., it is greater than *BD*).

But Keynes wanted his function to imply something stronger yet, namely that the *proportion* of income saved should rise and the *proportion* of income consumed should fall as *Y* rises. The function C_oF does indeed have this property. At Y_c, for example, the consumption/income ratio — or *average propensity to consume* — has a value of 1.0. At Y_a the average propensity to consume is $DY_a/BY_a = DY_a/OY_a$, which is less than 1.0; and at Y_b the average propensity to consume is HY_b/OY_b, smaller yet. By contrast, the consumption function we used in our discussions of the neoclassical model had a *constant* average propensity to consume. A function of that kind, drawn with the same marginal propensity to consume as the Keynesian consumption function C_oF is shown as the line *OJ* in Figure 1.

Keynes's speculations about the form and properties of his propensity to consume were quickly put to empirical test with very mixed results. For the 1930s in the U.S., the data on aggregate consumption and income did seem to conform reasonably well to a relation of the form

$$(1) \qquad\qquad C_t = \alpha + \beta\, Y_t,$$

with $0 < \beta < 1$ and $\alpha > 0$. The same sort of relation with positive intercept and slope less than unity was also found in budget studies of various occupational groups for certain years in the 30s, though the marginal propensities appeared to differ quite substantially between groups and regions. Longer ranging historical studies, however, disclosed no evidence of any systematic tendency for saving to rise relative to income as income rose and society grew richer. In terms of decade averages, the fraction of income saved in most of the 20th century did not appear systematically higher than in the 19th century.

Another serious blow to Keynes's conjecture came in the years immediately following World War II. Forecasts of postwar consumption spending obtained by extrapolating the propensity to consume of the 1930s grossly underestimated the levels of spending that actually occurred. Various *ad hoc* rationalizations were offered for these conspicuous prediction errors of the simple Keynesian model but by the early 1950s it had become abundantly clear that any attempt to explain consumption behavior by reference to current income alone, as in equation (1), was fundamentally inadequate and doomed to failure. For the economics profession, it was a case of "back to the drawing board."

Much of the essential content of the currently accepted theory of the consumption function was eventually provided in the middle 1950s by two of the then, as now, leading American economists, Milton Friedman and Franco Modigliani (the latter in collaboration with Richard Brumberg). The term "permanent income hypothesis" has come to be the accepted popular designation for the contribution of the former, and the term "life-cycle hypothesis" for that of the latter. The two positions, despite certain differences in emphasis, have much in common. In particular, both eschew any reliance on question-begging psychological "propensities" to save or consume. Instead, they base their analysis on an economic model of the saving decisions of an individual household that had been developed considerably earlier by the American economist Irving Fisher—a model, ironically, with which Keynes himself must surely have been thoroughly familiar.

In this book we shall be working mainly within the life-cycle framework. Some of the important features of the permanent income approach will be considered in an appendix to Chapter 5 after the basic structure has been sketched out.

CONSUMPTION, SAVING AND THE LIFE CYCLE

Before presenting the Fisherian model of saving behavior upon which the life-cycle hypothesis ultimately rests, it may be useful first to point out some of the principal features and regu-

FIGURE 4–2

Hypothetical wage and consumption pattern over the life cycle

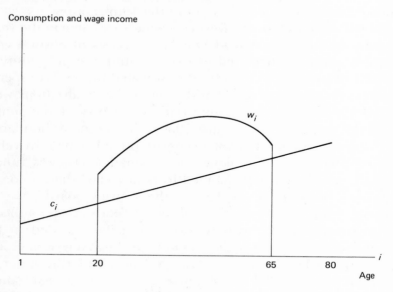

larities in observed life cycles that the formal apparatus seeks to explain. Consider, for example, the highly idealized economic life history of the bachelor portrayed in Figure 4–2. The x-axis shows what year of life he is in from the time of his birth at $i = 1$ until his death at the end of $i = 80$ (death presumably occurring in the midst of his 80th birthday party). The curve labeled w_i shows his wages or, as we shall sometimes call it, his nonproperty income, during each year of his life. As drawn, he is assumed to have no wage income whatever during the first 20 years of his life. After his 20th birthday he enters the labor force and works for the next 45 years, retiring at his 65th birthday. During his working life, his wage income rises steadily at first as he gains experience; reaches a peak at about age 55; and drifts slightly lower thereafter until retirement, when it ceases altogether.[1]

The curve labeled c_i shows the hypothetical level of consumption expenditures by our bachelor in each year of his life. Note

---

[1] The curve pictured might be appropriate for an engineer or similar employed professional worker. For unskilled and semi-skilled workers, the earnings profile would rise less steeply initially, peak earlier and fall off more sharply at the end.

that during his working years, from age 20 to age 65, he is consuming less than his wage income in each year. By contrast, he continues to spend for consumption during his retirement period, even though he no longer has any current wage income. To maintain himself through these golden years, he draws in one way or another on funds accumulated during the years when he was consuming less than his income. He is thus a net *dis-saver,* both then and during the childhood and schooling years before he enters the labor force. Presumably, the major part of the financing in his early years is provided by other members of his family, perhaps supplemented by some personal borrowing against his future earnings prospects (e.g., tuition loans).

Simplified as this possible life cycle is, it serves at least to remind us that savings and consumption patterns involve more than blind psychological urges for thrift or unthinking and mechanical responses to changes in the level of current income. Clearly, economic choices and allocations are being made, and it is to a more detailed study of these choices and the factors governing them that we now turn.

THE BASIC FISHERIAN MODEL OF THE SAVINGS DECISION

A review of the model of economic choice

One of the great beauties of the Fisherian approach to the theory of saving is that it treats the saving decision itself as merely a special case of the general problem of economic choice. The graphic representation of that problem presented in Figure 4–3 should seem thoroughly familiar to anyone who has completed a course in introductory price theory. The two axes represent units of two "commodities"—beef and pork, clothing and recreation, work and leisure, or any similar combination.

The curves labelled U are *indifference curves,* each showing, as the name implies, combinations of commodity 1 and commodity 2 between which the decision maker is indifferent. The numbers associated with each such indifference curve indicate relative preferences. That is, combinations of commodity 1 and commodity 2 lying on the curve labelled U_{54} are preferred by the decision maker to those lying on lower-numbered curves such as U_{33} or U_{21} and are regarded as inferior to combinations lying on higher-numbered curves such as U_{80}. The fact that we have drawn the curves with their rankings increasing in the northeast direction signifies that the decision-maker considers both goods desirable. If his preferences are consistent—in the sense that if he prefers combination A to combination B, and B to C, he always also prefers A to C— then the indifference curves never cross.

The slope of an indifference curve at any point—often referred to as the *marginal rate of substitution* (of commodity 1 for commodity 2)—is drawn to be negative throughout. Two combinations will thus only be equivalent for our decision maker if the one with the smaller amount of commodity 2 is compensated for by having a larger quantity of commodity 1. The indifference curves are also drawn as convex from below, so that more and more of commodity 1 would have to be added to the combination for each unit of commodity 2 removed in order to keep him on the same indifference curve. (We hasten to add that these assumptions about the decision maker's tastes are a good deal stronger in many respects than are strictly necessary. We make them here because they are the standard ones in elementary discussions and because they are the most interesting and fruitful for the kinds of problems that concern us here.)

The possible combinations from among which our decision maker must choose are represented in this case by the triangular area OEF. The point G represents his initial holding of the two commodities, OD units of commodity 1 and OH units of commodity 2. The line EF passing through G (often called the *budget line*) represents the additional combinations of commodity 1 and commodity 2 that he can obtain by swapping or trading one commodity for the other.[2]

In the absence of these trading possibilities, the decision maker would presumably have no alternative but to remain at the point G and hence on the indifference curve U_{27} which passes through

---

[2] As drawn, the rate at which one commodity exchanges for the other, given by the slope of EF at any point, is a constant independent of the quantities exchanged. That assumption about the opportunities available to the decision maker amounts to considering him as a very small trader in a well-organized market in which the cost of trading and of gathering information is small enough to be treated as of second-order concern. It is, needless to say, by no means the only assumption that might be made with respect to the possibilities for trading off or otherwise transforming one particular combination of commodities into another.

FIGURE 4–3

The graphic representation of the economic theory of choice

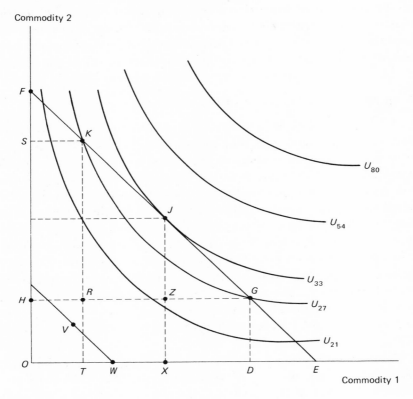

Commodity 2

U_{80}

U_{54}

U_{33}

U_{27}

U_{21}

Commodity 1

G. By trading along the line EF, however, giving up some of the commodity 1 with which he is relatively well stocked in favor of gaining additional units of commodity 2, he can reach the combination indicated by the point J which is on the higher indifference curve U_{33} and hence clearly preferable to G. Although further trading of commodity 1 for commodity 2 would be possible, it would clearly not be undertaken by the decision maker pictured. A point beyond J such as the point K lies on a lower indifference curve; the relative overabundance of commodity 1 at point G would simply have been changed into an overabundance on the opposite side. A point such as J can thus be thought of as the equilibrium combination of commodities 1 and 2 for our particular decision maker. It lies on the highest indifference curve he can reach starting from his initial endowment at G and trading at the rate of OF units of commodity 2 for each OE units of commodity 1. We can also characterize it as the point at which the decision maker's (subjective) marginal rate of substitution of commodity 2 for commodity 1 exactly balances the (objective) marginal rate of transformation of commodity 2 into commodity 1 in the market.

A reinterpretation in terms of the saving decision

Adapting this familiar model of economic choice to the saving decision begins with a relabelling of the axes. Instead of using the axes to represent two commodities to be consumed at a particular point in time, we want them to represent the total amount of resources our decision maker has available for the consumption of all commodities in two different periods of time. For concreteness, at this still early stage of the analysis, it helps to think of these periods as fairly long ones, say, the "working years" for period 1 and the "retirement" years for period 2; and to treat them as of equal length. It will also simplify matters to pretend that all payments are received, and made at the beginning of a period. The indifference curves of Figure 4–3 can then represent our decision maker's tastes for different patterns of standards of living in the two periods.

Patterns involving more consumable resources in both periods are surely to be preferred to those involving less, so that the preference ordering of the curves continues to be upward and to the right. The downward slope now reflects the supposition that our decision maker would never willingly consider a cut in his standard of living in any period without the promise of compensation in the form of an increase in his standard of living in some other period. And the convexity can best be thought of as a preference for "smooth" patterns of consumption over both periods, as opposed to patterns involving large changes in life style.

To expand on this important theme for a bit, consider the indifference curve U_{21} which has been recopied from Figure 4–3 onto Figure 4–4, where it can be studied in isolation. The points M and N represent two possible patterns of standards of living between which, by construction, our decision maker is indifferent. The pattern M gives total consumption of $400,000 in the first period to be followed by a standard of living of only $50,000 in

FIGURE 4–4

A graphical representation of the Fisherian theory of saving

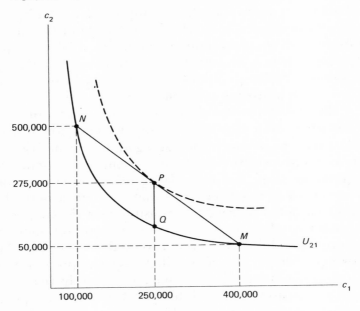

period 2. The pattern N has a time shape of the opposite kind: $100,000 in the first period followed by $500,000 in the second. Consider now a smoother pattern lying, for concreteness, exactly halfway between each of the extreme patterns M and N. That is, in the first year it calls for total consumption of

$$\frac{1}{2}\left(c_1^{(M)} + c_1^{(N)}\right) = \frac{1}{2}\,(400,000 + 100,000) = \$250,000;$$

and in the second, for

$$\frac{1}{2}\left(c_2^{(M)} + c_2^{(N)}\right) = \frac{1}{2}\,(50,000 + 500,000) = \$275,000.$$

Graphically, this new, smoother combination—the absolute difference in standard of living between the two periods being only $25,000 as compared to the $350,000 spread of M and the $400,000 spread of N—is the point P lying halfway between the points M and N on the straight line joining them. The convexity assumption thus amounts to the proposition that a smoothed out combination such as P lies above, and hence on a higher indifference curve than the more irregular patterns from which it was constructed.[3]

Before moving on to consider the appropriate reinterpretation of the opportunity set, a word is in order about the heroic abstraction involved in representing an individual's lifetime pattern of consumption as a single point. We face here another of the "aggregation problems" already encountered in our discussion of the production process and that we shall encounter repeatedly as we push on with the task of filling out our picture of the economy. For such comfort as it may bring, we may note that conditions do exist under which the aggregation over individual consumption items is entirely legitimate, though the conditions are fairly stringent (e.g., that the relative prices of all consumption goods are known and fixed; and that the satisfactions derived from a given dollar allocated to consumption in one period are independent of the composition of consumption spending in other periods, to indicate merely two of the more critical ones). Here as elsewhere, however, we shall take the position not that these requirements are in fact met, but merely that they are closely enough approximated for the broad-brush, qualitative uses we are making of the model in this book.

The transfer of resources between periods: Capital markets and interest rates

Turning now to the reinterpretation of the budget line or opportunity set, one should not feel inadequate if unable immediately to attach a meaning to the market tradeoff line *EF* illustrated in Figure 4–3. It is easy, in the ordinary two-commodity case, to imagine a market in which, say, beavers can be traded for deer; but how is one to visualize a market in which the dealing is in resources available for consumption at different points in time?

The answer is, of course, that like Molière's Monsieur Jourdain,

---

[3] Mathematically, the function $y = f(x)$ is said to be convex when, for any two points x_1 and x_2, $\alpha f(x_1) + (1 - \alpha)f(x_2) \geq f(\alpha x_1 + (1 - \alpha)x_2)$, for $0 \leq \alpha \leq 1$. When the inequality is reversed, the function $f(x)$ is said to be concave. In terms of Figure 4–4, P represents the point $c_2 = \frac{1}{2} f(400,000) + \frac{1}{2} f(100,000)$ and Q represents the point $c_2 = f\left(\frac{1}{2} (400,000) + \frac{1}{2} (100,000)\right) = f(250,000)$.

who was astonished to learn that he had been speaking in prose all his life, we are all active in precisely such a market at one time or another. We enter the market, for example, whenever we borrow to finance a car. The lender makes resources available to us in the current period; in return, we agree to make resources available to him in future periods (in this case, typically in the form of a series of interest and principal payments over 36 to 48 months). We enter the opposite side of the market whenever we buy a U. S. government savings bond or deposit money in a bank or buy a share of common stock. Despite their differences in outward form, essentially what we are doing in all of these cases is lending. All involve turning currently consumable resources over to the seller or issuer of the security or liability in return for the promise (or perhaps just the hope, as in the case of common stocks) of obtaining consumable resources in future periods.

In terms of Figure 4–3, the endowment point G along the line EF represents the initial combination of resources in the two periods available to our decision maker from his labor income or his previously accumulated wealth or from gifts or inheritances. If there were no opportunities to transfer consumable resources between periods, then the combination G would also be the pattern of his standard of living. He would have a consumption level of OD (say, 400,000 in period 1) and then have to take his belt in several notches and get by on OH (perhaps 150,000 as drawn) in period 2. But since there is a resource market, or *capital market* as it is usually called, any of the combinations lying along the line EF become available. Our decision maker can reach the combination K, for example, by lending current resources in the amount GR in return for the promise to receive RK of resources in period 2. Similarly, if he had started originally from K rather than G, he could increase the amount of resources available to support his standard of living in the current period by borrowing GR against the collateral of his income of OS(= TD) to be received next period. When period 2 comes and he receives his payment of OS, he turns SH(= RK) of it over to the lender in fulfillment of his bargain; and keeps the remaining OH(= TR) of resources for his own consumption.

As in the standard case, the slope of the line EF measures the rate of exchange between the two commodities, in this case between consumable resources available currently and consumable resources to be delivered at the start of period 2. The slope of the line is $-(OF/OE)$, meaning that the decision maker could obtain OE dollars currently in return for OF dollars next period (or GR dollars currently for RK dollars in period 2, etc.). For further concreteness, it may help to visualize the payment in the next period as being made up of two parts, one representing the initial sum or *principal* and the remainder the *interest*. Thus we would have

$$OF = OE + (OF - OE)$$

and the slope of the line could be expressed as

$$-\frac{OF}{OE} = -\left(1 + \frac{OF - OE}{OE}\right)$$

The term $\dfrac{OF - OE}{OE}$ is, of course, the familiar "rate of interest," which we shall designate as r[4]. Since real-world capital markets contain thousands of different kinds of securities with very different terms, the rate r must be thought of as the rate on a "representative" security. The relation between returns on different securities is presumably the concern of courses in finance.

Note, finally, that there is another and very useful way to characterize tradeoff lines such as EF. Just as OF is the amount obtained a period hence from an initial investment of OE when the interest rate is r, OE can be interpreted in the other direction as the current value in period 1 resources, or, more succinctly, the *present value*, of OF dollars to be delivered at the start of period 2. Note that OE is also the present value of any other point along the line EF, particularly including the initial endowment point G. And conversely, the present value of any arbitrary point V can be found by merely passing a line through the point V with a slope equal to $-(1 + r)$ and observing its intercept on the x-axis (in this case of V the amount OW).

Since the distance OE is the present value of G, the resources available to the decision maker over the entire two periods, we may also think of it as representing his current *wealth*.

---

[4] Recall that we have earlier used the same symbol r to stand for the net rental rate on capital goods. The reasons for using the same symbol in the two cases will be taken up later.

The existence of a capital market means that the decision maker can use his wealth to provide any one of the standards of living represented by the points lying along *EF*. He is not restricted to the particular combination *G*. As pictured, the decision maker will prefer the somewhat smoother combination *J* to his original pattern, *G*, available without using the capital market. He reaches it by saving *DX* out of his current income of *OD* and investing it in a representative security paying interest at a rate of 100*r* percent per period. At the start of period 2, he takes the proceeds of his loan plus the interest thereon, *ZJ*, adds this to the *XZ* of resources coming to him originally at the start of 2 and consumes the combined sum of *XJ* in period 2.

Such, then, is the essential kernel of the economic theory of saving. What the life cycle and associated developments seek to do is to give additional concreteness to the notion of consumption smoothing. They try to highlight, as it were, those events and times that produce the kinds of irregularity in income flows that call for smoothing. Before such matters can be considered in detail, the model of Figure 4–3 must be restated in general algebraic form to provide an apparatus that can readily encompass more than the two periods to which we are effectively limited in graphical presentation.

THE BASIC MODEL IN ALGEBRAIC FORM

The two basic elements of the graphical representation of the theory of consumption are the notion of the budget line *FE* representing the possible consumption patterns available to the decision maker, and the indifference curves such as U_{33} which represent his preferences for the different consumption patterns. Algebraic counterparts for these elements must be developed.

The preference function

The decision maker's tastes for patterns of consumption can be represented by a *utility function* or to use a more neutral term, by a *preference ordering function* which assigns rankings to each of the conceivable combinations of total consumption spending in each of the periods that make up the planning horizon. As in the case of our earlier discussion of production functions, we shall find it convenient to carry on the discussion in terms of a specific, and in some respects quite special, preference function. Mathematically it will be essentially the same function, viz

(2) $$\gamma_i \log c_i + \gamma_{i+1} \log c_{i+1} + \cdots + \gamma_{n_3} \log c_{n_3},$$

where, the c_i represent the total value of consumption in each period, and the γ_i (assumed to be positive) will be explained shortly. Note that we consider as consumption spending in this function only purchases of nondurables and the *services* of durables, all of which, for concreteness at this stage, may be thought of as being rented from the "banks" exactly as was done earlier in the case of productive capital goods. Note also that we shall assume the consumption spending c_i to be that of the decision maker only on his own behalf. The finite-lived bachelor decision maker neither receives income from his ancestors nor wishes to bestow any on his heirs. Though this is a strong assumption — this would be a very cold world in which to live — it is convenient to set aside all questions of bequests or intrafamily transfers for the present. These issues will be discussed more fully in Chapters 5 and 8.

The role of the γs in the preference function is to represent the weight the decision maker places on consumption in each time period. Other things equal, the greater the value of γ_i for any time period, the greater the utility of consumption during that period. Put another way, the relative values of the γs describe the decision maker's *time preference*. If we reduce potential consumption in, say, period 2 by γ_1 percent (where γ_1 is the coefficient on consumption in period 1), then we must add γ_2 percent to spending in period 1 in order to keep the decision maker indifferent. More generally, if $\gamma_i > \gamma_{i+\tau}$ so that the coefficient on period i in equation (2) is greater than that on the later period, $i + \tau$, it requires more than one percent of deferred consumption to compensate for the loss of one percent in more immediate consumption. Decision makers whose tastes have this property are said to exhibit *impatience* or to have *positive time preference*. By contrast, where $\gamma_i < \gamma_{i+\tau}$, the decision maker would be characterized by an economist as having *negative time preference* (and by a psychiatrist probably as an anal-obsessive). The case of $\gamma_i = \gamma_{i+\tau}$ is, not unnaturally, the case of *zero time preference*. Empirically, most people who have thought about it would probably regard positive time preference as the typical case, though examples of the reverse pattern can certainly be found. Fortunately there is no need for us to take a firm stand on the issue. None of the important results to follow derive crucially from the assumptions with respect to the γs (at least, as long as they stay within the realm of common sense). To emphasize this point, we shall hereafter normally assume zero time preference and take all the γs to have the same value (which, for further simplicity and without loss of generality, we can assume to be unity).[5]

The opportunity set

In constructing the opportunity set, the simplest and most revealing approach is to work backward, sequentially, starting from the last period. Consider the consumption possibilities open to a decision maker at the start of period n_3, the last period of his life. Since, by definition, there are no earnings in future periods against which he can borrow, his consumption cannot be greater than the wage or other nonproperty income he expects to earn in period n_3 plus any financial assets accumulated from past periods or minus any debts or liabilities for past borrowings that are still outstanding.[6] And since we have ruled out any bequests, there is no reason for his consumption in the last period to be less than his resources. Hence, his last-period constraint can be expressed as the equation

$$(3) \qquad c_{n_3} = a_{n_3} + w_{n_3} \equiv z_{n_3}$$

where a_{n_3} is the decision maker's financial net worth at the start of period n_3, w_{n_3} the nonproperty income, if any, that he will earn during n_3 and z_{n_3}, the sum of the two, is his total net wealth at the start of period n_3.

For our task, the key term in equation (3) is a_{n_3}, the net financial position, positive or negative at the start of n_3. By accounting definition, and by virtue of our conventions as to when payments are made and received, the net financial position at the start of n_3

---

[5] Geometrically, the case of zero time preference means that the indifference curves are symmetric around a 45-degree line drawn through the origin.

[6] We shall also use n_1 and n_2 to represent the individual's first and last periods in the labor force.

must equal its value as of the start of the previous period a_{n_3-1}; plus any additional saving s_{n_3-1} made from the income of the period (or minus any dissaving of previously accumulated assets to support a level of consumption in excess of income); and plus any interest earned at the rate r from lending the accumulated financial assets in the capital markets (or minus any interest paid if the individual was a net borrower for the period).

In symbols, we can express these accounting relations as

(4)
$$a_{n_3} = (a_{n_3-1} + s_{n_3-1})(1 + r)$$
$$= (a_{n_3-1} + w_{n_3-1} - c_{n_3-1})(1 + r).$$

Substituting the expression on the right-hand side of equation (4) for the a_{n_3} of equation (3), we have

(4′)
$$c_{n_3} = w_{n_3} + (a_{n_3-1} + w_{n_3-1} - c_{n_3-1})(1 + r)$$
$$= w_{n_3} + (a_{n_3-1} + w_{n_3-1})(1 + r) - c_{n_3-1}(1 + r).$$

With a little rearrangement we may express the opportunity line (4′) in what might be called present-value form as

(5)
$$c_{n_3-1} + \frac{c_{n_3}}{1 + r} = a_{n_3-1} + w_{n_3-1} + \frac{w_{n_3}}{1 + r} \equiv z_{n_3-1}.$$

In this formulation, z_{n_3-1} can be seen to be the maximum amount the decision maker could consume in the current period $n_3 - 1$ if he chose to set $c_{n_3} = 0$ (meaning no consumption next period). In other words, it is simply the algebraic counterpart to the point E in Figure 4–3, and consists of any financial assets accumulated from previous periods, a_{n_3-1}, plus any human wealth or *human capital* as we shall sometimes call it, $\left[w_{n_3-1} + \frac{w_{n_3}}{1 + r} \right]$.[7] The equation itself corresponds to the line EF, and the endowment point G on the line EF is the point with coordinates $(a_{n_3-1} + w_{n_3-1}, w_{n_3})$.

This reformulation of equation (4′) has the advantage of emphasizing how an individual's resources, in the sense of his finan-

---

[7] In referring to the expression in brackets as human capital, our usage of the term capital is consistent with that in the earlier chapters in which capital was treated as a *stock* yielding a *flow* of productive services in the current and future periods. In the human capital case, the expression above represents the value considered as the equivalent current stock of the flow of current and future earnings.

cial and human wealth, serve to limit the *level* of his standard of living as it were, but not necessarily its *pattern*. Given a capital market in which his resources can be reallocated over time by borrowing and lending, the individual can choose any pattern whose present value does not exceed the present value of his earnings plus his assets.

The same steps that led us from equation (3) for period n_3 to equation (4') for period $n_3 - 1$ can be obviously repeated again for period $n_3 - 2$ and so on, repeatedly, until we reach the first decision period, i.

Our opportunity set in present value form, will then be the following $n_3 - i + 1$ dimensional counterpart of the 2-dimensional equation (5)

$$(6) \qquad c_i + \frac{c_{i+1}}{1+r} + \frac{c_{i+2}}{(1+r)^2} + \cdots + \frac{c_{n_3}}{(1+r)^{n_3-i}} = z_i =$$
$$a_i + w_i + \frac{w_{i+1}}{1+r} + \frac{w_{i+2}}{(1+r)^2} + \cdots + \frac{w_{n_3}}{(1+r)^{n_3-i}}.{}^8$$

The equilibrium consumption function

The decision maker's problem can be represented formally as one of maximizing his preference function, equation (2), subject to his wealth constraint, represented by equation (6). The mathematics required to derive the solution to the decision maker's problem are beyond the level assumed for the text of this book, and the derivation has been relegated to an appendix. Here we will merely report some of the key steps that permit us to express the consumption function for our decision maker in a particularly compact and convenient way. Specifically, it can be shown that for this utility function the equilibrium relation between the consumption levels in the different periods will be

---

[8] For simplicity, we have taken the interest rate as constant over time. In the more general case in which interest rates were expected to be different in different periods, we would replace $(1 + r)^2$ with $(1 + r_i)(1 + r_{i+1})$ and so on, up to $(1 + r)^{n_3-i}$, which is replaced by the product, $\prod_{\tau=i}^{n_3-i} (1 + r_\tau)$. Some examples involving different rates for different periods are presented in the exercises to the next chapter.

$$c_{i+1} = c_i(1 + r)$$
$$c_{i+2} = c_{i+1}(1 + r) = c_i(1 + r)^2$$
$$\vdots$$
$$c_{n_3} = c_i(1 + r)^{n_3-i}$$

Substituting each of the terms on the right for the corresponding c's in the wealth constraint (6), the interest rate terms cancel from the numerators and denominators and we are left simply with

(7) $$c_i + c_i + \cdots + c_i = (n_3 - i + 1)\, c_i = z_i.$$

It follows, then, that

(8) $$c_i = \frac{1}{n_3 - i + 1}\, z_i$$

In words, the budgeted consumption in any period under our assumptions is proportional to total wealth at the start of the period, the factor of proportionality being equal to the total number of periods remaining.[9]

APPENDIX TO CHAPTER 4

DERIVATION OF THE CONSUMPTION FUNCTION

In this appendix we derive the consumption function, equation (8). Recall that the decision maker's problem in period i is to choose $c_i, c_{i+1}, \cdots, c_{n_3}$ so as to maximize

(A.1) $$\log c_i + \log c_{i+1} + \cdots + \log c_{n_3},$$

subject to the budget constraint that

(A.2) $$c_i + c_{i+1} \frac{1}{1 + r} + \ldots + c_{n_3} \frac{1}{(1 + r)^{n_3-i}} = z_i.$$

---

[9] The proportionality between consumption and wealth is a consequence of the general form assumed for the preference function, and in particular the fact that it is a *homogeneous* function, and not of our assumption that the γ_i are all equal. Where the γ_i are not equal, the consumption function is still of the general form, but the factor of proportionality is a weighted sum of the number of periods remaining of the form $\gamma_i / \sum_{\tau=i}^{n_3} \gamma_\tau$.

The simplest way to do this is to form the Lagrangian

$$\mathcal{L} = \log c_i + \log c_{i+1} + \ldots + \log c_{n_3}$$
$$- \lambda \left(c_i + c_{i+1} \frac{1}{1+r} + c_{i+2} \frac{1}{(1+r)^2} + \ldots + c_{n_3} \frac{1}{(1+r)^{n_3-i}} - z_i \right)$$

Differentiating partially with respect to each of the decision variables $(c_i, c_{i+1}, \ldots, c_{n_3})$ yields the following set of first order conditions:

$$\frac{1}{c_i} - \lambda = 0,$$

$$\frac{1}{c_{i+1}} - \frac{\lambda}{1+r} = 0,$$

$$\vdots$$

$$\frac{1}{c_{n_3}} - \frac{\lambda}{(1+r)^{n_3-i}} = 0.$$

In turn, these imply that

(A.3) $$c_i = \frac{c_{i+1}}{1+r} = \frac{c_{i+2}}{(1+r)^2} = \ldots = \frac{c_{n_3}}{(1+r)^{n_3-i+1}}.$$

In words, the consumption pattern chosen by a decision maker with such a preference function will have the property that the present value of the sum budgeted for consumption in each subsequent period is the same.

Substituting c_i for each of the terms constraint (A.2) we are left simply with

$$c_i + c_i + \cdots + c_i = (n_3 - i + 1)\, c_i = z_i.$$

It follows, then, that

(A.4) $$c_i = \frac{1}{n_3 - i + 1}\, z_i.$$

We leave it to you to show that if the γs are not equal so that in the equation (A.1)

$$\gamma_i \log c_i + \gamma_{i+1} \log c_{i+1} + \cdots + \gamma_{n_3} \log c_{n_3},$$

the consumption function becomes

(A.5) $$c_i = \frac{\gamma_i}{\sum_{j=i}^{n_3} \gamma_j}\, z_i.$$

That is, the consumption function is still of the general form of (A.4), but the factor of proportionality depends on the γs of the remaining periods.

PROBLEMS FOR CHAPTER 4

1. Figure 4–2 assumes that there is a discrete retirement age after which there is no wage income. Show how Figure 4–2 would look if it had been assumed instead that there was no retirement but merely a gradual diminishing of wage income as one got older.

(Exercises 2–4 use Figure 4–3.)

2. Show that an increase in wealth does not necessarily mean an increase in welfare (as measured by an increase in utility).

3. Show the effects on period 1 consumption of an increase in
    a. the interest rate.
    b. income in period 1.
    Hint: be sure to assume that consumption is a normal good with the right income and substitution effects.

4. What effect will a rise in the interest rate have on wealth and welfare for a person who initially is a saver? Who initially is a dis-saver?

5

Some properties of the life cycle model of consumption

CONSUMPTION OVER THE LIFE CYCLE: SOME NUMERICAL EXAMPLES

BEFORE SIMULATING the broader economic implications of our newly-derived consumption function, we will illustrate its main properties with some simple numerical examples. For comparison, we turn again to the bachelor whose life cycle of consumption and saving we have previously traced out graphically in Figure 4–1. For further concreteness, let us divide his life-span into four periods of equal length (each representing, say, 20 years of actual calendar time). The first period will represent his early childhood and schooling years during which he is assumed to earn no wage or other nonproperty income. His consumption expenditures during this interval must therefore be provided by his parents. For convenience of exposition at this point, we shall assume that his extremely cold-blooded parents actually keep track of all expenditures on his behalf and hand him a bill for these (plus accumulated interest) when he enters the labor force on his own at the start of period 2. (We again beg indulgence for continuing to postpone the subject of intrafamily transfers. We shall get there in due course.)

As for his earnings during his working years, suppose that he anticipates (and does indeed actually receive) wages of $300,000 for the period representing the first half of his career and

$630,000 for the second. Assume, finally, that the interest rate is expected to be, and does in fact turn out to be, 50 percent per period. (Remember that this is the rate for one of our 20-year periods. Fifty percent over 20 years is equivalent to only a little more than two percent compounded annually.)

The solution values for consumption, saving, wealth and its components in each of the four periods are presented in Table 5–1. At the start of period 1 our subject holds no financial assets, so that $a_1 = 0$. He does, however, expect to earn $300,000 in period 2 and $630,000 in period 3. At a rate of interest of 50 percent per period, the present value of these future earnings, entered in the column labeled h_1 (a mnemonic for the human component of wealth), is

$$h_1 = 300,000 \; \frac{1}{1 + .5} + 630,000 \; \frac{1}{(1 + .5)^2} = 480,000.$$

In period 1, h_1 is the only component of total wealth so that our consumption function tells us that budgeted consumption for the period will be given by

$$c_1 = \frac{1}{n_3 - i + 1} \, z_1 = \frac{1}{4 - 1 + 1} \, 480,000 = 120,000.$$

Because our subject earns no wage or interest income in period 1 — as shown in the column labeled y_i — his entire consumption spending constitutes dissaving and is entered as a negative value in the column labeled s_i. Having started with no financial assets, this dissaving of $120,000 also represents the principal amount of his terminal assets, in this case the principal amount of his borrowing.

At the start of period 2, interest at the assumed rate of 50 percent accrues on his borrowing, leaving him with a net liability of $120,000 \, (1 + .5) = 180,000$. The human component of his total wealth consists of (1) the wage payment of $300,000 for the current period, plus (2) the present value of the $630,000 to be received in period 3, which comes to $(630,000) \, \frac{1}{1 + .5} = 420,000$, making a combined total value of $h_2 = \$720,000$. After subtracting the initial indebtedness of $180,000, the bachelor's net wealth comes to $540,000. By the consumption function of Chapter 4, the desired consumption for the period is

TABLE 5–1

The bachelor's saving and consumption calculations over the life cycle

Period	a'_i Principal value of initial assets (+) or liabilities (−)	ra'_i Accrued interest income (+) or expense (−)	a_i Initial financial net worth	w_i Nonproperty income for the period	h_i Present value of all cur- rent and fu- ture nonprop- erty income
1	0	0	0	0	480,000
2	−120,000	−60,000	−180,000	300,000	720,000
3	− 60,000	−30,000	− 90,000	630,000	630,000
4	270,000	135,000	405,000	0	0

Period	z_i Total wealth	c_i Consump- tion	y_i Combined net income	s_i Saving	a'_{i+1} Principal value of terminal assets (+) or liabilities (−)
1	480,000	120,000	0	−120,000	−120,000
2	540,000	180,000	240,000	60,000	− 60,000
3	540,000	270,000	600,000	330,000	270,000
4	405,000	405,000	135,000	−270,000	0

$$c_2 = \frac{1}{n_3 - i + 1} z_2 = \frac{1}{4 - 2 + 1} \, 540,000 = 180,000.[1]$$

Note also that since the budgeted consumption of 180,000 is less than the net income for the period (i.e., less than wage income minus interest expense) our subject has positive saving of $60,000 for the period. These funds, in turn, are used to pay off a corresponding amount of the principal of the loans that were outstanding at the start of the period, leaving a balance of $60,000 of debts at the end of the period.

It is not until period 3 when the bachelor is well along in his career that his financial net worth builds up substantially.[2] Out of his wage earnings of $630,000 for the period, $30,000 is used to pay the carrying charges on his previous borrowing; $270,000 is budgeted for consumption (once again, a level 50

---

[1] Note that this value for c_2 checks with the value we would get for c_2 if we had directly applied the equilibrium conditions from Chapter 4 which imply $c_2 = c_1(1 + r)$. For example, $c_2 = 180,000 = 120,000\ (1 + .5)$.

[2] It may help make the example seem a bit less unrealistic to remember that, in principle, any durable goods owned (automobiles, homes, boats, etc.) are included in financial assets, with the rental value of the services thereon included in both income and consumption.

percent higher than in the previous period); and the remaining $330,000 is added to his financial assets. Netting out the initial liability of $60,000 leaves him a nest egg of $270,000 of net assets with which to start the final period. This fund, plus the $135,000 of interest earned thereon, affords him a standard of living of $405,000 during the years of his retirement, a level that represents, once again, an increase of 50 percent over that in the period immediately before.

To deepen your understanding of the consumption function, you may perhaps also find it a useful exercise at this point to compare the life cycle just described with the one that would have resulted in an economy in which the interest rate was considerably higher, say 100 percent per period rather than 50 percent. In particular, and before looking at the answers in Table 5–2, ask yourself how the consumption and saving levels in each stage of the life cycle will differ from those in Table 5–1. Some thought is necessary because the interest rate comes into the wealth constraint in two different ways. On the one hand, it serves as the discounting factor in the calculation of total wealth. Here, a higher rate of interest means a lower present value of future earnings and hence, presumably, a lower level of consumption spending. (Alternatively, we can think of the rate of interest in its role as the slope of the opportunity line and hence as the rate of exchange between present and future resources. A higher rate thus means a higher reward for lenders—or a higher cost for borrowers—and this should tend to encourage saving and discourage dissaving.) On the other hand, the interest earnings also enter directly into current wealth. The higher the interest rate, the higher the earnings on the financial assets accumulated and hence, presumably, the higher the indicated level of consumption. Which effects dominate in which periods? (Now you may look at Table 5–2.)

Comparing Table 5–2 with Table 5–1, we see that consumption starts in period 1 at a much lower level when interest rates are higher. In this period, there are no accumulated assets on which to earn interest income and the discount effect dominates completely. In period 2, consumption still remains lower in the high-interest-rate economy, but the gap is much smaller. The higher cost of borrowing in period 1, and hence the lower net financial liability carried over, has almost offset the effect on total

TABLE 5–2

Saving and consumption decisions when interest rate equals 100 percent per period

Period	a'_i Principal value of initial assets (+) or liabilities (−)	ra'_i Accrued interest income (+) or expense (−)	a_i Initial financial net worth	w_i Nonproperty income for the period	h_i Present value of all current and future nonproperty income
1	0	0	0	0	307,500
2	−76,875	−76,875	−153,750	300,000	615,000
3	− 7,500	− 7,500	− 15,000	630,000	630,000
4	307,500	307,500	615,000	0	0

Period	z_i Total wealth	c_i Consumption	y_i Combined net income	s_i Saving	a'_{i+1} Principal value of terminal assets (+) or liabilities (−)
1	307,500	76,875	0	− 76,875	−76,875
2	461,250	153,750	223,125	69,375	−7,500
3	615,000	307,500	622,500	315,000	307,500
4	615,000	615,000	307,500	−307,500	0

wealth of the heavier discounting of the period 3 earned income. By period 3, the patient sacrifice of consumption in the earlier periods finally begins to come to fruition and consumption is now higher along the high-interest-rate path. No future earnings remain to be discounted in periods 3 and 4, and the earnings effect of interest is now the dominant one. In the retirement period, in fact, the higher interest earnings on the funds accumulated permit a standard of living more than 50 percent higher than along the low-interest-rate path.

So much then for these two simple examples of life cycles of consumption and saving. We shall be referring back to them frequently in the course of the next two sections, in which we consider some of the broader economic implications of the life-cycle approach.

ESSENTIAL PROPERTIES OF THE LIFE CYCLE CONSUMPTION FUNCTION

The life cycle consumption function that we have derived differs from its simple Keynesian counterpart presented at the start of Chapter 4 in a number of important respects. The first and most obvious difference, of course, is that consumption is taken as a function of wealth and of age, and not simply of current income. This is not to say that the level of current income has no effect on current consumption under the life cycle hypothesis. Clearly, it does have an effect if for no other reason than that current income is one of the terms composing total wealth. Moreover, as we shall see in greater detail later, changes in current income may have an additional indirect effect on current consumption by leading to revised expectations of earnings in future years. But this is a far cry from the dominant role that Keynes and some of the latter-day Keynesians ascribe to current income. And we must not be surprised to find cases where the predicted responses to differences in current income under the two models differ quite drastically.

A second difference between the life cycle function and the function that Keynes seems to have had in mind is that the life cycle function does not imply that people will systematically become thriftier as they get richer. On the contrary, it says that consumption spending is strictly proportional to total wealth, so that if we were to compare two individuals of the same age, one of whom had twice the total wealth of the other, we would expect that his total standard of living would also be twice that of his poorer counterpart. Alternatively, we can say that when comparing two individuals of the same age the average propensity to consume out of total wealth is the same for both, and is equal to $1/(n_3 - i + 1)$, regardless of the level of total wealth.

The qualification of "of the same age" is important to keep in mind since wealth and age tend to be directly related. To see how age and income effects are easily confounded, consider the Keynesian consumption-income relation that seems to fit the data of Table 5-1. If we restrict our attention to individuals in the working periods 2 and 3, a cross-sectional budget survey at any point in time would turn up two consumption-income combinations: one with net income of \$240,000 and consumption of \$180,000 and the other with net income of \$600,000 and consumption of \$270,000. The average propensity to save out of current income at the first observation is $(240,000 - 180,000)/240,000 = .25$; whereas for the observation at the higher income level it has the much higher value of $(600,000 - 270,000)/600,000 = .55$. In this sense, then, it is certainly true, as Keynes conjectured, that the richer group saves more. But the difference is entirely due to the difference in age and hence in the position along the life cycle profile from which the observations were drawn; and not to any psycho-social tendency for "the motives towards accumulation" to become stronger after "a margin of comfort has been attained." (Cf., the descriptive passage from Keynes quoted near the beginning of Chapter 4.)

THE RESPONSE OF CONSUMPTION TO UNANTICIPATED CHANGES IN INCOME AND WEALTH

Up to this point all our discussion and illustrations of the life cycle model have assumed that the actual levels of income and wealth in any period were the same as those anticipated at the start of the life cycle. In practice, of course, it hardly needs mentioning that surprises, pleasant and unpleasant, continually arise. Some of the most striking differences between the life cycle and simple Keynesian consumption functions arise when their respective predictions of the response of budgeted consumption to these unanticipated changes in income and wealth are compared.[3]

Some numerical examples

Consider, for example, two life-time earnings profiles, one exactly as pictured in Table 5–1 and the other having a wage level of 10 percent less (i.e., wages of $270,000 in period 2 and $567,000 in period 3). If the lower level of earnings had been fully anticipated from the beginning, then, by virtue of the property of the life cycle consumption function that consumption is directly proportional to wealth, we know that consumption spending would also have been 10 percent smaller in every period. (For

[3] Strictly speaking, we should not be talking about "unanticipated" changes since our model was derived under the assumption that the decision maker knew all the relevant future values with perfect certainty. More general treatments of the saving decision in which uncertainty is taken into account explicitly have been developed in recent years, but they are far too complex for an introductory volume of this kind. Our certainty approach with "surprises" is admittedly inelegant, but it can serve as a reasonable first approximation to the more elaborate models for the class of macroeconomic problems that are our main concern.

TABLE 5-3

Saving and consumption decisions with cut of 10 percent in income

Period	a'_i Principal value of initial assets (+) or liabilities (−)	ra'_i Accrued interest income (+) or expense (−)	a_i Initial financial net worth	w_i Nonproperty income for the period	h_i Present value of all current and future nonproperty income	z_i Total wealth	c_i Consumption	y_i Combined net income	s_i Saving	a'_{i+1} Principal value of terminal assets (+) or liabilities (−)
Lower earnings fully anticipated										
1	0	0	0	0	432,000	432,000	108,000	0	−108,000	−108,000
2	−108,000	−54,000	−162,000	270,000	648,000	486,000	162,000	216,000	54,000	−54,000
3	−54,000	−27,000	−81,000	567,000	567,000	486,000	243,000	540,000	297,000	243,000
4	243,000	121,500	364,500	0	0	364,500	364,500	121,500	−243,000	0
Lower earnings not anticipated										
1	0	0	0	0	480,000	480,000	120,000	0	−120,000	−120,000
2	−120,000	−60,000	−180,000	270,000	648,000	468,000	156,000	210,000	54,000	−66,000
3	−66,000	−33,000	−99,000	567,000	567,000	468,000	234,000	534,000	300,000	234,000
4	234,000	117,000	351,000	0	0	351,000	351,000	117,000	−234,000	0

easy reference, the values for assets, consumption, income and saving are presented in Table 5–3, top panel.)

Suppose, however, that the lower wage level had not been anticipated at the start of period 1, but that the change had occurred rather at the start of period 2, after the first period's consumption spending and already taken place. The new level of consumption budgeted for period 2 will be given by

$$c_2 = \frac{1}{3} z_2 = \frac{1}{3} (-180{,}000 + 648{,}000)$$

$$= 156{,}000$$

which is thus even lower than the consumption level would have been if the 10 percent income falloff had been fully anticipated. The reason is, of course, that having spent too much in period 1 as a result of the overoptimistic projection of earnings, his liabilities are now too high in relation to his sustainable standard of living. An extra effort at belt-tightening, over and beyond that necessary merely to adjust to the new lower level of expectations, is required to work off this extra debt load during the limited working span remaining.

The short-run and the long-run consumption functions[4]

The level of consumption after an *unanticipated* change in earnings thus will differ, and in general differ quite substantially, from the value it would have had if the change had been anticipated. This property of the life cycle model helps to explain, among other things, why the relation of consumption to current income often seems to conform well to a simple Keynesian function with positive intercept over short periods or in cross-sectional budget studies and yet the average propensity to consume shows no tendency to drift downward when the readings are taken over longer intervals. For when we take a survey of actual consump-

---

[4] This section contains much of the essential message usually associated with the so-called permanent income hypothesis. To avoid distraction and digression at this point, however, we have relegated all formal discussion of the permanent income hypothesis to an appendix to this chapter.

tion spending and earnings in any given year, we are bound to turn up many individuals whose earnings differ from earlier expectations and whose consumption patterns are in the process of adjustment to new levels.

The situation is pictured graphically in Figure 5-1, which shows the relation between consumption and human wealth for some particular age-group i, all of whose members are assumed to have started their life cycles with the same anticipated earnings.

FIGURE 5-1
The long-run and short-run consumption functions

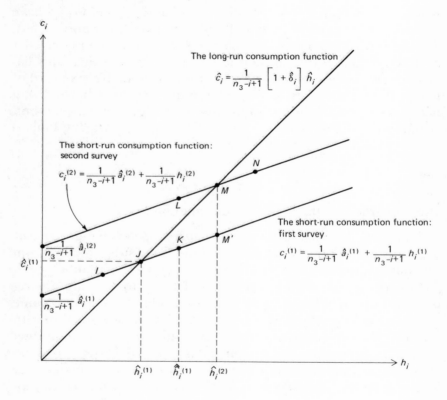

The line running through the points I, J and K is what might be called the *short-run consumption function* for the group at the time we take our first survey (indicated by the superscript 1). Algebraically, it is just our regular life cycle consumption function with the two wealth components stated separately, that is

$$c_i^{(1)} = \frac{1}{n_3 - i + 1} z_i^{(1)} = \frac{1}{n_3 - i + 1} \hat{a}_i^{(1)} + \frac{1}{n_3 - i + 1} h_i^{(1)}.$$

As drawn here, age group i is far enough along in the life cycle to have accumulated positive net worth as indicated by the positive value for the intercept $\hat{a}_i^{(1)}/(n_3 - i + 1)$. The slope of the line, or *short-run marginal propensity to consume* out of h_i, is, of course $1/(n_3 - i + 1)$.

The point J represents the consumption level that would have been chosen by any member of the group if his actual earnings had been exactly equal to his anticipated earnings, $\hat{h}_i^{(1)}$. The point K shows the consumption level for a member of the group who had just received an unexpected rise in his current and future wage income that has led him to revise his estimated human wealth up to the level $\hat{\hat{h}}_i^{(1)}$. His consumption is higher than $\hat{c}_i^{(1)}$ by the amount $\frac{1}{n_3 - i + 1} [\hat{\hat{h}}_i^{(1)} - \hat{h}_i^{(1)}]$ which is, of course, precisely what we mean when we say that $1/(n_3 - i + 1)$ is the short-run marginal propensity to consume. Similarly, the point I shows the level of consumption spending that would have been selected by an individual who had just revised his earnings expectations downward.

If we repeat the same survey a generation later, the short-run consumption function for a group then of the same age and relative earning position is represented by the line through the points L, M and N, reflecting a much higher absolute level of anticipated human capital, $\hat{h}_i^{(2)}$. The "on-target" level of consumption spending is now given by the point M which is, of course, considerably higher than the value at M' that would be predicted from a mechanical extrapolation of the earlier generation's short-run consumption function to the same value of anticipated earnings, $\hat{h}_i^{(2)}$. The line through the points, J and M, representing the "on-target" consumption of the two surveyed generations, is what might be called the *long-run consumption function* for age-group i. Its equation, in terms of target values for the variables, is simply

$$\hat{c}_i = \frac{1}{n_3 - i + 1} \hat{z}_i = \frac{1}{n_3 - i + 1} [\hat{a}_i + \hat{h}_i] = \frac{1}{n_3 - i + 1} [1 + \hat{\delta}_i] \hat{h}_i$$

where $\hat{\delta}_i = \hat{a}_i/\hat{h}_i$ is the on-target ratio of financial to human capital for age-group i. The *long-run marginal propensity to consume,* or slope of the long-run consumption function,

$$\frac{1}{n_3 - i + 1} \left[1 + \hat{\delta}_i \right]$$

is thus greater than the short-run marginal propensity, $\dfrac{1}{n_3 - i + 1}$,

for all age groups sufficiently far along the life cycle to have reached the point of positive net worth.[5]

Response to changes in the level of financial assets

Up to this point, our analysis of the response of consumption to unanticipated changes has focused on unanticipated changes in current and prospective wage earnings. There is another component to total wealth, however, namely financial net worth, and it, too, is subject to a variety of shocks, pleasant and unpleasant. Consider, for example, the effects of a sudden sharp drop in the stock market. An individual who directly or indirectly held a sizable fraction of his assets in that form now finds his previously planned standard of living no longer appropriate to his current wealth. He will thus cut back his current consumption by an amount equal to $1/(n_3 - i + 1)$ times the fall in his net worth, and move along thereafter on a parallel, but lower consumption track.[6]

---

[5] In the borrowing age groups $\hat{a}_i$ will be negative, as we have seen, so that the term in brackets is less than one, and the long-run marginal propensity is smaller than the short-run marginal propensity.

[6] Exactly the opposite effect occurs, of course, in the case of a rise in the stock market. This link between stock prices and savings helps explain, incidentally, why we can conduct our discussion of saving behavior entirely in terms of personal saving even though a large portion of aggregate saving technically takes the form of business saving (i.e., of undistributed corporate profits). As will be described in more detail in finance courses, these plowed-back corporate profits cause the price level of the typical common stock to be higher than it otherwise would. We assume that people smart enough to have assets to invest are smart enough, at least, eventually to recognize the increment to their personal wealth from this source as part of the "interest" return on common stock. If so, they will make the corresponding adjustments and save less in other forms so that our figure for total individual saving will indeed be

If the fall in the stock market is not also accompanied by a fall in his earned income, then the cutback in current consumption implies a corresponding surge in the average propensity to save out of current income. To a confirmed Keynesian, accustomed to thinking of consumption as adapting mechanically to current income, such surges are bound to seem mysterious. When they happen on a large scale, they often lead to searching "think pieces" in the financial pages in which the supposed sudden reluctance to spend is taken as further evidence of the imminent decline of the republic.[7]

Formally, the analysis of the response to unanticipated changes in financial assets proceeds exactly as in the case of human capital except for the reversal of the roles of a_i and h_i. That is, in the short-run consumption function

$$c_i = \frac{1}{n_3 - i + 1} \hat{h}_i + \frac{1}{n_3 - i + 1} a_i$$

the intercept becomes $\dfrac{1}{n_3 - i + 1} \hat{h}_i$, though the short-run marginal propensity to consume remains $1/(n_3 - i + 1)$. The long-run consumption function is simply

$$\hat{c}_i = \frac{1}{n_3 - i + 1} [1 + 1/\hat{\delta}_i] \hat{a}_i$$

Once again, the long-run marginal and average propensities are

---

approximately the same as the sum of corporate saving plus individual saving net of the increase in the value of corporate shares held.

A similar implicit "displacement" assumption is involved in our failure to give much prominence to such conspicuous features of present-day compensation arrangements as pension-plan contributions by employers. We assume that people are smart enough to make adjustments elsewhere, though there is no reason to believe the adjustment will be precisely one-for-one in any particular case (partly because the benefits are known to be far from certain for many companies and partly because the tax and other elements of subsidy involved may serve to change the perceived terms of trade on future versus present consumption). Some special problems arising in connection with social security are considered in Chapter 8.

[7] Amusingly enough, Keynes himself was quite aware that large swings in the stock market might have appreciable effects on the propensity to consume out of current income though he seems to have thought this was more likely to be true of Americans than of the less excitable British.

the same and both are higher than the short-run marginal propensity by the factor $[1 + 1/\hat{\delta}_i] = [1 + \hat{h}_i/\hat{a}_i]$.

CONCLUDING OBSERVATIONS

This brief disquisition on problems of adjustment to unanticipated changes in resources largely concludes our formal development of the microfoundations of the life cycle consumption function. We now have in hand most of the apparatus we need to consider the important implications of the life cycle hypothesis for the growth and stability of the economy as a whole. The macroeconomic models we use for this purpose will, not unnaturally, have many features in common with the neoclassical model of Chapters 2 and 3, especially in the areas of production and of income generation and distribution. But the consumption sector will be considerably more complicated. For some purposes, where the point being made is such that it can be conveyed adequately in a model involving no more than two age groups, we could reduce the aggregate consumption function to a single equation, though a much more elaborate one than the simple $C = \beta Y$ of the neoclassical case. In general, however, this involves too great a sacrifice of the richness of insight that the life cycle approach provides. We shall, therefore, find it a better strategy to maintain separate consumption functions for each of many age groups (sometimes as many as 80), and to estimate the aggregate effects of the various experimental shocks we give the economy (wars, taxes, inflation, etc.) by first tracing their impact on each of the major age groups, and then summing up over the entire population.

Before turning to these macroeconomic applications, however, we shall first finish up our discussion of the life cycle model with some observations on the long-postponed issues of intrafamily transfers and especially of the determination and financing of consumption expenditures during the early childhood, dependency periods.

We can deal with the matter briefly and somewhat cavalierly at this point, because once it is understood that we shall be maintaining a separate consumption function for each age group in our illustrative macro models, the issue of family versus individual consumption largely loses its significance. It becomes merely a question of how we choose to interpret the aggregation that is, in any event, going to be performed with the model. Consider, for example, a four-age-group model with numerical values taken for concreteness to be those of Table 5–1. And suppose further, for simplicity, that there are exactly four people in each age group. Then we have many equivalent ways of interpreting the aggregate consumption function.[8]

1. We can regard the population *as if* it consisted of 16 separate "households," four in each age group, with per capita consumption, income and wealth in each group as given in Table 5–1. (This is, in effect, the interpretation we have been giving to the life cycles so far.) Total consumption, summed over all the population, will be $3,900,000, as will be total income. Consumption and income per capita will be about $244,000.

2. We can regard the population as if it consisted of four identical families, each with four members: one child, one parent in age group 2, another parent in age group 3 and one retired grandparent. Total consumption and income for any one family during the current period will be the sum of the consumptions and incomes in each age group, namely $975,000 in each case, or again about $244,000 per capita.

3. We can regard the population as if it consisted of five different families with the compositions that are shown in Table 5–4.

We leave it to you to construct additional scenarios, real and imaginary.

In short, reasonable approximations of family consumption and saving patterns for many purposes can be obtained by assuming that families act *as if* they were composed of the atomistic bachelors described earlier. This still leaves unanswered the question of what happens when we explicitly incorporate intrafamily transfers such as bequests. We will return to that issue in Chapter 8.

---

[8] Keep in mind that the scenarios to follow are intended to be illustrative only and not indicative of actual magnitudes as they occur in practice. In terms of the findings in recent and past budget studies, the patterns below tend to give too much weight to the consumption of children. If we were striving for sharper accuracy at this point, we could adjust for this merely by varying the time preference γs in the preference function, and hence also in the consumption function. See the appendix to Chapter 4 on this point.

TABLE 5–4
Some hypothetical family consumption patterns

Family type	Number of family members in age group				Total family consumption	Total family income	Consumption per capita (in thousands of dollars)	Income per capita
	1	2	3	4				
Childless working couple............	0	0	2	0	540	1,200	270	600
Retired couple............	0	0	0	2	810	270	405	135
Young married couple with 2 small children............	2	2	0	0	600	480	150	120
Young childless couple living with her family............	0	2	0	2	1,170	750	293	188
Older working couple with twins............	2	0	2	0	780	1,200	195	300
Totals............	4	4	4	4	3,900	3,900	244	244

APPENDIX TO CHAPTER 5

THE PERMANENT INCOME HYPOTHESIS

A critical failing of the simple Keynesian consumption function is its prediction that the average propensity to consume will fall in the long run. The life cycle model of consumption was developed to show how the average propensity to consume could be constant in the long run, but fall with short-term increases in income. An alternative theory developed at about the same time as the life cycle model is the so-called permanent income model. Rather than clutter up the text with a comparison between the two theories, we have chosen to relegate it to this appendix.

The permanent income hypothesis

The *permanent income hypothesis* in its original and strongest form consists of the following definitions and assumptions:

1. An individual's actual income y_t in any period can be expressed as the simple sum of two components,

(A.1) $$y_t = y_t^* + y_t^T,$$

where y_t^* is his "permanent income" and y_t^T is his "transitory" income.

2. Actual consumption spending during the period also consists of a permanent and transitory component,

(A.2) $$c_t = c_t^* + c_t^T.$$

3. Permanent consumption is proportional to permanent income, with the factor of proportionality λ_i reflecting the individual's age, family structure and similar life cycle influences. Not only does permanent consumption depend on permanent income, but it depends *only* on permanent income and not at all on transitory income. In terms of permanent values, the consumption function is thus

(A.3) $$c_t^* = \lambda_i y_t^*$$

4. Transitory consumption is not systematically related either to permanent or transitory income.

Combining these assumptions and definitions, we thus get a function for total consumption of the form

(A.4) $$c_t = \lambda_i \, y_t^* + c_t^T$$

with c_t^T playing the role of a "random disturbance." In terms of propensities to consume, the relation (A.4) implies that the marginal (and average) propensity to consume out of permanent income is λ_i; and that the marginal propensity to consume out of transitory income is zero.

This difference serves to explain the crucial fact that the long-run and short-run average propensities to consume out of observed income are different. The situation for a particular age-group i is pictured in Figure 5A–1. The line OZ through the origin, with slope λ_i represents what might be called the permanent value consumption function. If we take our first survey at a time when the permanent income of a typical member of the group is $y^{*(1)}$, then we would expect to find a level of permanent consumption for that individual of $c^{*(1)}$. *Actual* consumption for any individual may well be somewhat above or below this value because of the transitory elements in consumption, so we might well observe a point off the line such as B or C for any given individual. Similarly, during the year we take our survey we are likely to find some individuals whose income has temporarily risen as a result of some piece of good fortune (say, an unexpectedly large Christmas bonus) that is regarded as unlikely to be repeated. Since such individuals will not adapt their permanent standard of living to such purely transitory increases in their income, we may well observe a point such as D where actual income $y_a^{(1)}$ is greater than permanent income $y^{*(1)}$, but actual consumption is still at a level of $c^{*(1)}$; or we may observe points such as E or F where there are some transitory elements in consumption as well as in income. In the other direction, some unlucky members of the group will find their current income, $y_b^{(1)}$, pushed below their permanent income, and for them we may find points such as G, H or I.

If we asked what line seemed best to represent the observed consumption-income combinations A through I turned up by our survey, it would have to be something very close to the line HAD. The fit would clearly not be exact; as drawn, there seems to be a lot of "scatter" about the line. But without knowing the mechanism producing the numbers, it would be hard to avoid the conclusion that HAD was a reasonably representative consumption function for the group. Note that the predicted average propensity to consume would be falling; the intercept would be approximately $c^{*(1)}$ and the apparent marginal propensity to consume out of measured income would be approximately zero.

Suppose now we take a similar survey of a corresponding segment of individuals in the same age group but a generation or two later. Permanent income for the group is now at the higher value $y^{*(2)}$ and permanent consumption at $c^{*(2)}$. There will still be transitory elements in the actual ys and cs so that the observations will again be scattered around a line of very flat slope, such as the line *RJN*. But if we compare the *average* income and *average* consumption for the two surveys, we will get, approximately, the points *A* and *J*; and since these points lie along or very close to

FIGURE 5A–1
Illustrations of the permanent income consumption function

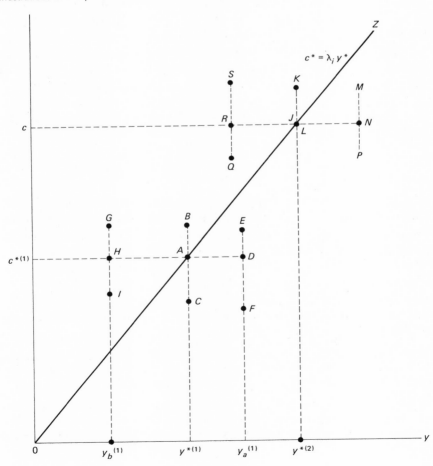

the line OZ we will find that there has been little if any change in the average rates of consumption to income between the two survey dates.

The life cycle view

There is clearly a very close similarity between the picture and scenarios of Figure 5A–1 and those we saw earlier in connection with Figure 5–1. One way of establishing the relation between them is to convert our earlier discussion which ran in terms of wealth stocks into one running in terms of income flows. Under the conditions assumed in building up our wealth model, this conversion really involves little more than some straightforward present value calculations. Consider, for example, an individual in age group 1 of Table 5–1. We know that the present value of his lifetime resources at the assumed interest rate of 50 percent is $480,000. A natural definition of his permanent income[9] would be the uniform flow of income during the four periods of his life that has exactly the same present value of $480,000, and is thus entirely equivalent to the sequence of earnings he actually anticipates.[10] In terms of the example, this means finding that value of X such that

$$X + \frac{X}{1 + .5} + \frac{X}{(1 + .5)^2} + \frac{X}{(1 + .5)^3} = 480,000$$

which, with a little calculation, is seen to be about $200,000.[11] More generally, it can be shown that the uniform lifetime income y_i^* starting in period i and equivalent to the value of wealth as of the start of period i is given by[12]

---

[9] So many investigators, following the lead of Friedman's original study, have approximated permanent income by an "exponentially weighted moving average" of past income that beginners may be pardoned for assuming that the two terms are interchangeable. They are not.

[10] Readers of British novels will recognize this as essentially the British way of indicating wealth — Lord So-and-So being worth £10,000 a year — in contrast to the more typically American balance-sheet approach to stating wealth.

[11] More precisely, $199,402.

[12] In some formulations, permanent income is defined rather as the income *in perpetuity* that would be equivalent to z_i, and which hence would be rz_i. The advantages of the perpetuity form are mainly those of mathematical simplicity, though economic rationalizations are sometimes offered in terms of estate-motive saving.

$$y_i^* = z_i \left[\frac{r(1 + r)^{n_3-i}}{(1 + r)^{n_3-i+1} - 1} \right].$$

Thus, by substituting for the value of z_i in our regular life-cycle consumption function, we get a consumption function restated in terms of permanent income of the form

$$c_i = \frac{1}{n_3 - i + 1} z_i = \frac{1}{n_3 - i + 1} \left[\frac{(1 + r)^{n_3-i+1} - 1}{r(1 + r)^{n_3-i}} \right] y_i^* = \lambda_i y_i^*.$$

If then we can identify permanent consumption with what we have previously called "on target" consumption, we have an exact correspondence between our long-run consumption function and assumption (A.3) of the permanent income hypothesis.

In the case of the transitory variables, however, the correspondence between the two models is much less direct. In fact, insofar as transitory consumption is concerned, there is nothing comparable in the life cycle model as we have developed it, though in principle we could certainly have added an equivalent random disturbance term to the life cycle consumption function. For transitory income, however, we can get at least an approximate counterpart by distinguishing among various kinds of unanticipated changes on the basis of the number of periods over which the change is expected to extend.

Consider, for example, two equivalent individuals, currently in the second period of their life cycles and having the same on-target consumption, assets and wealth up to this point. Suppose, for further concreteness, that both are given an unexpected raise of 20 percent, with, however, one difference: for one, the raise is in the form of a special one-shot bonus payable this year only; for the other, the raise is a promotion to a new and higher pay track for every year from now to retirement. Despite the fact that the increase in *current* income is the same for both individuals, the change in consumption implied by the life cycle model will be vastly different in the two cases. The man with the promotion has received a large increase in his wealth and will make a sizable upward readjustment in his standard of living. In the case of the data in Table 5–1, for example, an unexpected 20 percent increase in wages received at the start of period 2 and covering both periods 2 and 3 will raise wealth by $144,000 (20 percent of $720,000), and hence raise consumption by 1/3 of that amount, or $48,000. Since the rise in current income was

$60,000 (20 percent of $300,000), the apparent marginal propensity to consume is 48,000/60,000 = .8. By contrast, the man with the bonus has received an unexpected increase in wealth of only $60,000, which in turn, calls for an increase in consumption of only $20,000. Hence his apparent marginal propensity to consume out of current income will have the much lower value of 20,000/60,000 = .33.

PROBLEMS FOR CHAPTER 5

1. Suppose that the decision maker expects to live four periods and receive a wage income of $180,000 each period in periods 2 and 3, and that the interest rate is 50 percent per period. Calculate his consumption in each period of life.

2. Show how the consumption for period 4 can be calculated merely from knowing period 1's consumption and the rate of interest.

3. Using an interest rate of 100 percent, recompute the decision maker's consumption over his life.

4. Suppose the interest rate unexpectedly changed from 50 to 100 percent at the beginning of period 2 (and after the decision maker had paid interest on his period 1 debts). Recompute his lifetime consumption.

5. Suppose the annual wage rate the decision maker will receive unexpectedly drops by 50 percent after he had made his consumption decision for period 1. Recompute his lifetime consumption.

6. Compute the decision maker's consumption over the life cycle if the interest rate will be 50 percent in period 1 and 100 percent thereafter.

6

The neoclassical model
with a life cycle
consumption function

WE ARE NOW going to marry the life cycle consumption function
to the neoclassical model of economic growth. With this union
we can no longer completely rely on simple graphical analysis to
bring out the main points and must make heavier use of numerical
examples. For the computations involved in these examples, we
will rely on a computer program, though no knowledge of computers in general, or of the nuts and bolts of this program in particular, is required to follow the example.

STEADY-STATE EQUILIBRIUM PROPERTIES

As with the earlier example, we will use the Cobb-Douglas
production function to describe the relation between output and
inputs. In this case we will be working in terms of gross, rather
than net, values and we will slightly change the coefficients on
capital and the labor force so that gross national product (GNP)
is given by

$$Y_t = K_t^{.3} (N_t^*)^{.7},$$

where K_t = capital stock in year t, and N_t^* = number of effective
labor units in year t.[1] Table 6–1 presents some of the basic eco-

---

[1] A word of explanation about the shift in α from .5 to .3: the reader will
remember, if he has read the appendix to Chapter 3, that $1 - \alpha$ measures labor's
share of GNP, which has historically been about 70–75 percent in the United
States. The change in α is intended to reflect this oft-cited economic regularity.

TABLE 6–1

Basic economic data on NEUTRAL

Year	Labor force*	Capital stock†	Gross national product†	Consumption	Gross investment†	Wage rate††
1	308.4	8,912.2	2,765.5	2,072.9	692.6	6,276
2	311.1	9,250.1	2,869.9	2,151.2	718.7	6,458
3	313.7	9,597.8	2,978.3	2,232.4	745.9	6,645
99	709.9	337,350.9	104,665.0	78,452.4	26,212.7	103,214
100	715.9	350,062.5	108,618.3	81,415.3	27,203.1	106,206

* Millions of persons
† Billions of dollars
†† Dollars

nomic data on a hypothetical economy which we will call NEUTRAL. We are presenting data on only a few selected years; the reason for choosing these particular years will later become apparent.

A few calculations readily verify that NEUTRAL is in steady-state equilibrium. The wage rate is growing at a constant rate of 2.9 percent, reflecting the growth coming from technological change, an addition to the neoclassical model discussed in Chapter 3. The labor force is growing at an annual rate of .85 percent. The biological interest rate is $r_b = (1 + q)(1 + n) - 1 = (1 + .029)(1 + .0085) - 1 = .0377$, or 3.77 percent, and GNP, investment and consumption are all growing at that rate. Similarly, the Investment/GNP ratio (which is equal, of course, to the Saving/GNP ratio) is constant at 25 percent.

Another way to see that NEUTRAL is in steady-state equilibrium is to verify that all the capital investment represents capital widening, and none represents capital deepening (or "shallowing"). Table 6–2A presents the calculations for the aggregate capital stock, and Table 6–2B for the capital/effective labor unit ratio (assuming that capital depreciates at an annual rate of 4 percent). These calculations show that investment is proceeding at precisely the pace required for steady-state equilibrium.[2]

The model used in this example is similar, though not identical, to that of Chapter 2. Part of the difference comes from the addition of demographic detail. The new economy is composed of individuals living finite lives of 80 years, divided into three age periods of youth, work, and retirement. Naturally enough, all people are born in the first year of life, where, for simplicity, the Chinese convention of crediting people with a year of life at birth will be adopted. (Those with some experience

---

[2] Although we have chosen to make the time unit in the computer model a year we might equally well have used longer time units (such as the 20-year unit of the examples in Chapter 5) without changing any of the fundamental long-run properties of the model. Such a long time unit, however, would wash out most of the detail along the path to the eventual equilibrium. A unit shorter than a year such as a quarter or a month would in principle permit even more such detail to be displayed. But it becomes less and less plausible to pretend that equilibrium could be reached in all markets, especially the labor market, in every period in so short a time. Models in which the labor market does not adjust completely within one time period are considered in Chapters 16 and 17.

TABLE 6–2A

Aggregate capital accumulation (billions of dollars).

Year	Capital stock	Gross investment	Capital depreciation ($.04 \times$ col. 1)	Net investment	Capital widening requirements ($.0377 \times$ col. 1)	Next year's capital stock
1	8,912.2	692.6	356.5	336.1	336.1	9,248.3
2	9,248.3	718.6	369.9	348.7	348.7	9,597.0
3	9,597.0	745.9	383.9	362.0	362.0	9,959.0
99	337,350.1	26,212.7	13,494.0	12,718.1	12,718.1	350,068.2
100	350,068.2	27,200.5	14,002.7	13,197.8	13,197.8	363,266.0

TABLE 6–2B

Capital/effective labor ratio

Year	Effective labor units/worker	Labor force (millions), N	Total effective labor units, N^* (billions)	Capital/effective labor ratio, k	Investment/effective labor unit (gross)	Investment/effective labor unit (net of depreciation)	Required for capital widening ($.0377 \times k$)
1	5,432	308.4	1675.2	5.32	.413	.200	.200
2	5,589	311.1	1738.7	5.32	.413	.200	.200
3	5,751	313.7	1804.1	5.32	.413	.200	.200
99	89,325	709.7	63,394.0	5.32	.413	.200	.200
100	91,914	715.9	65,801.2	5.32	.413	.200	.200

at computer programming will appreciate the wisdom of the East.) A person in age group 19, say, will hereafter be referred to as a 19-year-old, though by Western standards he is only 18.

Although the assumption of certain death at 80 may seem to lack realism, remember that in macroeconomics the objective is to predict *aggregate* behavior. For this purpose the model need not do a good job of predicting individual behavior or life histories. All we are really saying with our fixed life-span assumption is that variations in the length of life of individuals cause perturbations in the totals that are small enough to be safely neglected.

Because people in this unisex population enter the labor force at age 20 and retire after age 65, the labor force is only a fraction of the total population.[3] The demographic data on NEUTRAL presented in Table 6–3 show that slightly over half of the population is in the labor force. Deaths (those reaching age 80) are .87 percent of the population while births are 1.72 percent. Hence the population growth rate, births minus deaths, is .85 percent per year.

TABLE 6–3
Demographic data on NEUTRAL (millions of persons)

Year	Population	Labor force	Births	Deaths
1	552.7	308.4	9.48	4.84
2	557.4	311.1	9.56	4.88
3	562.2	313.7	4.65	4.93
99	1271.9	709.9	21.82	11.15
100	1282.8	715.9	22.01	11.24

Another and very important difference between NEUTRAL and our earlier example is the saving process. Aggregate consumption and saving patterns in NEUTRAL are determined by individuals making their consumption and saving decisions according to the life cycle model of Chapters 4 and 5. Table 6–4

---

[3] Instead of assuming that people work a fixed number of years and retire, it would be possible to assume that "retirement" is characterized by declining wage income due to increased consumption of leisure and declining productivity. But as indicated earlier, nothing essential is lost by assuming a fixed retirement age.

TABLE 6–4

Individual financial data in dollars for NEUTRAL (year 1)

	Age 1	Age 20	Age 42	Age 65	Age 72	Age 80
Income statement						
Wages	0.0	6,276.2	6,276.2	6,276.2	0.0	0.0
Plus Earnings on assets	0.0	−2,151.5	1,463.8	4,836.1	3,410.4	456.3
Equals Net earnings	0.0	4,124.6	7,740.0	11,112.3	3,410.4	456.3
Less Consumption	1,442.7	2,243.0	3,738.8	6,379.9	7,506.6	9,038.9
Equals Net saving	−1,442.7	1,881.6	4,001.2	4,732.4	−4,096.2	−8,582.6
Wealth statement						
Initial assets	0.0	−42,621.5	28,997.9	95,801.6	67,559.6	9,038.9
Plus Present value of earnings	115,413.6	179,445.3	116,814.6	6,276.3	0.0	0.0
Equals Wealth	115,413.6	136,823.8	145,812.4	102,077.8	67,559.6	9,038.9
Consumption	1,442.7	2,243.0	3,738.8	6,379.9	7,506.6	9,038.9
Consumption/wealth ratio	0.0125	0.0164	0.0256	0.0625	0.1111	1.0000

presents data on the computation for individuals of selected age groups. Although the calculations are now too difficult to do by hand, these numbers are derived from exactly the same calculations as those in Chapter 5. Aggregate consumption expenditures in any year can be found by summing up these individual expenditures; that number has already been presented in Table 6–1.

In sum, we now have a model which, like those of Chapters 2 and 3, can explain the capital stock, the wage rate and the rental rate as a function of the saving rate; and like that of Chapter 5 can explain saving behavior. The difference is that this example can do all these things simultaneously.

THE ADJUSTMENT TO STEADY STATE

As with our earlier examples, we are interested both in what determines the steady-state equilibrium of an economy and how an economy moves back to a steady state after being disturbed.

The immediate requirement for seeing how NEUTRAL would adjust to a shock moving it away from its equilibrium capital/effective labor unit ratio is, of course, to have a shock. For concreteness, we will use a war. Suppose, in particular, that two countries initially exactly like NEUTRAL fight a brief but quite destructive war. In the country which lost the war—LOSER—10 percent of the population and 25 percent of the capital stock are destroyed. Consequently, the capital/labor ratio is reduced by approximately 15 percent. Although 10 percent of the population in the winning country—WINNER—is destroyed, there is no destruction of its capital stock. As a result, the capital/labor ratio is increased by approximately 10 percent.

Since this new computer model is an extension of the simple neoclassical model, let us look first at the predictions that the latter would make for these economies. As shown in Figure 6–1, the war raises WINNER's capital/labor ratio (or more precisely, the capital/effective labor unit ratio) from k_N to k_W. Consequently, output per *effective labor unit* rises from y_N to y_W, although total output falls. Because labor has become scarcer relative to capital, the wage rate rises and the capital rental rate falls in WINNER in the immediate postwar period. If the saving rate remains constant, this high level of output per effective labor unit is not sustainable and WINNER's capital/effective labor unit ratio will slowly drift down to its equilibrium level; i.e., to NEUTRAL's level of k_N. While this takes place, WINNER's growth rates will be below NEUTRAL's.

FIGURE 6–1
WINNER, LOSER, NEUTRAL and the neoclassical model

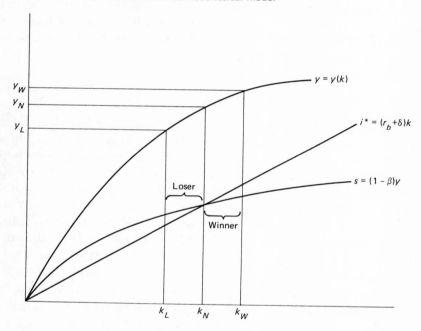

The neoclassical model predicts precisely the opposite effects for LOSER, whose capital/effective labor unit ratio falls from k_N to k_L. Capital has now become scarce relative to labor in LOSER so that its rental rate will rise and its wage rate will fall. However, this pattern is only temporary. LOSER's capital/effective labor unit ratio will slowly rise until it again reaches NEUTRAL's; its wage and rental rates will also move until they again reach NEUTRAL's level. In the short run, however, it will have a higher growth rate. These short-run predictions of the simple neoclassical model are summarized in Table 6–5.

TABLE 6-5
Rank predictions of the simple neoclassical model for the short run

	Country		
Variables	*WINNER*	*NEUTRAL*	*LOSER*
Rental rate	3	2	1
Wage rate	1	2	3
Growth rate	3	2	1

The role of the auctioneer

Let us now turn to developments in LOSER in the first year after the war.[4] As a consequence of the 10-percent decline in the labor force and 25-percent decline in the capital stock, its GNP is 15 percent below NEUTRAL's. This presents certain problems to the auctioneer. As regards the dual responsibilities of keeping both capital and labor fully employed, his response is clear: as we have just seen, he must raise the rental rate of capital and lower the wage rate in LOSER to compensate for its lower capital/effective labor unit ratio. In fact, given our numerical assumptions, he must raise the capital rental price from 5.32 percent to 6.56 percent and lower the wage rate from $6,276 to $5,972, though we can leave the details of computing these numbers to the auctioneer.

But the auctioneer has another task: ensuring that the demand for consumption and investment goods exactly equals the full-employment GNP that entrepreneurs will provide at the wage rate and rental rate he calls out. In the case of LOSER, this requires him to make sharp reductions in consumption and investment demand vis-à-vis NEUTRAL because of the smaller labor force and capital stock in LOSER.

What makes it possible for the auctioneer to adjust the demand to the supply is his power to announce *next* year's rental rate for capital. Because this rate effectively determines the capital stock firms will demand *next* year, it equivalently gives the auctioneer the power to control this year's investment demand. For example,

---

[4] For simplicity, we will only discuss postwar developments in LOSER; most of the effects in WINNER are exactly the opposite, and we will use data on that country for a series of questions at the end of the chapter.

if the auctioneer announces that next year's rental price will remain unchanged from this year's, there will be no change in the capital/effective labor unit ratio firms demand. The only demand for capital investment will be that required to permit capital widening. But if the auctioneer announces a lower rental price for next year, then the demand for capital investment will increase to permit capital deepening as well as capital widening. So, in the short run at least, we can think of both the demand for capital and the demand for investment as functions of the rental rate for next year.

When considered from the perspective of individual consumers, next year's rental rate for capital has another important economic role. Once the auctioneer announces the rental rate that firms must pay for the use of capital to the banks of Chapter 2 or whatever financial institutions are the immediate source of the capital, competition will force these institutions to pay the same rate as a rental rate for assets to the ultimate providers of that capital, the individuals whose assets they hold.[5] It is more common, of course, to refer to this as the *interest rate* paid by institutions and earned by individuals, rather than the rental rate of assets. For simplicity we will use the term interest rate to denote both the future payment to be made to individuals on their assets and the future payment (next year's capital rental rate) to be made by the users of capital.

As we have already seen in Chapters 4 and 5, changes in the interest rate will change individual wealth calculations and hence consumption demands. Thus the auctioneer's power to control the future rental price of capital — or, equivalently, the market interest rate — gives him the dual power to control both consumption demand and investment demand.

Figure 6–2 shows the demand curves for both consumption and investment goods as dependent on the market interest rate. We leave it to you to show that, under our assumptions, these demand curves are downward sloping. The interest rate which the auctioneer must call out is the rate r_1 where the sum of these two is exactly equal to the full employment level of GNP, Y_f. This

---

[5] We are, of course, ignoring the costs involved in running these financial institutions which could account for a difference between the rental price of capital and the return to savers. This assumption does not affect the argument.

FIGURE 6-2
The interest rate and equilibrium in the market for output

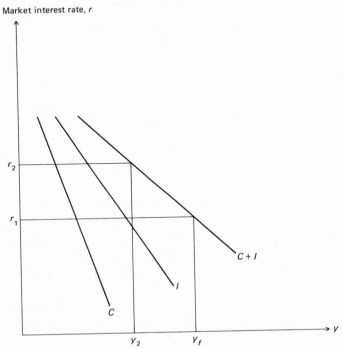

rate — and only this rate — will allow him to fulfill his task of en-suring that all output will be sold.

The rise in the investment/GNP ratio

Without going into the mechanics of how the auctioneer actu-ally computes this rate, let us simply note that in our example he will set the interest rate at 6.30 percent — below year 1's rental price of capital, 6.56 percent — but still above the steady-state rate of 5.32 percent for the rental rate of capital and the interest rate in NEUTRAL. Because it is below year 1's rental price, firms en-gage in capital deepening, and the capital/effective labor unit ratio in LOSER will increase from its value in year 1. Indeed, the data in Table 6-6 show this process of capital deepening continu-ing as LOSER returns to equilibrium.

This process should come as little surprise after our examina-tion of the neoclassical model. However, the speed at which it occurs is quite astonishing: the saving/GNP and hence also the

TABLE 6–6
Investment and consumption levels in LOSER (billions of dollars)

Year	Capital stock	GNP	Investment	Consumption	Investment/GNP ratio (%)
1	6,680.1	2,356.4	797.2	1,559.2	33.8
2	7,210.1	2,474.5	805.6	1,668.8	32.6
3 :	7,727.3	2,592.9	816.2	1,776.7	31.5

Year	Capital depreciation (.04 × capital)	Net investment	Capital widening requirements (.0377 × capital)	Rental rate of capital (%)	Market interest rate (%)
1	267.2	530.0	251.8	6.56	6.30
2	288.4	517.2	271.8	6.30	6.07
3	309.1	507.1	291.3	6.07	5.88

investment/GNP ratio in LOSER rises to 33.8 percent in year 1 as compared to only 25 percent in NEUTRAL. To understand this phenomenon, consider the effects of the war on individual consumption decisions, illustrated by the data in Table 6–7 for individuals in LOSER. A child aged 1 in LOSER immediately after the war would compute his wealth to be $79,000, not the $115,000 computed by his counterpart in NEUTRAL. LOSER's higher interest rate and lower wage rate mean lower wealth, and hence significantly lower consumption.[6]

The percentage decline in wealth is smaller among older persons. For example, the wealth of a 42-year-old declines by only 14 percent from $146,000 to $126,000: his nonhuman capital declines from $29,000 to $24,000[7] and his human capital declines from $117,000 to $102,000. But in all cases consumption falls, and by more than would be predicted by the crude neoclassical model which would have consumption fall in the same percentage as per capita GNP (5.3 percent).

---

[6] For simplicity we have constrained consumers in our examples to calculate their wealth on the assumption that interest rates in all future periods will be the same as this period's. Consumers also calculate their wealth on the assumption that the wage rate per effective labor unit will remain constant so that actual wages are expected to grow at a constant rate q.

[7] The war destroyed 25 percent of LOSER's capital, and hence 25 percent of its assets. However, 10 percent of the population was destroyed, with the result a 15 percent drop in per capita assets. We have assumed that this 15 percent drop was proportionately shared by all individuals. That is, every individual lost 15 percent of his assets. And individuals with negative assets also lost 15 percent of their liabilities.

TABLE 6–7

Individual financial data for LOSER (year 1)

	Age 1	Age 20	Age 42	Age 65	Age 72	Age 80
Income statement						
Wages	0.0	5,942.2	5,942.2	5,942.2	0.0	0.0
Plus Earnings on assets	0.0	−2,664.7	1,812.9	5,989.5	4,223.8	565.1
Equals Net earnings	0.0	3,277.5	7,755.1	11,931.6	4,223.8	565.1
Less Consumption	983.1	1,800.6	3,236.2	5,420.9	6,330.5	7,622.8
Equals Net saving	−983.1	1,476.9	4,518.9	6,510.7	−2,106.8	−7,057.7
			0.0	0.0	0.0	0.0
Wealth statement						
Initial assets	0.0	−35,945.5	24,455.8	80,792.2	56,974.9	7,622.8
Plus Present value of earnings	78,647.9	145,779.1	101,755.9	5,942.2	0.0	0.0
Equals Wealth	78,647.9	109,833.6	126,211.7	86,734.4	56,974.9	7,622.8
Consumption	983.1	1,800.6	3,236.2	5,420.9	6,330.5	7,622.8
Consumption/wealth ratio	0.0125	0.0164	0.0256	0.0625	0.1111	1.0000

In sum, the citizens of LOSER find themselves impoverished by the war and are led by the changes in wages and interest rates to reduce comsumption expenditures. As Figure 6–3, a graph of the saving/GNP ratio shows, this period of high saving and investment continues for some time; LOSER's saving ratio remains above NEUTRAL's until thirty years after the war. As a consequence, the time it takes LOSER to return to its original capital/effective labor unit ratio is relatively short. By the tenth year, the interest rate – a good proxy for this ratio – has dropped back to NEUTRAL's value.

Subsequent developments in LOSER

Two other developments are worthy of mention. First, as predicted by the neoclassical model, LOSER eventually returns to its original steady-state equilibrium. By year 100, its capital/effective labor unit ratio, interest rate, wage rate, etc., have all settled in at exactly the same values as in NEUTRAL. And indeed, there is no reason to expect a different result, since the war has done nothing to change the biological interest rate or long-run saving rate of LOSER. Of course this does not mean that LOSER's aggregate GNP is equal to NEUTRAL's. Its population is permanently 10 percent lower than it would have been, and consequently LOSER's aggregate variables will be 10 percent below NEUTRAL's.

The second phenomenon is that LOSER not only catches up with NEUTRAL very quickly but is also able to pass it! As Figure 6–4 shows, the rental rate of capital in LOSER drops below NEUTRAL's and stays there for about the next forty years, meaning that LOSER has a higher capital/effective labor ratio during this period. Were we to look at data on per-capita GNP, wage rates, etc., during this period, we would find them also higher in LOSER than in NEUTRAL. To be sure, LOSER's dominance is only temporary. By year 50, its capital/effective labor unit ratio has again fallen below NEUTRAL's, and thereafter oscillates in increasingly smaller cycles. This phenomenon of convergent cycling around the steady-state equilibrium is another difference between our model and the simple neoclassical model of Chapter 2. However, this cycling is a consequence of the specific numerical values used, and need not inevitably accompany the adjustment to equilibrium. But it may perhaps serve as a use-

FIGURE 6-3
Investment /GNP ratio

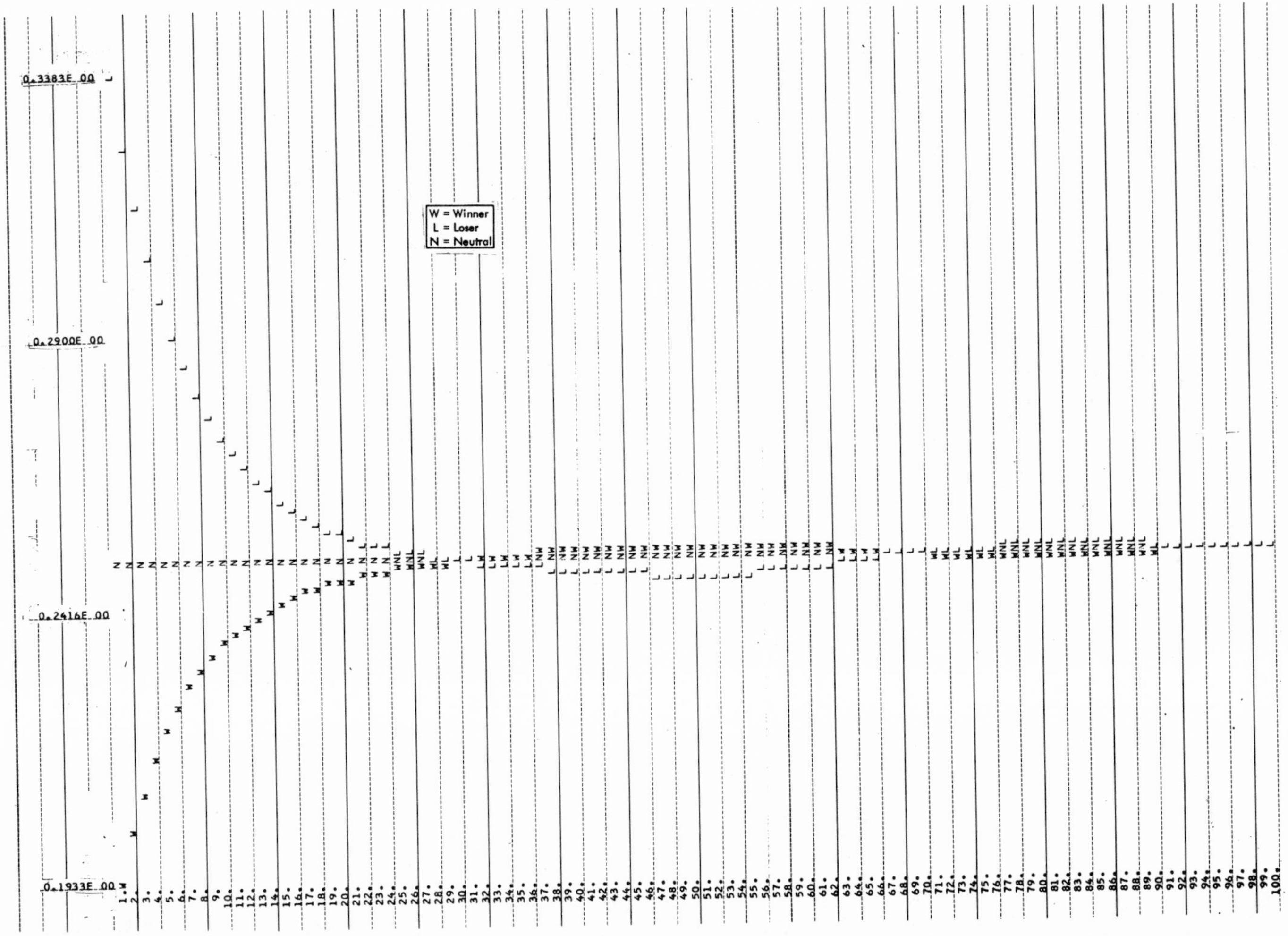

FIGURE 6-4
Capital rental rate

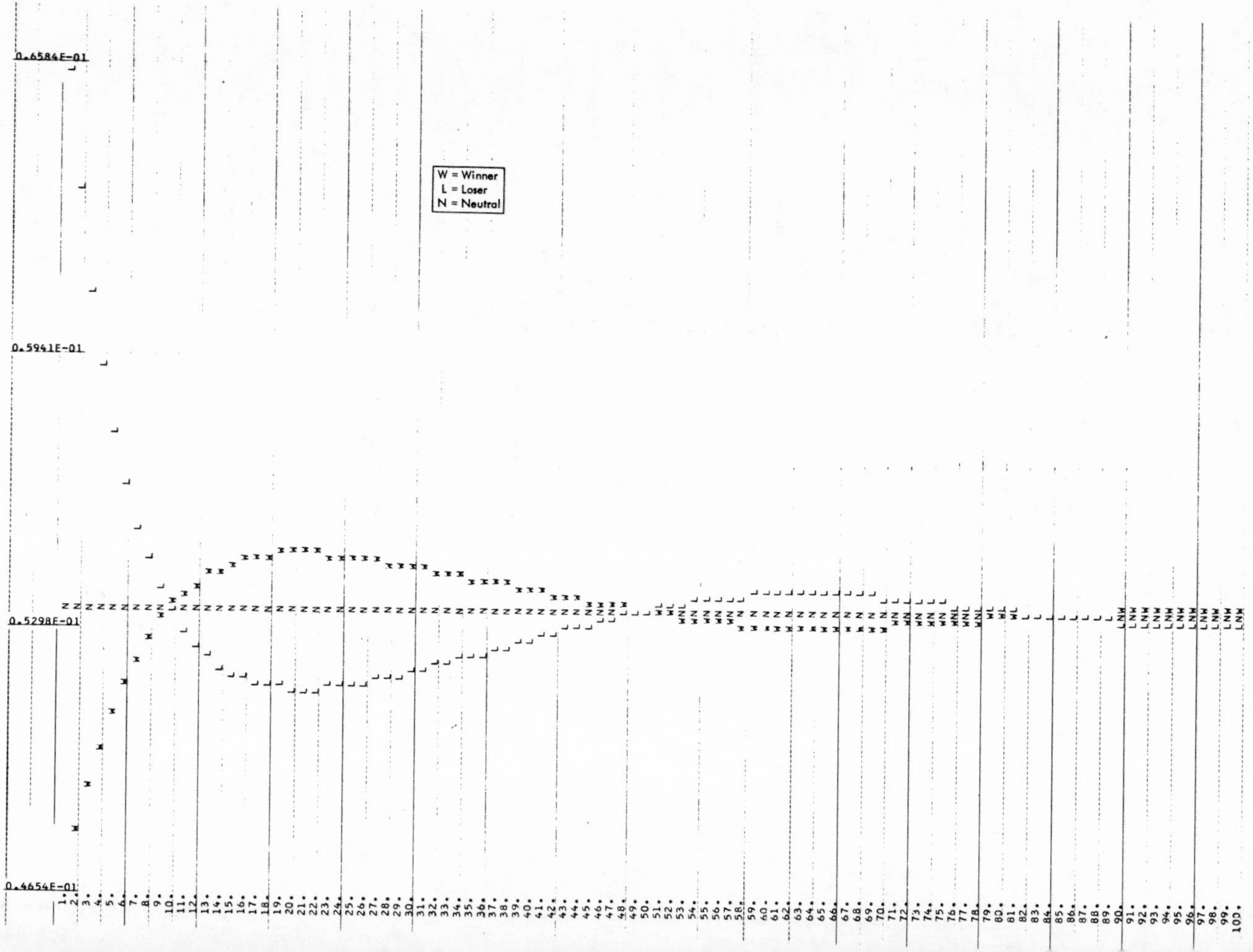

ful reminder that relative standings in the great growth race are not fixed and immutable. Today's leader may be tomorrow's laggard.

Implications for postwar economic growth

The important conclusion to be drawn from this experiment is that an economy subject to a shock such as the wartime destruction of its capital stock can recover much more quickly than the neoclassical model in Chapter 2 would seem to suggest. It can do so provided that it can raise its saving/investment rate. The life cycle theory of consumption suggests that such a rise will occur because the destruction of the capital stock will lead to a rise in the interest rate and a fall in the wage rate.

In the particular case of some of the "losers" of World War II (e.g., Germany and Japan), the end of the war was also marked by substantial inward migration. In Germany this came from Germans fleeing Eastern Europe; in Japan the migration was of Japanese returning from the lost colonies such as Manchuria, Korea, and Formosa. Since these migrations also provided a shock to the capital/labor ratio, pushing it down even further, the pressures for a high saving rate were increased beyond those from the war-related destruction alone.

It is common to hear the variations of saving and growth rates in the major industrial countries after World War II ascribed to supposed differences in "need for achievement" or in national character. Our results show that these disparities in rates can arise out of normal economic processes. We do not wish to suggest, however, that this experiment provides the complete explanation of the high saving and growth rates in Germany or Japan since the end of World War II. Economists would point to many other contributing factors, and we shall have more to say about some of them later.[8]

---

[8] It is precisely because these other factors are present that we have adopted our "one complication at a time" approach in terms of imaginary economies rather than attempting to work with real economies and real history. The experiments that nature provides, unlike that of WINNER-LOSER-NEUTRAL, are hard to read because she is rarely so accommodating as to present one causal event at a time, holding everything else constant. Statistical methods have been developed to analyze nature's experiments, but they must be left to more advanced courses.

DEMOGRAPHIC VARIABLES AND THE EQUILIBRIUM SAVING RATE

The WINNER-LOSER-NEUTRAL experiment involves two economies which make a speedy return to their initial steady-state equilibrium, providing some justification for placing so much stress on an economy's steady-state properties. In this section we shall begin to examine forces which can change that steady-state equilibrium, starting with an experiment of an economy adjusting to a change in one of its demographic characteristics: the retirement age.

We take up a country initially like NEUTRAL but where the retirement age is suddenly and without warning lowered from 65 to 60. We call it Country 60, and for symmetry refer to NEUTRAL as Country 65.

A warning is in order. Suggestions are sometimes made that the retirement age be lowered to "spread the jobs around," particularly in periods with substantial unemployment. Our experiment, however, is *not* concerned with the potential short-run effects of such a policy on the level of unemployment. The auctioneer will still be there to ensure that all resources are fully employed at all times. It is concerned with the long-run equilibrium and how it changes.

Immediate impact

The immediate impact in Country 60 is quite straightforward. As Table 6-8 shows, the lower retirement age reduces the labor force from Country 65's 308.4 million to 280.5 million, a decline of 9 percent. Since both countries initially have the same capital stock, Country 60's capital/effective labor unit ratio rises from

TABLE 6-8
Country 60 demographic data (millions of persons)

Year	Population	Labor force	Births	Deaths
1	552.7	280.5	9.48	4.84
2	557.4	282.8	9.56	4.88
3	562.2	285.3	9.65	4.93
99	1271.9	645.4	21.82	11.15
100	1282.8	651.0	22.01	11.24

5.32 to 5.85. As a consequence, the wage rate rises for those still working and the interest rate falls (see Table 6–7).

The sudden change in the retirement age and the consequent shift in wage rates and interest rates have some important effects on wealth and consumption patterns for the citizens in Country 60. A citizen aged 61 that year, for example, is in rather desperate straits. His wealth is only $86,000, while someone of the same age in Country 65 perceives his wealth to be $116,000. The difference: the person in 65 has human capital of $30,000, while his counterpart in 60 has none, thanks to the retirement edict.

Steady-state equilibrium

So far, Country 60 looks something like WINNER, which also had an immediate rise in the capital/effective labor unit ratio. But this is an illusory similarity for, unlike WINNER, there has been a *permanent* change in one of the fundamental demographic characteristics of the economy so that there is no reason to expect the ratio to return to its original level. We now turn our attention to predicting the long-run change in that ratio.

The most direct way to do this is to determine the shift in the equilibrium saving rate. Originally Country 60, like Country 65, devoted 25 percent of GNP to investment. In terms familiar from Chapter 2, that meant 60 had a saving rate equal to s_{65} and an equilibrium capital/effective labor unit ratio of k_{65}, as illustrated in Figure 6–5. Where the new equilibrium capital/effective labor ratio k_{60} will be relative to k_{65} is determined by the change in the equilibrium saving rate. If this rate rises to s_2, then k_{60} will equal k_2; a fall in the saving rate to s_1 means that k_{60} must equal k_1.

Now to the question: does the lower retirement age mean a rise or fall in the saving rate? Because the lower retirement age reduces the labor force by 9 percent, the aggregate GNP will be 9 percent smaller for any given capital/effective labor unit

TABLE 6–9
Wage and capital rental data, year 1

	Country 65	Country 60
Wage rate	6,276	6,458
Capital/effective labor ratio	5.32	5.85
Capital rental rate	5.32	4.72

FIGURE 6–5
Alternate possibilities for equilibrium with a lower retirement age

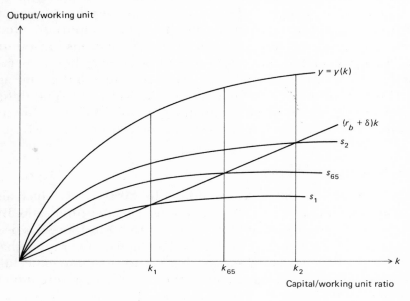

Output/working unit

$y = y(k)$

$(r_b + \delta)k$

s_2

s_{65}

s_1

k_1 k_{65} k_2 k

Capital/working unit ratio

ratio than it would be without the lower retirement age. But
though there is a decline in the labor force, there is no decline in
the population. Hence for any given capital/effective labor ratio,
per-capita consumption must fall by 9 percent simply to keep the
saving rate constant. Per-capita consumption will, of course, depend on individual wealth. Thus the question about the change
in the equilibrium saving rate is essentially a question about the
effects of the lower retirement age on individual wealth calculations.

The lower retirement age has three effects on wealth as it
would be calculated by a person aged one. Unfortunately, they
work in different directions:

1. Early retirement means an individual loses five years in the
   labor force. This 5/46 (10.9 percent) reduction in the working
   span would reduce his wealth by more than 9 percent.
2. But, the present value of these five years—the last years he
   spends in the labor force—is the least of any five-year span.
   This tends to reduce the impact of early retirement on wealth.
3. But, because of the constant rate of technological change, these

last five years will be the five years of highest pay. For example, a worker joining the labor force in year 1 in Country 65 will initially earn $6,458. In his last working year, technological change will have increased that wage to $34,253! This factor increases the weight of those lost five years in the wealth computations.

There are so many factors at work in this experiment that it is impossible to invoke simple principles to sort out their relative influences. It is best to look to the computer simulation of Country 60 for the answer. Figure 6–6, a graph of the investment/GNP ratio, shows that after some initial fluctuations Country 60's investment/GNP ratio settles in at a rate of 26.5 percent, meaning that its steady-state equilibrium capital/effective labor unit ratio is above Country 65's. This is confirmed by Figure 6–7, a graph of the capital rental rate in the two countries, which serves as a proxy for the ratio.[9] As we can see, there is an immediate drop in Country 60 (reflecting the 9 percent reduction in the labor force), eventually leading to an equilibrium rental rate of 4.79 percent, below Country 65's 5.32 percent.

Some policy implications

The fundamental difference between this experiment and that of WINNER-LOSER-NEUTRAL is the change in the steady-state equilibrium. You may be tempted to make some inference as to which country is better off. The data on GNP in Country 60, presented in Table 6–10, show that although output per worker may have risen, the increase is not enough to offset the decline in

TABLE 6–10
Country 60's gross national product (billions of dollars)

Year	Gross national product	Personal consumption expenditures	Gross investment
1	2,587.4	1,981.7	605.7
2	2,677.4	2,036.5	640.9
3	2,772.3	2,096.0	676.3
99	97,556.0	71,667.5	25,888.5
100	101,240.8	74,377.1	26,863.7

———

[9] Recall that the lower the capital/effective labor unit ratio, the higher the capital rental rate and vice versa.

FIGURE 6-6
Investment/GNP ratio

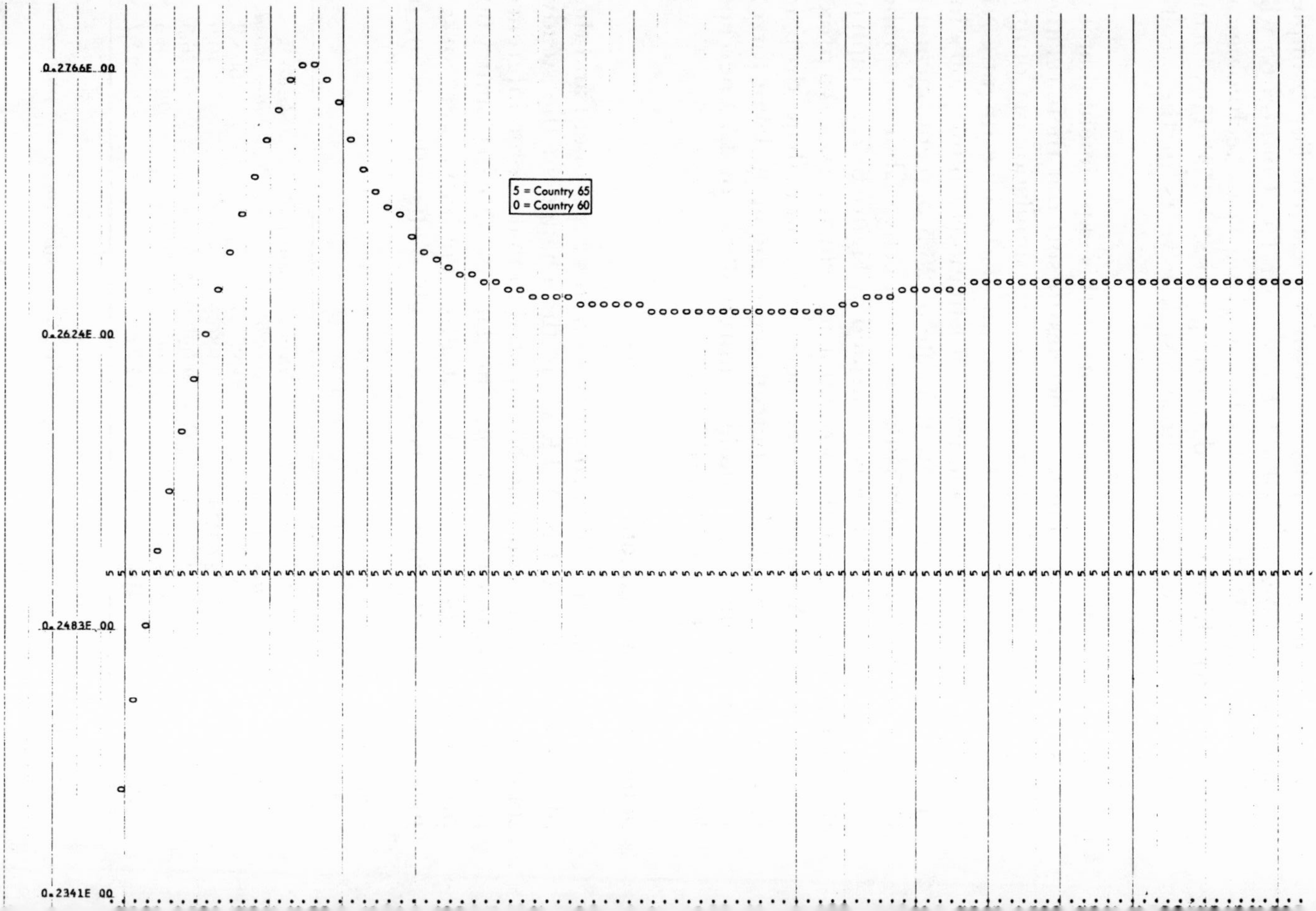

5 = Country 65
0 = Country 60

0.2765E 00   0.2624E 00   0.2483E 00   0.2341E 00

FIGURE 6–7

Capital rental rate

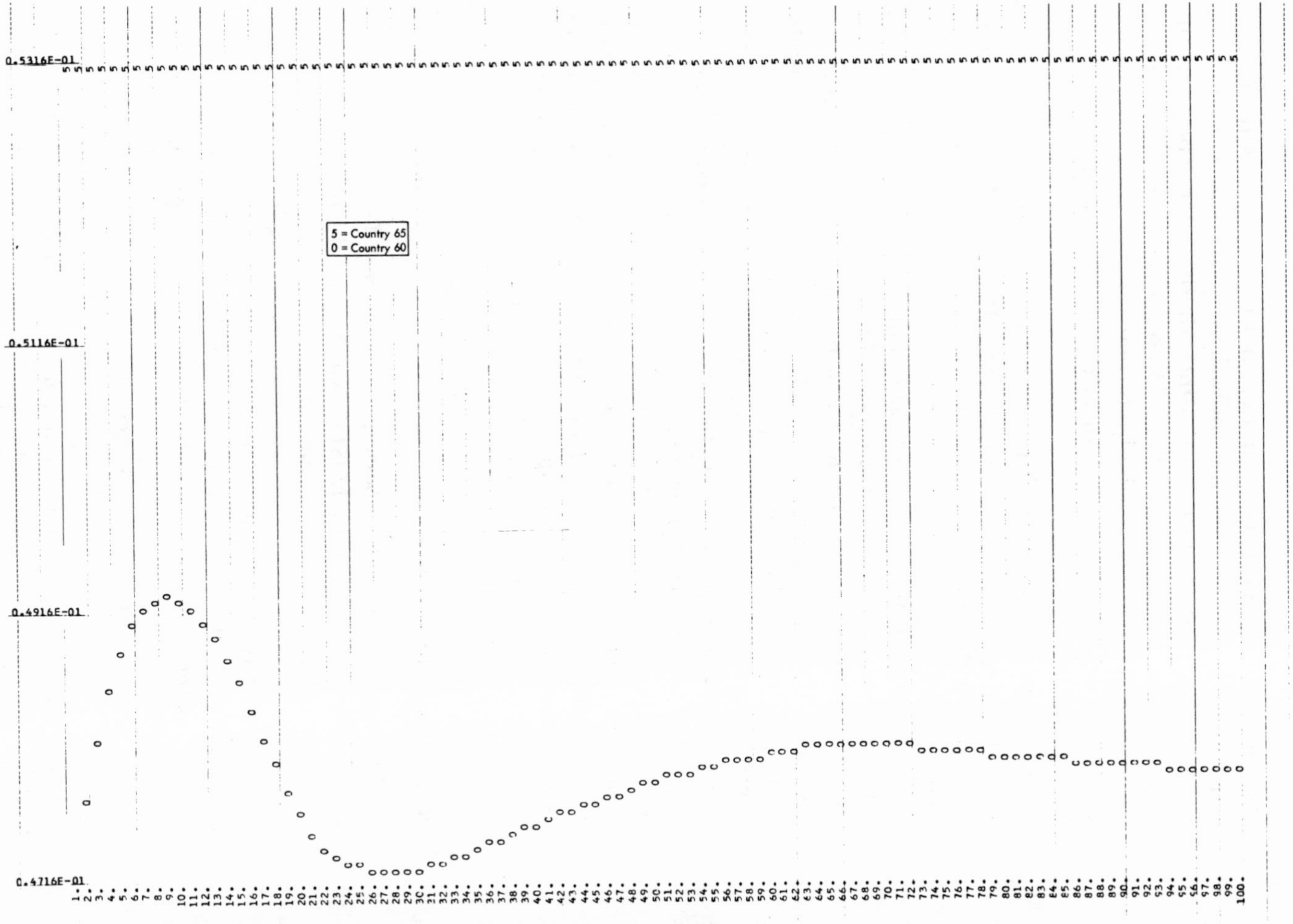

the labor force. As a consequence, both GNP and consumption expenditures per capita are now less in Country 60 than in Country 65.[10] But do not rashly conclude that 65 is a better country. If given the choice of the two countries with their mandatory retirement ages, individuals may consider the extra five years of retirement more than adequate compensation for the lower standard of living.

Of course, the best of all possible worlds would be attained if you could be born in Country 60 and given the freedom to pick your own retirement age. But that choice is not allowed in this experiment.

This is a good place to emphasize that these are experiments in positive, not normative, economics. This one shows how capital stocks change if the retirement age is lowered. One should not interpret the results as an argument against earlier retirement; they only make the obvious point that whatever the benefits, compulsory early retirement has certain costs as well.

You should keep this distinction in mind when we begin analyzing more controversial questions about the effects of government financial policies in the next chapter. As we shall see, the way in which the government finances its expenditures can change the equilibrium capital/effective labor unit ratio. But our emphasis, as here, will be on describing the effects of different policies, not on arguing whether they should or should not be adopted.

PROBLEMS FOR CHAPTER 6

1. Explain the low postwar saving rate in WINNER.
2. Suppose consumers in LOSER had accurately forecast that the interest rate would gradually drop from its postwar high. How would this have affected consumption spending in LOSER in year 1? In steady-state equilibrium?
3. What would be the effect on the capital/labor ratio and the saving rate in the short run and the long in a country which had a substantial
   a. in-migration of persons aged 20,

---

[10] Note that saving in Country 60 rose to 26.5 percent of GNP. In past examples, a rise in saving always meant a rise in consumption. We leave it to the reader to show why that does not apply here.

    b. outmigration of persons aged 20,

    c. outmigration of persons aged 65.

    In all cases you may assume that persons enter or leave the country with none of their accumulated assets (or liabilities).

4. What would be the effect on the capital/labor ratio of a rise in the "school-leaving age," the age at which one begins work, from 20 to 25?

5. Why does the rise in Country 60's saving rate not mean a rise in consumption?

6. Show that the curves in Figure 6–2 are, under our assumptions, downward sloping.

7. Consider an economy in equilibrium composed of four bachelors like those of Table 5–1, with one bachelor in each age group. Calculate national income, aggregate consumption, and aggregate saving. Now suppose that the population is growing and that, at a given point in time, the number of bachelors in age group i is equal to .9 times the number in age group $i-1$. Assume there are 1,000 bachelors in age group 1. Again calculate national income, aggregate consumption, and aggregate saving. Explain the difference in saving rates.

Bibliography for Section Two

Irving Fisher's contribution to the theory of saving is presented in

Fisher, Irving. *The Theory of Interest.* New York: Macmillan, 1930.

and the life-cycle interpretation of that theory is presented in

Modigliani, Franco, and Brumberg, Richard. "Utility Analysis and the Consumption Function: An Interpretation of Cross Section Data." In *Post Keynesian Economics,* Kenneth Kurihara, ed. New Brunswick: Rutgers, 1954.

Modigliani, Franco, and Ando, Albert. "The 'Life Cycle' Hypothesis of Saving: Aggregate Implications and Tests." *American Economic Review,* March 1963.

For the Permanent Income Hypothesis discussed in the Appendix to Chapter 5, see

Friedman, Milton. *A Theory of the Consumption Function.* Princeton: National Bureau of Economic Research, 1957.

The modern empirical literature on the consumption function is enormous. For one recent example, see

Nagatani, Keizo. "Life Cycle Saving: Theory and Fact." *American Economic Review,* June 1972.

For a very early discussion of the optimal plan of consumption and saving, see

Ramsey, Frank. "A Mathematical Theory of Saving," *Economic Journal,* December 1928.

The simulation model of Chapter 6 has a saving rate which is below the Golden Rule rate discussed in Chapter 2 and is therefore "efficient" in the sense that any change forces a choice between consumption now and consumption later. For a discussion of efficient and inefficient saving, see

Cass, David, and Yaari, Menahem. "A Reexamination of the Pure Consumption Loans Model." *Journal of Political Economy,* August 1966.

Samuelson, Paul A. "An Exact Consumption Loan Model of Interest With or Without the Contrivance of Money." *Journal of Political Economy,* December 1958.

section three

Government finance

PREVIOUS CHAPTERS have analyzed how saving and consumption decisions are made in a decentralized unplanned economy. Even where consumption and saving decisions are made on a voluntary decentralized basis, they are subject to a variety of indirect influences. One such influence, the way by which the government finances its expenditures, is the subject of this section.

The consequences of a shift from a tax on wage income to a tax on interest income are discussed in Chapter 7 as an illustration of how tax policy can influence the saving rate.

For simplicity, it is assumed in that chapter that the government adheres religiously to a "pay as you go" or balanced budget principle, though few governments do so. Chapter 8 therefore is addressed to the effects of deficit financing and the national debt on saving and consumption decisions.

7

The macroeconomics
of taxation

UP TO THIS POINT we have been proceeding as if an economy consisted solely of independent households and firms making voluntary exchanges of goods and services with each other in the appropriate markets. Modern economies, however, typically have a considerable governmental or public sector that draws on the productive resources of the private sector, supplying in return a variety of goods and services. Some activities of the public sector, such as the management of nationalized industries like the postal services, differ little in principle from those of the profit-motivated firms in the private sector. But many other kinds of government services, such as national defense or lunar exploration, are provided in response not to demands expressed in the marketplace but to demands expressed through various political processes. Since there are no market prices for such public services, the funds needed to pay for the resources used in supplying them must be obtained from taxes or borrowing (or from printing money.)

In this chapter and the next we shall see how the generalized neoclassical model we have been studying can be extended to allow for a public sector of this kind. Our main concern, however, will not be with the size of the public sector relative to the private nor with the composition of the government's output of services. These are important issues and indeed form the core of much recent political controversy in the United States and other countries. But they are not issues on which the neoclassical model as such has much to say, and their consideration is best deferred to specialized courses in public finance, industrial organization and political science.

The focus of our study will be the way the government's budget is financed. The generalized neoclassical model has something special (and sometimes something surprising) to contribute to tracing the implications of alternative financing schemes. In this chapter, we take up the effects of different types of taxes. The next chapter considers some of the effects of borrowing.

MODELING THE PUBLIC SECTOR

To represent the output of the public sector in any year, we shall assume an equation for the government sector of the simple proportional form

$$(1) \qquad\qquad G_t = \nu_t Y_t,$$

where G_t is the value of the resources used in the production of government services, Y_t is the output of the private sector, and ν_t is the fraction of total private product that the relevant political authority decides will be devoted to the provision of public services. The government services produced with these resources will be assumed to flow entirely to households. In principle, we could also allow part of these services to flow to firms and enter into the private-sector production function, but this would complicate the model beyond our needs.

In the same spirit, we shall assume that the satisfactions households derive from their consumption of privately produced goods and services are independent of those derived from their consumption of government services.[1] The actual expenditures of households on privately produced consumer goods will not be independent of the government services, of course. Those services have to be paid for through taxes and the taxes will show up in each household's budget constraint. Precisely how a tax will change a household's computed wealth and its expenditures for privately produced consumer goods depends on the particular tax. We shall get to these matters shortly.

---

[1] In mathematical terms, we are assuming that household preference functions are *separable* in the two kinds of consumption so that $U(C, G) = V(C) + V(G)$.

TABLE 7–1
Receipts and expenditures by sectors (in dollars)

Households

Receipts		Expenditures	
		Purchases of consumer goods	1,400,000
		Payments of taxes on wage income	346,000
Wages (including entrepreneurial returns)	1,730,000	Payments of taxes on interest income	44,000
Interest received	500,000	Deposited in bank	440,000
Total receipts from other sectors	2,230,000	Total payments to other sectors on income and capital account	2,230,000

Banks

Receipts		Expenditures	
Rents received	570,000	Payment of taxes on rental receipts	70,000
		Interest payments to depositors	500,000
New deposits by households	440,000	Purchases of newly produced capital goods	440,000
Total receipts from other sectors on income and capital account	1,010,000	Total payments to other sectors on income and capital account	1,010,000

Firms

Receipts		Expenditures	
Sales of consumer goods	1,400,000		
Sales of capital goods	440,000	Rental payments for capital equipment leased	570,000
Sales to government	460,000	Wage payments (including payment for entrepreneurial services)	1,730,000
Total receipts from sale of output to other sectors	2,300,000	Total payments for productive services used	2,300,000

Government

Receipts		Expenditures	
Taxes on wage income	346,000	Purchases of output from firms	460,000
Taxes on interest income	44,000		
Taxes on rental payments	70,000		
Total tax receipts	460,000	Total government expenditures	460,000

Government in the national income accounts

Before proceeding to these substantive issues, however, it may be useful to digress briefly by showing how a government sector of the kind we have been describing fits into the scheme of national income accounts sketched earlier in Chapter 2. The double-entry property of those accounts may help once again to clarify the interactions between the various sectors.

The receipts and expenditure accounts of the sectors are shown in Table 7–1. To facilitate comparison with the simpler model of Table 2–2 of Chapter 2, we have kept the total value of output by the firms in the private sector the same in the two cases. Twenty percent of that output, however, is now sold to the new government sector. To finance these purchases the government has levied three types of taxes: a tax on the wage income of households (at an average rate of 20 percent); a tax on the interest income of households (at 8.8 percent); and a tax on the rental receipts of the "banks" (of 12.3 percent). For this particular illustration, the government is following a *balanced budget* or pay-as-you-go policy in which its expenditures are exactly balanced by its tax receipts. (The case of an unbalanced budget or *deficit financing* is deferred until the next chapter.

As before, the national income and product totals can be derived from the sector accounts in a variety of equivalent ways. Table 7–2 summarizes the essentials in a format similar to those in the official tabulations published by most countries. It also illustrates two new concepts of income—*personal income* and *disposable income*—that we shall make use of here and in the chapters to follow.

Government and the neoclassical equilibrium

Figure 7–1 pictures the way in which a government sector of the kind we have been describing modifies the neoclassical equilibrium. As before, the curve $y = y(k)$ shows the national product per effective labor unit. But y no longer represents the amount available for private consumption and investment since we now have a government absorbing the fraction v of private output as an input in the provision of public services. The public's privately disposable income (national income per capita

TABLE 7-2
National income and product accounts (constructed from Table 7-1)

National product by purchaser		*National income by productive factor*		*National income by sector*		*National income by disposition*	
Consumption	1,400,000	Rental payments to capital	570,000	Wages received (including entrepreneurial returns)	1,730,000	Consumption by households	1,400,000
plus: Investment	440,000	*plus:* Wage payments (including payment for entrepreneurial services)	1,730,000	*plus:* Interest received	500,000	*plus:* Saving by households	440,000
plus: Government spending	460,000			Personal income	2,230,000	Disposable personal income	1,840,000
						plus: Personal taxes	390,000
						Personal income	2,230,000
				plus: Taxes on rentals paid by banks	70,000	*plus:* Taxes on rentals	70,000
National product	2,300,000	National income	2,300,000	National income	2,300,000	National income	2,300,000

net of government taxes) is given rather by the curve $y_{dis} \equiv y - g = (1 - v)y$. If a constant fraction β' of disposable income were to be consumed and the remaining fraction $(1 - \beta') = (1 - \beta - v)$ were to be saved, the equilibrium capital stock would be at k_e where the new saving function $s = (1 - \beta - v)y$ crosses the capital-widening line.

Two features of this equilibrium merit some further comment. Note first that since we have two kinds of consumption—consumption of private goods and consumption of public services—there are now two separate Golden Rule points of maximum con-

FIGURE 7–1

The neoclassical equilibrium with a public sector

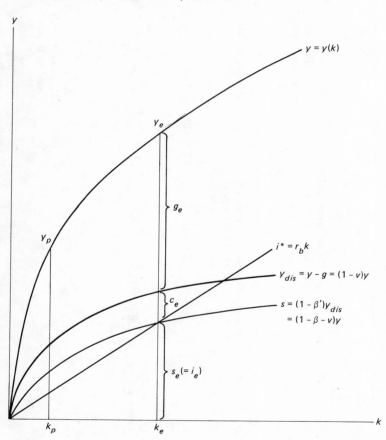

sumption. One is the point of maximum combined private and public consumption and is found at the value of k at which the slope of the aggregate production function is equal to the biological rate r_b, the slope of the capital-widening line. To keep the graph as little cluttered as possible, that value has been made to coincide with the previous illustrative equilibrium value k_e.

The second Golden Rule point is found at the value of k at which the slope of the disposable income curve $y_{dis} = (1 - \nu)y$ is equal to the biological rate r_b. It is shown as the point k_p and represents the maximum amount of private consumption possible for the given value of ν.

The distinction between efficient and inefficient saving rates continues to apply as before to each of the Golden Rule points taken separately. Any saving rate that led to an equilibrium value of k greater than k_e would be inefficient in that a lower saving rate would make possible a higher total of government expenditures plus private consumption both now and in the future. By the same token, saving rates leading to capital stocks less than k_p have the property that no increase in current private consumption is possible without the sacrifice of some future private consumption.

In the zone in the middle between k_p and k_e there is a seeming ambiguity with respect to efficiency. Cutting the saving rate would indeed raise both current and future *private* consumption per capita; but it would lead to a cut in *public* consumption per capita. In the broad sense, therefore, the range between k_p and k_e is not really a zone of inefficiency. The public might well want to make the trade of government for private consumption, but only because it places a higher relative value on the latter. It would not be getting something for nothing.[2]

The second noteworthy feature of the equilibrium pictured in Figure 7–1 is that the taxes used to finance the public sector are nowhere shown explicitly. They are present implicitly, however, in the allocation of disposable income as between consumption and saving. Precisely how taxes affect this allocation, and hence how government tax policies affect the equilibrium capital stock and all that flows from it, is the subject to which we now shall turn.

------

[2] Unless otherwise indicated, we shall assume in all subsequent illustrations that the economy is in the unambiguous zone to the left of k_p.

TAX POLICY AND THE EQUILIBRIUM CAPITAL STOCK

Consider an economy in steady-state equilibrium in which all the government revenue is being raised from a tax solely on wage income. Suppose that, for one reason or another, the rate of the wage tax is suddenly and unexpectedly reduced and that a new tax on interest income is imposed to make up the lost revenue. (The story to follow would be the same in all essentials if we had assumed the new tax to be levied on the rental income of the banks rather than on the interest receipts of households, but the interest-tax version is a bit easier to tell.)

A change in tax policy of this kind will push the economy out of its initial equilibrium and set in motion forces to change the capital/effective labor ratio. Which way the ratio will start to move depends on whether the tax shift leads to a rise in consumption or to a fall. To answer that question we can appeal once again to the life cycle model, extended now however to take the various taxes explicitly into account. In particular, if λ_w is the rate of tax on wage income and λ_r is the rate of tax on interest income, then the wealth of an individual of age i not yet in retirement can be expressed as

$$(2) \qquad z_i = a_i + h_i = a_i + \sum_{j=i}^{n_2} \frac{w_j(1 - \lambda_w)}{(1 + r(1 - \lambda_r))^{j-i}}, \qquad i \leq n_2,$$

where $w_j(1 - \lambda_w)$ represents after-tax or "take-home" wages and $r(1 - \lambda_r)$ represents the after-tax rate of interest earned on financial assets.[3] It follows from equation (2) that a cut in the wage tax, other things equal, will raise h_i; and since

$$c_i = \frac{1}{n_3 - i + 1} z_i,$$

c_i will rise in every age group (except for the elderly, already retired, who have no remaining human capital). Since a rise in the tax on interest income, other things equal, will also act to raise h_i and c_i, the answer to our initial question is thus clear: replacing a wage tax with a capital tax must lead to an immediate rise in con-

---

[3] For simplicity we assume that the government refunds, by one device or another, a fraction λ_r of interest payments made by individuals with negative financial assets.

FIGURE 7–2
Immediate effect of a tax on interest income

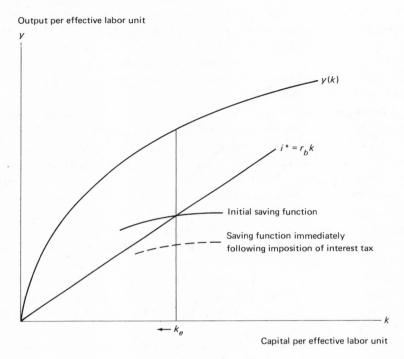

Output per effective labor unit

Capital per effective labor unit

sumption and decline in investment. The situation is pictured in Figure 7–2.

The long-run effects of the tax on interest income

Tracing the longer-run consequences of the shift to an interest tax is somewhat more complicated since we can no longer reason on an "all other things equal" basis. More consumption now also means less investment now, and thus less consumption at some future date. But need this shift in tax policy mean a decline in the *equilibrium* saving rate? That question must now be taken up.

The answer for the normal case can be seen with the help of Figure 7–3. (We use the term "normal case" because special cases, fortunately of little empirical relevance, can arise in which the conclusions would be reversed. Some of these exotica are taken up in the exercises.) Panel A merely reproduces Figure 7–2 with the initial equilibrium now designated as $k_e^{(1)}$. Panel B shows two ratios: first, capital widening investment to income, (i^*/y); second, the fraction of income saved in steady-state equilibrium, $(s/y)_e$ as a function of the equilibrium level of income y_e. The (i^*/y) function is necessarily upward sloping because i^* increases proportionally with k as k rises, while y increases less than proportionally with k.

The slope of the $(s/y)_e$ function is less clear cut. The $(s/y)_e$ function in the basic neoclassical model of Chapters 2 and 3 would plot as a horizontal straight line through the value $(1 - \beta)$. But in a life cycle world of the kind we have been working with, it can be shown that the $(s/y)_e$ function will be downward sloping. We will not provide a formal proof here. In common sense terms, what happens is that higher equilibrium values of y are associated with lower interest rates. The lower rate of interest, in turn, means that people get less return in terms of future consumption for reduced consumption today. And, in any economy except one in which people attach substantially higher weight to consumption during retirement years than to that in their working years, the lower rate of return on saving can be shown to reduce the saving/income ratio.[4]

The particular value of y_e at which the $(s/y)_e$ and the (i^*/y) curves intersect defines the long-run equilibrium point for the system. If the saving function is initially $(s/y)_e^{(1)}$, the equilibrium level of income is $y_e^{(1)}$. The problem of assessing the long-run effect of the tax switch has thus become one of showing how the switch shifts the $(s/y)_e$ curve. For the downward sloping function depicted, the direction of the tax-induced shift can readily be deduced. The tax shift has two effects. The first is to raise the effective or after-tax equilibrium wage rate associated with each value of y_e. This reduces the saving/income ratio by increasing wealth and hence the level of consumption associated with that value of y_e. The second effect of the tax shift is to lower the after-tax interest rate associated with each value of y_e. This also re-

---

[4] In the language of microeconomics we are saying that the "substitution effect" is normally the dominant one, but that it can conceivably be offset by the "income effect." In terms of our life cycle analysis of the saving decision, the perverse case described can arise if the γ_i in the individual utility functions are assumed to increase with age.

FIGURE 7–3
Long-run effect of a tax on interest income

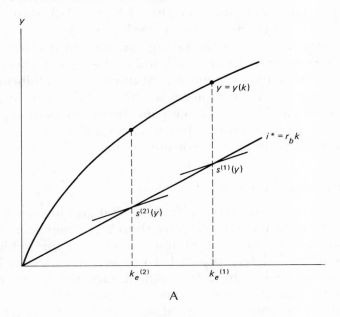

A

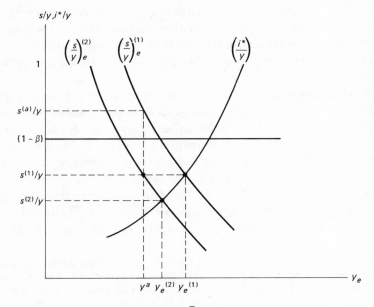

B

duces the saving/income ratio if, as assumed, lower interest rates lower the saving rate. Clearly then, the combined effect is to depress the saving rate and, in terms of Figure 7–3, shift the $(s/y)_e$ curve down and to the left from $(s/y)_e^{(1)}$ to $(s/y_e)^{(2)}$.[5]

The leftward shift of the saving function means that the new equilibrium level of income, $y_e^{(2)}$, will be lower as a consequence of the switch to a tax on interest. And since the equilibrium level of income is lower, so, in general, will be the level of consumption per capita. Thus the price paid for the immediate burst of consumption expenditures after the tax on interest was imposed is a lower long-run level of consumption.

The interest tax in practice

Raising the tax on income from capital and lowering the tax burden on wage income may have short-run benefits in the form of higher immediate consumption for most of the public while the cost is long-deferred and hard to see. This lesson has not been lost on legislatures. In point of fact, the U. S. and virtually all other developed economies now impose substantial taxes on the earnings of capital, though not always labeled as such. Interest and dividend earnings are included along with wage income for computing taxable income under the personal income tax. In addition, most countries impose a further tax on the profits of corporations — a tax equivalent, in our terms, to the tax on rental income of Table 7–1.

But while imposing substantial taxes on capital with one hand, legislatures have typically also levied special subsidies on the earnings from capital with the other. In the U. S., for example, purchasers of new capital equipment receive a so-called investment tax credit that currently amounts to 7 percent of the value of the equipment. Furthermore, taxes on that large part of the return from capital that takes the form of capital gains rather than a direct cash flow of interest or dividend payments is normally taxed at rates considerably below that on other sources of

---

[5] When the γ_i rise sufficiently with age, it is possible that for a miser-dominated economy the $(s/y)_e$ curve could be upward sloping so that lower interest rates increase saving rates. In this case the effect of the tax shift could be to shift the $(s/y)_e$ curve up and to the right and thus increase equilibrium output. But this case seems sufficiently unlikely that we defer it to an exercise.

income. Whether on balance these subsidies have offset or perhaps even more than offset the tax burden on interest income is an open question. But it should be kept in mind that the quadrennial call for closing the "loopholes" amounts to a call for heavier taxes on capital and hence for a policy of consumption now at the expense of consumption later.

The optimal combination of wage and interest taxes

To characterize a policy as being one of consumption now at the expense of consumption later is not necessarily to deplore it. What is deplorable is not to recognize that a trade-off is involved and to proceed as if there were no adverse consequences in terms of future consumption levels. But assuming these consequences are in fact recognized, nothing in our macroeconomic analysis of the problem to this point argues that such a policy ought not to be undertaken.

There are two reasons for this. First, all that we have established is that under the assumptions given there must be a cut in *aggregate* future consumption. It is entirely possible, however, that this lower aggregate might be distributed among the members of the community in a way that would lead to a higher level of aggregate satisfaction. Nor is this simply a matter of transferring consumption from the rich to the poor as visualized by the standard case for progressive taxation. Even in a world as egalitarian as our simulated economies of the previous chapter, individuals, if permitted to choose which steady-state to be born in, might well prefer to be born into the one with the higher tax on capital, despite its lower level of per-capita income and consumption.

The interest tax and consumption smoothing. To see why, turn to Figure 7–4 which is a reproduction of the figure used earlier in Chapter 4 to point up the significance of consumption smoothing in the Fisherian model of saving. The point N on the indifference curve labeled U_{21} involves the relatively low consumption level of $100,000 in period 1 and the very much higher level of $500,000 in period 2. By contrast, the point P has the smoother combination of $250,000 in period 1 and $275,000 in period 2. Note that the point P has less total lifetime consumption than N ($525,000 vs. $600,000). Yet as drawn, the point P clearly is pre-

FIGURE 7–4

A graphical representation of the Fisherian theory of saving

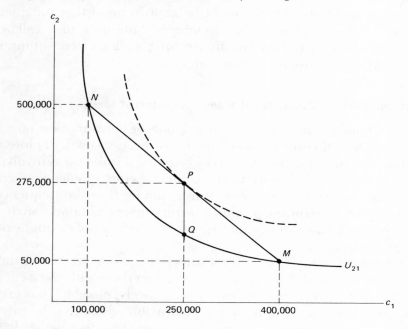

ferred to N. The smoother distribution in time has more than compensated for the lower aggregate.

But a smoother flow of consumption over the lifetime may well be one of the byproducts of a tax on interest income. This is certainly true, for example, for the utility function used in our derivation of the life cycle consumption function. The consumption patterns in that case have the property that consumption in different periods differs according to the relation $c_{i+\tau} = c_i(1 + r(1 - \lambda_r))^\tau$. The higher the value of λ_r the slower the "crescendo" of the consumption stream and hence the less the range of variation in consumption in different years. In such a world, the gains in satisfaction from having more of one's consumption in the early years of life can be shown to be substantial indeed.

The interest tax in the light of the alternatives. The second reason that we cannot automatically condemn an interest tax is that, in practice, the available alternatives may be as bad or worse. The only alternative we have so far considered has been a tax on wages. In our idealized neoclassical economy, such a tax does indeed lead to higher long-run levels of aggregate income and consumption than an interest tax of comparable revenue-raising potential. But remember that we have been assuming that the supply of labor is a biological datum independent of the wage rate. Hence we are ignoring completely any adverse effects that the wage tax might have on the incentive to work and in turn on the level of national output.

Nor are such potentially unpleasant side effects peculiar to a wage tax. Economists sometimes postulate a pure "lump-sum" tax with the property that it not directly affect or "distort" the trade-off between work and leisure or between consumption now and consumption late, or, for that matter, between any pair of commodities or services in the economy. Such a non-distorting tax, however, is only an expository device. All the taxes we know about — and in the course of the centuries an enormous number of different ones have been tried — involve distortions of one kind or another, as a rule increasingly so as the rate of tax rises.[6] Remember also, in this connection, the resources consumed in attempts by taxpayers to avoid or reduce their taxes, as well as in attempts by the taxing authorities to discourage such behavior.[7]

Pointing out the distortions inevitable in any tax program naturally leads to the question of whether there exist other methods of financing government that permit these wastes to be reduced or avoided. One such possibility, viz., financing by means of the sale of interest-bearing securities, is considered in the chapter to follow.

---

[6] An exception should be made for taxes on pollution or congestion. By leading to reduced output of products with "external diseconomies," to use the term from welfare economics, such taxes have the happy property of raising economic welfare and generating revenues at the same time. Though pollution is much in the news these days, the revenue-raising potential of such painless taxes is unfortunately (or perhaps fortunately) small.

[7] The complexity of the U. S. Tax Code has become legendary. Periodic attempts are made to "simplify" it and thereby reduce the costs of payment and collection. The 1969 Tax Reform Act, the latest in the long series of unsuccessful attempts at simplification, was promptly dubbed by cynics the "Lawyers and Accountants Relief Act of 1969."

PROBLEMS FOR CHAPTER 7

1. Suppose the initial capital/effective labor ratio had been to the right of k_p and to the left of k_e, and that the shift in the saving rate brought about by the shift in taxes had left the capital/effective labor ratio in this range. What effects would it have on equilibrium consumption in this case?

2. Suppose the new tax had been levied on the "banks" rather than on individuals. How would this have changed the results?

3. Suppose government spending increased from νY to $\nu' Y$ for year 1 and only year 1. What effect would this have on the capital/effective labor ratio in year 2 if financed by a temporary wage tax? In steady-state equilibrium? How would your answer change if the increase were financed by a tax on interest income?

4. Using the data of Table 5-1, compute the immediate effect on consumption by the bachelors in each of the four age groups of a 20 percent tax on wage income; a 20 percent tax on future interest income; an income tax of 20 percent that applies to both wage and future interest income.

8

The burden of the debt

FEW GOVERNMENTS have adhered to the pay-as-you-go requirement imposed on the government in the preceding chapter,
though conventional political etiquette requires deficit spending
be labeled as an unfortunate temporary departure. This chapter
will relax the pay-as-you-go assumption and analyze the economic implications of government borrowing. In particular we
will concentrate on two related questions:
1. Does deficit financing of current government expenditures
   impose a burden on future generations?
2. Under what conditions, if any, can a government avoid the
   pains of taxation by resorting to a policy of continual deficits?
   We first consider some general issues.

DOES THE DEBT MAKE A DIFFERENCE?

Many of the academic controversies over the consequences of
a government debt date from the policy of deliberate deficit
spending instituted by the Roosevelt administration in the U. S.
during the 1930s. These controversies intensified with the decision made at the start of World War II to finance a substantial
portion of the wartime increase in American military spending
by borrowing rather than by higher taxes.[1]

---

[1] Part of the spending was financed by printing money. But since money has
not yet been introduced into the model, we beg indulgence in deferring a
discussion of this option.

One argument against debt financing made at that time, which we do not propose to dwell on here, is that a government with a large debt is courting bankruptcy. Formerly this argument had considerable appeal. In the Middle Ages, for example, the king, as the richest landowner in the country, was expected to "live of his own" and pay for the government's expenses from the revenues of his estates. A king had some taxation powers, to be sure, but the collecting of taxes was at best uncertain. In a sense he was a private person, albeit an enormously wealthy one, and if he lived beyond his means he — and his government — faced the problems of any private person with substantial debts.[2] The argument, though still heard occasionally in newspaper editorials, has become outdated with the enormous increase in the ability of governments to collect taxes. Most modern governments — some oil sheikdoms excepted — are no longer expected to live "of their own." They typically have such substantial legal and physical powers to raise revenue that the risk of bankruptcy may safely be neglected.[3]

Another common objection to deficit financing in academic

---

[2] In fact it was to the kings' advantage to accumulate a substantial surplus during peacetime in anticipation of the possibility of a future war.

Elizabeth I of England inherited debts of nearly £200,000 from Mary Tudor upon her succession in 1558; a third of this was borrowed from Antwerp bankers at 14 percent. By 1575 she had paid off these loans, was accumulating a "war chest" which reached £300,000 by 1584 and was able to borrow at a more reasonable rate of 8–9 percent, while Philip II of Spain was paying 12–18 percent. Although Elizabeth acquired a reputation as a crabby penny-pincher in the process, the Crown's solvency proved decisive in 1588 when the Armada came. See R. W. Werham, *Before the Armada* (New York: Harcourt Brace, 1966).

[3] In the 19th century several U.S. state governments did in fact repudiate their bonds, to the great discomfort of British bondholders. After Pennsylvania repudiated its bonds in the Panic of 1837, the humorist Sydney Smith wrote a London newspaper: "I never meet a Pennsylvanian at a London dinner without feeling a disposition to seize and divide him; to allot his beaver to one sufferer and his coat to another — to appropriate his pocket-handkerchief to the orphan, and to comfort the widow with his silver watch, Broadway rings and the London Guide, which he always carries in his pockets. How such a man can set himself down at an English table without feeling that he owes two or three pounds to every man in company I am at a loss to conceive: he has no more right to eat with honest men than a leper has to eat with clean men." The London *Times* reported that "An American gentlemen of the most unblemished character was refused admission to one of the largest clubs in London on the sole grounds that he belonged to a republic that did not fulfill its engagements." (See "The Debts We Never Paid" by Robert Wernick in *American Heritage,* December, 1964.)

writings on the subject was the "deadweight loss" occasioned by the necessity to meet interest payments. The larger the debt, the heavier the tax burden required to effect the transfer to the bondholders. And, as was seen in Chapter 7, taxes distort a variety of key economic decisions, such as the consumption-saving decision.

This argument is correct as far as it goes. But it fails to consider the consequences of a remedy. Had the United States wanted to prevent the deadweight loss now being suffered from the World War II debt it would have done so by raising taxes in the 1940s. Those taxes, however, would have led to a deadweight loss in the 1940s. By the same token, the government could at this time prevent future generations from suffering the consequences of the debt by raising taxes now and paying off the debt.[4] Again, these tax increases would cause distortions. The question, in short, is one of distortion now versus distortion later.

Aside from a possible deadweight loss, does the size of the debt have any other consequences for an economy? Many critics of deficit financing have argued that since taxes must eventually be raised to meet the interest payments, borrowing now simply means transferring the burden of current government operations to future generations. Others have countered that the same future generations who pay the taxes also receive the interest payments so that the presumed burden is illusory. The real burden of the government expenditures, they argue, comes always in the year those expenditures are undertaken, when resources are diverted away from the private sector.

This is about where matters stood until the middle 1950s. The development of the life cycle model at that time made it possible to throw some new light on these long-standing controversies over the burden of the debt on future generations, and it is to these newer insights that we now turn.

We shall see that an increase in the government debt will lead

---

[4] Another possibility would be to reduce government spending. Some of the criticism of deficit spending is doubtless aimed at the spending, not the means by which it is financed. But our purpose is to examine the effects of financing a given level of government spending, and we will not consider this possibility.

Some would challenge the separability of questions of how much to spend and how to finance that spending, arguing that legislators are psychologically more inclined to increase spending when they can do so without raising taxes.

under certain conditions to a decrease in the equilibrium saving/ income ratio and consequently to a decline in the equilibrium capital/effective labor ratio. In this sense there will be a burden on future generations. This will happen even if the interest payments on the debt could be financed by nondistoring taxes. The fall in the saving rate will be marked, naturally, by a short-run increase in the level of consumption as well as by a decline in long-run per-capita consumption. That is, *under certain conditions,* the resort to deficit rather than tax financing is another instrument by which the government can affect the balance between consumption now and consumption later.

IMPLICATIONS OF AN INCREASE IN THE DEBT ON CONSUMPTION AND INVESTMENT DECISIONS

Let us return to the economy considered in Figure 7–1. Recall that it is in steady-state equilibrium; that the government finances its expenditures on a pay-as-you-go basis; and that there is no government debt. To simplify the calculation of examples, we shall also suppose that this economy has 80 inhabitants, one in each age group. Suppose now that the government gives each person a $1,000 bond, creating a national debt of $80,000, but thereafter adheres to the policy of a balanced budget.[5] What effects will this have on the economy in the first year and in steady-state equilibrium?

Changes in consumption and investment decisions, first year

As a consequence of this distribution of bonds, the auctioneer faces the immediate problem of having to call out a new interest rate. Figure 8–1 shows how he had initially determined the rate which would solve his task of keeping aggregate demand and sup-

---

[5] This program is effectively a *transfer payment* program, whereby the government merely transfers claims on resources from some individuals to others, but does not increase the government's demand on output. It thus leaves the aggregate amount of private consumption plus investment unchanged. Although this transfer payment program seems unusual, it does have precedents such as the 1936 Soldiers Bonus Bill, which gave government bonds to World War I veterans; we consider a more typical transfer payment program in the appendix to this chapter.

FIGURE 8–1

Changes in consumption and investment demand, first year

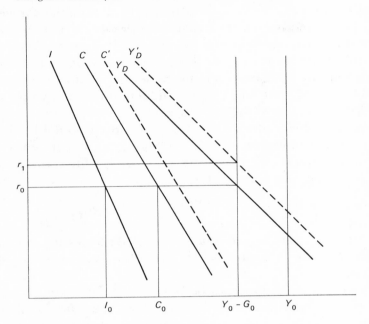

ply equal. (You saw a similar graph earlier in Figure 6–2.) The demand curves for consumption and investment are labeled C and I, respectively. Government spending is equal to G_0, so the amount of national product available for private use is $Y_0 - G_0$. Prior to the bond distribution, the auctioneer had called out the interest rate r_0 where the sum of consumption and investment demand, the Y_D curve, intersected the $Y_0 - G_0$ line. Consumption demand equaled C_0 and investment demand I_0.

How will consumption demand change as a result of the bond distribution? It clearly will rise if individuals are so foolish as to consider only the asset side of their wealth accounts. They will then conclude that the $1,000 bond windfall each has received is a net increase in wealth, and increase their respective consumption expenditures accordingly by $1,000/(n_3 - i + 1)$. But it would be irrational for the public to consider only the asset side of their wealth accounts. When the government returns next year to the pay-as-you-go principle, it must raise taxes to make the interest payments on the $80,000. When computing their wealth, individuals must take into account the present value of these future tax liabilities as well as the value of the bonds.

The net impact of the bond issue cum tax liabilities on wealth will depend on the nature of the taxes to be levied. Suppose, for example, the government can finance the interest payments by a uniform "head" tax. To facilitate comparisons, assume an interest rate of 5.32 percent, the same as prevailed in country NEUTRAL in Chapter 6.[6] Aggregate debt interest payments will be (.0532) (80,000) = 4,256, and each person will incur an additional tax liability of $53.20. To an individual aged 42, say, this means annual payments of $53.20 beginning a year hence and continuing for the remaining 38 years of his life. The present value of his tax liability will thus be:

$$\$53.20\left(\frac{1}{1+r}\right) + \$53.20\left(\frac{1}{1+r}\right)^2 + \ldots + \$53.20\left(\frac{1}{1+r}\right)^{38} = \$860$$

using the discount rate of 5.32 percent.[7] With this liability taken into account, the net effect of the $1,000 on his wealth is an increase of only $140.

The same calculations can be performed for a person of any age. For a person just being born who will pay the $53.20 each year for 79 years, the taxes have a present value of $983, while a person aged 80 will escape the taxes altogether. Summed over all

---

[6] The rate of interest paid by the government on its bonds will be taken as the same as that paid by "banks" to depositors. In practice, of course, government borrowing rates are typically lower than private rates, but the spread has no important bearing on the issues considered here. For further simplicity, we shall treat the government's bonds as one-year securities and thus avoid any question of capital gains or losses as a result of unexpected changes in interest rates.

[7] There is a trick to finding this summation. A simple expression for the sum of a geometric series is

$$x + x^2 + x^3 + \ldots + x^n = x\left(\frac{1 - x^n}{1 - x}\right).$$

In this case, the present value of the taxes equals

$$\$53.20(x + x^2 + \ldots + x^{38}), \text{ where } x = \left(\frac{1}{1+r}\right).$$

By the formula the taxes equal $\$53.20\left(\dfrac{1}{1.0532}\right)\left(\dfrac{1 - \left(\dfrac{1}{1.0532}\right)^{38}}{1 - \left(\dfrac{1}{1.0532}\right)}\right)$ or $860.

ages, these liabilities add up to $60,516. So, while the government's distribution of $1,000 bonds to each citizen amounts to an $80,000 debt, the value of the bonus net of the present value of the future tax liabilities equals only $19,484, less than one-fourth of the debt.

We see then that, even after considering the tax liabilities, each individual in this case will find his wealth increased by the bond distribution (though by less than the full amount of the bonus) and will therefore increase his consumption demand. In terms of Figure 8-1, this means the C and Y_D curves will shift to the right to C' and Y'_D, respectively, and the auctioneer must call out a higher interest rate, r_1.

How the picture looks in terms of the national income and wealth accounts is shown in Table 8-1. To facilitate comparison with the corresponding accounts in the balanced-budget economy of the previous chapter as well as with the earlier illustration in Chapter 2, we have kept the same values for all the key initial balance sheet items and for all the product account items except consumption and investment. These, of course, will be changed by the bond bonus scheme. To make sure that the change in consumption is not overlooked in the welter of numbers, we have changed it by considerably more than the discussion above would suggest.

Most of the individual entries are self-explanatory. Note, however, the new form of the saving/investment identity: saving equals investment plus the government's deficit. Note also that the balance sheets of the household sector as conventionally set up do not take explicit account of the future tax liabilities.

The effect of alternative tax schemes.   The size of the adjustment necessary to restore equilibrium in the current period will depend, of course, on the precise pattern of taxes to be imposed. Consider, for example, the same initial distribution of bonds, but suppose, now, that the tax is to be levied only on wage earners. Assuming individuals work only between the ages of 20 and 65, each person of working age must pay $53.20 $\left(\dfrac{80}{46}\right)$ or $92.52 per year. Again, it is possible to calculate the net effect of the bond distribution. Some sample figures are presented in Table 8-2 for both the wage tax and the across-the-board head tax discussed earlier.

TABLE 8–1

Receipts, expenditures, and final balance sheets by sectors

Households

Receipts		Expenditures		Assets		Liabilities	
Wages (including entrepreneurial returns)	1,730,000	Purchases of consumer goods	1,450,000	Initial deposits in bank	5,700,000	Initial net worth	5,700,000
Interest received	500,000	Payments of taxes on wage income	346,000	New deposits during year	390,000	Net saving during the year	470,000
		Payments of taxes on interest income	44,000				
		Deposited in bank	390,000	Private sector financial assets held	6,090,000		
				Initial government bonds	0		
Bonus transfer from government	80,000	Government bonds acquired	80,000	Government bonds acquired	80,000		
Total receipts from other sectors	2,310,000	Total payments to other sectors on income and capital account	2,310,000	Final total assets	6,170,000	Final net worth	6,170,000

Banks

Receipts		Expenditures		Assets		Liabilities	
Rents received	570,000	Payment of taxes on rental receipts	70,000	Initial stock of capital goods	5,700,000	Initial deposits	5,700,000
		Interest payments to depositors	500,000				
New deposits by households	390,000	Purchases of newly produced capital goods	390,000	Purchase of capital goods during the year	390,000	New deposits	390,000
Total receipts from other sectors on income and capital account	960,000	Total payments to other sectors on income and capital account	960,000	Total	6,090,000	Total	6,090,000

Firms

Receipts		Expenditures	
Sales of consumer goods	1,450,000		
Sales of capital goods	390,000	Rental payments for capital equipment leased	570,000
Sales to government	460,000	Wage payments (including payment entrepreneurial services)	1,730,000
Total receipts from sale of output to other sectors	2,300,000	Total payments for productive services used	2,300,000

Government

Receipts		Expenditures	
Taxes on wage income	346,000	Purchases of output from firms	460,000
Taxes on interest income	44,000		
Taxes on rental payments	70,000	Bonus transfer to households	80,000
Total tax receipts	460,000		
Deficit (increase in debt)	80,000		
Total receipts on income and capital account	540,000	Total government expenditures	540,000

The National Balance Sheet

Assets		Liabilities	
Initial capital stock	5,700,000	Initial net worth	5,700,000
Investment	390,000	Saving	470,000
Final capital stock	6,090,000		
Initial government debt	0		
Deficit	80,000		
Total	6,170,000	Total	6,170,000

TABLE 8–2
Present value of debt-related taxation

Selected age groups	Equal head tax on all age groups	Head tax on workers only
1	983	621
20	955	1,570
42	860	1,211
65	540	—
Total tax liability for all age groups....	$60,516	$68,326

Two points stand out in this table. First, the aggregate of the present value of the future tax liabilities is about $8,000 higher under the scheme of taxing those in the working-age groups. The distribution of tax liabilities is also quite different. Our 42-year-old, for example, finds that if the bond program is financed by a tax on the working-age groups, his wealth is actually *reduced* by some $211. Accordingly, the 42-year-old will reduce his consumption, as will those in many other age groups.

It happens that the bond program, tax liabilities included, increases aggregate consumption in year 1 for the particular numerical values chosen. Again the *C* curve shifts to the right, forcing a rise in the short-run equilibrium interest rate. But it is possible, depending on who gets the bonds and who pays the taxes, that a bond program may actually reduce aggregate consumption in year 1.[8]

These cases establish a critical principle about the short-run burden of an increase in the debt: *though an increase in the debt will, in general, change the level of consumption in the short run, the extent and even the direction of the change will depend on who expects to pay the future additional taxes.*

Changes in steady-state equilibrium

To show the effects of the initial bond distribution on a steady-state equilibrium, a technical modification to the pay-as-you-go assumption is required. The neoclassical model assumes an

---

[8] Suppose all the bonds are given to the young, say, and the interest is paid by taxes levied on the old. Then consumption will decline in year 1.

economy growing both from technological change and from population growth. Were the government to keep the size of the debt constant in such an economy, the relative size of the debt and hence its effects on the equilibrium capital stock would eventually become too small to be seen. To overcome this problem we will assume that the government sets taxes so as to keep the debt/GNP ratio constant—a policy which ensures that steady-state equilibrium will be characterized by a constant amount of debt per effective labor unit.

The mechanics of this policy are simple enough. The debt at the end of any year t, D_t equals last year's debt D_{t-1}, plus the difference between spending, $G_t + D_{t-1}r_t$, and taxes T_t. That is,

$$D_t = D_{t-1}(1 + r_t) + G_t - T_t.$$

In order to keep

$$D_t/Y_t = D_{t-1}/Y_{t-1},$$

this equation requires that the government's deficit in year t must be

$$\text{Deficit}_t \equiv G_t + r_t D_{t-1} - T_t = D_{t-1}\left(\frac{Y_t - Y_{t-1}}{Y_{t-1}}\right).$$

That is, if the debt/national income ratio is to be held constant, taxes must be set for year t so that the deficit during the year exactly equals the growth rate of national income times the amount of debt outstanding at the beginning of the year. In steady-state equilibrium this implies $\text{Deficit}_t = D_{t-1}r_b$.

This modification of the pay-as-you-go assumption allows the effect of the government debt on steady-state equilibrium to be represented in terms of Figure 8–2, the familiar graph of the neo-classical model. Initially the saving/investment rate per effective labor unit is $y - c - g$ (where c represents the consumption rate and g the level of government expenditures on goods and services). The equilibrium capital/effective labor ratio is $k_e^{(1)}$. The government bonds introduce two additional complications to the earlier analysis. First, people will include these bonds among their assets when computing their wealth. Were this the only factor, the saving curve would be pushed down to the dashed curve $y - c'' - g$. However, they must also subtract the increased

FIGURE 8–2
Long-run effects of an increase in government debt

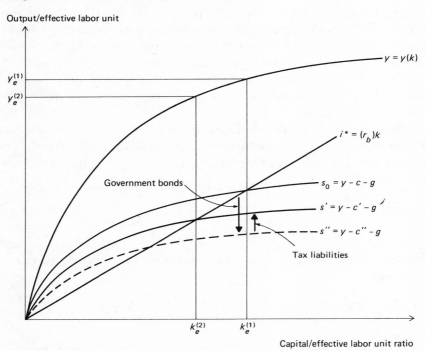

Output/effective labor unit

$y = y(k)$

$y_e^{(1)}$

$y_e^{(2)}$

$i^* = (r_b)k$

Government bonds

$s_0 = y - c - g$

$s' = y - c' - g$

$s'' = y - c'' - g$

Tax liabilities

$k_e^{(2)}$ $k_e^{(1)}$

Capital/effective labor unit ratio

tax liabilities for interest payments from their wealth and this will push the saving curve in the opposite direction.

In Figure 8–2, the tax liabilities have been assumed to offset only part of the impact of the bonds, as indicated by the middle saving curve, $y - c' - g$, giving an equilibrium capital/effective labor ratio of $k_e^{(2)}$, below the old value of $k_e^{(1)}$. Thus in the case pictured there is a burden of debt in the sense that the equilibrium capital/effective labor ratio and hence long-run per-capita consumption has been reduced by the bond distribution.

Figure 8–2 represents the outcome under either of the two tax programs we have considered, since, in each case, as Table 8–2 shows, the present value of the tax liabilities imposed in steady-state equilibrium is less than the value of the debt. More generally, given the assumption that individuals have no estate or bequest motive, the present value of the tax liabilities in the steady-state can be shown to be always less than the values of the outstanding bonds.[9] Therefore, given this critical assumption of no bequests, an increase in the government debt always implies a decline in the equilibrium capital/effective labor ratio, irrespective of its initial consequences on saving. Hence it implies that an increase in the national debt always throws a burden on future generations.[10]

The reason an increase in the government debt must have this effect is that government bonds constitute an alternative to capital as an asset individuals can hold in the process of smoothing out their consumption. That is, from the perspective of the consumer-saver, government debt is a substitute for bank deposits. To smooth out the process of paying the new tax liabilities engendered by the introduction of the bonds, individuals will want to hold additional financial assets, "bank" deposits plus bonds. The assumption that there is no bequest motive means that this increased demand for both assets as measured by the present value of future tax liabilities is always less than the increased supply of bonds. The increase in the supply of debt, therefore, *must* lead to a decrease in the demand for bank deposits.

---

[9] The proof is relatively straightforward. Let t_i denote the tax liabilities imposed on persons in age group i. Then T_i, the present value of the future tax liabilities of a person aged i, equals $\sum_{j=i+1}^{n_3} t_j (1+r)^{i-j}$ and the sum of all tax liabilities (the bottom line in Table 8–1), T^*, equals

$$\sum_{i=1}^{n_3} T_i = \sum_{i=1}^{n_3} \sum_{j=i+1}^{n_3} t_j/(1+r)^{j-i} = \sum_{i=2}^{n_3} t_i \left(\sum_{j=1}^{i-1} \left(\frac{1}{1+r} \right)^j \right)$$

The requirement that tax receipts equal interest payments means that $\sum_{i=1}^{n_3} t_i = rD$, where D is the size of the government debt. If all values of t_i must be non-negative (an important constraint we will return to in the appendix), then the largest possible value of T^* occurs when $t_1 = t_2 = t_{n_3-1} = 0$ and $t_{n_3} = rD$. Then

$$T^* = rD \left(\sum_{j=1}^{n_3-1} \left(\frac{1}{1+r} \right)^j \right) = D \left(1 - \left(\frac{1}{1+r} \right)^{n_3-1} \right) < D.$$

[10] To be sure, Table 8–2 also shows that for a person who is born after the bond distribution and thus gets no bonds, the program has a negative present value of either $983 or $621, depending on the tax scheme. These liabilities will cause the individual to reduce consumption in the first year of life and in all future years. Although this reduction in consumption on the part of those born after the bonus tends to offset the consequences of the debt, it can be shown to be only a partial offset.

But the counterpart of the bank deposits is society's stock of productive capital. Hence, if consumers hold smaller deposits, there is less capital available for production and this means less consumption.[11]

The bequest motive and the Immortal Consumer.   Now let us turn to that critical assumption: the absence of an estate or bequest motive. It has so far been assumed that the bachelor-consumers who populate the economy have no desire to make bequests to subsequent generations and hence that they die with zero assets.[12] This assumption was made for two reasons.

The first reason was to emphasize that bequest or estate motive saving is not necessary to explain why an economy accumulates capital, as some of both the foes and friends of the free market have maintained. The experiments in Chapter 6 clearly demonstrate, among other things, the error of this position: consumption smoothing over the life cycle was there seen to be capable of generating a capital/GNP ratio of 3.2. This is comparable to those found in modern economies.

The second reason is that, with one exception, introducing bequests into the model would not affect any of the answers to the economic issues discussed in this book. In light of this, and in light of the accounting complexities involved in introducing bequests, it seemed best not to introduce them. The one exception is the issue of government debt.

To avoid the algebraic complexities of including bequests into a model, economists have analyzed an alternative model of an economy populated by so-called *Immortal Consumers* who expect to live forever. Although this is patently absurd, it turns out to be an ingenious simplifying assumption.

We can see the ingenuity of the assumption of the Immortal

---

[11] If you are still unsure how government debt can displace physical capital, review the entries in Table 8–1, especially the National Balance Sheet.

[12] Remember that the assumption of this bachelor-consumer is really an "as-if" assumption: the reader is referred to the discussion in Chapter 5 of how families can be considered to be composed of such "bachelors" at various stages of the life cycle.

Some use the term "bequest" more broadly to include the consumption parents provide their children during their youth. In practice, this is the most important type of intra-family transfer. The more common usage of the word bequest, however, and the usage followed here, is the narrow one of a bequest as a transfer of wealth that takes place after the donor's death.

Consumer by looking at the steps involved in incorporating concern for future generations into the analysis. Consider a bachelor
who expects to live four time periods and whose utility from
consumption is

$$\log c_1 + \log c_2 + \log c_3 + \log c_4.$$

Now suppose that this bachelor has an heir whose life begins in
period 5, immediately on the death of the bachelor. Let his heir's
utility be equal to

$$\log c_5 + \log c_6 + \log c_7 + \log c_8,$$

(where $c_5 =$ the heir's consumption in his first period, which
would be the bachelor's fifth period, etc.). Finally, suppose that
the utility the bachelor obtains from the bachelor-heir's utility
equals

$$\rho(\log c_5 + \log c_6 + \log c_7 + \log c_8),$$

where ρ can be thought of as a measure of the affection in which
the bachelor holds his heir.

   Under these conditions, the bachelor may want to leave a bequest so that the heir's consumption is not limited by his lifetime
earnings. But how big a bequest? The bigger it is, the more
consumption during the heir's lifetime, and the less the consumption by the bachelor (there being no such thing as a free
bequest). One way for the bachelor to calculate the optimal bequest would be to maximize his utility

$$\log c_1 + \log c_2 + \log c_3 + \log c_4 + \rho\{\log c_5 + \log c_6 + \log c_7 + \log c_8\},$$

subject to a budget constraint consisting of the present value of
the income and consumption for both him and his heir, each of
whom receives wage income in the second and third period of his
life:

$$c_1 + c_2\left(\frac{1}{1+r}\right) + c_3\left(\frac{1}{1+r}\right)^2 + \ldots + c_8\left(\frac{1}{1+r}\right)^7 =$$

$$w_2\left(\frac{1}{1+r}\right) + w_3\left(\frac{1}{1+r}\right)^2 + w_6\left(\frac{1}{1+r}\right)^5 + w_7\left(\frac{1}{1+r}\right)^6.$$

In effect, the bachelor chooses the consumption pattern for his
heir as well. Although it may not be unusual for someone to *try*
to do this, the actual effort often fails. But by acting *as if* he

chooses for his heir as well, he can compute the amount of assets he should leave at the end of his life and thus influence his heir's consumption.[13]

In short, an individual leaves a bequest because he gets utility from the consumption it will provide his heirs, and it is useful to analyze his behavior by assuming he acts *as if* he maximizes the weighted sum of his utility function and his heir's.

Doubtless, the heir will also have an heir (referred to as the heir-heir, or H^2 for short) and this utility function should be extended to include H^2's consumption as well, if for no other reason than the heir will attach utility to H's consumption. Thus the utility function becomes

$$\log c_1 + \log c_2 + \log c_3 + \log c_4 +$$
$$\rho\{\log c_5 + \log c_6 + \log c_7 + \log c_8\} +$$
$$\rho^2\{\log c_9 + \log c_{10} + \log c_{11} + \log c_{12}\}.$$

Of course, there is no reason to stop with the third generation. One can extend the utility function to include the fourth and all subsequent generations. In that case, the utility function becomes

$$\log c_1 + \log c_2 + \log c_3 + \log c_4 +$$
$$\sum_{i=1}^{\infty} \rho^i(\log c_{4i+1} + \log c_{4i+2} + \log c_{4i+3} + \log c_{4i+4}).$$

That is, the bachelor acts as if he were planning a consumption stream to last forever. In other words, he plans his consumption as if he were an *Immortal Consumer*.

' The assumption of the Immortal Consumer is thus really meant as a simple way of representing the utility which people

---

[13] It is interesting to work out the solution to this maximization problem. The optimal consumption pattern is

$$c_i = \frac{1}{5 - i + 4\rho} \; z_i \qquad i = 1, \ldots, 4$$

where the bachelor is alive and

$$c_i = \frac{1}{5 - i} \; z_i \qquad i = 5, \ldots, 8$$

during the life of his heir.

attach to the well-being of their heirs, as evidenced by their willingness to make bequests.

The Immortal Consumer and taxes.   Suppose that the 80 people in the simple economy of this chapter are all Immortal Consumers. Suppose each of them receives a $1,000 bond from the government and is taxed $53.20 per annum to pay the interest on the debt. The present value of $1 per year in perpetuity is $1/r$. Thus, the present value of $53.20 is $\frac{\$53.20}{.0532} = \$1,000$[14] since the interest rate r equals .0532.

The present value of the tax liabilities is thus exactly equal to the asset represented by the government bonds, meaning that there is no burden of the debt. This is a straightforward extension of the principle laid down earlier that the impact of the debt can only be considered net of the present value of the tax liabilities required to finance the interest on the debt. For an economy peopled by mortal consumers, these tax liabilities will be less than the debt; in the case of Immortal Consumers, the tax liabilities will be equal to the debt.

It follows that if there is a bequest motive of this kind, the impact of the debt on individual wealth calculations is exactly offset by the present value of the tax liabilities, and an increase in the size of the debt will have no effect either on consumption or on investment decisions in the long run.

DEFICIT FINANCING AS A PERMANENT POLICY

The final question to be taken up is the viability of deficit financing as a permanent policy: can a government adopt a policy of financing a constant fraction of its annual budget by borrow-

---

[14] More formally, the present value is

$$\$53.20 \left(\frac{1}{1+r}\right) + \left(\frac{1}{1+r}\right)^2 + \left(\frac{1}{1+r}\right)^3 + \cdots.$$

Now the present value of $53.20 per annum for n years is

$$\$53.20 \left(\frac{1 - \left(\frac{1}{1+r}\right)^n}{r}\right).$$

As $n \to \infty$, this approaches $53.20/r$.

ing? It can certainly do so if the deficit is no greater than $r_b D_{t-1}$. For then the economy would be able to reach an equilibrium characterized by a constant amount of debt per effective labor unit. But what if the government attempted a policy of even larger deficits? The answer must be given in two parts, depending on what is assumed about the bequest motive.

If people do not have a bequest motive, the answer is no: any financing policy which leads to a constantly increasing debt/GNP ratio means a continuing displacement of capital by government debt and hence a continuing reduction in the equilibrium capital/ effective labor ratio.[15]

The answer is different in an economy peopled by Immortal Consumers. Increases in the size of the debt have no effect on the equilibrium/capital effective labor ratio. For example, suppose the government issued bonds each year to pay for all of its expenditures on goods and services, levying taxes only to pay for the interest on the debt. Though such a plan would lead to a constantly growing debt/GNP ratio, individuals would respond exactly as they would to government expenditures financed fully by taxation because the present value of the *future* tax liabilities required for those bond payments would have the same impact on wealth and hence consumption as the tax payments required to balance the budget.

The government might extend the scheme and finance all expenses, including interest payments, for one year by borrowing. This policy would change nothing; the Immortal Consumers would simply recognize that lower taxes now mean correspondingly higher taxes in future years so that the two effects on wealth exactly cancel. Hence, this modification of the scheme would have no effect on private decisions.

Suppose, however, that the government extended the scheme

---

[15] Do not conclude, however, that this precludes deficit spending on the scale followed in the United States since World War II. Even though national debt has been increasing, it has been increasing at a slower rate than GNP. That is, we have been reducing the debt/GNP ratio and, insofar as this element is concerned, increasing the equilibrium capital/effective labor ratio.

In the late 1940s, some economists argued that deficit financing posed no problem as long as the debt was not growing as fast as GNP. Our discussion shows that there is an important element of truth in this argument.

even further and financed all expenditures by borrowing year after year. In the short run this might appear to be the perfect financial scheme since it would avoid the distortions inherent in taxation. But this overlooks the fact that the equivalence of debt and tax financing presupposes that the government will eventually levy taxes to make interest payments on its bonds. If the government adopts a policy of continual deficit financing, individuals will ultimately realize that the government has no intention of levying taxes at some future date. When this happens, the scheme will collapse. The first individual to realize the government's intent will no longer include future tax liabilities in his wealth, his consumption will increase and there will be a reduction in the equilibrium capital/effective labor ratio. More critically there will come a day when all individuals will realize the government's intent. At that time the bonds will become worthless and the government will be forced to rely on taxation to finance its future operations.

A policy of 100 percent borrowing is thus a Ponzi scheme:[16] as long as it works, it is a good deal, but it ultimately must come to an end. It is impossible to predict when the government will be forced to end this kind of borrowing: all we can say is that it must eventually do so.

APPENDIX TO CHAPTER 8

An application to social security

The burden of the debt in an economy peopled by individuals who do not have a bequest motive depends critically on the nature of the taxes levied to finance the interest payments on the debt. The value of these liabilities is an offset to the value of the debt, and the present value an individual assigns to his liabilities depends on when those liabilities occur in the life cycle.

---

[16] Charles Ponzi was a Boston "money manager" of the 1920s who paid people 50 percent interest on funds deposited with him. He did so by using the proceeds of new deposits to pay off old depositors. While it worked, it was a good deal. Those who got in (and out) early made money, but the bubble eventually burst and those who still had deposits with Ponzi lost everything. A chain letter is a type of Ponzi scheme.

This two-sided feature of the debt provides a basis for discussing the role of government transfer payments generally, and we here take up the case of a social security program. Most of us will make positive payments to the social security program during our working years and, upon reaching 65, begin to make "negative" payments, or as it is usually put, begin to receive benefits.

As an example, consider the impact of a social security program in a simple 80-person economy that gives $1,000 a year to retired individuals, financed by a tax on wage earners. The present value for both the payments and taxes for selected age groups is presented in Table 8A–1.

TABLE 8A–1

Assets and liabilities from a social security program (for selected age groups)

Age group	Present value of benefits (at 5.32 percent)	Present value of taxes (at 5.32 percent)	Net value
1...............	368	2,189	−1,821
20...............	986	5,535	−4,549
42...............	1,211	4,269	−3,058
46...............	3,794	3,840	− 46
47...............	3,997	3,718	279
65...............	10,159	−	10,159
Total	275,033	240,809	34,224

For the young, the present value of tax liabilities far exceeds the worth of the social security payments; it is only for those past 46 that the value of the payments is greater than the tax liabilities.

Though the present value of these benefit payments or negative tax payments is probably represented physically by little more than a notation on some computer tape, it represents government debt just as much as do nicely printed bonds. Since the aggregate value of the liabilities falls short of the aggregate value of the payments by about $34,000, it is equivalent to a net government debt of this amount. The social security program can be analyzed in this respect as another way of issuing government debt, and, under the assumption of no bequest motive, as a way of shifting the equilibrium saving rate with all that implies.[17]

Transfer payment programs in a world with bequests. Following our analogy between the social security program and government debt, we should find that its effect on the saving rate disappear if there is a bequest motive. Here, of course, the assumption of Immortal Consumers seems a little forced—would Immortal Consumers ever retire?—though it is certainly plausible in an economy of mortal consumers with bequest motives. Again, returning to the example, suppose each individual takes into account the present value of the program to his heir. As we have seen, the program represents a net liability of $1,821 to each newborn citizen. Thus a bachelor who is mindful of the well-being of his heir will take the present value of the liability into account in computing his wealth. A bachelor who expects his heir to be born five years hence, say, will have an additional liability of

$$\left(\frac{1}{1.0532}\right)^5 \$1,811 = \$1,405.$$

Indeed, a bachelor truly mindful of all his heirs will take the present values of their tax liabilities into account as well.

The consequences are summarized in Table 8A–2 below (for simplicity, we have assumed that each bachelor's heir is born upon his death).

If individuals take into account the impact of the social security program on only the next generation, then the net debt

---

[17] It should be noted, however, that government expenditure on these transfer payment programs differs in a critical way from the government expenditures discussed in earlier chapters. Those expenditures involved purchases of goods and services by the government and directly reduced the output available for private consumption and investment in the short run. Transfer payment programs do not have that effect. In the short run, a $1 billion increase in social security payments would not reduce expenditures by the private sector, but simply transfer assets (or the right to consume and save) from social security taxpayers to recipients of social security.

Social security benefits sometimes induce early retirement, so that an increase in the benefits could lower the labor force and hence reduce the GNP available to the private sector even in the short run. In that case the conceptually neat distinction between transfer payments and government expenditures on goods and services would break down.

TABLE 8A–2
Net value of social security program (for selected age groups)

Age	Net value to bachelor	Present value of program to bachelor's heir	Present value of program to all future heirs
1	− 1,820.72	− 28.80	− 29.26
20	− 4,549	− 77.10	− 78.34
42	− 3,058	−241.17	−245.04
46	− 46	−296.73	−301.50
47	279	−312.52	−317.54
65	10,159	−794.46	−850.17
Total	34,224	−33,683	−34,224

implicit in the program is \$34,224 − \$33,683 = \$541, a rather picayune amount. And even this \$541 disappears if we assume that individuals take all future generations into account.

In short, the impact of this form of debt on the equilibrium saving rate disappears if there is a bequest motive.

PROBLEMS FOR CHAPTER 8

1. Using the data and assumptions of Table 5–1 (that people live for four time periods and receive wage income of \$300,000 and \$630,000 in periods 2 and 3 and that the interest rate is 50 percent), calculate the change in wealth for persons of each age group from a gift of a \$10,000 bond to each person if
    a. the interest is to be financed by a uniform head tax on all age groups,
    b. the interest is to be financed by a head tax on workers only,
    c. the interest is to be financed by a tax on interest income (with a "deductible" clause for interest payments by the younger age groups).
    You should assume that there is an equal number of persons in each age group.

2. Also using the data assumptions of Table 5–1, calculate the lifetime consumption for a bachelor just born whose utility function is

    $$\log c_1 + \log c_2 + \log c_3 + \log c_4 +$$
    $$\rho(\log c_1^* + \log c_2^* + \log c_3^* + \log c_4^*),$$

    where c_1^* is the consumption of the bachelor's heir in the first period of the heir's life. For simplicity, you may assume that $\rho = 59/135$ and that the heir is born at the end of the bachelor's life. What bequests (assets at time of death) does the bachelor leave? How would it change his consumption had his ancestor left him a like bequest?

3. What effects would an increase in the national debt have on the equilibrium capital/effective labor ratio if half of the population had a bequest motive and half did not?

Bibliography for section three

A useful comprehensive reference on the economics of taxation is

Musgrave, Richard. *The Theory of Public Finance*. New York: Mc-Graw-Hill, 1957.

The following sources discuss the effect of various taxes on steady-state equilibrium and take up the question of optimal tax structure.

Arrow, Kenneth J., and Kurz, Mordecai. *Public Investment, the Rate of Return and Optimal Fiscal Policy*. Baltimore: Resources for the Future, 1970.

Diamond, Peter A. "Incidence of an Interest Income Tax." *Journal of Economic Theory*, September 1970.

Diamond, Peter A., and Mirrlees, J. A. "Optimal Taxation and Public Production." *American Economic Review*, March-June 1971.

A discussion of the implications of deficit financing somewhat along the lines taken here is

Modigliani, Franco. "Long Run Implications of Alternative Fiscal Policies and the Burden of the National Debt." *Economic Journal*, December 1961.

This article as well as some others on the subject are reprinted in

Ferguson, James M. *Public Debt and Future Generations*. Chapel Hill: University of North Carolina, 1964.

A somewhat later discussion of these issues is

Diamond, Peter A. "National Debt in a Neoclassical Growth Model." *American Economic Review*, December 1965.

section four

Money and the price level

THE DISCUSSION in previous sections has made no reference to the role of money. And for good reason. We have been able to discuss such key macroeconomic questions as the determinants of the standard of living and economic growth without reference to money; one could stop at this point and have a fairly complete framework for discussing many important issues in aggregate economics. Indeed, as frequent references to the "veil of money" in the writings of economists indicate, the introduction of money into the discussion often serves to obscure the issues.

Still, there is good reason to take up money at this point. The power to create money gives government another tool in addition to taxes and, borrowing for diverting resources from the private sector. It is a tool whose consequences are even more difficult to trace out and whose workings are often counter-intuitive.

The study is introduced by a series of parables in Chapter 9 that illustrate the essential properties a demand-for-money function should have. A microeconomic function with such properties is developed in Chapter 10; its behavior is illustrated with some numerical examples like those of Chapter 5.

The first step in integrating money into the aggregate analysis is taken in Chapter 11 which focuses on short-run effects on the price level of unexpected increases in the quantity of money. Chapter 12 completes the integration by discussing the effects of a change in the rate of growth of the money supply on various steady-state equilibrium parameters such as the equilibrium inflation rate.

Chapter 13 discusses the costs of various inflation rates, anticipated and unanticipated, and takes up the question of the socially optimal rate of money creation. Chapter 14 shows how the price level is influenced both in the short run and in the long by government spending, taxing, and borrowing. The introduction to money is completed in Chapter 15, which discusses the role of commercial banks and central banks in the provision and management of the money supply.

9

The microeconomic foundations of the demand for money

INTRODUCTION

UP TO THIS POINT, our analysis of the workings of an economy has presumed, in effect, that payments to and from households are made in kind. The worker receives a wage consisting of w units of output. Some of these units he consumes directly; some he turns over to the government in settlement of his tax liabilities; some he lends back to the productive sector, which in turn incorporates them into new productive equipment. In the economy we see around us, of course, payments in kind between economic units are the exception rather than the rule. Some college students may receive room and board in return for babysitting services provided; but most workers are paid in cash, rather than in the output of their firm (though, even here, some part of the wage is typically also given in the form of securities of the firm, such as pension rights or options to buy shares). Some may (or may have to) make their contribution to government programs in the form of direct transfers of labor services to the armed forces; but most citizens are able to settle their obligations by a transfer of money to the tax collector. Some farmers can invest their corn crop of this year directly into their pig crop of next year; but most new capital is acquired by firms by a payment of cash (or issuance of securities, with many subsequent flotations and retirements of securities for cash or cash and security packages.) In sum, money is the medium through which most exchanges are effected.

But while direct exchanges in kind are the exception, and indirect exchanges via money the rule, there is nothing anomalous in our having delayed the introduction of money until the ninth chapter 'of this book. It is a remarkable fact—and one quite clearly recognized at least as far back as Adam Smith—that the answers to the questions we have been concerned with so far would in no essential way be changed if we had allowed for the more roundabout process of exchange through the medium of money. They would only be somewhat harder to see; hence, the frequent references in the economics literature to the "veil" of money.[1]

Why then introduce money at this late point and complicate an otherwise straightforward picture of how the standard of living is determined and how it grows? For two reasons, essentially. First, money in modern economies can be produced by governments, giving them another policy instrument for attracting resources away from the private sector and for distributing the cost of government services among the citizenry. Second, many economists believe that the policies governments have actually followed (directly and indirectly through their official banking arms) with respect to the production of money have been major contributing factors to the boom and bust sequences that have so plagued modern industrial economies. There is a good deal of dispute still over how important a contributing factor monetary policies have been, and as to what alternative policies might have served society better. But few today would deny the vast potential for mischief in poorly conceived monetary management by governments.

The introduction of money as the medium of exchange in the model takes us from a one-commodity to a two-commodity world. We must, therefore, (*a*) add equations describing the demand for this new commodity, (*b*) specify a production function governing its creation, and (*c*) show how the equilibrium rates of exchange are established both between money and the generalized output commodity and between money and such

---

[1] Note for the possibly too-hasty reader: we are not saying that social well-being is unaffected by the presence or absence of the institution of money. Clearly, relying entirely on barter would involve enormous waste of resources. But, given that money has somehow been invented and hence that the need to incur the costs and risks of barter has been obviated, little is lost and much is gained by proceeding *as if* the exchanges took place on a costless barter basis.

other financial assets as government bonds. As before, we shall try to proceed in easy stages. This chapter and the next concentrate on the micro foundations of the demand for money, very much in the spirit of Chapters 4 and 5. Subsequent chapters take up the macro demand function for money and the determination of the rates of exchange between money and the output commodity and between money and financial assets. To focus more sharply on the critical issues at this stage, the production function assumed for money will be a relatively simple one. The final chapter in the sequence, Chapter 15, will then attempt to fill in some of the omitted institutional detail about the money supply in modern economies.

THE ESSENTIAL PROPERTIES OF THE DEMAND FUNCTION FOR MONEY

Although we have made repeated references to the "demand for money," you need feel no embarrassment if unable immediately to visualize such a function. The words "demand function" inevitably conjure up the familiar diagram of consumption theory in which the quantity of some commodity, say pounds of beef demanded per year, is measured along one axis and its price per unit on the other. Other things equal, the lower the price—that is, the fewer the units of money that must be given up for each pound of beef obtained—the greater the quantity of beef demanded. But if money itself is to be the commodity demanded, what is to constitute *its* price per unit? And if the money demanded is to be given up in exchange for other commodities, what is to be put on the quantity axis?

The answers to these and related questions about the demand for money will be developed here in two steps. First, we shall work through some simple numerical examples of cash management by a household in an economy similar in its essentials to those we have been studying so far, but using money as a medium in all exchanges. These examples are intended as fables or parables, each with its appropriate moral, and taken together they should make it easier to see the essential qualitative properties required of a demand function for money. Chapter 10 takes the next and key step of deriving an explicit demand function for money with the desired properties, and relating it to our life cycle demand function for consumption.

Strategies for cash management: A parable

Consider an individual just about to start work for a new employer at a wage of $100 per week. Given the current level of his total wealth, he finds $60 per week the rate of consumption spending appropriate to his stage in the life cycle, with the remaining $40 to be added to his holding of assets. For simplicity, imagine that the $60 per week of consumption spending will be dribbled out at a steady rate of $10 per day for each of the six days, Monday through Saturday. Sundays he watches TV.

As a new employee, he must first report to the controller's office and get his pay arrangements settled. The kindly old gentleman there with the green eyeshade asks whether our subject would care to sign up for the automatic bond purchase program. Of course it's not compulsory to do so, he is told; but Mr. Connally, his immediate supervisor, has always prided himself on the 100 percent rate of participation by his division, and would hate to see this record spoiled.

Since our subject is proposing to save $40 of his pay in any event, authorizing a check-off of that amount will certainly involve no hardship. (It might, of course, in a world where governments sought to convince the more unsophisticated of their citizen-savers that buying securities yielding less than the market rate of interest was an act of patriotism. But who could believe such a thing?) The question is, rather, whether he should authorize a still larger deduction and thereby enhance his image in Mr. Connally's eyes.

If he were to authorize, say, $70 to be taken out of his pay, he would run short of cash by the middle of the week. He could always cash in $30 of the bonds to carry him to the end of the week, but this would be a bit of a nuisance. He'd have to walk a few blocks out of his way home from work on Thursday and then waste another few minutes standing in the queue in front of the teller's cage at the bank. He might also have to pay a service charge.

But while cashing bonds in the middle of the week may be a nuisance, it need not be a completely unmitigated one. More interest income is earned from holding the $30 of bonds from Monday to Thursday than from holding the $30 in cash. In fact, to make the point of the parable stand out in boldest relief, we shall assume (until further notice) that money yields no interest whatever; and, in the other direction, that bonds or other earning assets can under no circumstances be used for making purchases. Neither asset, in sum, completely dominates the other.

How a choice of a bond deduction policy might be made under these conditions is sketched in Table 9–1. The first column lists various bond deduction policies and the second the corresponding cash balance with which our subject would then open the week. The third column shows the number of trips to the bank to cash in bonds that would be required to get through the rest of the week under each policy. Thus, if only $40 is taken out for bonds, the initial $60 in cash is adequate to cover all subsequent expenditures. At a deduction of $70, however, a trip to the bank will have to be made on Thursday; at $80, two trips will have to be made, one on Wednesday, and one on Friday. At a deduction of $90, a trip to the bank would have to be made every day from Tuesday on.[2] Suppose, for concreteness, that 6 cents is the cost of each such trip to the bank — that is, the cost of the shoe leather used up plus any service charge, plus the cash-equivalent cost of the otherwise enjoyable leisure time that has to be wasted standing in line. Then the total cost of the trips associated with each bond deduction will be that shown in column (4).

Against these costs must be set the corresponding interest earnings which, in this example, will be taken at .0015 dollars per dollar per day (equivalent to an annual rate of about 50 percent, i.e., to .5 dollars per dollar per year). The policy of taking only $40 in bonds in the initial deduction means that $40 will be in bonds every day during the week, making 240 dollar days of holdings in all, as shown in column (5). Raising the initial deduction to $70 means an extra 90 dollar days of interest earning power, since the additional $30 is held for 3 days and cashed in on Thursday. An initial deduction of $80 gives 360 dollar days (2 days at 80, 2 at 60, and 2 at 40); and one of $90 gives 390 dollar days. The total interest earned (neglecting the negligible amount of interest on the interest) under each policy is then found simply by multiplying the dollar day figure of column (5)

---

[2] To keep the table simple, we consider only policies involving an integral number of equally-spaced trips per week (treating Monday as if it were a trip for this count).

TABLE 9–1

The bond/money decision

(1) Initial bond deduction	(2) Initial cash balance 100 − Col. (1)	(3) Number of trips to the bank required	(4) Total cost of trips .06 × Col. (3)	(5) Total dollar days of bond holdings	(6) Interest earned during week .0015 × Col. (5)	(7) Net earnings Col. (6) − Col. (4)
40	60	0	0	240	.36	.36
70	30	1	.06	330	.495	.435
80	20	2	.12	360	.54	.42
90	10	5	.30	390	.585	.285

by the assumed daily interest rate of .0015 as shown in column (6). Subtracting out the cost of the trips to the bank gives the net gain under each policy, shown in column (7).

As can be seen, the highest net gain under the conditions given is $.435 per week, representing the policy of $70 for the initial deduction. The choice problem we raised is thus solved. But notice that in solving it we have been able to give a straightforward meaning to the notion of a demand for money. Since our subject's total pay is $100, saying that he demands $70 of bonds to start the week is equivalent to saying that his demand for money at the start of the week is $30.

But there is more. Not only has the parable suggested what to put on the quantity axis of a demand for money function, but it also indicates some of the key factors influencing the size of that demand. For suppose that the cost of a trip to the bank had been not 6 cents per trip, but only 1 cent per trip. Then the best policy, other things equal, would be the one calling for a bond deduction of $90, and a cash payment of only $10. We would say that our subject's demand for money was lower because one of the services rendered by an opening cash balance had fallen in value, namely the service of being able to go shopping without having to make so many trips to the bank during the week. And in the other direction, suppose that the value for the rate of interest had been only a tenth of that used in Table 9–1. Then the optimal initial cash balance would have been $60 rather than $40, the greater demand for money reflecting the reduced cost (in the form of reduced loss of interest earnings) of obtaining the services rendered by an opening cash balance.

This is still only part of the story. The rest of it, however, requires us first to extend our parable a bit.

Money holdings and purchasing power

Suppose that shortly after our subject has started work a currency reform occurs, of the kind that actually took place in France on January 1, 1960. A law is passed replacing each old dollar (symbol $\$_O$) with 2 new dollars (symbol $\$_N$). (In France it happened to be 100 old francs for 1 new franc). Furthermore, and this is most important to the tale, it is decreed that any and all pre-reform contracts denominated in old dollars are to be regarded as having been renegotiated into new dollars at the official rate of 2$_N$ for each 1$_O$.

What change in bond deduction policy would our subject now want to make? The answer itself is surely obvious, but it will be useful for later purposes to have a counterpart to Table 9–1 in which the elements of the decision problem are restated in terms of the new currency unit. Thus in Table 9–2, the entries in columns (1), (2) and (5) are each exactly twice those of Table 9–1, since our subject now earns $_N$200 per week and spends at the rate of $_N$20 per day, $_N$120 per week. Column (3), as before, shows the number of trips to the bank that would be necessary to get through the week under each policy, and column (4) the total cost in new dollars of those trips. Note that since the same amount of time and shoe leather is involved in each trip as it was before the reform, the monetary equivalent cost of each trip, restated in the new currency unit, will be twice that of Table 9–1. Column (6) shows the interest earnings. Note that the interest *rate* shown in the column heading is unaffected by the change in currency unit and the reinterpretation of contracts even though the interest *payments* (and the principal value of the bond holdings) would be. The interest rate, as the name suggests, is the *ratio* of dollars earned per day to dollars invested per day and hence is unchanged by a simultaneous doubling of both the numerator and denominator. Column (7), finally, shows the net earnings in new dollars associated with each bond deduction and hence each initial cash balance policy. Since all the entries in the column are exactly twice those of the corresponding entries in Table 9–1, the relative ranking of the policies is unaffected. The best strategy remains the second one, that is, the one calling for one trip to the bank on Wednesday. This calls for a bond deduction of $_N$140 and a demand for money of $_N$60.

The demand for real cash balances.   That the quantity of money demanded changes exactly in proportion to any "split" or reverse-split in the monetary unit is a point that can be stated in a variety of more or less equivalent ways. One of the most common ways, and most important in terms for the discussion to follow, is the proposition that the demand for money is a demand for *real* cash balances.

By a real economic magnitude we mean, in this context, one expressed in units of the output commodity. Thus suppose that

TABLE 9–2

The bond/money decision following a currency revaluation

(1) Initial bond deduction	(2) Initial cash balance 200 − Col. (1)	(3) Number of trips to the bank required	(4) Total cost of trips .12 × Col. (3)	(5) Total dollar days of bond holdings	(6) Interest earned during week .0015 × Col. (5)	(7) Net earnings Col. (6) − Col. (4)
80	120	0	0	480	.72	.72
140	60	1	.12	660	.99	.87
160	40	2	.24	720	1.08	.84
180	20	5	.60	780	1.17	.57

the ruling rate of exchange between the physical output commodity and money in Table 9–1 is 4 "boxes" of output for each 1 old dollar. (Equivalently, and more familiarly, we could say that the price of output in terms of money is $\$_o0.25$ per box). Then, since our subject's weekly wage in money units (or, to use another common synonym, his *nominal* wage) was taken as $\$_o100$, his real wage is $\dfrac{\$_o100/\text{week}}{\$_o0.25/\text{box}} = 400$ boxes/week. That is the amount of physical commodity that he could buy with his paycheck at the ruling price level. Similarly, we would say that the real cost of a trip to the bank to cash in bonds is $\dfrac{\$_o0.06/\text{trip}}{\$_o0.25/\text{box}} = 0.24$ boxes/trip. And in the same way we say that the real cash balance our subject chooses when he authorizes the deduction of $\$_o70$ in bonds from his pay is $\dfrac{\$_o30}{\$_o0.25/\text{box}} = 120$ boxes.

Note what happens to the various real and nominal magnitudes after the currency reform. All the nominal magnitudes are doubled, including, of course, the nominal value of a box of output. Hence all the real magnitudes, which are expressible as *ratios* of two nominal values—the nominal magnitude itself and the nominal value of a unit of output—are left unchanged. Real wages, for example, are: $\dfrac{\$_N200/\text{week}}{\$_N0.50/\text{box}} = 400$ boxes/week; the real cost of a bank trip is $\dfrac{\$_N0.12/\text{trip}}{\$_N0.50/\text{box}} = 0.24$ boxes/trip; and, most directly to the point at the moment, the real value of the cash balance demanded under the optimal strategy (or, equivalently, the purchasing power equivalent of the cash held at the start of the week under the best policy) remains $\dfrac{\$_N60}{\$_N0.50/\text{box}} = 120$ boxes.[3]

---

[3] Since we are still in a one-output commodity world, we can go from nominal to real magnitudes unambiguously merely by dividing by a single price, viz., the price per unit of output. In a multi-commodity world, we would have to face an "index number problem"—that is, the problem of finding a weighted average price to represent the heterogeneous group as a whole. Except under very special conditions, there is no way to construct such an average without involving some ambiguity in comparisons of the resulting real magnitudes for different individuals, or even for the same individual at different times. The difficulties, however, are not really critical for the issues considered in this book and are best left to courses in price theory.

In this and subsequent chapters, we shall find it useful to distinguish between real and nominal variables by writing all nominal variables in **boldface,** and real variables in lightface. This convention is similar to the one already employed, and which we shall continue to employ, of using capital letters to represent aggregate concepts and lower-case letters to represent per-capita variables.[4]

A digression on real interest rates, nominal interest rates and Fisher's Law. Just as we distinguish between real and nominal wages, so we must distinguish between real and nominal returns from holding assets. Consider, for example, an individual who bought one hundred old dollars' worth of bonds on Monday of the week just before the currency reform and cashed them in on Monday morning of the week just after the reform became effective. Neglecting the cost of bond cash-ins, his nominal realized rate of return on the bonds in terms of original dollars is

$$\frac{(\$_o100 + \$_o.0015 \cdot 100 \cdot 6) \cdot 2 - \$_o100}{\$_o100} = 1.018,$$

or 101.8 percent for the week. But we know that this apparently spectacular investment performance is an illusion. In terms of real purchasing power invested and received, the realized rate of return for the week has been only

$$\frac{\$_N201.8/\$_N0.50 - \$_o100/\$_o0.25}{\$_o100/\$_o0.25} = \frac{3.6 \text{ boxes}}{400 \text{ boxes}} = .009,$$

i.e., nine-tenths of one percent or .15 percent per day, exactly as in the original parable.

Using more general notation, if we let r stand for the realized real rate of return on an asset, $\boldsymbol{r}$ for its money or nominal rate of return and $\boldsymbol{\eta}$ for the rate of change in the nominal value of a unit of output over the return interval (i.e., $\boldsymbol{\eta} = \boldsymbol{p}_N/\boldsymbol{p}_o - 1$), then we can express the relation between realized real and money returns as

(1) $$r = \frac{(1 + \boldsymbol{r})/\boldsymbol{p}_N - 1/\boldsymbol{p}_o}{1/\boldsymbol{p}_o} = (1 + \boldsymbol{r})\frac{\boldsymbol{p}_o}{\boldsymbol{p}_N} - 1 = \frac{1 + \boldsymbol{r}}{1 + \boldsymbol{\eta}} - 1$$

---

[4] Thus Y = real gross national product, $\boldsymbol{Y}$ = nominal gross national product, y = per-capita real gross national product, and $\boldsymbol{y}$ = per-capita nominal gross national product. There are some exercises on this distinction at the end of the chapter.

or, rearranging a bit into a somewhat more compact and transparent form as

(2)
$$r = \frac{r - \eta}{1 + \eta}.$$

That is, the realized real rate of return is the money rate of return minus the rate of change in prices ("discounted" by $\frac{1}{1 + \eta}$ to reflect our treatment of time as discrete and hence our assumption that the entire price change occurs at the start of the period following the initial investment).[5]

Note that equation (2), as we have derived it, is an identity. It *defines* the realized real rate of return (plus unity) as the money rate of return (plus unity) corrected for the change in prices. There are some circumstances, however, in which equation (2), with suitable change in interpretation, would also hold in terms of the *promised* rates of interest on contracts made at the start of the period. To use some common economists' jargon, equation (2) would be said to hold in terms of *ex ante* (i.e., forward looking) rates, and not merely as an identity *ex post* (i.e., looking backward). Suppose, for example, that there exist loan contracts denominated in real terms. For concreteness, think of them as "purchasing power bonds" — which incidentally do exist in a number of countries — in which the number of money units paid to the investor on maturity of the contract is adjusted in the light of the price level then ruling so as to maintain a stipulated real return. Or, equivalently, think of them as direct rentals of real capital goods with payment made with units of real output — as we did, in effect, in previous chapters whenever we spoke of the interest rate as the return on capital. Suppose further that there also exist loan contracts denominated in money units, as is the case with ordinary bonds. Then if all traders in the capital market agree as to the values of the current price level and next period's price level, there can be one and only one relation between the money rate of interest and the real rate of interest in equilibrium in a perfect capital market, namely

---

[5] In a continuous time framework, equation (2) would be

(2′) $e^r = e^r/e^\eta,$

implying the familiar $r = r - \eta.$

(3)
$$r = \frac{r - \eta_e}{1 + \eta_e}$$

Or

(3')
$$r = r + \eta_e + \eta_e r.$$

where η_e is the rate of change in the equilibrium price level antici-pated by all participants. Any other value for r, given η_e and r, would make it possible to earn a nonzero return with no net in-vestment (e.g., if $r \lessgtr r + \eta_e + r\eta_e$, borrow **$100** and invest in $100 of purchasing power bonds which will yield $100(1 + r)$ in real terms and $100[1 + r + \eta_e + r\eta_e]$ when the real yield is converted back to money units at the start of next year. Use $100(1 + r)$ of the converted money proceeds to pay off the borrowing, and pocket the difference of $100[r - (r + \eta_e + r\eta_e)]$. Such free-ride profit opportunities are incompatible with equilibrium in the capital markets.)

The proposition that the equilibrium money rate of interest is equal to the real rate plus the anticipated change in prices (plus the cross-product term) is often called Fisher's Law in honor of the great American economist Irving Fisher, who, along with his many other contributions (cf. Ch. 4), was among the first to state the proposition and develop some of its major implications. It is, as we shall see, an extremely important proposition and one which we shall be making use of repeatedly in the course of our discussions of monetary policy in subsequent chapters.[6]

Real rates, nominal rates and the demand for money. Given two distinct rates of interest, a real rate and a nominal rate, which rate or which combination of rates governs the demand for money? To see, suppose that the currency revaluation of Table 9–2 were pushed forward to Tuesday of the week in Table 9–1, so that from Tuesday on the price level would be $0.50 per box of output. Suppose, further, that instead of the automatic re-scaling of all contracts previously assumed, we leave the job to the natural workings of Fisher's Law. That law assures us that if the

---

[6] For the most part we shall use it in the simple form derived above without any explicit further corrections for uncertainty on the part of investors as to the prices that will actually rule next period. For the problems we shall be consider-ing, the costs of a more systematic treatment of uncertainty about prices would far outweigh any benefits.

price level is known to be $0.50 per box from Tuesday on, then we cannot have at one and the same time on Monday (a) a price level at the original value of $0.25 per box, (b) a real rental rate for capital of 0.0015 boxes per box per day, and (c) a money rate of interest on bonds purchased on Monday and maturing on Tuesday or thereafter of 0.0015 dollars per dollar per day. Let us assume, for maximum dramatic effect, that it is the original price level and real rental rate that remain unchanged. Then the nominal rate of interest ruling on the Monday before the price level doubles must be $r = r + \eta_e + \eta_e r = .0015 + 1.0 + (1.0)(.0015) = 1.003$ per dollar per day. (Any bonds bought on Tuesday or thereafter will again carry a money rate of 0.0015 dollars per dollar per day, since no further *change* in the price level is anticipated.)

Table 9–3 shows the implications of this scenario for the Monday bond/money decision. Columns (1) and (2) are the bond and money strategies to be considered, with the previous optimum indicated by a single asterisk. Column (3) is the opening cash balance on Tuesday morning under each strategy ($10 less than the entries in column (2) because of Monday's consumption spending). Column (4) shows the nominal value of bonds held as of the start of Tuesday, principal plus interest (column (1) times $(1 + 1.003)$). Column (5) is the sum of columns (3) and (4) and thus gives the nominal value of financial assets as of Tuesday. The corresponding real value of those assets (column (5)/$0.50 per box) is given in column (6).

A quick glance down column (6) shows that the original demand for $30 of cash on Monday is no longer optimal. Even if our subject were to make a trip to the bank every day for the rest of the week, the cost of those trips would be only 4×0.24 boxes/trip $= .96$ boxes. By contrast, cutting the initial cash demand back from $30 to $20 would increase real wealth by 20.06 boxes; and cutting it further to $10 would add another 20.06 boxes.

Thus a change in the money rate of interest has indeed changed the demand for money even though the real rate of interest and the real cost of trips to the bank have remained the same. Nor is this merely an artifact of the particular numbers used in the parable. A price increase, whatever its size, must reduce the real value of assets denominated in money units, such as cash or bonds. If the increase is anticipated, the bond buyers

TABLE 9-3

The money/bond decision in anticipation of a currency revaluation

(1) Initial bond deduction	(2) Initial cash balance $100 - Col.\ (1)$	(3) Opening cash balance Tuesday morning $Col.\ (2) - 10$	(4) Nominal value of bonds held as of Tuesday morning $Col.\ (1) \times (1 + 1.003)$	(5) Total nominal assets $Col.\ (3) + Col.\ (4)$	(6) Real value of nominal assets $Col.\ (5) \div 0.50$
40	60	50	80.12	130.12	260.24
70	30*	20	140.21	160.21	320.42
80	20	10	160.24	170.24	340.48
90	10	0	180.27	180.27	360.54

receive compensation in the form of higher interest payments for the loss in real value of the principal. Holders of noninterest-bearing money, however, would benefit from no such adjustment. Hence the opportunity cost of holding money rather than bonds has two components: (a) the real return that would be foregone by holding money rather than earning assets even if prices were constant; plus (b) the loss in real purchasing power due to an anticipated price increase (or minus the gain in real purchasing power due to an anticipated fall in prices). The sum of these two costs of holding money is, by virtue of Fisher's Law, the nominal rate of interest.

The demand for money and the level of expenditures

The parable of Table 9–1, it will be recalled, described the choice of a bond deduction by an individual spending at the not very princely, but computationally very convenient, rate of $60 per week (of six days). We saw that under the other conditions given, his optimal strategy implied a demand for money, in the sense of a demand for an opening cash balance, of $30. How would this demand compare to that of an individual spending at a higher rate, say $120 per week, assuming all other conditions of the problem are the same?

The answer depends, alas, on precisely how we choose to interpret the phrase, "all other conditions of the problem are the same." There is no difficulty with keeping the interest rates or the price level unchanged. But what of the cost of cashing a bond? That cost, as described in the parable, had the following three components: (*a*) the time spent walking to the bank and standing in the queue at the teller's cage; (*b*) the shoe leather consumed in the extra walking and standing; and (*c*) any fees or service charges made by the bank. Consider the first. Even if we can assume that our two subjects spend precisely the same amount of time per trip to the bank, we cannot assume that the money equivalent of that time is the same for each of them. If the individual with the higher expenditure level is earning a higher wage, he will presumably attach a higher value to his own time. How much higher and whether more or less than in proportion to the difference in wages and wealth, we have no way of saying for sure, but some difference there must surely be. Similarly, with the shoe leather cost. The wear and tear on a pair of hand-sewn calfskin oxfords by Gucci comes to a lot more than that on a pair of Thom McAn's.

Even the service charge component is unlikely to be the same for all transactions at any given point in time. And it can certainly not be taken as constant over time in any context in which increases in real wages are being considered. For a major element in bank and brokerage charges (in real terms) is the (real) cost of the clerical and other labor services used to process the transactions.

Fortunately, these unavoidable ambiguities in the notion of an "unchanged" cost of getting from cash to earning assets and back do not have to be completely resolved. Under any reasonable interpretation of the term "unchanged cost," a higher rate of expenditures is likely to be associated with a higher demand for money. How much higher, and, in particular, whether the increase in money demanded tends to be more or less than in proportion to the change in expenditures, are questions we can leave to be answered in the light of the empirical record.

For the United States, at least, the empirical evidence suggests that over long periods of time real per-capita money balances have tended to grow at roughly the same rate as real per-capita expenditures so that a value of unity for the long-run elasticity of real money balances with respect to real per-capita expenditures would certainly be an acceptable first approximation.

Over shorter intervals, however, the picture is somewhat less clear. The important point is that although the ratio of money stock to expenditures has varied somewhat over time, there appears to be no discernible trend of a kind incompatible with the assumption of a long-run elasticity equal to unity. The development of a demand-for-money function with this property, as well as with the other properties suggested by these parables, is the task of the next chapter.

PROBLEMS FOR CHAPTER 9

1. Suppose that the production function is $y = \sqrt{k}$, that there are 10,000 workers, $k = 45$ and $P = 5$. Compute Y, $\mathbf{Y}$, y, and $\mathbf{y}$.
2. Compute the optimal amount to put into Mr. Connally's bond program for the decision maker depicted in Table 9–1 if
   a. he wants to spend $15 per day,

   b. trips cost 4¢ each,

   c. the interest rate is .0012,

   d. all of the above are true.

3. Suppose that the real rate of interest is 5 percent, that the expected inflation rate is 3 percent, and that interest income is taxed at a rate of 20 percent. Calculate

   a. the nominal interest rate (before taxes),

   b. the nominal interest rate (after taxes),

   c. the real rate of return after taxes.

10

A consumption interpretation of the demand for money

So MANY PROPERTIES essential to a demand-for-money function have now been specified that you may well be wondering whether any simple function with those properties does in fact exist. And, if it does exist, whether it can be derived from an underlying microeconomic model of individual behavior. The answer to both questions is yes.

A LIFE CYCLE DEMAND FUNCTION FOR MONEY

Consider, for example, a demand-for-money function of the following form:

$$(1) \qquad m_i(t) = \xi \, c_i(t) \, \frac{1 + \mu}{\mu}$$

where

$m_i(t)$ = the *real* value of cash balances demanded at the start of period t by an individual aged i.

$c_i(t)$ = the level of *real* consumption spending during period t by an individual aged i.

$\mu = (1 - \lambda_r)\tau$ = the after-tax *money* rate of interest.

ξ = a positive constant whose value may, in principle, be different for different age groups.

207

It is easily verified that this function does indeed possess the essential properties outlined in the preceding chapter. The demand for real cash balances described by equation (1) is a decreasing function of the nominal rate of interest and, implicitly, an increasing function of the costs of transferring funds between cash and earning assets. No term directly represents such costs, but they are impounded in the parameter ξ. The higher such costs, the higher the value of ξ and the higher the demand for initial balances. The term $c_i(t)$ makes the demand for real balances an increasing function of the level of real consumption expenditures planned for the period. It also suggests how the demand for real balances might be expected to behave over time, relative to real income. In a world in which real consumption is governed by a life cycle process of the kind we have developed, we know that along an equilibrium growth path, real consumption, real wealth and real income will all be growing at the same rate. Equation (1) thus implies an equal growth rate for real cash balances under such conditions.

THE BASIS OF THE DEMAND FUNCTION FOR MONEY

To derive this life cycle demand function we begin, as usual, with the utility function. Since our world has both money holdings and ordinary consumption expenditures, the simple functions that we have so far been working with must be expanded accordingly. The natural extension of previous utility functions is one of the form:

$$(2) \qquad \gamma_i \log c_i + \gamma_{i+1} \log c_{i+1} + \ldots + \gamma_{n_3} \log c_{n_3} +$$
$$\xi_i \log m_i + \xi_{i+1} \log m_{i+1} + \ldots + \xi_{n_3} \log m_{n_3}$$

where m_i is the real value of cash balances held at the start of period i and c_i the real value of consumption during period i.[1]

Economists of a generation ago would have regarded putting money holdings into the utility function as fundamentally incorrect. It might seem to imply that the decision maker is a

---

[1] We again repeat the caution that some of the properties derived from this utility function are specific to its explicit functional form, particularly the fact that it is a *separable* utility function. We shall call your attention to some of these special properties when they arise in this and subsequent chapters.

miser who loves money for its own sake, deriving pleasure from viewing the handsomely engraved portraits of the presidents. Actually, the justification for putting money into the utility function is simply this: like an automobile, a house or a suit, a cash balance, too, is a durable consumer good that provides a flow of valuable services to the holder. What are these services? Essentially, as we have seen, the ability to avoid or reduce transactions costs that would otherwise have to be incurred in implementing consumption and saving programs during that period. Admittedly, one usually thinks of the services yielded by durables in more positive terms (though surely some part of the services rendered by an automobile are the avoided costs of hailing a taxi on a rainy day). But in economics, minus a minus is as good as a plus.

Certainly a more elegant way of handling those costs would be to exhibit them explicitly (as in the parables of Chapter 9), along with the appropriate policies for optimal cash management. But it is also a much more complicated way than merely assuming that the utility individuals obtain from money balances is a function of the stock of money they hold at the beginning of a period. Since the essential qualitative predictions of the two approaches can be shown to be the same, we opt for simplicity.

Because the next step, the derivation of the budget constraint, involves some tedious algebra, we defer it to an appendix. Taking the γs and ξs of the utility function (2) as constant (except for setting $\xi_{n_3} = 0$, for reasons which should become clear after a reading of the appendix and footnote 4), for simplicity, setting $\gamma = 1$ as was done in Chapter 4, and using the budget constraint derived in the appendix, it can be shown that the utility-maximizing program for our decision maker will have

$$c_j = c_{j-1}(1 + \mu)$$

$$m_j \frac{\mu}{1 + \mu} = \xi\, c_j,$$

for all periods except for the last where,

$$m_{n_3} = 0.$$

The second equation means that the decision maker has adjusted his money holding so that the cost of holding money balances is equal to $\xi\, c_j$. That cost, as we saw in Chapter 9, consists not only of the real return forgone on the funds tied up in cash balances, but also of any depreciation or appreciation of the real value of cash balances due to changes in the price level. Hence, it is the money rate of interest reflecting both components combined that measures the cost of cash balances.[2]

The utility maximizing program for a decision maker can further be shown to lead to a revised life cycle consumption function for an individual of age i:

$$(3) \qquad c_i = \left(\frac{1}{n_3 - i + 1 + \xi\,(n_3 - i)} \right) z_i,$$

and as the demand-for-money function.

$$(4) \qquad m_i = \xi\, c_i \frac{1 + \mu}{\mu}.$$

The demand function can equivalently be expressed as

$$(5) \qquad m_i = \frac{1}{n_3 - i + 1 + \xi\,(n_3 - i)} \, \xi \, \frac{1 + \mu}{\mu} \, z_i.$$

Equations (4) and (5) mean that the demand-for-money function can be appropriately interpreted as either a "wealth" or "transactions" demand, depending on the context.[3]

MONEY HOLDINGS AND CONSUMPTION OVER THE LIFE CYCLE: SOME NUMERICAL ILLUSTRATIONS

Consider once again the bachelor whose 4-period life cycle of consumption was traced out in Table 5–1. Let his earning opportunities in real terms be exactly as before. We assume now, however, that our bachelor lives in an economy which uses money. In particular, let him expect his nonproperty income in period 2 to be \$300,000, and in period 3 to be \$630,000, both measured in terms of period 1 purchasing power. Let the real rate of in-

---

[2] For what it is worth, this is exactly analogous to the real cost of consuming any other durable good. The cost of the transportation services provided by an automobile, operating and maintenance costs aside, consists of the sum of the (real) rate of interest and the depreciation rate times its capital value.

[3] Thus, in the great debate among economists over the "wealth" vs. the "transactions" approach to the demand for money, we are in the happy position of being able to say that our function is compatible with either interpretation.

terest again be 50 percent per period. Then his wealth at birth will also have exactly the same value as in the earlier example, namely, $480,000 (i.e., $h_1 = 0 + \dfrac{300,000}{(1 + .5)} + \dfrac{630,000}{(1 + 5)^2} + 0 = 480,000$).

Suppose that the price level is expected to rise at a rate of 50 percent per period in each period thereafter. Then it will also be the case, thanks to Fisher's Law, that the nominal rate of interest per period will be

$$r = \mu = (1 + .5)\,(1 + .5) - 1 = 1.25,$$

i.e., 125 percent per period. (Note that, until further notice, we are assuming that $\lambda_r = 0$.)

Because our bachelor will now have to make a cash balance decision as well as a consumption decision at the start of each period, we must specify values for the ξ_i in his utility function. To simplify the number work—and only for that reason—it is convenient to set $\xi = 1/3$ for each of the first three periods. Our simplifying assumption requires $\xi_4 = 0$, as was noted earlier. The consumption and money demand functions for our bachelor will thus be:

$$(3')\qquad \begin{cases} c_i = \dfrac{1}{(5 - i) + \dfrac{1}{3}\,(4 - i)}\; z_i, & i = 1,\,2,\,3 \\[2em] c_4 = z_4, \end{cases}$$

and

$$(4')\qquad \begin{cases} m_i = \dfrac{1}{3}\, c_i\, \dfrac{2.25}{1.25} = .6 c_i, & i = 1,\,2,\,3 \\[1.5em] m_4 = 0. \end{cases}$$

Turn now to Table 10–1, which presents our bachelor's consumption and cash balance decisions, along with the summary accounting information. Notice that the table is in two parts. The bottom panel, labeled "In nominal terms," records all events in the normal accounting way, that is, in current dollars. The top panel, labeled "In real terms," shows the same events expressed in terms of period 1 dollars, that is, in terms of dollars adjusted for changes in the purchasing power of a dollar after period 1.

For period 1, but only period 1, current dollars and period 1 dollars are the same, so that the entries in the two panels are the

TABLE 10-1

The bachelor's consumption and cash balances with an inflation rate of 50 percent per period

Period	(1) a'_i Nonmonetary assets carried over	(2) $a_i = a'_i(1+r)$ Carryover plus real return on nonmonetary assets	(3) m'_i Money balances carried over	(4) w_i Nonproperty income for the period	(5) h_i Present value of future nonproperty income	(6) z_i Total wealth	(7) c_i Consumption	(8) m_i Money holdings	(9) a'_{i+1} Terminal value of nonmonetary assets (2)+(3)+(4)−(7)−(8)	(10) Price level
A. In real terms (constant period 1 dollars)										
1	0	0	0	0	480,000	480,000	96,000	57,600	−153,600	1.00
2	−153,600	−230,400	38,400	300,000	720,000	528,000	144,000	86,400	−122,400	1.50
3	−122,400	−183,600	57,600	630,000	630,000	504,000	216,000	129,600	158,400	2.25
4	158,400	237,600	86,400	0	0	324,000	324,000	0	0	3.375
B. In nominal terms (current-period dollars)										
1	0	0	0	0	480,000	480,000	96,000	57,600	−153,600	
2	−153,600	−345,600	57,600	450,000	1,080,000	792,000	216,000	129,600	183,600	
3	−183,600	−413,100	129,600	1,417,500	1,417,500	1,134,000	486,000	291,600	356,400	
4	356,400	801,900	291,600	0	0	1,093,500	1,093,500	0	0	

same. In both, the first entry is the $480,000 in column 5, representing the present value of expected future nonproperty income. We can get this figure either by discounting the expected real earnings by the real rate of interest or by discounting the expected nominal earnings at the money rate of interest, viz.

$$h_1 = 0 + \frac{450,000}{2.25} + \frac{1,417,500}{(2.25)^2} + 0$$

$$= 0 + \frac{(300,000)\,(1.5)}{[(1.5)\,(1.5)]} + \frac{(630,000)\,(1.5)^2}{[(1.5)\,(1.5)]^2} + 0 = 480,000.$$

Computed either way, it represents our subject's sole source of wealth at the start of period 1. Applying (3′) and formula (4′) with $i = 1$, we then have for our decision variables:

$$c_1 = \frac{1}{4 + \frac{1}{3}\,(3)}\,480,000 = \frac{1}{5}\,480,000 = 96,000,$$

and

$$m_1 = .6c_1 = 57,600.$$

Note that the value of consumption in period 1 is substantially less than in the earlier life cycle example of Chapter 5, where we had simply

$$c_1 = \frac{1}{n_3 - i + 1}\,z_1 = \frac{1}{4}\,(480,000) = 120,000.$$

Even though initial real wealth is the same in the two cases, the bachelor in the money-using economy must keep a portion of that wealth in the form of noninterest-bearing cash balances. The desired crescendo of consumption — that is, the desired growth of consumption at a rate equal to the real rate of interest — is sustainable only if it starts from a lower level.

Because our subject started the period with no financial assets, his consumption of $96,000 in period 1 plus his cash holding of $57,600 puts him $153,600 in debt by the end of the period. By our timing convention, interest on that debt is added as of the start of period 2. Since the nominal rate of interest is 125 percent per period, the nominal value of his debt thus becomes $345,600 (see column 2 of panel B) as of the start of period 2, and its value in terms of period 1 purchasing power is simply

$$\frac{345,600}{1 + \eta} = 230,400 = (153,600)[1 + r] \text{ (see column 2 of panel A)}.$$

Against this liability, our subject has his cash balance as a financial asset.[4] Its value in nominal terms is still the same $57,600, but because of the price rise of 50 percent since period 1, its value in real terms has fallen to $38,400 $= \dfrac{\$57,600}{1.5}$. In addition to these financial liabilities and assets, our subject also has his nonproperty earnings during period 2, plus the present value of the earnings expected next period. Netting out the assets against the liabilities yields a net wealth for period 2 of $792,000 in nominal period 2 dollars, and of $528,000 in period 1 dollars. And given these values for total wealth, formula (3′) sets the level of consumption in real terms in period 2 at

$$c_2 = \frac{1}{3 + \dfrac{1}{3}\,(2)}\,528,000 = 144,000 = c_1(1 + \mu) = 96,000(1.5),$$

and in nominal terms at

$$c_2\,(1 + \eta) = 144,000(1.5) = \frac{1}{3 + \dfrac{1}{3}\,(2)}\,792,000 = 216,000.[5]$$

Formula (4′) then sets the value of the desired initial cash balance in real terms at

$$m_2 = .6c_2 = (.6)(144,000) = 86,400,$$

and in nominal terms at

$$m_2(1 + \eta) = (86,400)(1.5) = (.6)(216,000) = 129,600.$$

And so on, in similar fashion, for the rest of the table.

---

[4] Note that our decision maker ends the period with the same amount of money he started with. One way to relate this convention to the cash management parables of Chapter 9 is to assume that there are many in and out cycles within a single period. The beginning and ending cash balances are recorded at the same stage in the cycle but the decision maker changes his cash policy and hence sets up a new cycle pattern at the start of each period.

[5] Note that since consumption is strictly proportional to wealth, we can use the same formula (3′) to compute either real or nominal consumption as the context may happen to require.

The effect of a higher anticipated rate of inflation

Suppose that the rate of price inflation in the example had been set at 100 percent per period, rather than 50 percent per period. How would the life cycle of real consumption and money holdings have been affected?

For money holdings, the answer must surely be that they will be lower throughout. The higher rate of anticipated inflation implies a higher nominal rate of interest and hence a higher opportunity cost of maintaining a cash balance. Our bachelor can thus be expected to try to economize on his money holdings. But what of his consumption spending? What proportion of the wealth released from cash balances will be consumed, and what proportion merely transferred to other earning assets? (Think out your answer before looking at Table 10-2, which presents the complete life cycle and supporting accounting information for a world with an inflation rate of 100 percent per period, but otherwise identical to that of Table 10-1.)

A glance down column 7 of the top panel will show that despite the difference in the rate of inflation, the level of real consumption spending by our subject is precisely the same in every period. The complete insensitivity of real consumption to the anticipated rate of inflation arises because real consumption in our formulation depends only on real wealth; and real wealth, in our examples, is unaffected by the rate of inflation of the nominal magnitudes. It is true that lower real cash balances are carried throughout, and to that extent a higher level of earning assets (or lower level of interest-bearing liabilities) is maintained in each period. But the added real interest earnings are just balanced by greater erosion of such cash balances as are in fact held. (E.g., in period 1 of Table 10-1, the cash balance was set at $57,600, and it fell in real terms to $38,400, as a consequence of the 50 percent inflation between periods 1 and 2. In Table 10-2, our subject's first period cash balance was only $48,000 to start with, but it suffered a decline in real value of $24,000 when the price level doubled. Note that the real return on the difference in initial cash balances (i.e., $(57,600 - 48,000)(r) = (9,600)(.5) = 4,800$) is exactly equal to the difference in the loss of real purchasing power of the cash balance in the two cases, i.e., $(48,000 - 24,000) - (57,800 - 38,400) = 4,800$).)

TABLE 10–2

The bachelor's consumption and cash balances with an inflation rate of 100 percent per period

Period	(1) a'_i Nonmonetary assets carried over	(2) $a_i = a'_i(1 + r)$ Carryover plus real return on nonmonetary assets	(3) m'_i Money balances carried over	(4) w_i Nonproperty income for the period	(5) h_i Present value of future nonproperty income	(6) z_i Total wealth	(7) c_i Consumption	(8) m_i Money holdings	(9) a_{i+1} Terminal value of nonmonetary assets (2)+(3)+(4)−(7)−(8)	(10) Price level
A. *In real terms (constant period 1 dollars)*										
1	0	0	0	0	480,000	480,000	96,000	48,000	−144,000	1.0
2	−144,000	−216,000	24,000	300,000	720,000	528,000	144,000	72,000	−108,000	2.0
3	−108,000	−162,000	36,000	630,000	630,000	504,000	216,000	108,000	180,000	4.0
4	180,000	270,000	54,000	0	0	324,000	324,000	0	0	8.0
B. *In nominal terms (current-period dollars)*										
1	0	0	0	0	480,000	480,000	96,000	48,000	−144,000	
2	−144,000	−432,000	48,000	600,000	1,440,000	1,056,000	288,000	144,000	−216,000	
3	−216,000	−648,000	144,000	2,520,000	2,520,000	2,016,000	864,000	432,000	720,000	
4	720,000	2,160,000	432,000	0	0	2,592,000	2,592,000	0	0	

It is a property of utility functions of the special (separable) kind we have been using that the real consumption pattern of the bachelor over his life cycle is completely unaffected by the rate of price inflation. But even for these kinds of utility functions, great care must be taken in generalizing from this seeming "neutrality" of money. Remember, first of all, that the conclusion is strictly a *partial equilibrium* one based on given real rates of interest and given wage rates. Before we could conclude that inflation had no affect on real consumption, we would have to see whether cash balances might displace private capital as a store of wealth, and thereby change real rates of interest and real wage rates. This class of problems will be taken up in the next chapter after a full general equilibrium model of a monetary economy has been set down.

Second, even within a partial equilibrium setting, it is important to keep in mind that our conclusion with respect to inflation and real consumption must not be taken as suggesting that the higher rate of inflation in Table 10–2 had no adverse consequences for our hypothetical bachelor. In fact, if asked to choose whether to live out his span in the Table 10–1 world or the Table 10–2 world, our subject would unhesitatingly opt for Table 10–1. To see why, recall the form of our subject's utility index, viz.,

$$\sum_{i=1}^{4} \log c_i + \xi \sum_{i=1}^{3} \log m_i.$$

Since real consumption would be the same in both worlds, the first summation offers no basis for distinction. But thanks to the higher rate of inflation, we know that desired real cash-balance holdings will be less in the world of Table 10–2. Hence, the value of the preference index will also be lower for a life cycle lived in that world.

Nor is this merely an artifact of the particular preference function we happen to be using. Recall what getting along with a smaller cash balance requires. As we saw in our parables of cash management policy in Chapter 9, it means using up more time and shoe leather in the queues at the bank, and incurring higher levels of transaction costs in the management of one's earning assets. We have chosen to model these costs indirectly by putting a positive weight on cash holdings in the utility index. But we must not lose sight of the fact that the loss of utility from inflation is ultimately a matter of the higher costs of cash management that must be incurred when prices rise more rapidly.

Finally, before generalizing about the relation between inflation and real consumption, keep in mind that we have been concerned so far only with inflations that have been fully anticipated in advance. The effects on real wealth and real consumption of an *unanticipated* change in the rate of inflation are quite different. In fact, failure to distinguish adequately between the two types of inflation has been a major source of confusion in discussions by economists in and out of government concerning the economic consequences of inflation.

Even without a full general equilibrium model, of the kind to be set out in the next chapter, some of the key differences between the two kinds of inflation in their impact on real wealth can readily be illustrated. Table 10–3, for example, traces out a 4-period life cycle in which the first two periods are exactly the same as those of Table 10–1. At the end of period 2, further continuation along the lines of Table 10–1 is being anticipated, when the price level at the start of period 3 suddenly and unexpectedly jumps by 167 percent to a value of 4.0. Thereafter, the price level is expected to increase by 100 percent per period, and it does in fact proceed at that rate, reaching a value of 8.0 at the start of 4.

That this unexpected price rise has pushed our subject off his original path of real consumption is clear from comparing the values in column 7 of Table 10–3 with those in Table 10–1. Period 3 consumption falls to $204,858 from the earlier $216,000, and period 4 consumption to $308,495 from $324,000. What has happened is that the unexpected price rise at the opening of period 3 has produced an unexpected fall of $25,200 in the real value of the cash holdings carried over from period 2, reducing them from the $57,600 level of Table 10–1 to $32,400.[6] The lower level of wealth, in turn, requires a lower consumption path over the remaining years of the life cycle. An *unexpected* inflation, in short, acts in part like an unexpected tax — a fact that seems to have been

---

[6] Note that to keep the example simple we have assumed in effect that all his nonmonetary assets (and liabilities) are kept in real form, and hence are insulated from price-level changes. To the extent that this is not the case, there will be additional wealth effects of the unexpected inflation. We shall postpone discussion of them, however, until the next chapter.

TABLE 10–3

The bachelor's consumption and cash balances with unexpected inflation

Period	(1) a'_i Nonmonetary assets carried over	(2) $a_i = a'_i(1+r)$ Carryover plus real return on nonmonetary assets	(3) m'_i Money balances carried over	(4) w_i Nonproperty income for the period	(5) h_i Present value of future nonproperty income	(6) z_i Total wealth	(7) c_i Consumption	(8) m_i Money holdings	(9) a'_{i+1} Terminal value of nonmonetary assets (2)+(3)+(4)−(7)−(8)	(10) Price level
A. *In real terms (constant period 1 dollars)*										
1	0	0	0	0	480,000	480,000	96,000	57,600	−153,600	1.0
2	−153,600	−230,400	38,400	300,000	720,000	528,000	144,000	86,400	−122,400	1.5
3	−122,400	−183,600	32,400	630,000	630,000	478,800	204,858	102,429	171,513	4.0
4	171,513	257,280	51,215	0	0	308,495	308,495	0	0	8.0
B. *In nominal terms (current-period dollars)*										
1	0	0	0	0	480,000	480,000	96,000	57,600	−153,600	
2	−153,600	−345,600	57,600	450,000	1,080,000	792,000	216,000	129,600	−183,600	
3	−183,600	−734,400	129,600	2,520,000	2,520,000	1,915,200	819,432	409,716	686,052	
4	686,052	2,058,240	409,716	2,520,000	0	2,467,956	2,467,956	0	0	

well understood by kings and governors long before any formal economics was being written.

APPENDIX TO CHAPTER 10

Derivation of the demand function for money

Although the arguments of the utility function are *real* consumption and *real* cash balances, the decision maker keeps his accounts in money terms. To distinguish the nominal from the real magnitudes in the course of the derivation, we continue to follow the notational convention that nominal values will be in **boldface** and their corresponding real counterparts in lightface. Thus $m_t = \boldsymbol{m}_t/\boldsymbol{P}_t$ says that real money balances in period t are nominal balances divided by (or deflated by) the price level of period t and similarly for all other real and nominal magnitudes.

At the start of period $j + 1$, but before he has actually made his plans for the period, our decision maker's total wealth, $\boldsymbol{z}_{j+1}$, will be

$$\boldsymbol{z}_{j+1} = \boldsymbol{m}_j + \boldsymbol{h}_{j+1} + \boldsymbol{a}_{j+1},$$

where $\boldsymbol{m}_j$ is the cash balance carried over from the previous period, $\boldsymbol{h}_{j+1}$, the value of his human capital, and $\boldsymbol{a}_{j+1}$ the value of all nonmoney financial assets owned (owed). These entries, in turn, can be expressed in terms of the accounting statements of the previous period as

$$(A.1) \quad \boldsymbol{z}_{j+1} = \boldsymbol{m}_j + (\boldsymbol{h}_j - \boldsymbol{w}_j(1 - \lambda_w))(1 + \boldsymbol{r}(1 - \lambda_r)) + \\ (\boldsymbol{a}_j + \boldsymbol{m}_{j-1} + \boldsymbol{w}_j(1 - \lambda_w) - \boldsymbol{c}_j - \boldsymbol{m}_j)(1 + \boldsymbol{r}(1 - \lambda_r)) \\ = (\boldsymbol{z}_j - \boldsymbol{c}_j)(1 + \boldsymbol{r}(1 - \lambda_r)) - \boldsymbol{m}_j \, \boldsymbol{r}(1 - \lambda_r)$$

where $\boldsymbol{w}_j$ is the wage income earned in period j, λ_w is the tax rate on wage income, λ_r is the tax rate on interest income, and $\boldsymbol{r}$ is the before-tax nominal rate of return received on the funds put into the capital market.[7] For concision let $\boldsymbol{\mu} = (1 - \lambda_r)\boldsymbol{r}$ stand for

---

[7] Note that (A.1) maintains our assumption that the cash balances earn no interest whatever. This is a much stronger assumption than necessary, but helps to sharpen the contrast between money and other forms of holding wealth. More general models in which money holdings of individuals do bear interest are presented in Chapter 15.

the nominal after-tax rate of return. Then repeating the substitution of (A.1) successively gives the following as the resource constraint, expressed in nominal terms, for an individual of age i:

$$(A.2) \quad c_i + \frac{c_{i+1}}{1+\mu} + \frac{c_{i+2}}{(1+\mu)^2} + \cdots + \frac{c_{n_3}}{(1+\mu)^{n_3-i}}$$

$$+ m_i \frac{\mu}{1+\mu} + m_{i+1} \frac{\mu}{1+\mu} \left(\frac{1}{1+\mu}\right) +$$

$$m_{i+2} \frac{\mu}{1+\mu} \left(\frac{1}{1+\mu}\right)^2 + \ldots + m_{n_3-1} \left(\frac{\mu}{1+\mu}\right)\left(\frac{1}{1+\mu}\right)^{n_3-i+1}$$

$$= z_i$$

The consumption levels and cash balances of the resource constraint (13) (A.2) are nominal values, whereas those of the utility function (2) are in real terms. The conversion of (A.2) to conform with (2) is easily accomplished, however. Dividing both sides of (A.2) by the current price level P_i and multiplying each $c_{i+\tau}$ and $m_{i+\tau}$ by $P_{i+\tau}/P_{i+\tau}$ gives

$$(A.3) \quad c_i + c_{i+1} \left(\frac{P_{i+1}}{P_i}\right) \frac{1}{1+\mu} + c_{i+2} \left(\frac{P_{i+2}}{P_i}\right)\left(\frac{1}{1+\mu}\right)^2$$

$$+ \cdots + c_{n_3} \left(\frac{P_{n_3}}{P_i}\right)\left(\frac{1}{1+\mu}\right)^{n_3-i} + m_i \frac{\mu}{1+\mu}$$

$$+ m_{i+1} \frac{\mu}{1+\mu} \left(\frac{P_{i+1}}{P_i}\right) \frac{1}{1+\mu} + m_{i+2} \left(\frac{\mu}{1+\mu}\right)\left(\frac{P_{i+2}}{P_i}\right)\left(\frac{1}{1+\mu}\right)^2$$

$$+ \cdots + m_{n_3-1} \frac{\mu}{1+\mu} \left(\frac{P_{n_3}}{P_i}\right) \left(\frac{1}{1+\mu}\right)^{n_3-i-1} = z_i.$$

The terms $P_{i+\tau}/P_i$ incorporate any changes in the price level and can be expressed in terms of previous notation as $\frac{P_{i+\tau}}{P_i} = (1+\eta)^{\tau}$.[8]

---

[8] Here, as throughout this derivation we have assumed that interest rates and inflation rates are constant over the decision maker's life span. This substantially simplifies the exposition without detracting from its import. If inflation rates differed in these years, then $P_{i+\tau}/P_i$ would be given by

$$(1+\eta_{i+1})(1+\eta_{i+2}) \cdots (1+\eta_{i+\tau}).$$

Like adjustments would be made in the formulas to allow for μ being different in different time periods.

Using Fisher's Law, the real after-tax interest rate, μ, is given by

$$\mu = \frac{1+\mu}{1+\eta} - 1,$$

and making the corresponding substitutions

(A.4)

$$c_i + c_{i+1}\frac{1}{1+\mu} + c_{i+2}\left(\frac{1}{1+\mu}\right)^2 + \cdots + c_{n_3}\left(\frac{1}{1+\mu}\right)^{n_3-i}$$

$$+ m_i\frac{\mu}{1+\mu} + m_{i+1}\left(\frac{\mu}{1+\mu}\right)\frac{1}{1+\mu} + m_{i+2}\left(\frac{\mu}{1+\mu}\right)\left(\frac{1}{1+\mu}\right)^2$$

$$+ \cdots + m_{n_3-1}\left(\frac{\mu}{1+\mu}\right)\left(\frac{1}{1+\mu}\right)^{n_3-i-1} = z_i.$$

The final steps on the road to the demand-for-money function of equation (1) are similar to those covered in the appendix to Chapter 4. We will not repeat them here.

PROBLEMS FOR CHAPTER 10

1. Suppose that the bachelor decision maker expects to live four periods and receive a wage income of $180,000 in real terms in both periods 2 and 3, and that the real and nominal interest rates are 50 and 80 percent per annum, respectively. Further, suppose that $\xi = 1/3$. Following the format of Table 10-1, calculate the decision maker's consumption and money holdings for all periods in both real and money terms.

2. Recompute these numbers using a real interest rate of 100 percent. (Hint: what will this do to the nominal interest rate?)

3. Suppose the expected inflation rate were 100 percent per period. What effect would this have on the nominal interest rate? On consumption and money balances over the life cycle?

4. Suppose prices were falling at 25 percent per period. What effect would this have on the nominal interest rate? On consumption and money balances over the life cycle?

5. Suppose the decision maker's assets and liabilities were all denominated in nominal terms and that the price level unexpectedly doubled at the start of year 2 (instead of increasing at the expected rate of η percent). Complete the effects this would have on consumption and money balances, in real and nominal terms, over the life cycle.

11

The Quantity Theory
of Money

THE ANALYSIS of the demand for money has stressed the distinction between the nominal value of a unit of money such as a dollar and its real value, the number of units of output that could be obtained for a unit of money. But it has left for this chapter the question of what determines that real value. If you were asked what determined the real value of a commodity such as wheat, your automatic response would have been "the law of supply and demand." The money price of wheat would be such that the demand for wheat — at that price — exactly equalled the supply of wheat — at that price. So, too, with money itself: its value is governed by the balancing of supply and demand.

The balancing process for money, however, is a good deal harder to visualize than the partial equilibrium framework used to describe the process for wheat. Because of this, modern monetary theorists often introduce this part of economic theory by means of parables or fables which permit the essentials of the equilibrating process to stand out more clearly, an example followed earlier in the introduction of the demand for money. We shall again follow that example here.

We will suppose initially that the only money in the economy is *fiat money*. The government simply prints up notes of various denominations which everyone thereafter accepts in payment for a sale of goods, services or securities. We will thereby postpone a discussion of the complexity of modern monetary institutions until Chapter 15. (If you find it hard to imagine why a seller would accept such notes without some "backing," you may suppose that the government has passed a "legal tender" act compelling the acceptance of its notes "for all debts, public and private.")

We will also suppose that all of the money is held by households and that none is held by firms as a third factor of production along with labor and capital. This is not to say that the demand for money by firms is unimportant. In practice, something close to a quarter of the money balances in the U.S. are held by corporations rather than by households. But virtually all the important qualitative properties of an economy with money can be obtained from the approach of the previous chapter and in a much simpler fashion.

THE EFFECT OF AN UNANTICIPATED CHANGE IN THE SUPPLY OF MONEY

Imagine that the task of finding an equilibrium solution for our neoclassical economy with money is once again entrusted to the all-knowing auctioneer first encountered in Chapter 3. To date he has been assigned two tasks: first, to bring about full employment of the economy's labor and capital resources; second, to see to it that the demand for consumption and investment goods exactly equals the total output produced at full employment. He satisfies the former of these assignments by calling out a capital rental rate equal to the marginal product of capital at the full employment capital/effective labor unit ratio: (Equivalently, he can call out a wage rate equal to the marginal product of labor at full employment.)

The auctioneer has the interest rate to work with for his second assignment of making sure that the demand for output by households and firms exactly equals the full-employment supply of output. By calling out this rate, really next period's capital rental rate, he permits each household to compute the human capital component of its wealth, and hence to enter a figure for its consumption demand on the auctioneer's book. Announcing the rate also permits entrepreneurs to compute the capital/effective labor ratio desired for next period. Knowing next period's full-employment labor force, the auctioneer converts these desired capital/effective labor ratios to an estimate of the total desired capital stock. By subtracting out the current capital stock he can then calculate the investment demand at that market rate. If the sum of these demands for output exceeds the supply, the auctioneer can reduce the excess by calling out a higher interest rate, reducing the current demands for consumption and investment. Further adjustments can be made in this fashion until both sides of the auctioneer's books have been brought into balance.

The introduction of fiat money as a medium of exchange does not change these parts of the auctioneer's assignment. The specific value of the real interest rate that happens to equilibrate the supply and demand for total output need not be the same as before, of course. After all, we know that the form of the consumption function will be different — with $\dfrac{1}{(n_3 - i + 1) + \xi(n_3 - i)}$ replacing $\dfrac{1}{n_3 - i + 1}$ as the coefficient of wealth in the consumption function. And we know that real wealth at the start of any period now includes the real value of any money balances carried over from the previous period. But up to this point, at least, the auctioneer would still find himself on basically familiar ground.

The introduction of money will now create a third assignment for the auctioneer: to balance the supply and demand for money. Until further notice, we rule out any possibility of bringing about that balance by changes in the number of monetary notes in circulation. The auctioneer is simply told the number of notes that have been issued by the monetary authorities and for which he must somehow find the necessary demand.

Since the life-cycle demand function for money for a representative household of age i developed in the previous chapter is of the form

$$m_i = \xi \, c_i \, \frac{1 + \mu}{\mu} = \frac{\xi}{(n_3 - i + 1) + \xi(n_3 - i)} \, z_i \, \frac{1 + \mu}{\mu}$$

$$i = 1, 2, \ldots, n_3 - 1,$$

the auctioneer does not lack tools for carrying out his new assignment. Anything he can do to raise real wealth and hence real consumption will also raise the demand for real balances. He can also affect the demand for real balances to the extent that he can change the nominal rate of interest μ. He does not, of course, have complete freedom to set that rate at any level he pleases. Fisher's Law requires

$$\mu = (1 + \mu)\,(1 + \eta_e) - 1,$$

where μ is the real rate of interest after taxes, and η_e is the rate of inflation expected next period.[1] The expected rate of inflation, whatever it may be, must be treated by the auctioneer as something beyond his control.

Finally, note that the money supply and money demand are stated in different units of measurement: the demand is for *real* cash balances, whereas the government supplies only the *nominal* units. The auctioneer can determine how much real purchasing power the government issue represents, and hence how much real demand he has to generate by calling out a value for P. In equation form, his equilibrium condition would thus be:

$$(1)\qquad \sum_i^{n_3-1} L_i m_i = \sum_i^{n_3-1} L_i m_i / P = \xi \sum_i^{n_3-1} c_i\, L_i\, \frac{1+\mu}{\mu} = M_s / P$$

where L_i, as before, represents the number of individuals in the ith age group, c_i and m_i are real consumption and real balances, m_i are balances in nominal terms, P is the price level, and m_s is the nominal supply of fiat money.

A simple example

To show how the new equilibrating mechanisms work, we propose to give the system a shock as we have done before, and then look over the auctioneer's shoulder as he tries to rebalance his

---

[1] Recall that the symbol $\eta_e(t)$ stands for the expected rate of price change from period t to period $t + 1$, that is, for the expected value of $\left(\dfrac{P(t+1)-P(t)}{P(t)}\right)$. We assume that this expectation is made as of the start of period t, *before* the equilibrium price level for that period, $P(t)$, has become known. The symbol η stands for the actual rate of inflation during period t, that is, $\dfrac{P(t)-P(t-1)}{P(t-1)}$. The expectation could alternatively be stated in terms of the price level expected for period $t + 1$. Given our simplifying assumption that $\eta_e(t)$ is formed before P_t is known, the two methods are equivalent.

books. Before this shock the economy is in long-run, steady-state equilibrium. For further simplicity we will suppose that no net population growth or technological change is taking place. The government sector is also quite rudimentary. No resources are used by the government, no taxes are levied, and no interest-bearing debt is floated. Money, moreover, is the only financial asset in the system, with all other assets and the returns thereon denominated in real terms (as in the numerical examples in the last part of Chapter 10). The price level is constant and there is no expected change; that is $\eta_e = 0$.

Suppose now that an employee of the Treasury, returning home from the Department's annual Christmas party and over-come with impulses of goodwill toward others, had taken the key to the printing presses, set them in operation and printed addi-tional notes with a total face value exactly equal to the face value of the notes previously circulating. He entrusted the notes to Santa Claus, who happened to be flying past the Bureau of En-graving and Printing at just the right time. Santa was instructed to deliver the new notes to the people in proportion to the money balances they already held—an instruction not fully in keeping with the spirit of Christmas, perhaps, but which simplifies the telling of the subsequent story.

The auctioneer can be pardoned for not sharing in the general rejoicing on Christmas morning since the events on Christmas Eve will have created serious imbalances between demand and supply in both of the markets that he has been assigned to clear. In the money sector, the supply of money has doubled. The de-mand for money has increased since the money found in the Christmas stockings will have increased everyone's wealth. From the money-demand equation, we know that desired cash holdings will increase by the same proportion as any increase in wealth. But money holdings are only a part of total wealth. Hence the doubling of money holdings represents less than a doubling of wealth, and less than a doubling of demanded balances. Thus there is an imbalance between demand and supply. Meanwhile, in the market for output, the demand by consumers will be higher as a consequence of the increase in wealth on Christmas morning. Since the economy had previously been in a no-growth steady-state equilibrium implying consumption exactly equal to total income, the auctioneer will find that desired consumption will now exceed the total output that could be produced with the labor and capital resources available.

Confronted with these imbalances, the auctioneer might be tempted to turn first to the tool that served him so effectively as an equilibrator in the simpler economy, the rate of interest. By calling out a higher value for that rate, the auctioneer can reduce the value that households place on their future earnings stream and induce them to cut back their consumption demands. But trying to balance the output market in this fashion will only serve to aggravate his problem of finding parking places for the legacy of the Treasury's Christmas party, the additional money units. Lowering wealth by raising the real interest rate will reduce the demand for cash balances. Furthermore, the real rate of interest is one of the components of the cost of holding money. Assuming for the purposes of this first scenario that everyone continues to expect a zero inflation rate for the next period, raising the real interest rate raises the nominal rate as well. Therefore, the cost of holding money rises and the demand for cash balances, already deficient, falls still further.

Fortunately the auctioneer has another tool to work with, the price in money of a unit of output. Calling out a different price level than the one that had ruled in the previous period will set up two different chains of adjustments. First, the change in the price level changes the real value of wealth by changing the real value of nominal cash balances. To this extent, raising the price level will have essentially the same effects as raising the real interest rate. But raising the price level and reducing the real value of nominal balances will also, by the same token, reduce the real value of the stock of money balances that the auctioneer must manage to get parked. This reduction in the effective supply, moreover, must clearly be greater than any countervailing reduction in the demand for real balances. The cut in real supply is in direct proportion to the change in the price level, whereas the cut leads to a less than proportionate cut in real wealth since money holdings are only a part of total wealth and hence, given our money demand equation, to a less than proportionate cut in the demand for real money balances.

Suppose that, having made this analysis, the auctioneer were to try out successively higher and higher values for the price level. Could he restore the equilibrium of the system and, if so, at what price level? Under the given assumptions, the answer is quite simple: after an unanticipated, one-shot doubling of the money supply, the auctioneer can restore the economy to steady-state equilibrium by doubling the price level. By doing so, he cuts the total *real* value of the money supply back to its previous value, so that there is no additional net supply to be parked. At the same time, with no increase in real balances, there is no increase in real wealth and hence no increase either in the demand for consumption goods or for real balances. Thus, as so often seems to be the case, the unexpected present greeted so joyfully on Christmas morning has failed to yield any lasting satisfaction.[2]

THE QUANTITY THEORY OF MONEY

An equivalent way of stating the auctioneer's decision to double the price level is to say that he has decided to halve the equilibrium value of a unit of money relative to a unit of output. Put this way, it is hardly surprising that the value of money should decline when the number of money units increases. The standard apparatus of supply and demand from ordinary price theory would suggest that result for any commodity whose supply is doubled. What makes the money case so remarkable is that, under the assumptions given, the value of a unit of money in terms of goods falls off in a very special way; in inverse proportion to the increase in the supply. That is, the total real value of the stock of money is the same regardless of the number of nominal units in circulation. Economies that behave in this fash-

---

[2] This situation in our fable is sometimes described as a case of "too much money chasing too few goods," or equivalently as a case of *demand-pull inflation*. Under this interpretation, the economy is pictured as adjusting to the injection of money by holders of excess money balances rushing out to spend the money and in the process, bidding up the money price of real goods. Our reasons for not adopting this scenario but instead continuing to rely on the scenario of an auctioneer calling out tentative prices and interest rates until the two markets clear are discussed in more detail later in this chapter.

The term demand-pull inflation is sometimes contrasted to *cost-push inflation*, supposedly caused by firms passing through the cost of higher wage demands. This distinction is basically one of journalists — to whom all inflation looks like cost-push — and we shall have no further need of it.

ion are said to conform to the *Quantity Theory of the Value of Money,* usually abbreviated to either the *Quantity Theory of Money* or the *Quantity Theory.*

The Quantity Theory is one of the most venerable and cele-brated propositions of economic theory, and rightly so. It is a classic example of how systematic theorizing can lead to conclu-sions strikingly at variance with those likely to be reached on the basis of unaided "common sense." Common sense would suggest that getting more money always makes you better off, but the Quantity Theory says not if everyone gets more. Common sense would suggest that a government could increase the purchasing power of its citizens by printing more money; but the Quantity Theory says the government has no control whatever over the total real value of the money stock.

The velocity of money

These same conclusions are often presented in terms of the *income velocity of money* (or *velocity* for short), the ratio of national income during a particular year to the stock of money as of, say, the start of that year. In symbols, $V = YP/M$. Historically the term velocity comes from the fact that if the flow of income for the year is, say, \$100 and if the stock of money is \$25, then, on the aver-age each dollar can be thought of as turning over (i.e., entering into somebody's income) four times a year. When the definition of velocity is rearranged as

$$M\,V = P\,Y,$$

it is known as the Quantity Equation. Like so much else of mone-tary theory, the terms Quantity Equation and velocity of circula-tion are associated with Irving Fisher. When the relation be-tween the stock of money and the flow of income is expressed as the reciprocal of velocity, i.e., as the ratio of money to income, it is often called "the Cambridge k" because of the preference for this form by John Maynard Keynes and his colleagues at Cambridge University in the 1920s.

Historical antecedents aside, velocity (or more properly, the reciprocal of velocity) can really be thought of as a way of measur-ing the real money balances individuals hold without having to measure the price level. For example, if velocity is equal to 5 the real money stock is equal to 10.4 weeks' national income. The prediction of the Quantity Theory that the stock of real money balances is independent of the nominal money supply can thus be restated as saying that velocity is not systematically affected by changes in the level of the nominal money supply.[3]

Money and spending

Just as some writers prefer to work with velocity rather than with real balances, so many prefer to express the equilibrating mechanism in terms of "spending," i.e., in terms of the product of real consumption and the price level, rather than simply *P* itself. Although this formulation, correctly presented, is completely consistent from the formal point of view with the discussion here, the spending approach has two expository advantages that account for its great popularity. First, like the concept of velocity, the concept of spending makes it possible to tell the story of adjustment to equilibrium without having to specify exactly what prices or price indexes do the adjusting. More important, perhaps, is the fact that spending is an activity that everyone has experienced. Hence, the scenario has a more appealing and realistic air when stated in terms of spending than when stated in terms of a bloodless auctioneer who simply marks the prices up to their new equilibrium values. But precisely because the notions of spending and "demand pull" are so vivid, their use can sometimes mislead the unwary into believing that the asserted propositions about the consequences of changes in the money supply are somehow either different or, at least, more firmly grounded than when those propositions are stated in terms of an auctioneer adjusting

---

[3] A common error is to interpret the Quantity Theory as requiring that velocity not simply be independent of changes in *M,* but independent of the level of interest rates as well. Such is not the case, and our demand-for-money function

$$M = \xi \, C \, \frac{1 + \mu}{\mu},$$

which implies a "consumption velocity" of $\frac{C}{M} = \frac{1}{\xi} \frac{1 + \mu}{\mu}$, permits the demand for real money balances and hence velocity to be a function of nominal interest rates. Yet, as we have seen, this function obeys the Quantity Theory.

the price level. The two approaches might differ if we considered scenarios which specified precisely who manages to acquire goods at other than equilibrium prices and precisely how these transactions affect the subsequent evolution of the economy. But no such well-specified "dynamic" monetary theory has yet been developed. To avoid the misleading "dynamical" connotations of the spending scenario, we shall continue to rely on the fiction of an auctioneer who reequilibrates the price level instantaneously after a monetary disturbance.[4]

Some qualifications to the simple version of the Quantity Theory

Many simplifying assumptions have been invoked along the way to reach these sharp conclusions that the price level changes in proportion to changes in the nominal money supply. The best way to see which are really crucial ones is to consider some cases where the Quantity Theory does not hold, or, as some might prefer to put it, where it holds, but in a weaker form.

Suppose that all the facts of the previous illustration were the same except that money is not the only asset denominated in nominal terms. In particular, let the debt instruments issued by individuals in the early stages of their life cycles, and the interest thereon, be denominated in money, rather than in real terms. When the auctioneer now cries out a price level twice that of the previous period, he will succeed once again in reducing the real value of cash balances to their pre-Christmas amount, and in doing the same for the real value of total wealth. But there will have been a substantial redistribution of real wealth as between the generations. Those early in their life cycles will find their debts less onerous. They can look forward to paying their debts back in 50-cent dollars, as it were. Their gain, however, is at the expense of those in the later stages of the life cycle whose retirement funds are correspondingly eroded by the unanticipated price inflation.

Since the marginal propensity to consume out of real wealth is higher among older age groups, the transfer of wealth from old to young leaves the auctioneer with a projected level of real con-

---

[4] Some special cases in which the auctioneer cannot clear certain markets instantaneously are considered in Chapters 16 and 17.

sumption below that of total output. He will be out of balance as well in the money sector, since the demand for money is proportional to consumption and will fall *pari passu* with any cutback in consumption. Thus a simple increase in the price level in the same proportion as the increase in money, i.e., a doubling, can no longer be counted on to do the job. The other tools in the kit, and in particular the real rate of interest, must also be brought into action.

Once wealth transfers occur so that the second equilibrating variable has to be invoked, a precise prediction of how much the price level will change after a given change in the nominal money stock is no longer possible. That will depend on the actual magnitudes involved. Some qualitative properties of the full solution, however, can be established with the aid of Figure 11-1.

FIGURE 11-1
Conditions for equilibrium in the money and goods markets

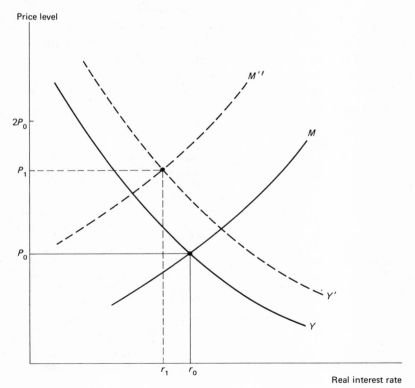

The Y curve shows all the combinations of P and r which the auctioneer could use to ensure equilibrium in the market for output in the initial pre-Christmas period. It is easy to see that the curve is downward sloping. If the auctioneer calls out a lower value for P, he raises the real value of the nominal cash balances, and, to this extent, he raises everyone's real wealth. The higher levels of real wealth imply higher levels of desired consumption. This demand for additional current consumption will be further reinforced by the transfer of wealth from young to old brought about by lowering the value for P. To cut total consumption and investment back to fit the total output available, the auctioneer will thus have to cry out a higher value for r.

The M curve shows the equilibrium combinations of P and r available to the auctioneer in the money sector. This curve slopes upward. Calling out a higher value for P cuts the real value of the stock of money that must be held. It will also thereby cut everyone's real wealth, and, with that, their demand for real balances; but as we saw earlier, the effect on supply dominates the effect on demand. Hence the demand for money will exceed the supply, a condition that the auctioneer must remedy by raising r. This must be the case, moreover, even after allowing for any wealth transfers occasioned by the rise in prices.[5]

The intersection of the two curves indicates the values of P and r consistent with an equilibrium in both sectors simultaneously.

---

[5] To see why, consider some equilibrium combination of P and r; and now imagine that the auctioneer were to call out a higher value for P. Since the stock of the nominal balances remains the same at M_0, the auctioneer would have to lower his value for r (implying a downward slope to the curve) only if at the new higher value for P the public did not want to hold as much as M_0 in nominal balances. But even an individual who held all his wealth in nominal form and whose real wealth was therefore cut in proportion to the price rise would not cut his demand for nominal balances. He would cut his demand for *real* balances, of course, but the price rise would cut the real value of his nominal balances by the same percentage as his demand (given our demand-for-money function), thus leaving his demand for nominal balances unchanged. Going to the other extreme case in which all wealth is in real form, it is easy to see that the price rise which leaves real wealth unchanged, and hence also the demand for real balances, must therefore increase the demand for nominal balances. Consequently, in any intermediate case in which some assets are held in real form and some assets (or liabilities) are held in nominal form, the demand for nominal balances must rise after a rise in P. Since these cases exhaust the possibilities, the M curve must slope upward.

This is the position, with the price level and interest rate equal to specific values P_0 and r_0, respectively, that the auctioneer had presumably been able to reach before the events of Christmas Eve. In terms of the diagram, those events amount to a shifting of each of the curves to the new positions indicated by the dotted curves Y' and M'. The Y curve shifts upward and to the right because the new Christmas money would raise wealth and consumption, thereby causing excess demand for output at the previous values of P_0 and r_0. One or both of those values would have to be raised to find a new point of equilibrium (and once one such point is found, the rest of the curve can be derived from the same reasoning invoked earlier to account for the slope of the curve). Meanwhile, the M curve is being shifted upward and to the left. The Christmas gift generates an excess stock of real balances at the original price level, but an equilibrium can be restored either by raising P or by lowering r, or by any combination of P and r along the curve M'.

The new full equilibrium is indicated by the point P_1, r_1, at the intersection of the two dotted curves. What can be said about this point relative to the original equilibrium P_0, r_0? One thing certain is that the new price level P_1 need not be exactly twice the old, as would be predicted by the simplest version of the Quantity Theory. As drawn, it is less than $2P_0$ but it could be greater. The most we can say is that as a consequence of the additional money, the new equilibrium price level will be higher than before. The fact that the curves have opposite slopes and have both been shifted upward guarantees that. How much higher, however, there is no way to tell without specifying actual numerical magnitudes for all the variables, and grinding through to a solution.

What of the new value for r? Here we cannot be quite so confident even about the direction of change. The answer will depend on how the injection of money affects the level of real consumption. If the demand for real consumption falls, as it does in our fable because of the transfer of real wealth from the elderly to the young, the auctioneer will have to call out a lower interest rate. (This is the situation depicted in Figure 11–1.) We could change the story so that the new money is distributed not across the board, but in a way that would transfer wealth on balance from the lower to the upper age groups, even with a doubling of the price level. In this case the shift in the Y curve would be sufficiently greater than that in the M curve so that the equilibrium interest rate rises.[6]

Note, finally, that the results in Figure 11–1 refer only to the *immediate* consequences of the change in the nominal money supply. We saw earlier in Chapter 6 that a neoclassical economy, with no government spending or taxes, might be pushed off its long-run growth path for a while by a disturbance in the amount or distribution of its stock of wealth. But the shock would work its way out of the system and eventually the long-run, steady-state growth path would be reattained. The same is true when the shock comes from unexpected increases in the nominal money supply and from wealth transfers induced thereafter by the unexpected inflation. Eventually, the initial intergenerational wealth transfers wash out of Figure 11–1 and the long-run equilibrium solution will have the same value for r and for all the other real variables as would have occurred without the shock. The price level would have to be different, of course, but by the same reasoning as given before it is clear that a price level twice that of the pre-shock era will do the job. The simple Quantity Theory of Money is thus a good deal more robust when taken as a statement of long-run tendency than it is in the short run, where distributional and other short-term effects may obscure its working.

The Quantity Theory and repeated changes in the supply of money

The predictions of the simple Quantity Theory may also be falsified in the short run even when no changes, direct or indirect,

---

[6] Although it matters some who gets the new money, it does not matter much whether the new money comes in as a transfer payment from the government (albeit an unauthorized transfer), or as a payment for securities purchased, which is the more usual route for monetary expansion. Since the latter route involves an *exchange* of assets between the government and the public, it might seem at first glance that there would be no change in total real wealth at the initial value for P and hence no reason for the Y curve in Figure 1 to shift upward. But the acquisition of interest-bearing securities by the government in exchange for money will permit a corresponding decrease in tax levies.

To a first approximation, that is to say, up to distributional effects (and "burden of the debt effects" of the kind discussed in Chapter 8), the surrender of the securities and the reduction of the tax liabilities cancel each other out and the money payment remains as a measure of net increase in real wealth at the initial value of P. The subsequent history will be the same apart from distributional effects as in the simpler and more transparent case of an outright gift of money.

in the distribution of wealth occur in the wake of the injection of new money. Suppose, for example, that everyone on Christmas morning were to revise his or her expectations as to next period's inflation from the zero of our original fable to 100 percent. Do not concern yourself, for the moment, with why they might have changed their minds or how they all happened to hit on the same value. Let's first see what the consequences would be.

Our auctioneer could, as before, try a value for P_1 double P_0, thereby keeping the new money from having any effect on total real wealth. Assuming money to be the only nominal asset, as in the original fable, we know that this value for P will keep the market for real output in its original equilibrium. Doubling P will also restore the real value of total balances to their pre-Christmas level. But the money sector will not be in equilibrium. The 100 percent inflation now anticipated for next period will raise the cost of holding money and hence push the demand for real balances below the real supply even at a price level twice that of the pre-shock era. Our auctioneer will thus have to try a still higher price level, which will then put the output market out of equilibrium, requiring still further adjustments in r and P.

The eventual outcome will be of the kind pictured in Figure 11-2. The Y curve is shifted upward and to the right of the original to Y', but we know from before that it must run through the point labeled Q at which the real rate still has its original value r_0 and the price level equals $2P_0$, exactly double its initial value. Had inflationary expectations remained at their pre-Christmas level of 0, the post-Christmas M curve would also have run through Q, as indicated by the line M'. But, given that they have jumped to 100 percent, the M curve is displaced even further upward and to the left, to the position indicated by the curve M''. Thus, under the assumptions given, the new equilibrium involves a higher price level and a lower real interest rate than the simple Quantity Theory would predict.

To call this result a failure of the Quantity Theory would hardly be fair, of course, if the sudden leap in inflationary expectations that led to the extra rise in current prices were entirely arbitrary and unmotivated. But it would be just as arbitrary to assume that no change in expectations of future inflation would occur in the wake of monetary changes of the kind being considered.

Here, as before, the Quantity Theory is still satisfactory for explaining long-run behavior even though it breaks down in the first year. To see how the changes in expectations of future monetary expansions can influence equilibrium, suppose that the events of Christmas Eve, instead of being unique and unexpected, actually became an accepted tradition. Each year, a ritual theft of the keys to the printing press is reenacted, and the money supply is doubled. Eventually, after many generations have come and gone, and after any initial perturbations like those discussed above have washed out, we can surely safely assume that everyone anticipates a doubling of M come Christmas Eve.[7]

Assume now that our auctioneer, after much trial and error, has somehow been able to get the economy back on a long-run growth path, though not necessarily the same one. His problem each Christmas morning, then, is merely to hold it to that path, and to do so in a way that is consistent with the public's expectations. Since neither population growth nor technological change is taking place, the level of per capita consumption and total consumption along the steady-state path must be constant, and the same must be true for per capita and for total real wealth. But how can the auctioneer hold wealth unchanged from period to period in the face of the massive annual injections of new money? Clearly, one way would be with a price increase sufficiently large to offset the new injection, which, in this case, means a doubling of the price level.[8] Would this be a consistent and sustainable policy? Clearly, yes, as long as the tradition of an annual doubling of the money supply at Christmas-time is honored and is expected to continue to be honored.

---

[7] One slight technical change in the scenario must be made. We can no longer assume that new money is distributed among households in proportion to the money balances they hold. If the new money were always known to be so distributed, the annual injection would come to be regarded as equivalent to the payment of interest on money holdings. Extension of the model to allow for explicit and implicit interest payments on money can be done, but is best deferred to Chapter 15. For the remainder of this one, imagine that new money coming in is distributed at random, or by some rule or principle that serves to make the amount each household expects to receive be independent of its initial money holdings.

[8] It is an artifact of our discrete model of the economy that the price level doubles on Christmas morning. In practice, the price level would rise continuously over the year in anticipation of the annual injection. But it is a harmless expository simplification to assume that all changes in prices must take place on only one day of the year.

FIGURE 11-2

Consequences of repeated changes in the supply of money

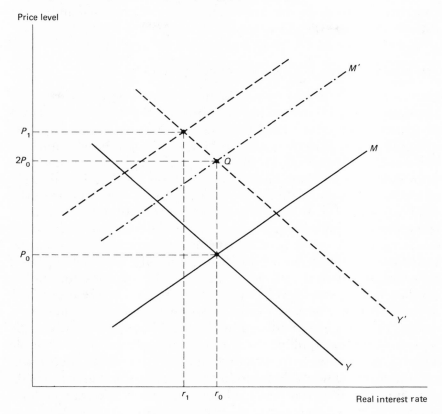

Thus we see that expectations of future changes in the money supply and in the price level need not invalidate the predictions of the simple Quantity Theory.[9] The conditions for expectations under which this proposition is true, however, are quite restrictive. They include, among others, the expectation of no further change in the rate of change of prices. Unfortunately, there ap-

---

[9] One important qualification must be entered. There is almost, but not quite, complete symmetry between the cases of anticipated monetary expansion and contraction. The breakdown of symmetry arises because a monetary contraction compatible with long-run equilibrium must not proceed so fast that the gain from holding idle balances, that is, the rate of fall in the price level, exceeds the rate of return from holding capital at full employment.

pear to be no circumstances, other than those of our modified fable, in which such expectations would also be "sensible"; and therein lie many of the unsolved problems, both of monetary theory and monetary practice.

THE FORMATION OF INFLATIONARY EXPECTATIONS

The general theoretical problem of how inflationay expectations are formed is one of the great unsolved problems of macroeconomics, and currently the subject of intensive controversy. As a simple example to show the problems involved in modeling the process by which the public forms inflationary expectations, suppose that it forms them entirely on the basis of the inflation actually experienced over the past year. In terms of the scenario of the fable presented in this section, in which the annual doubling of the money supply becomes routine after the first year, this would mean that in the year of the first injection — year 1 for concreteness — the public was expecting a zero rate of inflation for period 2 (since no inflation was taking place in the steady-state era befor the first injection). (In our notation, $\eta_e(1) = 0$. See footnote 1 above.) From previous reasoning we know that, for such an expectation, the simple Quantity Theory prediction will hold exactly in year 1 and the equilibrium price level in that year will be double that of year O. By the postulated rule for updating expectations of inflation we know that households in year 2 will then be expecting an inflation of 100 percent for year 3, since that was the level they actually experienced in the previous year, year 1. But as we saw when considering the case of an expected 100 percent inflation for the period after the initial unexpected doubling of the money supply, an increase in the rate of inflation expected for period 3 will cause the price level in period 2 to increase by more than the doubling predicted by the simple Quantity Theory. Suppose the increase is 130 percent. Then in year 3, when the public updates its expectations again, an inflation rate of 130 percent will be anticipated. But since this would be an increase over the rate of inflation that had previously been anticipated, the actual rate of inflation occurring in year 3 will again be higher than 100 percent and could well be higher than 130 percent. Whether this happens will depend on the precise form of the money demand function. Were it to happen, it would lead to a still further upward revision of expectations in year 4, and so on, in a never-ending upward spiral. Nor would the effects of this upward explosion of the price level be confined entirely to the monetary sector. Because the price level is increasing at a faster rate than the money supply, the real value of the money stock is eroding away. Hence, real wealth must also be falling, and along with it real consumption and the real rate of interest. Clearly, something has gone dreadfully wrong.

The explosive problems associated with adjustments in inflationary expectations would undoubtedly be more severe than this example suggests. Suppose that the public eventually came to realize, as it surely would, that the rule it was following was leading to an underestimate of the actual rate of inflation, year after year, without fail. Then a new rule would come to be adopted which led to a higher predicted rate of inflation than the old rule. But this anticipation of an even faster rate for next period would also cause the current rate of inflation to be higher than it would be under the old scheme of expectations, and thus to an even more rapid explosion of the price level. Note, moreover, that this explosion would take place even if the new forecasting rule were so "sensible" that it succeeded in hitting the actual rate of inflation right on the nose!

Adaptive expectations

One way out of this difficulty is to assume that people do not place such heavy weight on recent experience. The rules verbally discussed above are special cases of the so-called *adaptive expectations* model. That model assumes that people revise their expectations of inflation according to the rule:

(2) $$\eta_e(t) = \eta_e(t-1) + \lambda(\eta(t-1) - \eta_e(t-1)).$$

That is, the rate of change in price from period t to period $t+1$ expected as of period t equals the rate of change that had originally been expected from period $t-1$ to period t; plus an adjustment proportional to the difference between what had been expected and what actually happened in period t. In our first explosive example, we were assuming, in effect, that $\lambda = 1$, so that (2) reduced to

(3) $$\eta_e(t) = \eta(t-1).$$

In our second and presumably more "sensible" case (but also, alas, more explosive), we were in effect taking $\lambda > 1$. Suppose, however, we were to move in the opposite direction and try lower values for λ, implying a slower rate of adaptation of forecasts to observed past forecast errors. We know that in the extreme case of $\lambda = 0$, implying that past experience has no effect whatever on the expected rate of inflation, we could surely achieve stability. Any scheme that led to unchanging expectations of inflation would get us back to the simple Quantity Theory. This would suggest, then, that there may well be some value for λ between 0 and 1 that would allow expectations to change with experience, but not so rapidly as to produce an explosion. Such in fact is the case, though we must leave a rigorous proof to more advanced courses. We can always guarantee stability, in sum, as long as we are prepared to believe that people are sufficiently slow to learn from their past mistakes.

If people did form their expectations according to this model, expected inflation would lag behind actual inflation for an enormously long time. In a model like that of Chapter 6 with our money demand function and with the money supply growing at, say, 6 percent per year, λ could not exceed .075 for stability to be achieved. At that value, it would take over 20 years for the expected inflation to make 80 percent of the eventual adjustment required from a change in the rate of increase in the money supply.

Herein lies the dilemma confronting models of inflationary expectations: just as a model which makes the economy explode into ever-increasing hyperinflation every time the rate of growth of the money supply is increased is unacceptable as a description of how people form expectations, so, too, is one which implies they are systematically fooled about inflation rates. It would violate an important principle of economics summarized in the well-known saying of Abraham Lincoln: "You can't fool all the people all the time."

A digression on Lincoln's Law

As applied to the particular problem of inflationary expectations, this principle, which we shall call Lincoln's Law, says essentially that "you can't use the Quantity Theory to beat the bond market." Nominal interest rates must reflect *all* the information and wisdom available to traders and this must certainly include that provided both by the Quantity Theory and its well-recognized qualifications. If this were not the case, and interest rates were based on inflationary expectations that lagged systematically behind actual inflation rates—Fisher, himself, for example thought it might take 20 or 30 years for long-term interest rates to catch up—then either of two things would happen. The relatively few people who knew the Quantity Theory would make above-normal returns from speculating on interest rates; or more likely, they, their students and their followers would rush into the market with such speed and in such volume in their search for these easy profits that interest rates would be driven out of their sluggish adaptive patterns.[10]

This is not to say that the marketplace is always right, for a second part of Lincoln's Law is that you can fool all the people some of the time. There is always uncertainty about future inflation rates, and the market will often turn out to be wrong *ex post*. Lincoln's Law simply means that the market cannot be wrong in any manner that can be exploited for systematic profits.

In short, a "realistic" model of how inflationary expectations are formed in the marketplace must include two crucial properties:

1. The economy must not explode with every change in the rate of growth in the money supply.
2. Consistent with Lincoln's Law, actual and expected inflation cannot differ in any way which permits systematic profit.

Unfortunately, construction of a model meeting these two tests is no simple task. We can, however, take a major step toward constructing a model that meets the requirements of Lincoln's Law as well as converging rapidly toward the new equilibrium path by the simple expedient of setting the expected rate of in-

---

[10] This is clearly not the place to describe how one might make profits by speculation. One possible route has already been briefly discussed in connection with Fisher's Law in Chapter 9.

In any event, the reader is cautioned against attempting such speculation because few famous economists (Lord Keynes perhaps excepted) appear to have earned returns from speculation greater than could be attributed to the normal processes of chance. On the other hand, there are enormous masses of statistical evidence showing that bond and stock prices do not behave in ways that would permit anyone to make systematic profits by any mechanical rules whatever. (Readers familiar with recent research in the field of finance will recognize the above as a reference to the so-called *efficient markets hypothesis*. We shall return to the subject in a somewhat different context later.)

flation equal to the expected rate of monetary expansion rather than to the rate of inflation most recently experienced. To solve the problem in this ingenious fashion requires one to believe, of course, that the public knows about the Quantity Theory. But we do know, at least, that some of them have managed to get this far in the book, and even more of them are regular readers of the columnists in *Newsweek*.

The Friedman surge effect

Changes in expectations of inflation, even where not of the explosive variety, may still have important practical consequences. Recall the events surrounding the first doubling of the money supply. When we assumed that the public expected no further increases, we found that the simple Quantity Theory applied and the price level doubled. We also found that in the long run, after the public had come to expect a doubling in *M* every year, the price level would also double every year. But what if the public came to expect that annual doubling in *M* and *P* right from the start? An equilibrium in the first year could then not be reached merely by a doubling of *P*. We saw why in our example in which a future 100 percent rate of inflation was anticipated. The rise in the expected rate of inflation from zero to 100 percent per year increased the cost of holding cash balances and hence decreased the demand for money. The price level, therefore, had to more than double so as to cut the excess supply of money back to meet the reduced level of demand.

A change in the *rate of change* of the money supply (in this case from a rate of change of zero per year to one of 100 percent per year) must therefore lead, in the short run, to a rate of inflation *higher* than the sustainable long-run rate of inflation (in this case, 100 percent per year). We shall refer to this inevitable consequence of a change in the rate of change of the money stock as the Friedman surge effect, in honor of the economist Milton Friedman, who first called attention to it and to some of its more unpleasant implications. These unfortunate side effects cannot fully be appreciated within the context of our still very simple model with its instantaneously adjusting prices, wages and interest rates. But we shall encounter them in full measure in later chapters when we have added more detail to our picture of the economy.

Granted that there must be an interval in which the Friedman surge pushes the rate of inflation above its long-run sustainable rate in the case of an increase in the rate of increase in M (or below its long-run sustainable rate in the case of a decrease in the rate of change), can anything be said about how long the interval will be, or how far from its equilibrium rate the surge will carry the rate of inflation? The answer is no, without further specification of the structure of the economy and the orders of magnitude of the key parameters. It was in part for exploring questions of this kind that we developed our numerical computer model and we return to it in the chapter to follow.

PROBLEMS FOR CHAPTER 11

1. Suppose that, instead of Santa Claus, an avenging angel had come on Christmas Eve and destroyed half the money balances. What actions both in the short run and in the long would the auctioneer have taken if money was the only nominal asset? If there were other nominal assets?

2. When the Christmas Eve Caper became an annual doubling of the money supply, the story was modified so that the annual distribution of money was not proportional to money holdings. How would it have affected the story had this modification not been made?

3. Derive the Y and M curves if consumption and investment demand are not functions of the interest rate.

4. Derive the Y and M curves if real wealth is not affected by changes in the price level.

5. Suppose the demand function for money was of the form

$$M_D = \xi Y.$$

What would the Y and M curves then look like?

6. Suppose the demand function for money depended on output, not consumption, and was of the form

$$M_D = \xi \frac{1 + \mu}{\mu} Y.$$

What would the Y and M curves then look like?

7. Show how the conclusions reached in this chapter can be restated in terms of velocity.

8. Give a numerical example of how one could make money if the expected inflation rate systematically differed from actual inflation rates.

12

Money and the price level in a growing, full employment economy

THIS CHAPTER presents and puts through its paces a new computer model. It will have real sectors essentially the same as those of the country we called NEUTRAL in Chapter 6, though the mechanics of government taxation and spending will be detailed along the lines discussed in Chapters 7 and 8. But now all exchanges of goods and services will be assumed to be made through the medium of a fiat money of the kind discussed in Chapters 9–11.

Combining real and monetary sectors into a single model is clearly a major step in building up our picture of how present-day economies function. But it is still only one step along the way. Be very careful, therefore, about matching up recent economic events with what may seem to be similar patterns in our experimental simulation.

Keep in mind, first of all, that modern economies make use not only of fiat money, but of a variety of other money-like instruments or money substitutes supplied by banks and other financial firms. But since nothing of substance is changed by allowing for the presence of some of these privately produced monies, (although the landscape takes on a more familiar look), we shall relegate this class of extensions to Chapter 15 and here keep to the simpler story line.

Forty or fifty years ago we could not have been quite so cavalier in downplaying the banking system even in an elementary text, since the banking system was then still subject to periodic and violent collapse. Under modern conditions, however, the waves of bank failures and consequent crises of confidence of the kind experienced in the early 1930s are virtually unthinkable. Some of the reasons why will be explained in Chapter 15.

Not only are we suppressing much institutional detail with respect to the banking sectors but we shall continue to proceed on the assumption that prices, wages and interest rates are free to move quickly (in fact, instantaneously) to eliminate any excess demand or excess supply in the markets for output, factors of production, and money. Some real world markets, however, sometimes seem to behave as if the relevant prices were not completely free to change, and where such is the case, part of the initial response to shocks will take the form of generating or taking up some "slack" in the economy. Some of these additional adjustment mechanisms will be explored in subsequent chapters. Other mechanisms, however, must be deferred to specialized advanced courses.

Remember, finally, that our concern is economics and not econometrics. The numerical values assigned to the various parameters in the equations, such as α, δ, q or ξ, and hence the relative numerical magnitudes generated in the simulations, are intended to be representative only of modern economies in general and not of any one economy in particular.

These caveats having been duly entered, we turn now to the experiment. As before, the experiment is conducted in terms of three countries, each identical initially, and all proceeding placidly along the common, long-run growth path. Two of the countries are then shocked and their subsequent behavior contrasted with that of the control country still moving on its original trajectory. The control country will be named SIX, because its distinguishing feature is a money supply that increases initially and throughout at the constant rate of six percent per period. We begin by presenting some essential "historical data" on SIX, which we ask you to take on trust without attempting their recomputation.

THE ANATOMY OF LONG-RUN EQUILIBRIUM
IN A MONETARY ECONOMY

Table 12–1 shows the GNP of country SIX in constant year 0 prices for a number of years starting with year 1. This economy has many features in common with NEUTRAL of Chapter 6. In

TABLE 12–1
Country SIX real gross national product (billions of year 0 dollars)

Year	Gross national product	Personal consumption expenditures	Gross investment	Government purchases of goods and services
1	2,516.9	1,525.8	506.0	485.1
2	2,612.0	1,583.5	525.1	503.4
3	2,710.7	1,643.3	545.0	522.4
99	95,257.4	57,749.2	19,149.8	18,358.4
100	98,856.3	59,930.8	19.873.7	19,051.8

particular, it has the same production function, labor force and
population characteristics, and biological growth rate. The
government, a new feature, is taking each year 20 percent of last
period's GNP, and, operating under the modified pay-as-you-go
rule of Chapter 8, pays for its expenditures by a combination of
personal income taxes (at a rate of 20.85 percent), money creation, and borrowing calculated to keep the debt/GNP ratio constant. The equilibrium saving/investment rate turns out to be 20
percent versus NEUTRAL's 25 percent. (Some of the main reasons will come out in the course of the discussion; others will be
deferred to the exercises.) This explains why SIX has a lower level
of real GNP than NEUTRAL. Since they share a common value
of r_b of 3.77 percent, their real growth rates are, of course, the
same.

Table 12–2 shows the GNP of Country SIX for the same
years, but expressed in current-year prices. Notice that nominal
GNP and all its components are larger than the corresponding
magnitudes expressed in year 0 prices, and that the nominal magnitudes are growing more rapidly. Clearly price inflation must be

TABLE 12–2
Country SIX gross national product (billions of current dollars)

Year	Gross national product	Personal consumption expenditures	Gross investment	Government purchases of goods and services	Price level (year 0 = 100)
1 ..	2,570.9	1,558.5	516.9	495.5	102.1
2 ..	2,725.1	1,562.0	547.9	525.2	104.3
3 ..	2,888.7	1,751.2	580.8	556.7	106.6
99 ..	776,348.1	470,656.3	156,070.9	149,620.9	815.0
100 ..	822,924.3	498,891.0	165,437.4	158,595.9	832.4

taking place, and this surmise is confirmed by a glance at the last column of the table. Prices are increasing at the steady rate of 2.14 percent per year. We know, therefore, that the growth rate of nominal GNP and its components must be given by the relation:

Growth rate of
   nominal GNP = (1 + Growth rate of real GNP)(1 + Growth rate
               of prices) − 1
             = (1 + .0377)(1 + .0214) − 1 = .06.

Money, debt, and capital

From the analysis in Chapter 11, the natural supposition is that the growth in the price level reflects, at least in part, a corresponding growth in the money supply. The essential information about how the money supply has in fact been growing in country SIX is presented in the next four tables. Tables 12–3 and 12–4 show the nation's wealth by major categories valued at year 0 and at current-year prices. We see that Country SIX began year 2 with a capital stock worth 6,752.0 billion dollars in year 0 dollars. During the year, additional productive capital worth 525.1 billion dollars at year 0 prices was installed, while the deterioration of original capital stock amounted to 270.1 billion dollars in year 0 prices. Thus the stock of physical capital at the end of the period came to 7,007.0 billion dollars in year 0 prices, representing a growth rate of real capital in the economy of 3.77 percent, the biological interest rate. The real value of the government debt — here and throughout assumed to consist entirely of interest-bearing securities of precisely one-year maturity — also increased at the biological interest rate from 1,136.1 billion to 1,179.0 billion of year 0 dollars.

The last component of the nation's wealth is its stock of fiat money. At the end of year 2, the value of the money stock in year 0 prices was 106.4 billion dollars, which again represents a growth in real terms of 3.77 percent over the level of the previous period.

As was true of the relations between the real and nominal magnitudes in Tables 12–1 and 12–2, the growth of real wealth at a rate of 3.77 percent per year combines with a growth in the price level of 2.14 percent per year to give a growth in all the

TABLE 12–3

Country SIX national wealth (billions of year 0 dollars)

Year	Capital stock (start of year)	Plus: Gross investment	Less: Depreciation	Equals: Capital stock (end of year)	Plus: Government debt	Equals Nonmoney assets	Plus: Money stock	Equals: Total private assets
1 ..	6,506.2	506.0	260.2	6,752.0	1,136.1	7,888.1	102.5	7,990.6
2 ..	6,752.0	525.1	270.1	7,007.1	1,179.0	8,186.1	106.4	8,292.5
3 ..	7,007.1	545.0	280.3	7,271.8	1,223.5	8,495.3	110.4	8,605.7
99 ..	246,236.7	19,149.8	9,849.5	255,537.0	43,006.1	298,543.1	3,879.2	302,422.3
100 ..	255,537.2	19,873.7	10,221.5	265,189.2	44,631.4	309,820.6	4,025.8	313,846.4

TABLE 12–4

Country SIX national wealth (billions of current dollars)

Year	Capital stock (start of year)	Plus: Gross investment	Less: Depreciation	Equals: Capital stock (end of year)	Plus: Government debt	Equals: Nonmoney assets	Plus: Money stock	Equals: Total private assets
1 ..	6,645.7	516.9	265.8	6,896.8	1,160.5	8,057.3	104.7	8,162.0
2 ..	7,044.4	547.9	281.8	7,310.5	1,230.1	8,540.6	111.0	8,651.6
3 ..	7,467.2	580.8	298.7	7,749.2	1,303.9	9,053.2	117.6	9,170.8
99 ..	2,006,829.0	156,070.9	80,273.1	2,082,626.8	350,499.6	2,433,126.4	31,615.3	2,464,741.7
100 ..	2,127,204.0	165,437.4	85,088.1	2,207,552.0	371,531.8	2,579,085.1	33,512.3	2,612,597.4

nominal magnitudes, including that of the nominal money stock, of 6 percent per year. These figures are given in Table 2–4.

The process by which this 6 percent annual expansion in the nominal stock of money is brought about is shown in Table 12–5, which presents the essential details of the government's budget. Notice that in year 2, for example, government expenditures totaled 640.2 billion dollars, of which 525.2 billion dollars represented purchases of output and 115.0 billion dollars represented interest payments at a rate of 9.91 percent on the 1,160.5 billion dollars of government debt outstanding at the start of the year. Budgetary receipts, consisting entirely of personal income taxes, came to 564.3 billion dollars, thus leaving a deficit of 75.9 billion dollars for the year. Of this amount, 69.6 billion dollars was met by the sale of additional interest-bearing debt, and the remainder of 6.3 billion dollars by printing new money.

TABLE 12–5
Country SIX government budget (billions of current dollars)

Year	Purchases of goods and services	Plus: Interest on government debt (at 9.91%)	Equals: Total expenditures	Less: Receipts	Equals: Surplus of deficit (−)
1 ...	495.5	108.5	604.0	532.4	−71.6
2 ...	525.2	115.0	640.2	564.3	−75.9
3 ...	556.7	121.9	678.6	598.2	−80.4
99 ...	149,620.9	32,770.5	182,391.4	160,760.4	−21,631.0
100 ...	158,595.9	34,736.1	193,332.0	170,395.2	−22,936.8

Household financial and wealth data

Where this new money eventually wound up can be seen from the income statements and balance sheets of representative individuals at various ages shown in Table 12–6. Each 42-year-old, for example, started year 2 with accumulated assets of $25,639.70, of which $181.30, amounting to about 60 percent of a week's wages, was in the form of cash. His human capital was worth $88,013.10, so that his total wealth came to $113,834.10. Given this value for wealth, the derivation of his consumption level proceeds in a manner similar to the earlier nonmonetary models,

TABLE 12-6

Country SIX household financial data in year 2 (current dollars)

	Age 1	Age 20	Age 42	Age 65	Age 72	Age 80
Income statement						
Wages	0.0	0.0	6,132.3	6,132.3	0.0	0.0
Plus: Earnings on assets	0.0	−2,901.4	2,355.4	7,279.1	5,186.2	664.7
Less: Personal taxes	0.0	673.7	1,769.9	2,796.7	1,081.5	138.6
Equals: Net earnings	0.0	2,557.2	6,717.8	10,614.7	4,104.7	526.1
Less: Consumption	1,010.6	1,648.4	2,904.7	5,251.6	6,288.7	7,727.5
Equals: Net saving	1,010.6	908.8	3,813.1	5,363.1	−2,184.0	−7,201.4
Less: Changes in money balances	69.5	10.5	18.4	33.3	39.8	−482.3
Equals: Changes in other assets	−1,080.1	898.3	3,794.7	5,329.8	−2,223.8	−6,719.1
Wealth statement						
Initial assets	0.0	−31,578.9	25,639.7	79,237.4	56,454.5	7,345.2
Plus: Initial money stock	0.0	102.9	181.3	327.8	392.5	482.3
Plus: Present value of earnings	81,245.9	132,518.4	88,013.1	4,853.7	0.0	0.0
Equals: Wealth	81,245.9	101,042.5	113,834.1	84,418.9	56,847.0	7,727.5
Consumption	1,010.6	1,648.4	2,904.7	5,251.6	6,288.7	7,727.5
Money balances	69.5	113.3	199.7	361.0	432.3	0.0
Consumption/wealth ratio	0.0124	0.0163	0.0255	0.0622	0.1106	1.0000
Money/wealth ratio	0.0009	0.0011	0.0018	0.0043	0.0076	0.0

namely by multiplying wealth by the appropriate life cycle parameter, which we know from Chapter 10 is $\dfrac{1}{n_3 - i + 1 + \xi(n_3 - i)}$.
For this age group it has a value of 0.0255 and yields a figure for
consumption of \$2,904.70.

This consumption level in turn is one of the elements governing his decision as to how large an initial cash balance to hold.
Recall that the demand-for-money function for an individual of
age i in period t can be written as

$$m_i = \xi c_i \frac{1 + \mu}{\mu},$$

where μ is the nominal, one-period interest rate (after taxes).
For country SIX the value of μ is 7.84 percent in period 2, and
indeed in every other period as well, since Country SIX is in
steady-state equilibrium on its long-run growth path. Thus
$\dfrac{1 + \mu}{\mu}$ has the value 1.0784/.0784 = 13.76. For the remaining
coefficient ξ a value of 0.005 has been assigned here and throughout the chapter. Our forty-two-year old's demand for money at
the start of period 2 is thus

$$\xi c_i \frac{1 + \mu}{\mu} = (.005)(2904.7)(13.76) = 199.7,$$

which is an increase of \$14.50 over the balance held during the
previous period. Conducting a similar calculation for each age
group and summing over the whole population would account
for the entire 6.9 billion dollar increase in the stock of money.

Real and nominal interest rates

Not only does the steady price inflation of 2.14 percent per
year in Country SIX produce the divergences we have seen between the real and nominal values of income and wealth, but it
leads to a corresponding divergence between real and nominal
market rates of interest and between real and nominal realized
rates of return. These differences are summarized in Table 12–7.
Begin with the figure 7.61 percent in the column headed Net real
marginal product of capital. This is the net real rate of return
that the owners of the capital at the end of year zero expected to

earn during year 1. Because prices were expected to rise by 2.14 percent, the nominal rate of return expected by the owners was 9.91 percent (since $(1.0761)(1.0214) - 1 = .0991$). That was also the rate that the government had to offer the public on its one-year debt securities. (Remember that we are assuming that the public recognizes no differences in risk between privately issued and government securities so that the promised yields must be the same.) The return expected on either government or private securities is subject to the personal income tax. The personal tax rate in year 0, applying uniformly to both wage and interest income, was 20.85 percent, and that is also the tax rate that investors are projecting for interest income to be received in year 1. Hence the after-tax nominal return expected for year 1 is 7.84 percent, and this is the value for μ that entered the demand functions for money in year 0. It is not, of course, the rate that individuals use in computing their human capital. The relevant rate for that purpose must be the *real* after-tax expected return which in this case is 5.58 percent (since $(1.0784)/(1.0214) - 1 = .0558$).

TABLE 12–7

Reconciliation of interest rates, Country SIX

Net real marginal product of capital	7.61 percent
Plus: Allowance for expected inflation	2.30
Equals: Rate on government bonds	9.91
Less: Allowance for tax on personal interest income (at rate of 20.85 percent)	2.07
Equals: Private nominal return	7.84
Less: Allowance for expected inflation*	2.26
Equals: Expected private after-tax real return	5.58

* The difference between the two allowances for expected inflation simply represents the different way in which the two corrections come into the calculation, and not any difference in expectations.

Note that the various rates of return in Table 12–7 are the rates *expected* by investors for the periods indicated. They will also be the rates investors actually receive in year 1 and in every year thereafter as long as Country SIX remains in steady-state equilibrium along its growth path.

So much, then, by way of introduction to our model of a neo-classical economy with money. There are clearly many other aspects of the money mechanism and its interactions with the real sectors that remain to be explored. But they are perhaps best seen and understood by considering how the economy responds to shocks that jolt it off the original equilibrium path.

THE RESPONSE TO CHANGES IN THE RATE OF GROWTH OF THE MONEY SUPPLY

As indicated earlier, the shocks to be studied consist of shifts to new rates of growth of the money supply that are unanticipated when they occur in year 1, but are maintained and are expected to be maintained indefinitely thereafter. One such switch will be an increase in the rate of growth of money from a level of 6 percent per year to one of 8 percent per year; for contrast, the other will be a decrease to a rate of 4 percent per period.

Figures 12–1 and 12–2 portray subsequent rates of growth of prices and the paths of real GNP in Countries FOUR and EIGHT relative to that of Country SIX for the 100 years following the initial shifts. (Before actually turning to the graphs, you might find it a useful exercise to think back to the discussion of the Quantity Theory in Chapter 11, and the discussion of the real parts of the system in Chapters 6, 7 and 8, and sketch out the patterns you would expect to see.)

Inflation rates and real growth rates in the long run

The discussion in Chapter 11 suggested, among other things, that a new steady-state growth path would eventually be reached after the initial disturbances had worked their way out of the system. Figures 12–1 and 12–2 confirm this supposition. After some large displacements in the early years, the rate of inflation in Country FOUR oscillates in waves of diminishing amplitude, and ultimately approaches a new equilibrium value of 0.21 percent per year. The pattern of ups and downs is somewhat different in Country EIGHT, and the amplitude of the cycles somewhat less. But again, there is a homing in to a new steady-state value which in this case is 4.07 percent per year. The rate of growth of real GNP also eventually settles down to a steady-state level, but it is the same level, 3.77 percent a year, in both Country

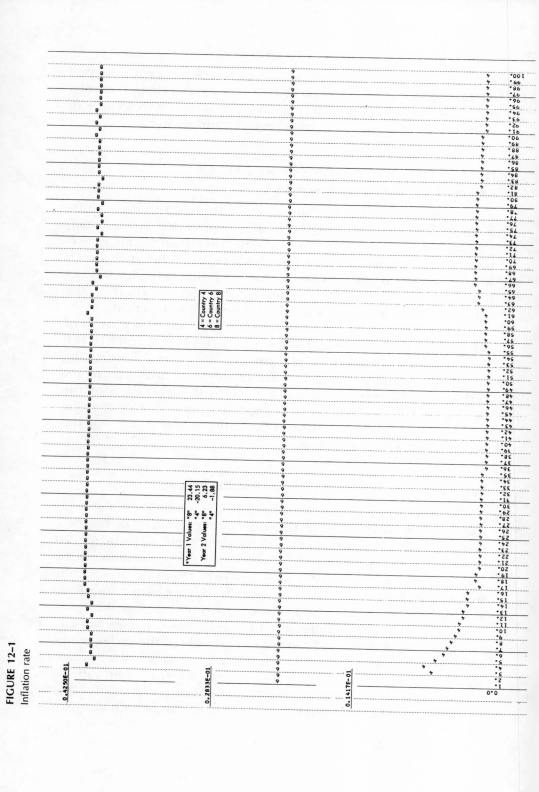

FIGURE 12–1
Inflation rate

FIGURE 12-2
GNP ("6" base)

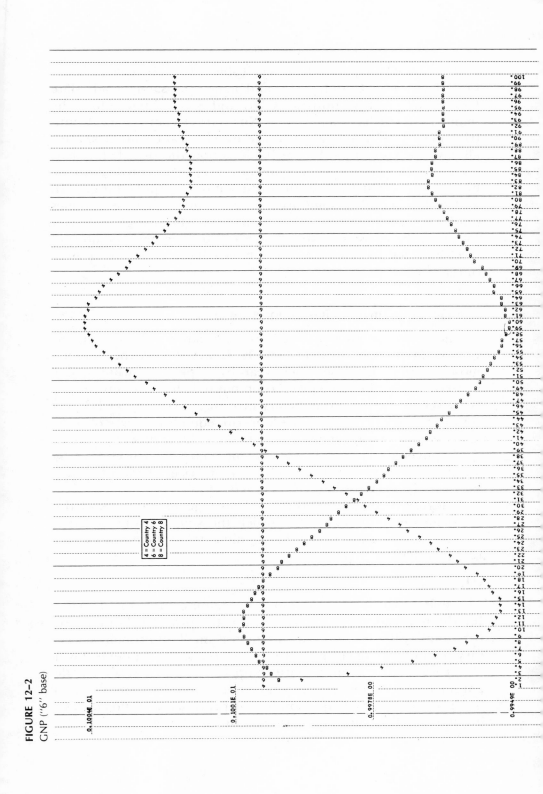

FOUR and Country EIGHT (cf. Table 12–1). In fact, it is the same level as in Country SIX and hence the same steady-state level from which Countries FOUR and SIX started before the monetary disturbances in year 1. Nor is this a coincidence. Countries FOUR, SIX and EIGHT are neoclassical economies, after all, and we know that, by mechanisms now thoroughly familiar, their growth rates of real income must eventually converge to the biological interest rate r_b. Since the rates of population growth and technological change are the same in all three economies (and the same as in the earlier simulations), the biological interest rate must be the same. Note, however, that the new equilibrium levels of GNP are different; we will have more to say about these differences later.

The Quantity Theory adjusted for growth

The results so far presented are at variance with the simplest version of the Quantity Theory. In Country SIX, the nominal money supply increases each year by 6 percent, while prices increase not in the same proportion but only by 2.14 percent per year. When the rate of monetary growth is raised by 33 1/3 percent to 8 percent per year, the long-run equilibrium rate of price increase goes up by almost 100 percent to 4.07 percent per year. And conversely, when the rate of monetary growth was cut by a third to 4 percent per year, the rate of price inflation fell by a factor of 10 to 0.214 percent per year.

The results, however, do obey a more general version of the long-run Quantity Theory of which the simple proportionality rule is a special case. Recall that equilibrium of the money sector requires that

$$(1) \qquad\qquad M_s = M_d = P \, \xi \, C \, Z$$

where M_s = the stock of nominal fiat money; M_d = the demand for the nominal stock of balances; P = the price level of output; C = total real consumption (minus the small adjustment necessary for individuals in the last year of life). Z = the interest term $(1 + \mu)/\mu$, expressed in a more compact form, and ξ, is the scale parameter in the demand-for-money function. Dividing through by the corresponding equation for the previous year and expressing the resulting ratios in terms of growth rates gives

(2) $\left(1 + \dfrac{\Delta M}{M_s}\right) = \left(1 + \dfrac{\Delta P}{P}\right)\left(1 + \dfrac{\Delta \xi}{\xi}\right)\left(1 + \dfrac{\Delta C}{C}\right)\left(1 + \dfrac{\Delta Z}{Z}\right).$

To isolate the pure monetary supply effects, we must abstract from any autonomous changes in demand, and hence we shall here (and throughout this chapter) set $\dfrac{\Delta \xi}{\xi}$ equal to zero.[1] The interest component $\dfrac{\Delta Z}{Z}$ will zero out by itself once the long-run growth path is attained, since the real rate of interest, the tax rate and the expected rate of inflation will all have reached their eventual unchanging steady-state values. Thus (2) will reduce to

(3) $\left(1 + \dfrac{\Delta M_s}{M_s}\right) = \left(1 + \dfrac{\Delta P}{P}\right)\left(1 + \dfrac{\Delta C}{C}\right)$

In our neoclassical setting we know that $\dfrac{\Delta C}{C}$ in turn must be equal in equilibrium to the biological rate of interest r_b, so that we can express the long-run relation between rate of change in prices and the rate of change in the money supply as

(4) $\dfrac{\Delta P}{P} = \dfrac{\dfrac{\Delta M_s}{M_s} - r_b}{1 + r_b}.$[2]

Notice that when $r_b = 0$, implying that no growth in real magnitudes is taking place, as we assumed for simplicity in Chapter 11, Equation (4) reduces to the simple proportionality case. But when $r_b > 0$, part of the monetary expansion is absorbed by the growth in the demand for balances and only that part of the expansion of money in excess of r_b requires an equilibrating adjustment in the price level. In particular, for Countries FOUR,

---

[1] Some circumstances which can lead to shifts ξ are described and analyzed in Chapter 15.

[2] The proposition that the real money stock is growing at the biological interest rate depends critically on the assumption introduced in Chapter 9 of a unitary wealth elasticity of the demand for money. Although other values of that elasticity are possible in the short run, they have implications about the ratio of money balances to other assets that make them unsuitable for analysis of long-run steady state. If the elasticity were less than unity, money balances would shrink to relative insignificance; if greater than unity, money would become the overwhelmingly dominant asset.

SIX and EIGHT, we have $r_b = .0377$ and hence the values of 0.0021. 0.0214 and 0.0407, respectively, for $\Delta P/P$.[3]

Note finally that under the generalized version of the quantity theory, as in the simpler earlier version, it remains the case that the monetary authorities can control the growth of the money supply in nominal, but not in real terms. Whether the authorities in our experimental countries choose to pump in money at a rate of 4, 6 or 8 percent per year, the equilibrium rate of growth of real balances, like that of all other real magnitudes, remains the 3.77 percent per year, the system's biological rate r_b.

The short-run response to a change in the rate of change in the money supply

Although the Quantity Theory, adjusted for growth, gives an accurate prediction of the steady-state rate of inflation in our experimental economies, the relation between the change in money and the change in prices is inevitably much harder to pin down in the early years after an initial equilibrium is disturbed. In terms of the links in the chain between money and prices as given by Equation (2), we know, for one thing, that the interest rate effect $\Delta Z/Z$ cannot be taken as zero in the short run. The expected future rate of inflation is one of the components of the nominal rate of interest and this expectation must be allowed to change to reflect the new conditions. The consequences of this change in expectations are, of course, what we have earlier dubbed the Friedman surge. Nor, in addition, can we replace $\Delta C/C$ by the long-run real growth rate, r_b. To the extent that unanticipated changes in the price level occur, changes will also occur in the real values of all assets denominated in money terms. Where such changes are not offset by corresponding changes in the value of nominal liabilities (and remember that almost by definition there are no direct liabilities anywhere in the system to offset a pure fiat money) real wealth will change and with it the demand for real consumption and real balances. We have earlier seen this effect in Chapter 11. Real wealth effects

---

[3] This formula is derived under the assumption of a unitary wealth elasticity of demand for money. If the wealth elasticity is not equal to one, the important properties of equation (4) are still true: equilibrium is characterized by a constant rate of inflation that increases with rises in $\Delta M/M$ and decreases with rises in r_b.

of this kind following after a change in *M* are often called Pigou Effects in the monetary literature (in honor of the British economist A. C. Pigou, who invoked this line of argument to attack a particularly heterodox and provocative proposition in Keynes's *General Theory*). Nor are these two classes of effects the only ones that must be taken into account. The governments in our experimental economies have a variety of revenue-raising options in addition to merely printing money, and the particular policies followed will also affect the response of prices to a change in monetary policy. Precisely how can best be seen after we have probed a bit more deeply into the history of the early post-change years in our experimental economies.

The Friedman surge. Figure 12–1 shows that in year 1, when the rate of monetary expansion in Country EIGHT was suddenly raised from 6 to 8 percent per year, that country experienced an immediate rise in prices of 23.44 percent. Most of this jump is the Friedman surge consequent on the sharp change in the rate of inflation expected by the public for years 2 and beyond. Those expectations have been computed on the assumption made in Chapter 11 that the public understands the Quantity Theory (and in its general growth-adjusted form at that); and that it takes the long-run equilibrium inflation rate under the new conditions as its new estimate of inflation. Numerically, this implies a change in the expected inflation rate from 2.14 percent a year to 4.07 percent a year.[4]

That such an increase implies in turn a value of $\Delta Z/Z$ that explains much of the 23.44 percent change in the price level is easily verified. From Table 12–7 we see that the before-tax real rate of return is expected to be 7.61 percent in year 1. With inflation now anticipated at 4.07 percent per year, the government

---

[4] We can now check how well this rule of inflationary expectations meets the criteria laid down in Chapter 11. As to the question of stability, there is no problem: the economy does not explode. However, the rule is not entirely consistent with Lincoln's Law. The problem is not in year 1 where the discrepancy between actual and anticipated inflation is quite large. This comes from the Friedman surge, and by assumption no one could predict the change in the rate of growth of the money supply. There are some errors in subsequent years, however which should have been anticipated. By far the largest occurs in year 2 when the inflation rate is 6.8 percent; subsequent errors are much smaller. These errors are substantially smaller than would have arisen with a rule of adaptive expectations and justify the claim of Chapter 11 that the rule used here is a substantial improvement. But it is not perfect; confronted with this situation, the marketplace would have done even better.

bond rate must rise from 9.91 percent to 11.99 percent per year. Assuming for simplicity that taxpayers project the currently ruling tax rate, which is 20.78 percent in Country EIGHT in year 1, the expected after-tax nominal return μ becomes 9.468 percent. Hence the component $(1 + \mu)/\mu$ of the demand for money in EIGHT has the value 11.56, which is 16.2 percent smaller than the corresponding value for Country SIX. It follows, then, that even if real consumption were the same in EIGHT in year 1 as in year 0, the price level in EIGHT would have to rise by 28.8 percent to equilibrate the demand and supply of cash balances since from Equation (2) we would have

$$\frac{\Delta P}{P} = \frac{1 + \Delta M_s/M_s}{1 + \Delta Z/Z} - 1 = \frac{1 + .08}{1 - .162} - 1 = .288.$$

A price surge of this magnitude in response to seemingly so small a step-up in the rate of monetary expansion may seem extremely unreal at first glance. And certainly there have been few cases of price movements of this size, although movements in the wholesale price index almost this large have occurred recently in the course of a single year in the U. S. But by the same token, there have also been few if any cases that conform to the very stringent conditions of our controlled experiment. Country EIGHT has been enjoying a long period of growth completely free from wars, depressions and other calamities, man-made or natural. Suddenly the monetary environment is changed. The public not only understands immediately the full implications of the new policy, but knows with confidence that this change is permanent, and that no further changes in the rate of monetary expansion, up or down, will ever recur. Real-world monetary shifts are rarely seen so clearly against the background of other events. And to the extent that they are not, the surge to the new price level track, though it will still be there, will be spread out over a longer interval, and hence will be a good deal harder to detect than it was in our controlled experiment.[5]

---

[5] Even after these qualifications, our surge of 23.44 percent in the price level would strike most economists as being on the high side for a country such as the U. S. It implies an interest elasticity of the demand for money of close to minus one (since the expected after-tax nominal rate of interest rose from 7.84 percent to 9.50 percent). Empirical estimates of this elasticity based on the U. S. experience have typically been well below this in absolute value.

Pigou Effects. Tables 12–8 and 12–9 summarize the value of money balances and nonmoney assets respectively in both nominal and real terms for a sample of individuals of different ages in Countries SIX AND EIGHT at the start of year 1.

As can be seen by comparing the entries in Table 12–8, the individuals in both countries started the eventful year 1 with nominal balances rising with age, but identical within each age group. The unanticipated price surge in EIGHT thus lowered the real value of accumulated cash balances across the board.

TABLE 12–8
Real and nominal value of money balances for selected individuals in Countries SIX and EIGHT, beginning of year 1

	Age 20	*Age* 42	*Age* 65
Nominal value in			
SIX and EIGHT	100.00	176.20	318.50
Real value (year 0 prices) in			
SIX	97.90	172.51	311.83
EIGHT	81.01	142.74	258.02

TABLE 12–9
Real and nominal value of nonmoney assets for selected individuals in Countries SIX and EIGHT, beginning of year 1

	Age 20	*Age* 42	*Age* 65
Nominal value in			
SIX	−30,047.20	24,392.60	75,383.20
EIGHT	−34,379.60	27,909.60	86,252.30
Real value (year 0 prices) in			
SIX	−29,416.30	23,880.40	73,800.40
EIGHT	−27,850.50	22,609.20	69,870.00

Notice from Table 12–9 that the real value of initial assets other than money is also lower in EIGHT (at least for all age groups with positive assets) even though the nominal values of initial assets are higher. The reason is that the nonmoney financial assets are of two fundamentally different types. About 82 percent of the assets at the start of the period are in the form of claims to productive capital; that is, deposits in the "banks" of Chapter 2. These assets are, of course, real assets, which is to say that they have what amounts to a built-in adjustment or escalator for any changes in prices during the period. Neither their real value nor their real before-tax return is affected by the 23 percent surge in prices. The remaining 18 percent of the assets, however, are in the form of government bonds, which are dominated in nominal terms. Such assets, too, have some built-in protection against inflation, but only to the extent that the inflation is anticipated. In the present case, this anticipation was for a price rise of 2.14 percent, so that the apparent nominal return of 9.91 percent on the bonds actually represented a substantial loss for the year in real terms.[6]

A Pigou effect of the same kind, but of the opposite sign, will be experienced by those in the younger age groups who start the year with an accumulated net financial liability. Thus for age-group 20, for example, the real value of accumulated liabilities is $27,850 in Country EIGHT, as compared with $29,416 in Country SIX. This difference, of course, is a classic example of the debtor's gain from unanticipated inflation. In practice, the gain and consequent intergenerational wealth transfer might well be larger since we have assumed, for simplicity of calculation, that the debts of young people are denominated in real and nominal terms in exactly the same proportion as society's assets. Hence only 18 percent of the early-age borrowing is in nominal form — the part corresponding to the share of nominal government bonds in total assets.

Tax effects. The price surge in year 1 has cut the real value of that portion of total wealth held by the public in Country EIGHT in the form of money and government bonds. The surge, however, has not led to a fall in aggregate real wealth or, consequently, in aggregate real consumption (cf. Tables 12–1 and 12–10). Apparently some additional adjustments are taking place that are offsetting, and in fact more than offsetting, the Pigou real-balance effects. Comparison of the real wealth figures for different age groups in Countries SIX and EIGHT in year 1 shows that the human capital component of real wealth is uni-

---

[6] This loss will be offset to a large extent, of course, by the reduction in tax liabilities engendered by the reduction in the real value of the government debt; in a world of Immortal Consumers, it will be fully offset. As will be seen later this offset applies as well to the effect of the Friedman surge on money balances.

TABLE 12–10
Gross national product in Country EIGHT

Year	Gross national product	Personal consumption expenditures	Gross investment	Government purchases of goods and services
		billions of year 0 dollars		
1.....	2,516.9	1,532.2	499.6	485.1
2.....	2,611.3	1,580.1	527.8	503.4
3.....	2,710.3	1,640.1	547.9	522.3
99.....	94,897.0	57,705.9	18,901.4	18,289.7
100.....	98,482.2	59,885.6	19,616.3	18,980.3

Year	Gross national product	Personal consumption expenditures	Gross investment	Government purchases of goods and services
		billions of current dollars		
1.....	3,107.0	1,891.4	616.8	598.8
2.....	3,424.2	2,072.0	692.1	660.1
3.....	3,699.0	2,238.4	747.8	712.8
99.....	6,000,662.0	3,648,939.0	1,195,203.0	1,156,520.0
100.....	6,480,925.0	3,940,960.0	1,290,910.0	1,249,055.0

formly higher in Country EIGHT. The real wage rate currently being earned and the real wage rate projected for future years are the same for both countries. Hence the discrepancy must be arising from the discount factor being applied to those projected wage earnings. But a check back to Table 12–3 shows that the real capital stock at the end of year 1 is virtually the same in EIGHT as in SIX. The before-tax real return on capital expected in the two countries must thus also be virtually the same. Specifically, the rate in Country EIGHT is 7.62 percent per year, which is only slightly higher than the 7.61 percent expected in Country SIX. Hence differences in the before-tax real rate of return of capital cannot account for the higher present value of future earnings in Country EIGHT.

One possible explanation might be that the tax rate has fallen, and hence that expected after-tax wages have risen and pulled up the value of human capital. That the tax rate must fall when the rate of monetary expansion rises is a necessary consequence of the pay-as-you-go principle. More government money being issued means the government need raise less of its revenue via taxation. In the particular case of Country EIGHT, the new value for the personal tax rate is 20.78 percent in year 1. This value is indeed lower than the 20.85 percent value for the year in the control Country SIX, but a difference this small could hardly account for the observed differences in real human capital in the two countries.

Is there perhaps some other and subtler tax effect that we have not hitherto encountered, and which may be driving down the expected after-tax real return in Country EIGHT? The answer is yes, and to see what it is, recall the figures that investors in EIGHT and SIX are taking in year 1 as their expectations of future nominal before-tax returns, viz., 11.99 percent per year and 9.91 percent, respectively. These yields look deliciously high at first glance, but we know that to a considerable extent they represent merely so much "running in place." An investor of $100 in EIGHT, for example, has to earn 4.07 percent just to stay even with the expected inflation. The tax collector, however, makes no allowance for the purely nominal character of the gain in such a case. An income tax on the 4.07 percent return would still have to be paid at the indicated expected personal income tax rate of 20.78 percent. Hence an investor who earned 4.07 percent in nominal terms and thus just broke even in real terms would actually wind up with a net loss in real terms by the time he had settled with the Internal Revenue Service.

For someone earning the 11.99 percent market return in EIGHT, the outlook is, of course, not quite so bleak. He will wind up with a positive real return after taxes, but it will be a smaller real return than if there had been no inflation or if the inflation were at the slower rate of 2.14 percent per year as in Country SIX. Numerically, we have for Country EIGHT

Expected real rate
of return after taxes

$$= \frac{(1 + [(1 + r)(1 + \eta_e) - 1](1 - \lambda))}{(1 + \eta_e)} - 1 =$$

$$\frac{(1 + [(1 + .0762)(1 + .0407) - 1](1 - .2078))}{(1 + .0407)} - 1 = .0522,$$

where λ is the personal tax rate. By contrast, if there had been no inflation we would have had the value

Expected real rate
of return after taxes $= (1 + .0762)(1 - .2078) - 1 = .0606,$

and if the inflation rate had been 2.14 percent we would have had the value

Expected real rate
of return after taxes
$$= \frac{(1 + [(1 + .0762)(1 + .0214) - 1](1 - .2078))}{(1 + .0214)} - 1 = .056.$$

The lower real return from capital resulting from inflation has consequences similar to those we saw earlier in Chapter 7. There the extra burden on the income from capital was the result of imposing a tax on interest income; here it results from the fact that the effective weight of the personal income tax on returns from capital is increased relative to the weight on returns from labor by basing the tax on the nominal rather than the real rate of return. But the economic consequences are essentially the same. In both cases there will be a weakening in the inducements to save, and eventually, other things equal, a reduction in the size of society's stock of productive capital.[7]

---

[7] This statement is true even though the income tax is levied on nominal rather than real wages. To convince yourself, consider two individuals in a given year t, each with an expected income of $10,000, one entirely from wages and the other entirely in the form of return on capital. Suppose, further, that the $10,000 return on capital is the interest on a one-year "index-adjusted" bond that promises holders a 10 percent rate of return per year in real terms before taxes. At the start of year t the bond is therefore selling for $100,000.

If the tax rate is 20 percent, each will have the same tax liability of $2,000 in year t and the same after-tax nominal and real income of $8,000. Let the price level now double unexpectedly during year t. If the wage earner were then to receive $20,000 before taxes, he would pay taxes of $4,000 and be left with an after-tax income of $16,000. He would, it is true, be paying more dollars in taxes than if the price jump had not occurred, but he would have suffered no loss in real after-tax income.

How much do the issuers of the bond have to pay the holder in order to make good on their promised 10 percent return before taxes in real terms? Clearly $20,000 won't be enough. That amount in interest plus return of the original $100,000 principal would leave the holder with a net *loss* in real terms. His nominal terminal wealth of $120,000 would be worth only $60,000 in before-inflation purchasing power. To give him a 10 percent real rate of return, they would have to pay him $120,000 in interest plus his principal of $100,000. But the tax on $120,000 of interest would come to $24,000 or about 6 times that paid by a wage earner with the same before-tax real income. The bondholder's after-tax real rate of return is actually negative, −$2,000 in preinflation purchasing power $((220,000 - 24,000)/2 - 100,000)$.

So much, then, for our analysis of the short- and long-run effects of a sudden increase in the rate of growth of the money supply. To complete the picture, we might trace out what happens in the short run when the growth rate is suddenly cut, as in Country FOUR. The patterns are sufficiently symmetrical, however, that that task can be left as an exercise. (Some specific questions to direct the inquiry as well as some helpful hints are given in the problems at the end of the chapter.) We turn instead in the next chapter to consider some of the broader economic and policy issues raised by this experiment.

PROBLEMS FOR CHAPTER 12

1. Calculate the income velocity in years 1 and 100 in countries SIX and EIGHT. Explain the differences.

2. Consider an economy in steady-state equilibrium with a biological interest rate of 3 percent per year and with an annual rate of growth of the money supply of 5 percent per year. Assume that the price level today is 1.0.

    (a) Assuming that the economy remains in steady-state equilibrium, what will the price level be a year hence? Five years hence? Draw a graph with P on the vertical axis and time on the horizontal axis showing the path of the price level over the next five years.

    (b) Suppose that the monetary authorities begin to increase the money supply at a rate of only 3 percent and intend to maintain that new rate forever. On the same graph draw the new time path of the price level over the next five years and explain its main features. (This question really asks for the qualitative properties of your graph; do not worry about the precise numerical values.)

    (c) Suppose that instead of the policy in (b) the monetary authorities announce that, in addition to the normal 5 percent annual injection of money, there will be a special injection today which doubles the money supply. Thereafter, they will resume the 5 percent annual injection. There is absolutely no reason to doubt that they will so behave. Again, on the same graph, draw the time path of the price level and explain its main features.

    (d) How would you change your answer to (c) if the special injection were announced today for one year hence?

3. What rate of monetary expansion in a country like SIX would lead to price stability?

Tables A, B and C present some data on Country FOUR which will be useful in answering the following questions.

TABLE A

Real gross national product in Country FOUR (billions of year 0 dollars)

Year	Gross national product	Personal consumption expenditures	Gross investment	Government purchases of goods and services
1	2,516.9	1,543.4	488.5	485.1
2	2,610.0	1,603.9	502.7	503.4
3	2,706.1	1,660.1	524.0	522.0
99	95,427.1	57,763.8	19,273.1	18,390.2
100	99,033.9	59,946.3	20,002.5	19,085.1

TABLE B

Gross national product in Country FOUR (billions of current dollars)

Year	Gross national product	Personal consumption expenditures	Gross investment	Government purchases of goods and services	Price level (year 0 = 100)
1	2,009.7	1,232.4	390.0	387.3	79.8
2	2,044.8	1,256.6	393.8	394.4	78.3
3	2,133.5	1,308.8	413.1	411.5	78.8
99	92,171.5	55,793.1	18,615.6	17,762.8	96.6
100	95,852.9	58,020.8	19,360.0	18,472.1	96.8

TABLE C

Real and nominal values of money balances and nonmoney financial assets for selected individuals in Country FOUR, beginning of year 1

	Age 20	Age 42	Age 65
Money balances			
Nominal value	100.00	176.20	318.50
Real value	125.20	220.60	398.90
Financial assets			
Nominal value	−25,520.70	20,717.90	64,026.80
Real value	−31,961.90	25,946.90	80,186.70

4. Assuming no change in the real interest rate or in the personal tax rate, calculate for FOUR for year 1
   a. the government bond rate,
   b. the nominal after-tax rate of return,
   c. the real after-tax rate of return.

5. Country FOUR's price level falls by 20.2 percent in year 1. What rate would be due to the Friedman surge? Explain the difference.

6. Why does Country FOUR's real gross national product decline for several years after the shock, even though it eventually has a higher level than SIX?

7. Suppose SIX initially had no government debt. Would the difference between the steady-state equilibrium values of GNP in FOUR and SIX be larger or smaller?

13

Inflation as a tax

THE GOVERNMENTS in the hypothetical countries of Chapter 12 were constrained to follow different policies with respect to the rate of growth of the money supply. Suppose that they had been free to make their own choices after due consultation with their economic and political advisers. Suppose further that questions about the relation between inflation and unemployment (questions to be taken up in Chapter 17) are put aside. How might they have decided which policy was the best of the three and whether there might be still other policies that were better yet?

MONEY CREATION AS A REVENUE DEVICE

Some of their economic advisers might lead off any discussion of such policies by pointing out that selecting a rate of monetary growth was really a problem in taxation. Admittedly, this is not the "commonsense" approach to inflation. Admittedly also, economists often state their propositions in a provocative way so as to command the attention of their audience. But this one can hardly be completely surprising to anyone who has come thus far through the book. It was clearly foreshadowed, for example, in the life cycle examples at the end of Chapter 10. The focus of the discussion there, however, was on an unanticipated inflation where some of the tax-like effects of inflation are easy to see. But the analogy between inflation and taxation extends equally to the case of inflations that are fully anticipated.

The point is important enough for an understanding of what follows to merit some further elaboration and illustration before proceeding to the pros and cons of the policy decision.

Inflation as a tax on cash balances

Tables 13–1 and 13–2 contain the essentials of the government budgets of the three experimental countries in the year 100 after they have all moved to their long-run growth paths. The level of real government spending remains essentially the same in the three countries. The nominal levels differ enormously, of course, after a century of compounding of the seemingly small differences in the annual rates of inflation. The three countries differ also in the extent to which they rely on various revenue sources. Country EIGHT, for example, makes less use of the personal income tax than do the other two countries. Real income tax receipts in year 100 are $19,714 billion in Country EIGHT, representing 103.9 percent of budgeted real spending on goods and services. By contrast, real income tax receipts in Country FOUR cover 113.2 percent of real spending on goods and services. Country EIGHT also raises the smallest amount in

TABLE 13–1
Government expenditures and receipts, year 100, in countries FOUR, SIX and EIGHT

	trillions of current dollars		
	FOUR	*SIX*	*EIGHT*
Purchases of goods and services	18.5	158.6	1,249.1
Interest on government debt	5.4	34.7	190.1
Total expenditures	23.9	193.3	1,439.2
Income tax receipts	20.9	170.4	1,297.4
Money creation	.2	1.9	16.1
Borrowing	2.8	21.0	125.7
Total receipts	23.9	193.3	1,439.2
	trillions of year 0 dollars		
	FOUR	*SIX*	*EIGHT*
Purchases of goods and services	19.08	19.05	18.98
Interest on government debt	5.59	4.17	2.89
Total expenditures	24.67	23.22	21.87
Income tax receipts	21.60	20.47	19.71
Money creation	.20	.23	.25
Borrowing	2.87	2.52	1.91
Total receipts	24.67	23.22	21.87

TABLE 13–2

Government revenues as a percent of government expenditures on goods and services (year 100)

	FOUR	SIX	EIGHT
Income tax	113.2	107.4	103.9
Money creation	1.0	1.2	1.3
Borrowing	15.1	13.3	10.1

Government revenues as a percent of total government expenditures (year 100)

	FOUR	SIX	EIGHT
Income tax	87.5	88.1	90.2
Money creation	.8	1.0	1.1
Borrowing	11.7	10.9	8.7
Addendum:			
Personal income tax rate	22.77	20.85	19.49

real terms from new issues of interest-bearing debt—$1,910 billion, or 8.7 percent of its total budget, as compared with $2,870 billion and 11.7 percent in Country FOUR. What permits the government of Country EIGHT to get by with lower taxes and borrowing than the other countries even though diverting approximately the same level of resources away from private use? The answer is that the government of EIGHT is making greater use of another revenue-raising device and that, of course, is its power to print money. In the year 100, the government of Country EIGHT printed up and distributed $16,094 billion of new money. At the price level ruling that year—65.808 on a year 0 base of 1.0—this sum in newly-printed nominal money represented $245 billion in real purchasing power, or about 1.3 percent of the total spending for the year by the government on goods and services. The corresponding percentage figures for Countries SIX and FOUR are 1.2 and 1.0 respectively.

That inflation is essentially a tax is equally clear when viewed from the standpoint of the private sector at the paying end of the tax. Households in Country EIGHT started year 100 with initial cash balances totalling $201.1 trillion in nominal value. The government issued an additional $16.1 trillion, and the price level rose from 63.234 to $(1 + \eta)\, 63.234 = (1 + .0407)\, 63.234 = 65.808$. If the government had issued no new cash balances, then— neglecting any surge effects—equation (12–4) tells us that the price level would have fallen by 3.65 percent to 60.933. The actual price level of 65.808 is 8 percent higher than this number. The difference of 8 percent in the price levels implies a reduction in the real value of the opening cash balances from 201.1/60.933 = \$3,300 billion to 201.1/65.808= \$3,055 billion. The difference of \$245 billion is the amount that we calculated earlier as the government's real revenue from the monetary expansion. The inflation, in short, is essentially the same as an excise tax levied on holders of cash at a rate equal to the rate of expansion of money. The only difference is that the inflation tax is a hidden one. No internal revenue agent actually has to come around and collect it.

Is an inflation tax inequitable?

In weighing the inflation tax against available alternatives, the monetary authorities and their expert advisers would try to distinguish between questions of equity or fairness on the one hand and questions of economic efficiency on the other. Many of the citizens of some present-day countries believe, for example, that fairness requires taxes to be progressive. The rich should pay a larger fraction of their incomes in taxes than the poor. The ethical views of others, however, might lead them to believe that the percentage should be equal across the board. Where, by these standards of equity, does an inflation tax fit? Is it a progressive tax or a regressive tax?

Our model and experiments can shed little light on these questions directly. Our imaginary countries, after all, are egalitarian, with every worker receiving the same wage. The only differences in wealth are those arising naturally in the course of passage through the stages of the life cycle. In these countries money holdings are proportional to wealth so that an inflation tax is neither progressive nor regressive. The age-related differences in wealth and its composition are important, however, for weighing the burden of an inflation tax, and typically figure prominently in controversies over inflation.

Inflation as a tax on the elderly. How often, for example, do we not hear references to inflation as the "cruelest tax"? Those so characterizing inflation presumably have in mind such episodes as the hyperinflations in Germany and other Central European countries after World War I, or the much smaller but still far from trivial increases in prices in the U. S. and in the Western European countries after World War II.[1] These episodes were certainly cruel, indeed, to those whose wealth was in the form of currency, bank accounts, annuities, pensions and similar assets fixed in nominal terms. For the elderly and the retired, of course, financial assets are normally the major or sole component of wealth and a major portion of financial assets, in turn, is typically held in money-fixed claims. Thus the special cruelty associated with the inflation tax is that of finding a heavy cut suddenly made in the nest-egg so painfully accumulated from a lifetime of labor.

The cruelty of such episodes, however, is more properly attributed to the *unanticipated* nature of the price rise than to the inflation tax as such. Once a steady state is reached, the holders of interest-bearing nominal assets will be insulated from any further erosion of purchasing power. The nominal interest rate will be high enough to compensate for the inflation (apart, of course, from the kinds of tax effects discussed at the end of the previous chapter).

The existence of the inflation premium included in nominal interest rates and related kinds of protection against inflation such as cost-of-living adjustments in wage contracts — and now in social security payments in the United States — are often overlooked in popular discussions of inflation. But they are not a complete solution to the problem of inequities under an inflation tax. Holders of noninterest-bearing cash balances are not compensated, after all. Furthermore, unless we are prepared to assume that the steady state had existed from the beginning of time, a transition from a previous rate of inflation to the current one must presumably have occurred somewhere along the way. Unanticipated transitions of this kind, as we have seen, involve surges in prices and unanticipated changes in the real value of nominal assets. For those elderly citizens caught in the transition to a new, higher level of inflation the knowledge that the elderly

---

[1] The German inflation and similar episodes have come to be called *hyperinflations* because prices were increasing at incredibly rapid rates. At the height of the German inflation in October 1923, for example, prices were increasing at the rate of 40 percent a day, and increased by a factor of 32,500 that month alone. The Hungarian inflation rate averaged 244 percent a day during July 1946.

of future generations will feel little pain from the new inflation can hardly be expected to provide much solace.[2]

THE OPTIMAL RATE OF MONEY CREATION[3]

Even if the distribution of the burden of a fully anticipated inflation tax were considered satisfactory, the economic efficiency of this method of taxation relative to the available alternatives would still have to be appraised. As we first pointed out in Chapter 7, all taxes involve a certain amount of economic inefficiency, and the inflation tax on money balances is no exception. An example on the inefficiency of tolls and excise taxes may perhaps be the best way of making clear the precise meaning of economic efficiency in this context.

The inefficiency of tolls and excise taxes generally

Suppose that a government levied a special toll of $1.00 per ton on merchandise shipped by truck over a turnpike between two cities, AAA and ZZZ. Suppose further that trucking is an un-regulated, competitive, constant-cost industry and that the labor, fuel and other costs incurred in sending a truck on the AAA-ZZZ turnpike come to $4.00 per ton. The pre-tax and post-tax equilibrium freight rates charged by the truck companies and the quantities of merchandise shipped are pictured in Figure 13–1. Before the tax was levied, the competitively-set freight rate was $4.00 per ton. The demand schedule for shipments at various freight rates being DD', the quantity of merchandise shipped was q_0 tons per year. After the toll is imposed the equilibrium-freight rate rises to $5.00 per ton. The traffic level falls to q_1 tons per year and the government collects $(q_1 \cdot \$1.00)$ in toll revenues annually (represented by the rectangular area $EFGH$).

To see why this method of raising revenue is inefficient, consider the cost situation as it might appear to a shipper located in

---

[2] On the other hand, a government anxious to step up the rate of inflation, but concerned about the adverse effects on the elderly of the initial surge, could reduce or eliminate the blow by a once-and-for-all compensating payment to those who would otherwise be hurt.

[3] The issues discussed in this section are essentially those treated in the literature of monetary theory under the rubric of "the welfare costs" of inflation.

town BBB, some 50 miles from AAA. Before the toll was levied, the alternatives available to him might have been:

Costs per ton

BBB to ZZZ via CCC		*BBB to ZZZ via AAA*	
BBB to CCC		BBB to AAA	
(30 miles)	$0.50	(50 miles)	$0.60
CCC to ZZZ		AAA to ZZZ	
(650 miles)	$4.50	(600 miles)	$4.00
Total	$5.00	Total	$4.60

The route to ZZZ via CCC costs more because the CCC-ZZZ leg is longer, hillier and slower than the AAA–ZZZ leg, and the higher fuel, tire and other costs incurred on that leg more than offset the savings of the shorter initial leg.

The imposition of the toll, under our assumptions, will clearly shift the balance of advantages away from the AAA–ZZZ route for this shipper. Total costs on that route including toll will rise to $5.60 per ton as compared to only $5.00 on the longer and hillier route via CCC. Thus the use of the $1.00 toll as a revenue device will have forced this shipper to burn up an additional $0.40 worth of gas, oil, rubber and time that otherwise would have been available to produce something useful.

FIGURE 13–1

Demand for trips as a function of the freight rate per ton

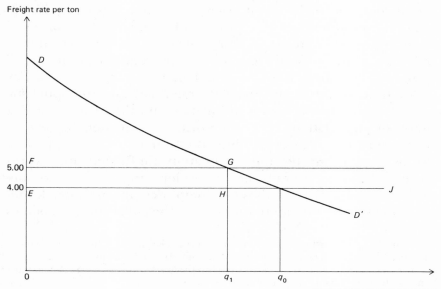

The wastes of an inflation tax

A direct analog to this type of economic waste exists under an inflation tax on cash balances. In terms of Figure 13–1, substitute the volume of real money balances for the number of tons shipped on the quantity axis and substitute the nominal rate of interest for the freight rate per ton on the price axis. The curve DD' would then be an ordinary demand-for-money function. The distance OE would represent the cost (ink, paper, press time, etc.) of producing the money;[4] and q_0 that quantity of money for which the value of a unit of money to the public, as measured by the money rate of interest, was exactly equal to the cost of producing that unit. By raising the equilibrium money rate of interest to OF, the quantity of money demanded falls to q_1. At this higher cost for holding money, some individuals are led to incur time, shoe leather, or other costs to economize on cash, just as our shipper from BBB to ZZZ was led to take a costly roundabout route to economize on toll expense.

We have allowed for waste of this sort indirectly in our model by including money balances in the utility function of consumers. Higher rates of inflation imply lower money holdings and hence lower values of any individual's utility or preference index. (Recall the discussion at the end of Chapter 10.)

Our way of indirectly representing the economic waste under an inflation tax by the loss in utility from money balances is adequate for considering long-run rates of inflation on the order of those experienced in the U. S. and Western European countries in recent years (typically less than 10 percent per annum). For substantially higher rates of inflation, however, the particular utility function for money we have used may give too optimistic a picture both of the wastes of inflation and the revenue-raising power of the inflation tax. In the world of our model, the government could always divert additional resources away from private use by stepping up the rate of inflation still further. Real world citizens, however, usually have a wider range of inflation-tax avoidance devices than those encompassed in our model, and these devices eventually put a limit on the collection possibilities

---

[4] Normally, this cost is so small relative to the face value of the money printed that it can be taken to be zero. In a few cases of extreme hyperinflation, however, the presses were unable to keep up with the price rise and the currency actually came to be worth more as paper than as money.

of the tax. As the inflation rate steps up, for example, workers can be expected to demand more frequent pay periods, more frequent and longer "shopping breaks," and eventually to demand to be paid in whole or part in kind. In fact, after a point, inflation may actually become counterproductive as a tax. Prices eventually may rise so much faster than the rate of production of new money that the real value of government purchases actually falls.[5] Furthermore, production of goods and services by the private sector may be so reduced by the wastes of barter, shopping breaks and the like, that total government revenue in real terms may fall even though the fraction of GNP diverted to the government by its inflation tax may still be increasing.

What monetary policy minimizes the wastes of inflation?

Granted that inflation leads to wastes and inefficiencies, what monetary policy keeps these wastes at a minimum? At first sight, that policy might seem to be one of zero price inflation, implying a rate of monetary expansion equal to the biological interest rate. Actually, however, a government may be able to find policies that reduce waste even further.

The case for a falling price level.   Suppose, for example, that a government decided to abandon inflation as a method of raising revenue, and hold its money supply constant. Equation (4) of Chapter 12 tells us that, in steady state, prices would actually *fall* each period, since we would have

$$\frac{\Delta P}{P} = \frac{-r_b}{1 + r_b}.$$

The cost of holding cash would no longer be the real rate of interest *plus* the rate of loss of purchasing power of money; but rather the real rate *minus* the rate of gain of purchasing power of money. Reducing the cost of holding balances in this fashion would increase the demand for balances and thereby reduce the amount of resources wasted in attempting to economize on cash.

---

[5] For this to occur, the elasticity of demand for real balances with respect to the expected rate of inflation must be greater than −1 in absolute value. Such can never be the case in our model because that elasticity can range there only from 0 to −1. In some of the hyperinflations of the 1920s, however, it appears that values above −1 in absolute value were in fact eventually reached.

But if economic waste is less when prices fall at a rate of $\dfrac{r_b}{1 + r_b}$ than when the price level is constant, why not continue on? Why not actually raise other taxes and use the proceeds to *retire* money already outstanding? The price level would then fall even faster and the costs of holding money and the wastes attendant thereon would be reduced still further.

Clearly, however, this reasoning cannot be extended indefinitely. If the price level were made to fall at a rate greater than the real rate of interest, the money rate of interest required by Fisher's Law would have to be negative. But no one would want to lend at such a rate because a higher return could be earned merely by holding cash. At most, a policy of deliberate deflation could be carried in general only to the point where the money rate of interest became zero. (And, in the special case of our model, not even this far, thanks to our logarithmic utility function which would make the demand for money infinite, given a zero rate of interest and hence a zero cost of holding money).

Offsets to the gains from reduced inflation.   Granted that a policy of deliberate deflation cannot be pursued beyond the point where the nominal or money rate of interest becomes zero (or, strictly speaking, equal to the cost of producing money), can a case be made for pushing even that far? It would seem so if we were to look only at the wastes avoided in the monetary sector. But remember that cutting the money supply requires some other tax to be raised. And unless this tax leads to less waste of resources than that occasioned by the economizing on cash holdings, there will be no net gain to society, or perhaps even a net loss, in substituting one form of taxation for the other.

In the specific case of our FOUR-SIX-EIGHT experiment, the substitution of income taxes for inflation taxes by Country FOUR actually happened to prove beneficial on balance. Not only was the long-run level of real balances highest in Country FOUR, but so also was the level of real consumption. Such an outcome, however, is almost certainly an overstatement of the gains likely to be achieved in practice from reducing the rate of inflation in favor of other sources of revenue.

For one thing, much of the damage to the capital stock in the higher-inflation Countries SIX and EIGHT was occasioned, as we saw, by the taxation of that part of the return to capital that represents merely a nominal appreciation in capital value. Any country proposing to rely systematically on inflation as a long-run revenue source would presumably exempt such nominal gains from ordinary taxation. Had we, too, built such an exemption into our experiment, Country FOUR with the lowest rate of inflation would also have had the lowest capital stock and consumption in the long run, rather than the highest. The reason is that after the adjustment for nominal returns, Country FOUR would have had the highest level of personal income taxation in real terms. And as we saw in Chapter 7, any tax that falls in whole or in part on interest income, as would a personal income tax, is likely to reduce the incentive to save. Hence it would lead to a smaller national output of goods and services than could be achieved under a tax that did not distort the tradeoff terms between consumption now and consumption later.

Even if we could somehow find a perfectly nondistorting tax to substitute for inflation, switching to a policy of greater deflation might still not increase wealth. The announcement that the rate of growth of the money supply is henceforth to be cut will produce an immediate downward surge in the price level. This surge, in turn, will lead to a rise in the real value of cash balances and, consequently, to a rise in the perceived value of real wealth. At the same time, however, the announcement that other taxes will henceforth be higher leads to a fall in the perceived value of real wealth (because the present value of those new taxes has to be subtracted from wealth). Which of the two effects dominates and hence which way wealth changes cannot be settled a priori, but depends on the specific numerical values assumed for the various factors entering into the wealth equation.[6]

To be fully realistic in appraising all the economic conse-

---

[6] The fact that the two wealth effects will not, in general, cancel out exactly implies, among other things, that money will not be "neutral." By neutrality in this sense economists mean that changes in the nominal money supply leave unchanged the equilibrium values of the real variables in the system (such as the real rate of interest or the real capital stock). We have previously seen many other instances of the nonneutrality of money in our models (e.g., the reduction in the capital stock due to the taxation of interest income whether real or nominal), but some might prefer to attribute these effects to the inefficient taxes used to substitute for inflationary finance rather than to money itself. Since it is difficult to imagine any feasible tax that would be nondistorting—even the mythical head tax, if one were actually to be instituted—the issue of neutrality and the controversies surrounding it are of little practical interest at best. For what it may be worth, our discussion suggests that neutrality is of little interest even from the theoretical point of view.

quences of an inflation tax, allowance would also have to be made for other kinds of distortions that we have kept out of the model in the interests of simplicity. High income taxes or consumption taxes, for example, will encourage households to devote more time to untaxed leisure activities and less to paid labor. Taxes will affect the balance between risky and safe investments. And by no means least, in comparing the wastes of taxation with those of inflation, we must not forget the direct costs of collection under the tax approach, as well as the non-trivial fraction of the services of the accounting and legal professions enlisted in the practice of tax avoidance.

Stability rather than optimality as a goal for monetary policy

We can summarize the discussion to this point by saying that inflation appears to be neither so bad a tax as to make its elimination a matter of urgent social concern nor so good a tax as to justify any very much larger role that it currently plays in countries such as the U. S. or Canada, or in the more developed nations generally. All taxes, inflation included, are wasteful to some extent, and the attendant waste tends to increase as the rates of taxation rise. Here, as elsewhere, an optimal policy in principle is one that will equate at the margin the disadvantages and drawbacks of all the policy alternatives considered together (including, of course, their interactions as in our earlier demonstration of the particularly adverse consequences of taxing purely inflationary nominal interest income). There is certainly no strong reason to believe that the rate of money creation in such an optimal tax program will be negative or zero, but there is no way to pin it down more closely, given our limited knowledge of the structure of the economy and the very severely limited powers of computation currently available.[7]

For these reasons, economists have tended to stress considerations other than merely efficiency of revenue collection as a basis for choosing a rate of monetary expansion or contraction. The leading monetary theorists of the pre- and post-World War I

---

[7] Fuller treatment of this class of optimality problems, often referred to as "the economics of the second-best," is best left to advanced courses in price theory or welfare economics.

period, such as Irving Fisher or the early Keynes, tended to favor a policy of price-level stability, implying a policy of monetary growth at about the biological rate. Having a stable standard of value, they felt, would not only simplify economic planning and calculation by firms and households but would avoid the bitter political debtor-creditor struggles that had occurred in response to the wide swings in the price level in the 19th century. Modern monetary theorists, aware that these benefits can be obtained even with nonzero rates of price change, provided they are fully anticipated, have tended to place greater emphasis on the stability of the rate of growth of money than on the level of the rate itself.

PROBLEMS FOR CHAPTER 13

1. Suppose the government's annual injection of money is made by distributions to individuals proportional to their holdings of fiat money. What will be the wastes of inflation in that case?

2. Several persons have advocated that the government (and others) issue *purchasing power bonds* whose nominal value would be increased every year in proportion to the change in the price level. Others have argued that these bonds are unnecessary because of the inflation premium in nominal interest rates. Under what circumstances would purchasing power bonds be equivalent to more conventional bonds?

3. Suppose purchasing power bonds were freely available. How would their existence affect the wastes and redistributional effects of inflation?

4. Suppose that a privately produced commodity such as gold served as money for an economy. What would determine the rate of expansion of the money supply (that is, the rate at which gold was mined)? What would be the optimal rate of growth of the money supply?

14

Fiscal policy and the price level

Up to now, the only disturbances to the price level considered have been abrupt changes in the rate of money creation. Eliminating such disturbances, however, does not mean that an economy will remain placidly at the long-run steady-state rate of inflation. Monetary stability is only a necessary but not a sufficient condition for steady-state equilibrium. Shocks coming from elsewhere in the system will be transmitted to prices and interest rates via the money supply/demand mechanism. As an example of such shocks, we will here consider the effects of changes in government spending and taxation policies.

There is, however, a fundamental difference between shocks to the money supply itself and shocks arising in the nonmonetary sectors. Played out against a background of monetary stability, those of the latter type can affect the rate of inflation in the short run, but damp out and leave no trace on the rate of change of prices in the long run.

THE EFFECTS OF AN INCREASE IN GOVERNMENT SPENDING

To see the differing effects on the two types of shocks, consider an economy similar to that in Chapter 12, in steady-state equilibrium with government expenditures on purchases of goods and services equal to a constant fraction ν of national income. These expenditures are assumed to be fully financed by two sources of revenue: an annual injection of money and a tax on wage income. It will simplify matters to assume that the growth rate of the money supply is equal to the biological interest rate r_b. For further simplicity, we will also suppose that the government has no debt and is not allowed to issue any. (This constraint will be relaxed in due course.)

Suppose now that the government permanently increases its spending from vY to $v'Y$. To follow the pay-as-you-go principle, it increases the annual tax on wage income by $(v' - v)Y$. What effect will this increase in spending have on the price level and on the inflation rate, in the first year of the change and in the long run?

Immediate changes in the inflation rate

The solid Y and M curves in Figure 14–1 illustrate what the position of the economy would have been in year 1 without the increase in spending. These curves show the combination of the price level and the real interest rate that would have equated the demand and supply of both real output and money prior to that year. (If you are unsure what these curves represent, you should review the derivation of those curves in Chapter 11 before proceeding.) The point at which they cross indicates the price level P_0 and the real interest rate r_0 in the steady-state equilibrium prior to the shock.

Under the program of increased spending, the auctioneer must satisfy an additional demand for goods and services by the government equal to $(v' - v)Y$. At the same time, the new wage tax will reduce private wealth and hence consumption demand. However it can be shown that the drop in consumption demand will normally be less than the rise in government spending.[1] Were the auctioneer therefore to attempt the previous combination of P_0 and r_0 he would find that aggregate demand exceeded aggregate supply by the difference between the in-

---

[1] There are special cases, depending on the γs in the individual utility function, in which the consumption demand will drop by more than the increase in government spending. However, as with Chapter 7, we will here discuss only what we consider to be the more plausible cases.

FIGURE 14–1
Determination of price level and interest rate, year one

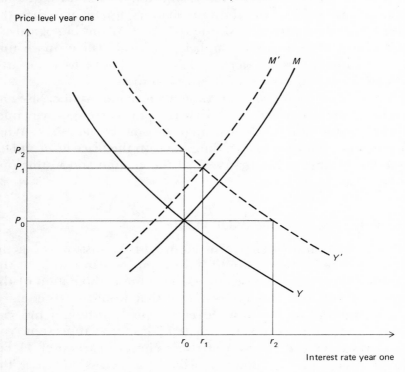

crease in government spending and the decrease in consumption demand.

One way he could bring the demand for output in line with supply would be to raise the interest rate to r_2 and to depress consumption and investment demand; alternatively, he could raise the price level to P_2, and rely on the unanticipated inflation to depress consumption demand. Many other combinations, indicated by the Y' curve to the right of the Y curve, would achieve the purpose of keeping demand and supply in balance: the purpose in drawing attention to these two points is to show that the Y curve has indeed shifted to the right to Y'. As to the M curve, we leave it to you as an exercise to show that the reduction in wealth resulting from the additional tax will shift it to the left to M'.

The changes on the price level and the interest rate which result from the increase in government spending are shown in Figure 14–1. The price level is raised to P_1. As the Y' and M' curves are drawn, the interest rate rises from r_0 to r_1, but this is clearly dependent on the way in which those curves are drawn; it is possible that the interest rate might fall.[2]

Long-run changes in the price level and inflation rate

Granted then that the shift in government spending will raise the price level and the rate of inflation when that shift occurs, will there be any effect on the price level and the inflation rate when the economy returns to steady-state equilibrium? As to the inflation rate, the answer is clearly no.

The inflation rate. The inflation rate for any year can be found from equation 2 of Chapter 12

(1) $$\left(1 + \frac{\Delta M_s}{M_s}\right) = \left(1 + \frac{\Delta P}{P}\right)\left(1 + \frac{\Delta C}{C}\right)\left(1 + \frac{\Delta Z}{Z}\right)\left(1 + \frac{\Delta \xi}{\xi}\right).$$

Now in steady-state equilibrium $\Delta\xi = \Delta Z = 0$ and furthermore $(1 + \Delta C/C) = 1 + r_b$. Thus the equilibrium inflation rate will be given by equation 4 of Chapter 12

(2) $$\frac{\Delta P}{P} = \frac{\frac{\Delta M_s}{M_s} - r_b}{1 + r_b}.$$

Because the government is also expanding the money supply at the biological interest rate, it follows that equilibrium must here be marked by a zero inflation rate. We may thus conclude that *although government spending and taxation policies can influence the inflation rate in the short run, they have no influence on the long-run rate. That rate is dependent only on the rate of monetary expansion and the biological interest rate.*

The level of prices in the long run. The change in the equilibrium price *level* will depend on how, if at all, steady-state

---

[2] If the demand for money depended on national output and not consumption alone, then there would be no shift in the M curve; in this case, both the price level and the interest rate are unambiguously raised. Still, none of the key propositions in this chapter depends on the assumption that money demand is proportional to C rather than Y; an exercise along this line is provided at the end of the chapter.

equilibrium has changed. It is possible to show—though we will not do so here—that an increase in government spending financed by a wage tax leads here to a decreased equilibrium saving rate and hence to a decline in the equilibrium capital effective labor ratio. This decline will lead to a decline in consumption/effective labor unit and hence to a decline in the demand for real money balances per effective labor unit. In addition the lower capital/effective labor ratio means a higher interest rate, also tending to reduce the demand for real money balances per effective labor unit. Because the government's policy of expanding the nominal money supply at the biological rate keeps nominal money balances per effective labor unit constant, it is clear that the auctioneer must respond to this reduced demand by raising the price level to reduce the supply of real money balances per effective labor unit.

MUST AN INCREASE IN GOVERNMENT SPENDING BE INFLATIONARY?

It is not surprising that an increase in government spending can lead to a rise in the price level both in the short run and in the long run. The fact is, however, that it is not the spending that causes the inflation, but how that spending is financed. Indeed, there are circumstances under which the financing of an increase in government spending could cause prices to fall! We will illustrate one such case in this section.

Immediate effects of a rise in government spending financed by a tax on interest income

Suppose that the government had decided to finance the increase in spending by a tax on interest income like that considered in Chapter 7. As we saw there, such a tax would reduce the rate μ at which an individual discounts his human capital and would thereby increase his wealth. The increase in consumption demand, coupled with the increase in government spending, will shift the Y curve to the right to Y', as illustrated in Figure 14-2. At the same time, the tax on interest income will have two effects on the demand for money and hence on the M curve. Recall that this demand is given by

$$(3) \qquad m_i = \frac{\xi}{(n_3 - i + 1) + \xi(n_3 - i)} \frac{1 + \mu}{\mu} z_i.$$

Not only does the tax increase z_i, but it also reduces μ, the nominal after-tax interest rate. Both factors tend to increase the demand for money balances. An increase in the demand for money also shifts the M curve to the right, to M'.

FIGURE 14–2
Changes in equilibrium with an increase in government spending financed by a tax on interest income

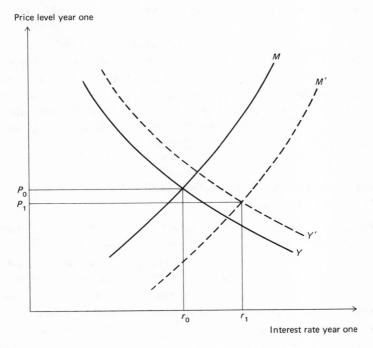

As drawn in Figure 14–2, the new intersection of the Y and M curves involves a rise in the interest rate (before taxes) from r_0 to r_1 and, most important, a fall in the price level from P_0 to P_1! Of course, this is only one possibility, though not an implausible one. It does serve to remind that a tax which increases the demand for real money balances produces deflationary pressures.

Changes in steady-state equilibrium with a tax on interest income

The effect on the equilibrium price level is more difficult to determine. We know that output and consumption per effective labor unit will be lower, and the before-tax interest rate r will be higher with an interest tax than with the wage tax. We saw those results in Chapter 7. But the demand for money depends not only on consumption but also on the after-tax rate $\mu = (1 - \lambda_r)r$. Though r is higher with an interest tax than with the wage tax, μ may indeed be lower. If so, that will tend to increase the demand for real money balances and hence could lead to a *lower* price level.[3]

In short, one cannot conclude that government spending need be inflationary. All one can say is that the inevitable shocks to equilibrium resulting from a change in government spending produce secondary shocks to the demand for money which cause the inflation rate to differ from the equilibrium rate. The magnitude as well as the direction of the change in prices depends on how that spending is financed.

IS DEFICIT FINANCING MORE INFLATIONARY THAN TAX FINANCING?

There are other ways to finance an increase in government spending other than by those considered so far. In particular, what about deficit financing? Is it true, as is popularly believed, that a deficit-financed spending increase is more inflationary than an increase financed by taxation? To see the consequences of deficit financing, let us reexamine the influence of the permanent increase in government spending from νY to $\nu' Y$, now supposing the first year of the increase to be financed entirely by borrowing. For the sake of comparison, suppose that the government returns to the pay-as-you-go principle the following year, paying for the interest on the debt by a tax on wage earners.

We already know from Chapter 8 that, in an economy populated by Immortal Consumers, the present value of current and

---

[3] Given the demand-for-money function used here, this can be shown to indeed be the outcome.

future tax liabilities is exactly equivalent under debt and tax financing. The only difference is the timing of the payments, and that has no effect on consumption expenditures. If consumers do not have a bequest motive, however, the reduction in wealth from the present value of the future tax liabilities will be less than it would be were the spending financed on the pay-as-you-go basis. Therefore, the reduction in consumption demand in the first year will also be less and the Y curve, instead of shifting to Y', will shift even further to the right to Y'', as illustrated in Figure 14–3. However, the same increase in wealth will shift the M curve part of the way back to M'' to the right of M'. As a consequence, the effect on the price level is ambiguous. As drawn here, the price level rises to P_3, higher than P_1, the level attained under a balanced budget, so that the rate of inflation

FIGURE 14–3
Determination of price level with deficit-financed spending increase

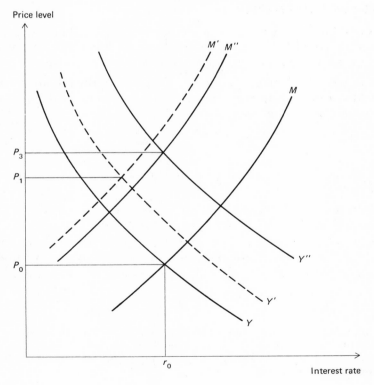

from deficit financing in the short run $(P_3 - P_0)/P_0$ is higher than the rate from a pay-as-you-go policy, $(P_1 - P_0/P_0)$.[4]

Thus there may be some truth in the proposition that debt financing is more inflationary than tax financing. But where consumers discount the future tax liabilities that a debt represents, the difference is considerably less than the popular view would suggest.

Some economists have argued, in defense of this popular view, that individual consumption decisions are unaffected by these future tax liabilities. This may be true for the first year but it will not be true for the second when the debt-induced tax increase is forcefully called to their attention. We very much doubt, however, that these tax increases always come as a surprise. They might the first time deficit financing is used. But Lincoln's Law tells us not to expect the public to be fooled consistently by a policy of deferring taxes by deficit financing.

PROBLEMS FOR CHAPTER 14

1. Show how an increase in government spending financed by borrowing could be less inflationary than one financed by taxation in a world peopled by consumers with no bequest motive.

2. Suppose the demand for money depends on the level of output Y and not on consumption alone. That is, the money demand function is (say) of the form

$$M_d = \xi \frac{1 + \mu}{\mu} Y.$$

    Show how an increase in government spending could be deflationary even in this case.

3. Show that the increase in government spending financed by a wage tax will shift the M curve in Figure 14–1 to the left.

4. Suppose the increase in government spending from νY to $\nu' Y$ was for one year only, thereafter returning to νY; and that the duration of the spending increase had been announced in advance. If the

---

[4] On the other hand, it is possible that the effect will be to lower the price level, as you can readily verify. If the demand for money is proportional to output and not consumption alone, there is no shift in the M curve and the price level unambiguously rises.

increase were to be financed by a one-year special surcharge on wage income, what would this shock do to the price level in year 1? To the price level in steady-state equilibrium? Compare your answer with the case of a permanent increase in spending.

5. Show the consequences of a wage-tax-financed increase in government spending if

    a. the demand function for money is of the form

$$M_d = \xi \frac{1 + \mu}{\mu} Y,$$

    b. the demand function for money is of the form

$$M_d = \xi Y,$$

    c. consumption and investment demand are not functions of the interest rate,

    d. wealth is not affected by changes in the price level,

    e. (a) and (c) are both true,

    f. (a) and (d) are both true.

    Hint: Recall the Y and M curves derived in the problems of Chapter 11 for these cases.

6. Show the consequences of an increase in the money supply for each of the six cases above, paying particular attention to whether consumers have a bequest motive.

15
Money and banking*

IN MODERN ECONOMICS, only part of the money stock is fiat money supplied by the government. The rest, and usually the far larger part, is "produced" by the private sector. This chapter brings into the analysis this *inside money*, as it is often called in contrast to fiat or *outside* money. We start with a brief sketch of the commercial banks, whose deposit liabilities are the principal element in the inside money stock. Demand functions for the two kinds of money are then derived and the conditions for equilibrium of the money sector set down. Although the economy is found to respond in much the same way as before to an increase in outside money, the introduction of inside money creates new kinds of linkages with the price level and new sources of monetary disturbance. These, in turn, have led to the establishment of central banks such as the U. S. Federal Reserve System in an attempt to mitigate such disturbances. The effects of the major tools of central banks on the economy are briefly described at the close of this chapter.

THE BUSINESS OF BANKING

Extending our picture of the economy to include an inside money, supplied entirely by banking firms in the private sector, is a relatively straightforward matter. We have already made con-

---

* This chapter may be skipped without loss of continuity.

siderable use of the notion of "banks" as financial intermediaries whose liabilities, called "deposits," are taken as representative of the financial assets in which households keep their savings. We need now only assume that the deposit liabilities of one particular class of banks—a class called *commercial banks*—are so easily and cheaply transferred from one holder to another (e.g., by writing a check) that they have come to be used in lieu of currency for making purchases or settling debts.[1]

How have commercial bank deposits come to achieve this dual status as both asset and money? Two explanations may be offered, depending on which of the banks' business activities we choose to stress. One explanation, which might be called the "warehouse receipt" interpretation, starts from the observation that substantial costs must be incurred by the holder to maintain a cash balance in the form of fiat currency or *commodity money* such as gold. The risk of fire and theft is ever-present. Rather than each household maintaining its own stronghold—or perhaps chancing it with mattress or sugar bowl—there are clearly economies in having central safe-keeping facilities. Providing such facilities has traditionally been one of the most conspicuous services of the banking industry, and it is no accident that banks usually manage to have the huge vault doors prominently visible to the public. In this light, the "deposits" of the bank can be thought of as literally that: the physical transfer of currency to the bank for safe keeping with a receipt given in the form of a credit to a deposit account in the depositor's name. Checks written against such accounts direct the bank to transfer title to the funds deposited and hence their "moneyness" is basically a carry-through of the moneyness of the underlying currency.

Banking as an exchange of I.O.U.s

Though the warehouse-receipt interpretation of the moneyness of commercial bank deposits has considerable intuitive ap-

---

[1] Commercial banks typically have two kinds of deposit accounts: checking accounts or *demand deposits*, and savings accounts or *time deposits*. The former, as the name implies, are payable on demand. In the U. S., at least the bank has the technical right to require 30 days' notice before honoring a withdrawal from a time deposit. (In practice this right to notice is rarely invoked.) Unless otherwise indicated, we shall be using the term commercial bank deposits to refer to demand deposits subject to check.

peal, it is by no means the whole story or even the most important part of it. Under modern conditions, commercial bank deposit accounts need not arise from the physical deposit of currency. They can be created by the bank itself in the course of its lending operations. When an individual or a firm receives a bank loan, proceeds of the loan are typically turned over in the form of a fully paid-up deposit account. Yet the only thing the borrower has deposited in the bank's vault is his own I.O.U.[2]

The paradox would largely disappear if we used the less graphic term "bank liabilities" or "bank securities" rather than bank deposits. As the previous account makes clear, what commercial banks do essentially is, for a price, swap their own liabilities for those of their customers. The customers are willing to pay this price because they find it easier and less costly to settle claims against them by offering the bank's I.O.U. rather than their own. One reason is that their creditors have to do much less checking of the banks' I.O.U.s. The banks' elaborate program of loan investigation, their cushions of equity capital (and, in the U. S. at least, the government insurance of bank deposits) stand behind their liabilities. A second, related reason is that the cost of transferring this class of liabilities is much lower than for most other securities. No lawyers' fees, brokerage charges, insurance, or title search are involved; merely a form directing the bank to change the name of the owner of the account. It is these attributes of safety and convenience that lead to the kind of widespread acceptability that is associated with the term money. And they could be expected to do so even in an economy with no fiat currency whatever.[3]

---

[2] In Britain and a number of other countries the creation of deposits is streamlined still further by the granting of "overdraft" privileges. As the name implies, these permit the writing of checks in excess of the balance in the account, with the automatic conversion of the excess into a loan at an agreed-upon rate of interest when the check is presented for collection. U. S. banks are not permitted to extend overdraft privileges to their customers, but with characteristic ingenuity have developed more complicated arrangements which amount to much the same thing.

[3] Safety, convenience and acceptability are clearly matters of degree, and hence it should not be surprising that disputes sometimes arise as to where along the spectrum to draw the line between money and other assets.

The simultaneous currency of inside and outside money

While a cashless society in which commercial bank deposits are used to the exclusion of currency is entirely conceivable, all modern economies have mixed monetary systems in which currency and inside bank-created money circulate simultaneously.[4] There are several reasons for this. First, in countries such as the U. S., Canada and Britain the standard payment system makes the substitution of bank credit for individual credit only a partial one. The check instructing the bank to change the name on the account is handed over in the first instance not to the bank, which could immediately verify the status of the account, but to the creditor who must then route it back to the bank. Where the creditor cannot easily validate the customer's ownership of the bank liability he will demand cash instead (as any traveller stranded in a strange town on a weekend can readily testify).[5]

Second, some of the very features of bank accounts that make them so convenient for settling accounts in some circumstances can be most inconvenient in others. An obvious case in point is the documentary record or "audit trail" that a bank account (with the possible exception of one in Switzerland) normally leaves. Not for nothing has the attaché case full of $100 bills become a cliché. Still another quite important reason is that governments typically add to the demand for fiat money by requiring it to be used for certain purposes. Chief among these is the re-

---

[4] It would be conceivable to have an economy with no outside money; we have, in effect, seen essentially such an economy in the "real" models of Chapters 1 through 8. The main difference between such real models and the outside-money models of Chapters 9 and beyond is that the real models have no "price level." They have relative prices, and they may well use some abstract monetary unit like the dollar for record-keeping purposes. But there is no stock of such units and hence no need to determine the rate of exchange between units of output supplied by the private sector and units of currency supplied by the government.

[5] The sending of the check by the creditor back to the bank for collection takes time and thereby makes possible a common practice called "kiting" checks or "playing the *float*" as corporate treasurers prefer to call it. By paying its east-coast suppliers with checks on its west-coast bank, the customer firm can continue to use the funds in its business during the collection period.

Some European countries have adopted systems called *giro systems* in which the drawer directs his own bank to pay the creditor who is notified only when the funds have actually been put at his disposal.

quirement that commercial banks hold among their assets an amount of government-produced, outside money equal to a substantial fraction of their own deposit liabilities. It is true that, even in the absence of such government regulation, banks would find it economical to hold some *vault cash,* as it is called, for essentially the same reasons as would the subjects in our cash balance parables in Chapter 9. But under normal conditions, the amounts of outside money held by banks in response to government-imposed *reserve requirements* are well above the amounts they would hold if they were completely free to choose the composition of their own portfolio of assets.

MONETARY EQUILIBRIUM WITH INSIDE AND OUTSIDE MONEY

The supply function for bank money

For present purposes, the important consequence of these reserve requirements is the considerable simplification they make possible in constructing the supply function of inside bank money. There is no need to spell out the complete details of the process whereby a bank finds its profit-maximizing level of reserves of fiat money. The imposed reserve requirement means that reserves and deposits for any (and hence every) bank must meet the condition

$$(1) \qquad M^R \geq \phi M^d \text{ or equivalently } M^d \leq \frac{1}{\phi} M^R,$$

where M^d is the level of deposit liabilities supplied, ϕ is the required reserve ratio and M^R the level of reserves. The assumption that the reserves required by law are greater than those that would be voluntarily maintained means that the constraint (1) is binding and hence that it can be replaced by the corresponding equality

$$(2) \qquad M^d = \frac{1}{\phi} M^R = \frac{1}{\phi} (M^b - M^c),$$

where M^b is the *monetary base,* the total amount of outside money supplied by the government, and M^c is the portion of the monetary base held by the public outside of banks.

To say that (1) and (2) apply to "any and every" bank is not to suggest that an individual bank can or would make loans equal to the multiple $1/\phi$ of any newly acquired reserves. If the borrowers used their newly created accounts to pay their creditors and if these creditors happen to be depositors in other banks, then the first bank will suffer a deficiency in its required reserve account. The safe course, therefore, for an individual bank is to lend out no more than the fraction $(1 - \phi)$ of any newly-acquired reserves. When transferred to another bank this permits a further expansion by that bank of $(1 - \phi)^2$ times the original inflow, and so on thereafter. The sum of the series of deposits created following an inflow of \$1 of reserves is thus $1 + (1 - \phi) + (1 - \phi)^2 + \ldots$. This is a geometric series which will sum to $1/\phi$ as long as $\phi < 1$. A competitive banking *system,* in short, behaves in accord with the supply function (2) even though no individual bank would ever expand its deposits by a multiple of its reserves.[6]

Note finally that (2) tells us only the amount of deposits supplied by the banking system for any given level of reserves held. It doesn't tell us how much of the monetary base will actually end up as reserves held by the banks and how much as currency held by the public. To answer that question, we must first take a closer look at the factors underlying the public's demand for outside and inside money.

The demand functions for inside and outside money

In sketching out the demand side we shall continue to assume that we can adequately represent the desirable properties of a cash balance by including it as an argument in the household's utility function. In fact, we shall continue to use the same form of utility function, since, as we have seen, it leads to very compact and transparent demand functions. Warnings will be duly given whenever the analysis leads to conclusions that are special to the functions used.

---

[6] A qualification must be entered for systems in which some individual banks have such a large share of the market that they can count on a substantial re-deposit of any funds that its borrowers transfer to their creditors. With a value for ϕ of .2 and a market share of .5 (approximately that of the Bank of America in the state of California) the safe limit is not .8 of a new deposit, but 2.5.

With two kinds of money balances, the utility function of Chapter 10 now becomes

$$\log c_i + \quad \log c_{i+1} + \ldots + \quad \log c_{n_3} + \ldots +$$

$$(3) \quad \xi_c \log m_i^c + \xi_c \log m_{i+1}^c + \ldots + \xi_c \log m_{n_3-1}^c + \ldots +$$

$$\xi_d \log m_i^d + \xi_d \log m_{i+1}^d + \ldots + \xi_d \log m_{n_3-1}^d,$$

where m^c represents the real value of currency holdings at the start of the period and m^d the real value of bank demand accounts.

The resource constraint can be extended in an analogous way. For further generality, however, we shall now assume that bank deposits, but not currency, bear interest. We will use ρ to represent the rate individuals earn, net of taxes, on their deposits. The only essential restriction on ρ is that it be less than μ, the nominal after-tax market rate of interest on nonmoney financial assets; otherwise, of course, no one would ever want to hold any financial assets other than bank balances.

But we can say a bit more about the value of ρ if we are willing to specify a bit more about the banking industry and its cost structure. In particular, suppose that all the clerical and search costs of processing checks and loans are covered by direct service charges. Then, if we let μ, as before, stand for the after-tax rate of interest on financial assets, the maximum rate of interest on deposits that any bank could pay without incurring a loss would be $\rho = (1 - \phi)\mu$. If we also suppose the industry to be competitive and to be subject to no regulatory restrictions on deposit interest rates, then $(1 - \phi)\mu$ is also the *minimum* that any bank would have to pay in order to retain its depositors.[7]

Under these assumptions, the opportunity cost of holding a bank balance thus becomes $\mu - \rho = \phi \mu$ as compared with an opportunity cost of μ, as before, for noninterest-bearing currency. Taking these different costs into account, the resource constraint (in real terms) derived in the appendix of Chapter 10 can now be rewritten as:

---

[7] The U. S. is one of the few developed countries in which the payment of interest on demand deposits is prohibited by law. As we shall see, however, this prohibition has so little effect on the substance of the analysis that it is more sensible to work from the outset in terms of the more general formulation of which $\rho > 0$.

$$z_i = c_i + c_{i+1} \left(\frac{1}{1+\mu}\right) + c_{i+2} \left(\frac{1}{1+\mu}\right)^2 + \ldots + c_{n_3} \frac{1}{(1+\mu)^{n_3-i}} +$$

$$m_i^c \left(\frac{\mu}{1+\mu}\right) + m_{i+1}^c \left(\frac{\mu}{1+\mu}\right)\left(\frac{1}{1+\mu}\right) + m_{i+2}^c \left(\frac{\mu}{1+\mu}\right)\left(\frac{1}{1+\mu}\right)^2$$

$$+ \ldots +$$

$$(4) \quad m_{n_3-1}^c \left(\frac{\mu}{1+\mu}\right)\left(\frac{1}{1+\mu}\right)^{n_3-i-1} +$$

$$m_i^d \left(\frac{\phi\mu}{1+\mu}\right) + m_{i+1}^d \left(\frac{\phi\mu}{1+\mu}\right)\left(\frac{1}{1+\mu}\right) +$$

$$m_{i+2}^d \left(\frac{\phi\mu}{1+\mu}\right)\left(\frac{1}{1+\mu}\right)^2 + \ldots + m_{n_3-1}^d \left(\frac{\phi\mu}{1+\mu}\right)\left(\frac{1}{1+\mu}\right)^{n_3-i-1}.$$

It then follows that the demand functions obtained by maximizing the utility function (3) subject to the constraint (4) will be:

$$c_i = \frac{1}{(n_3 - i + 1) + \xi_c(n_3 - i) + \xi_d(n_3 - i)} \cdot z_i$$

$$m_i^c = \xi_c \cdot c_i \cdot \frac{1+\mu}{\mu}$$

$$m_i^d = \xi_d \cdot c_i \cdot \frac{1+\mu}{\phi\mu}.$$

Summing over all households, we then have as the aggregate demand for each of the two kinds of money balances

$$\sum_i m_i^c \cdot L_i \equiv M^c = \xi_c \cdot C \cdot \frac{1+\mu}{\mu}$$

and

$$\sum_i m_i^d \cdot L_i \equiv M^d = \xi_d \cdot C \cdot \frac{1+\mu}{\phi\mu}$$

in real terms and

$$M^c = \xi_c \cdot C \cdot P \frac{1+\mu}{\mu}$$

$$M^d = \xi_d \cdot C \cdot P \cdot \frac{1+\mu}{\phi\mu}$$

in nominal terms.

Equating each of these demand functions with the corresponding supply function we have

(5) $M^d_{\text{Supply}} = \dfrac{1}{\phi} M^R = \xi_d \cdot C \cdot P \cdot \dfrac{1 + \mu}{\phi\mu} = M^d_{\text{Demand}},$

$M^c_{\text{Supply}} = M^b - M^R = \xi_c \cdot C \cdot P \cdot \dfrac{1 + \mu}{\mu} = M^c_{\text{Demand}},$

which can in turn be combined into the single equilibrium condition for the money base

(6) $M^b = (\xi_d + \xi_c) \cdot C \cdot P \cdot \dfrac{1 + \mu}{\mu} = \xi_b \cdot C \cdot P \cdot \dfrac{1 + \mu}{\mu}.$

Note that equation (6) is formally identical with the equilibrium condition originally developed in Chapter 11 while still assuming that all money was outside money. The only differences are in interpretation. The single-shift parameter ξ of Chapter 10 has now been decomposed into one with two elements ξ_d and ξ_c in recognition of the fact that part of the base of outside money is held directly by households and part indirectly in the form of bank reserves. But, and this is the important point, *all the previous analysis of how the economy responds to changes in the supply of outside money continued to apply as before even though we now have inside money circulating along with outside money.*[8]

The money multiplier

It is true, of course, that the *absolute size* of the nominal money supply, given the money base, will necessarily be larger when we have fractional-reserve bank money as well as hand-to-hand currency. But under our assumptions, the combined sum of currency plus commercial bank checking deposits—a sum usually designated by the symbol M_1 in the monetary literature—can be shown to be a constant multiple of the monetary base. Hence, a doubling of M_1 still involves a doubling of the stock of fiat money, and equation (6) and its dynamic variants can be used to trace out the consequences exactly as before.

The ratio of the money balances held by the public to the *high-powered money* base supplied by the government is called the *money*

---

[8] The key assumptions that produce this result are: (1) that the reserve ratio is binding and (2) that the wealth and interest elasticities of demand are the same for both types of money. The consequences of relaxing some of the assumptions will be taken up in later sections.

multiplier. Under our assumptions the money multiplier has the value

$$M_1/M^b = \frac{1 + \theta}{\theta + \phi},$$

and the *deposit multiplier* has the value

$$M^d/M^b = \frac{1}{\theta + \phi},$$

where $\theta = \xi_c \phi/\xi_d =$ the public's desired ratio of currency holdings to deposit holdings. The derivation of these multipliers is left to the exercises at the end of the chapter.

THE FATAL FLAW IN A FRACTIONAL RESERVE BANKING SYSTEM

Though the presence of a fractional reserve banking system may not affect the response of the system to exogenous changes in the stock of outside money, it does create new channels by which monetary disturbances can reach the price level. In particular, any change in the public's preferences for outside money relative to inside money can upset the equilibrium in the money sector even though there may be no change in the demand for aggregate money balances, M_1. The reason is that under a fractional reserve system a dollar of hand-to-hand currency demanded represents a demand for $1 of the monetary base, whereas a dollar of deposits demanded represents a demand for only the fraction ϕ of $1 of the monetary base. Hence, in terms of the equilibrium condition (6), a shift from cash to deposits represents a fall in ξ_b, and from deposits to cash a rise in ξ_b, with all that implies for compensating shifts in the equilibrating variable P.

An example may help to fix these ideas. Suppose that the reserve ratio $\phi = .2$, that initially $\xi_c = .003$ and $\xi_d = .002$. Then the public's desired currency/deposit ratio will be $\theta = \frac{\phi \xi_c}{\xi_d} = .3$ and the various money multipliers will be

$$\frac{M^c}{M^b} = \frac{\theta}{\theta + \phi} = .6 \qquad \frac{M^d}{M^b} = \frac{1}{\theta + \phi} = 2.0 \qquad \frac{M_1}{M^b} = \frac{1 + \theta}{\theta + \phi} = 2.6.$$

Table 15–1 shows the sector balance sheets under the assumed conditions for an economy with $1,000,000 in its monetary base

TABLE 15–1
Initial balance sheets of the household and banking sectors (in current dollars)

Households

Assets		Liabilities	
Currency	600,000	Loans from commercial banks	1,600,000
Commercial bank checking accounts	2,000,000	Loans from other banks	2,500,000
Balances in other banks (i.e., nonmoney financial assets)	7,400,000	Household net worth	5,900,000
Total	10,000,000	Total	10,000,000

Commercial Banks

Assets		Liabilities	
Required reserves	400,000	Balances in checking accounts	2,000,000
Loans to households	1,600,000		
Total	2,000,000		2,000,000

Other Banks

Assets		Liabilities	
Value of real capital	4,900,000		
Loans to households	2,500,000	Balances	7,400,000
Total	7,400,000	Total	7,400,000

of outside fiat money. Note that to simplify comparison with corresponding accounts in earlier chapters we continue to maintain the fiction that title to the goods making up the capital stock (including the commercial bank vaults and premises) is vested in a special type of bank that leases the capital goods to operating firms. We shall expand their capabilities, however, to include the granting of loans to households and firms in competition with the commercial banks.

Suppose now that a change in the public's preferences for the two kinds of money balances takes place with ξ_c falling to .0025 and ξ_d rising to .0021. The fact that the fall in ξ_c has been assumed equal to $1/\phi$ times the rise in ξ_d means that the change is simply a desire on the part of the public to convert a portion of its present currency holdings to checking account balances without altering the value of its combined money holdings. Nevertheless, this simple switch has thrown the monetary sector out of equilibrium.

Panel A of Table 15–2 shows how the public's demand for money balances would look on the auctioneer's book immediately after the shift in preferences. Panel B shows the quantity of deposit balances that the commercial banks would want to supply. The banks want to supply substantially more balances than before because the deposit of the now redundant currency by the public has created additional reserves and thereby loosened the reserve constraint on supply.

The banks not only want to expand their deposit liabilities, but they can readily do so. From Table 15–1 we see that other competitive types of banks are currently lending some $2,500,000 to households. The commercial banks thus need merely approach the debtors and offer to refinance these loans at terms slightly more favorable in order to pick up the desired increment in their earning assets and hence in their deposit liabilities. The term *intermediation* has come to be applied to this substitution of commercial bank credit for other credit (and the term *disintermediation* when the flow is reversed).

TABLE 15–2
Desired balance sheets of the household and banking sectors following a shift in preferences toward deposits

A. Household Desired Balance Sheet

Assets		Liabilities	
Currency	500,000	Loans from commercial banks	1,600,000
Balance in commercial bank checking accounts	2,100,000	Loans from other banks	2,500,000
Other	7,400,000	Household net worth	5,900,000
Total	10,000,000	Total	10,000,000

B. Commercial Bank Desired Balance Sheet

Assets		Liabilities	
Required reserves	500,000	Balances in checking accounts	
Loans to households	2,000,000		2,500,000
Total	2,500,000	Total	2,500,000

The auctioneer must therefore turn to his other equilibrating variables, P and μ, in the hope of finding some way of boosting the level of nominal deposits desired by households up to the level that banks want to supply. If the shift in preferences has led to no change in the rate of inflation expected for *next* year — and there is no reason why next year's rate should change — then there will be no change in μ. The auctioneer's problem is essentially a one-shot·fall in the $(\xi_c + \xi_d)$ component of the equilibrium condition (6) from .005 to .0046 or by 8 percent. We are now on familiar ground. Simple Quantity Theory considerations tell us that, distributional effects aside, a rise of 8 percent in the price level would be required to cut the real supply of money balances back to equal the real demand (or, equivalently, to expand the nominal value of balances demanded up to the level of nominal balances supplied).

Shifts in preferences between cash and deposits of this kind, and the disturbances left in their wake have played a conspicuous role in the monetary history of the U. S. Some economists have argued that such a shift was a major factor aggravating the Great Depression (or, as they would prefer to call it, the Great Contraction or Great Deflation) of 1929–1933. After 1929, people began to lose confidence in the banking system. And small wonder, since an increasing number of bank failures were occurring. These failures and rumors of further impending failures led to an increase in the demand for currency at the expense of bank deposits which, in turn, triggered more failures as the price level fell and "good" loans turned sour. (Remember that bank loans are stated in nominal, not real, terms.) The increase in the demand for the monetary base that such a shift out of deposits represents was only partly met by the increase in the base that the monetary authorities actually supplied. From the end of 1929 to the beginning of 1933, the money base increased by about 14 percent. But the total money supply contracted by about 30 percent over that interval; and the price level fell by nearly 50 percent.

CENTRAL BANKS AND THE MANAGEMENT OF A FRACTIONAL RESERVE BANKING SYSTEM

The fact that the money base was actually increasing throughout most of the period shows, among other things, why a monetary authority attempting to stabilize the price level could not safely follow a policy of simply stabilizing M^b, the monetary aggregate under its direct control. Only if the public's preferences for inside as opposed to outside money never changed would such a policy work. But where such shifts in preferences do occur, the only way to keep them from perturbing the price level would be to allow M^b to change in response — increasing M^b when the public wants more currency and decreasing it when the shift is in the other direction. In sum, faced with the prospects of such shifts in preferences, and the consequent shifts in the demand for the money base, a policy of stabilizing the rate of change of prices implies stabilizing the growth of the total money stock M_1, and not M^b.[9]

Federal Reserve liabilities and the monetary base

In this light, the monetary collapse in the U. S. in the 1929–1933 period is doubly ironic since the Federal Reserve System had been set up less than twenty years earlier, largely with such shift-induced money panics in mind. The essence of the new system was to create a bankers' bank (or central bank as it is more commonly called) whose liabilities would be part of the country's monetary base.[10] Those commercial banks compelled to join the system (and this included most of the large commercial banks) had to hold their required reserves in the form of (noninterest-bearing) deposit accounts in the appropriate regional Federal Reserve Bank. Should the public want to withdraw cash from the banking system, then the needed cash could be obtained from the Federal Reserve whose circulating liabilities, called Federal Reserve Notes, were to be a major form of circulating currency. If the public wanted to hold less cash and more deposits, then the commercial banks would deposit the redundant notes in their

---

[9] For related reasons, some economists have proposed that the monetary authorities aim to stabilize the growth of an even broader aggregate, dubbed M_2 and consisting of M_1 plus time deposits in commercial banks. Exploration of these and other monetary targets is best left to specialized advanced courses.

[10] In practice, of course, nothing in banking is ever quite this simple. Over the course of the years, the money base in the U. S. has included such things as gold coins, gold certificates, silver certificates and Treasury notes; but their role is now minor and further consideration can safely be deferred to more specialized courses.

accounts at the Federal Reserve, which in turn would extinguish them.

As originally envisioned, the Federal Reserve was to play mainly a passive role in this switching between currency and deposits. As the commercial banks needed to replenish their stocks of currency they were expected to borrow from the Federal Reserve Bank in much the same way as their customers borrowed from them. As it turned out, however, the Federal Reserve usually found itself forced to set such a low rate of interest on borrowings by the banks that banks had enormous incentives to borrow and, in the process to enlarge the economy's money base. To keep the money supply from expanding completely out of control, therefore, the Federal Reserve resorted to rationing its below-cost credit by devices that would today be called "arm-twisting" or "jaw-boning," but in that more innocent age went by the name of "moral suasion."[11]

Open-market policy

The rate charged by the System for member-bank borrowing, though normally a bargain, was changed so infrequently that it was sometimes actually above the market rate of interest. Bank borrowing from the System naturally ceased and with it much of the revenue supporting the Federal Reserve System and its operations. The managers of the System sought to meet this problem in the same way as they would have done under corresponding circumstances in the commercial banks from which they came; and, by another of the ironies of U. S. monetary history, they stumbled thereby on what has since become their major tool of monetary management, *open-market policy*.

Open-market policy, as the name implies, is the purchase and sale of securities (almost invariably government securities) through the normal channels of trade. It corresponds, at the Federal Reserve level, to the intermediation and disintermediation

---

[11] For reasons we needn't go into, the act of borrowing was technically called *rediscounting* and the borrowing charge was (and is) known as the *rediscount rate*. Hence the picturesque phrase "slamming the discount window" to describe the denying of Federal Reserve credit privileges to banks taking more than their supposedly fair share of the Fed's bargain credits.

in the case of commercial banks described earlier, but with one critical difference. *When the Federal Reserve swaps its liabilities for earning assets it expands the monetary base.*

An open-market purchase is thus formally the same as the printing of fiat money by the government. In fact, under modern conditions most governments actually create money by a technical sale to the central bank of some or all of the securities issued to cover a budgetary deficit. This is not to suggest, however, that a current budgetary deficit is either a necessary or a sufficient condition for monetary expansion. Strictly speaking, even if the government were adhering to a pay-as-you-go tax policy, a central bank could, in principle, always expand or contract the monetary base by an appropriate open-market operation.

To the extent that a central bank did expand the money supply on its own initiative by "monetizing the debt" through an open market operation it would, of course, be levying an "inflation tax" on the community of essentially the same kind discussed earlier in Chapter 13. The tax paid by the public would be the loss in the real purchasing power of the money base due to the price rise. (Note that the tax falls only on the base even though the total money supply is many times larger. Remember that the public's losses in its capacity as lender to the banks are offset by its gains as borrowers.) The proceeds of the tax are used to retire a corresponding amount of interest-bearing debt and thus, in effect, to reduce the amount of ordinary taxes that would otherwise have to be paid by the public in order to meet the interest payments to the bondholders.[12]

It is precisely because the open-market operations of central banks are essentially tax policies that few countries today do more than preserve the fiction of an independent central bank. The U. S. is the last and most conspicuous exception, but even there the concept of a monetary authority independent of the governing administration has come under increasing attack.

---

[12] In the U. S. the monetary base in mid-1973 was approximately $100 billion (of which about $60 billion was in currency and $40 billion in reserves against demand deposit liabilities of $200 billion). Each percentage-point increase in the rate of monetary expansion and inflation, therefore, would represent no more than $1 billion in tax revenues.

Changes in reserve requirements

In addition to open-market operations most central banks have another, though much less frequently used, method for controlling the quantity of money in the hands of the public: namely, changing the rate of reserves required against deposits. From our earlier discussion of the supply function of the banking industry and the money multiplier, we know that a cut in ϕ will increase the supply of M^d and M_1. But the cut in ϕ will permit (and in a competitive environment, will force) banks to pay higher interest rates on their deposit accounts and this in turn will increase the demand for M^d and M_1. If the increase in demand is not equal to the increase in supply, then the auctioneer will have a disequilibrium to contend with and will have to undertake some compensating adjustment in P.

The particular demand function for deposits that we developed earlier had the form

$$M^d_{Demand} = \xi_d \cdot C \cdot P \cdot \frac{1+\mu}{\mu-\rho} = \xi_d \cdot C \cdot P \frac{1+\mu}{\phi\mu}.$$

Hence, in this case, a halving, say, of ϕ would lead to a doubling of the demand for deposits. Since the supply function is of the form

$$M^d_{Supply} = \frac{1}{\phi} M^{\dot{R}},$$

the halving of ϕ would also lead to a doubling of the supply of deposits. Unlike a change coming from a change in the supply or demand for the monetary base, a change in the reserve ratio would change M^d and M_1 but would have no effect on the price level or anything else of consequence.

This somewhat paradoxical result occurs because with our demand-for-money function the demand for M^c does not depend on the cost of M^d and because the elasticity of demand for bank balances with respect to the interest rates paid by banks happens to be precisely unity. If that elasticity were less than unity, then a halving of ϕ would lead initially to a doubling of the supply of deposits but to less than a doubling in the demand for deposits. An equilibrating move in the price level would thus be required, but it would be less than in proportion to the increase in M_1. Only in the extremely unlikely case of zero interest elasticity would the predictions of the simple Quantity Theory, as applied to M_1, seem to be borne out.[13]

A FURTHER LOOK AT SOME OF THE ASSUMPTIONS

We have carried out all our analysis of inside money to this point on the basis of two convenient simplifying assumptions, viz. (1) that competition compels the banks to pay interest on their deposit accounts and (2) that the required reserve ratio is always binding. We shall conclude our discussion of money and banking by considering briefly some modifications to previous conclusions when for one reason or another these assumptions no longer hold.

The effects of prohibition of interest payments on deposits

Since the passage of the Glass-Steagall Banking Act of 1933, U. S. banks have technically been forbidden by law to pay interest on their demand deposit accounts. There are two approaches that might be taken to analyzing the effects of this prohibition. If we assume that such prohibitions can indeed be effective, then we would have to retrace the steps in the derivation of our demand-for-deposits function equation (5), this time with $\rho = 0$. A glance at those steps shows that the only change required will be that of replacing $\phi\mu$ with just μ as the opportunity cost of holding deposits.

This change in turn has two consequences worth noting. First, it means a lower money multiplier since θ, the desired cash/deposit ratio, will be higher—understandably so since the advantages of deposits relative to cash have been drastically reduced. Second, the complete prohibition of interest would by definition prevent any change in interest rates offered to account holders when the required reserve ratio is changed. Thus a change in

---

[13] For completeness we might note that if the interest elasticity of the demand for money were actually greater than unity (as implied, for example, by the usual textbook picture of a Keynesian "liquidity preference function") then we would have the weird result of a cut in the reserve ratio leading simultaneously to an increase in M_1 and to a *fall* in the price level. Some examples of the price level response under various assumptions about interest elasticity are provided in the exercises.

reserve ratios would require an adjustment in the equilibrium level of prices even in a world whose money demand functions, like those of (5), had unit elasticity with respect to interest rates.

The second and more realistic approach is to assume that the prohibition of interest on demand deposits is about as effective as any other kind of price control, which is to say, not very effective at all once the gap between the controlled price and the competitive price becomes large enough to create incentives for evasion. Of course, banks are too much in the public eye and in the regulatory eye to engage in open flaunting of the rules, but under the pressure of competition they have been able, over the years, to come up with a variety of "free services" to depositors (especially business depositors) that have much the same effect on the demand for deposits as if interest were in fact being paid. We say only "much the same" because here as elsewhere the presumption is that the free services are valued less by the recipient than a corresponding direct cash payment. In fact, for some holders, they may be worth nothing at all. (On the other hand, the fact that some of these services need not be reported as income subject to the personal income tax may actually make them worth more to high-bracket taxpayers than a corresponding interest payment.) Until the prohibition is ended and banks are forced to "unbundle" we will never know for sure just how close an approximation to interest payments these bank services really are and hence whether the zero interest or the full interest model is the better approximation. Our own guess is that the interest payment model has been closer to the mark in recent years. Fortunately, however, as we have seen, there are relatively few issues in monetary theory or policy for which the difference in models would give substantially different results.

Banking in a world of nonbinding reserve requirements

When we relax our second working assumption, that the reserve ratio is always binding, the necessary modifications of previous conclusions are also relatively minor (except for one special set of circumstances to be noted below). Under normal conditions, the main difference between a system with and a system without binding reserve constraints is that the money multiplier in the latter would not be a constant but a variable, changing with each change in the fraction of their assets that the banks decide to hold in the form of outside money. As noted earlier, the banks could be expected to choose that fraction along essentially the same lines as our householder in the parables of Chapter 9 went about choosing an opening cash balance. That is, they would try to balance off the income lost on any assets held in the form of outside money against the costs of converting cash to and from earning assets. The lower the rate of interest the higher the fraction of assets it is economical to hold in the form of cash to avoid the costs of transacting, and hence the lower the money multiplier.

If the market rate of interest should happen to be extremely low, it is even conceivable that the most economical level of reserves desired by banks might actually be higher than the reserve required by law. When this is the case, the banking system is said to be holding *excess reserves*.

The presence of excess reserves lowers the *marginal* deposit multiplier which, in the extreme case of interest rates close to zero, becomes equal to one. Should the public then deposit additional currency in the banks, the deposit total would go up by the amount of the deposit, but there would be no further expansion of deposits of the kind we described earlier. The returns from lending, net after the cost of making loans, would no longer be high enough to get the banks to undertake the intermediation. This means, of course, that the shift from currency to deposits would not set up the kind of imbalance between the supply and demand of deposits that would require a movement of the price level to equilibrate. In short, when nominal interest rates are effectively zero, the monetary mechanism tends to work in a way that is fundamentally different from the way it behaves when interest rates are significantly higher than the cost of making loans.

Some monetary historians have argued that something very much like the situation pictured actually happened in the U. S. in the period immediately after 1933. To bring the panic runs on the banks to a halt, President Franklin Roosevelt proclaimed a Bank Holiday of indefinite duration in March 1933, and, at the same time, introduced various banking laws designed to restore public confidence in the soundness of the banking system, notably Federal insurance of bank deposits. As public confidence in the soundness of those banks allowed to reopen increased, currency began to flow back into the banking system and hence into bank reserves. But by 1933 the collapse that had begun in 1929–1930 had carried the economy into a severe deflation. And with that severe deflation came extremely low levels of nominal interest rates. Hence the reflow of funds into the banks merely led to excess reserves and not to the kind of price movement that might have reversed the price falls caused by the earlier outflows of reserves into currency holdings by the public.[14]

The episode of the huge post-1933 pile-up of excess reserves had a most unfortunate legacy. More than any other fact or theory it was probably responsible for the dominant view among economists in the 1930s and 1940s—and indeed even in more recent years—that monetary expansion would normally have little visible effect on the economy and could certainly not be counted on to reflate an economy out of a recession. The money would simply wind up in excess reserves and the monetary authorities would find themselves "pushing on a string."

It is important to remember, therefore, that what leads banks to hold excess reserves, as in the 1930s, is their belief that using the funds to refinance old loans or to make new ones would not be profitable. It takes nominal interest rates extremely close to zero for this to be the case.

PROBLEMS FOR CHAPTER 15

1. Consider an economy with a competitive banking system in which the money base is ten billion dollars and banks are required to hold reserves equal to 20 percent of their demand deposits. Initially the public is holding an amount of currency equal to 20 percent of demand deposits.
    a. What is the money supply (M_1)?
    b. Suppose the reserve requirement on banks were lowered to 10 percent. What would happen to the money supply and its components?
    c. What would happen to the price level if money demand is given by equation (5)?

    ---

    [14] A further contributing factor may have been a voluntary increase by banks in their reserves as a precaution against further runs.

2. Suppose the demand function for deposits were of the form

$$M^d_{Demand} = \xi_d\, C\, P\, \sqrt{\frac{1+\mu}{\phi\mu}}\,.$$

What effect would a halving of the reserve requirement then have on the price level?

3. Why does the "inflation tax" fall only on the money base and not on all of M_1?

4. Suppose that initially $\xi_c = .003$, $\xi_d = .002$, $\phi = .2$ and that all other variables are as depicted in Table 15–1. Suppose that ξ_c falls to .0025 and ξ_d rises by an equal amount. What effect would this have on M_1? On M^b? On the price level?

5. Show that the money multiplier has the value $(1 + \theta)/(\theta + \phi)$ and that the deposit multiplier has the value $1/(\theta + \phi)$ where $\theta = \xi_c\phi/\xi_d$ and ϕ is the ratio of required reserves.

Bibliography for section four

On the microeconomic foundations of the demand-for-money function, see

Barro, Robert J. "Inflation, the Payments Period and the Demand for Money." *Journal of Political Economy*, Nov./Dec. 1970.

Baumol, William J. "The Transactions Demand for Cash: An Inventory Theoretic Approach." *Quarterly Journal of Economics*, November 1952.

Miller, Merton H., and Orr, Daniel. "A Model of the Demand for Money by Firms." *Quarterly Journal of Economics*, August 1966.

Orr, Daniel. *Cash Management and the Demand for Money*. New York: Praeger, 1971.

Tobin, James. "The Interest Elasticity of the Transactions Demand for Cash." *Review of Economics and Statistics*, August 1956.

For completeness we should also mention

Tobin, James. "Liquidity Preference as Behavior Toward Risk." *Review of Economic Studies*, February 1958.

However, this article is more appropriately viewed as an important part of the literature on portfolio theory than as part of the literature on the demand for money.

There are several well-known statements of the modern Quantity Theory. In particular, see

Friedman, Milton. "The Quantity Theory of Money: A Restatement." In *Studies in the Quantity Theory of Money*, Milton Friedman, ed. Chicago: University of Chicago Press, 1956.

————. "Money, Quantity Theory." In *International Encyclopedia of the Social Sciences*. New York: Macmillan and Free Press, 1968.

Much of the empirical work on the demand for money is summarized in

> Laidler, David. *The Demand for Money: Theories and Evidence*. Scranton, Pa.: International Textbook, 1969.

An interesting recent empirical study of the behavior of velocity is

> Gould, John P., and Nelson, Charles R. "The Stochastic Structure of the Velocity of Money." *American Economic Review*, forthcoming.

As to the distinction between real and nominal interest rates, Fisher's contributions are presented in

> Fisher, Irving. *The Theory of Interest*. New York: Macmillan, 1930.

The issues we have discussed under the heading of Lincoln's Law are closely related to the theories of *rational expectations* and *efficient markets*. The classic reference to rational expectations is

> Muth, John P. "Rational Expectations and the Theory of Price Movements." *Econometrica*, July 1961.

The efficient markets hypothesis is discussed in

> Fama, Eugene. "Efficient Capital Markets: A Review of Theory and Empirical Work." *Journal of Finance*, May 1970.

For some recent evidence on the relation between nominal interest rates and future inflation rates, see

> Fama, Eugene. "Short Term Interest Rates as Predictors of Inflation." Mimeographed, 1973.

The problem of stability discussed in Chapter 11 is treated in

> Black, Fischer. "The Uniqueness of the Price Level in Monetary Growth Models with Rational Expectations." *Journal of Economic Theory*, forthcoming.

> Cagan, Phillip. "The Monetary Dynamics of Hyperinflation." In *Studies in the Quantity Theory of Money*, Milton Friedman, ed. Chicago: University of Chicago Press, 1956.

> Sidrauski, Miguel. "Rational Choice and Patterns of Growth." *American Economic Review*, May 1967.

> Stein, Jerome. *Money and Capacity Growth*. New York: Columbia University Press, 1971.

The relationship between the real and monetary sectors of an economy is rigorously developed in

> Patinkin, Don. *Money, Interest and Prices*. Second Edition. New York: Harper and Row, 1965.

For an early attempt to marry a monetary sector to a growth model, see

> Tobin, James. "Money and Economic Growth." *Econometrica*, October 1965.

A later model is presented in the Sidrauski article referenced above.

A detailed monetary history of the United States with emphasis on monetary disturbances is given in

Friedman, Milton, and Schwartz, Anna J. *A Monetary History of the United States, 1867–1960.* Princeton: National Bureau of Economic Research, 1963.

For a somewhat critical review of this volume, see

Tobin, James. "The Monetary Interpretation of History." *American Economic Review,* June 1965.

For a discussion of hyperinflation, see Cagan's article and, more recently, Barro (1970).

Money creation as a form of taxation is discussed in

Bailey, Martin J. "The Welfare Cost of Inflationary Finance," *Journal of Political Economy,* April 1956.

Barro, Robert J. "Inflationary Finance and the Welfare Cost of Inflation." *Journal of Political Economy,* Sept./Oct. 1972.

Friedman, Milton. *The Optimum Quantity of Money and Other Essays.* Chicago: Aldine, 1969.

———. "Government Revenue from Inflation." *Journal of Political Economy,* July/August 1971.

Friedman's book is also the source for the proposition we have called the Friedman surge.

For a discussion of conventional approaches to banking and the money multiplier, see

Jordan, Jerry L. "Elements of Money Stock Determination." *Review.* Federal Reserve Bank of St. Louis, October 1969.

and for a discussion of some of the inadequacies of that approach, also see

Tobin, James. "Commercial Banks as Creators of Money." In *Banking and Monetary Studies,* Deane Carson, ed. Homewood, Ill.: Irwin, 1963.

section five

Unemployment

THE PREVIOUS SECTIONS assumed that the economy was always at full employment. We are now ready to relax that assumption and discuss how a variety of shocks to the economy can cause unemployment and how the economy responds to those shocks.

Chapter 16 analyzes the basic microeconomic foundations of unemployment and shows how temporary unemployment can occur when some price such as the wage rate cannot adjust immediately to its market level. Chapter 17 then takes up the implications of unemployment at the macroeconomic level and discusses what the government can and cannot do to hasten the return to full employment.

16

The microeconomic foundations of unemployment

IN THE PREVIOUS CHAPTERS we have assumed the existence of an auctioneer who calls out prices ensuring that the demand and supply are equated in all markets. We turn now to see what happens when the auctioneer cannot perform his function and prices do not adjust instantly in response to changes in demand or supply. This chapter will focus on the process of price adjustment in a single market. The major emphasis will be on adjustment in the labor market. The implications of this process for short- and long-run equilibrium in the economy as a whole are taken up in Chapter 17.

PRICE ADJUSTMENT IN A SINGLE MARKET

As an example of the microeconomic process, consider a market for freshly-cut flowers. Suppose that a quantity of flowers is cut each day for sale in a central marketplace. Because cut flowers wilt, any left over at the end of the day must be thrown away. The market is illustrated in Figure 16–1. The demand curve D gives the quantity of flowers customers are willing to buy on any day as a function of the price charged, and the supply curve S indicates the quantity of flowers that will be brought to market, also a function of the price producers expect to receive. The equilibrium price of flowers is P_0, and the equilibrium quantity cut for sale — and sold — each day is Q_0.

FIGURE 16-1
The demand and supply of flowers

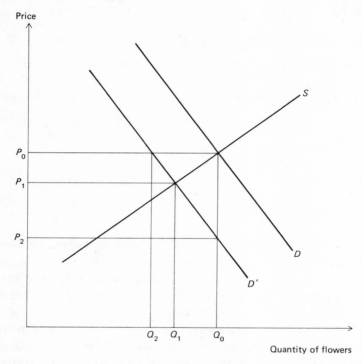

Quantity of flowers

The consequences of a shift in demand in a centralized market

Suppose now that because of a change in income or in tastes, the demand curve for cut flowers shifts to D'. The new equilibrium quantity of flowers bought and sold each day will be Q_1, the new equilibrium price will be P_1, and the market price will drop to that level as soon as people are aware of the shift in demand.

On the first day after the shift in demand, however, suppliers, unaware of the change, bring the old quantity of flowers Q_0 to the market. Demand, however, is equal only to Q_2 at the old price. If a law forbade a change in the price of flowers without advance notice, there would be a surplus of unsold flowers. A quantity $Q_0 - Q_2$ would wilt and be thrown away at the end of the day.[1]

---

[1] For most nonperishable commodities it would be possible to store the surplus for possible sale at a later date. To keep the story simple enough to handle by graphical analysis, we have chosen a commodity that cannot be stored.

But suppose there is no such law. Can surpluses then exist? Certainly not if the auctioneer is on the job. He need only call out a price for flowers equal to P_2 and the quantity demanded that day will rise to Q_0. All that is really required is that the price fall to P_2, although clearly the explanation of how the price gets there must be a little more complicated in the absence of the *deus ex machina* of the auctioneer. One might explain it in terms of sharp-eyed customers realizing the reduced demand and cutting the price they are willing to pay. An alternative scenario might attribute the decline in price to nervous suppliers who in their anxiety to ensure that their flowers are not the ones unsold at the end of the day start a price war. Which story is best? As long as we are assuming the price level will adjust *instantly and costlessly* to the new equilibrium, all three stories are really the same. The marketplace acts *as if* greedy customers bid the price down *and as if* anxious suppliers lowered the price *and as if* there were an auctioneer shouting out the price that balanced supply and demand.

The case of a decentralized market

In a centralized market for a homogeneous commodity such as we have been describing it would be hard *not* to believe that prices move quickly to clear the market. With all buyers and sellers congregating at one location, information about who was doing what would flow freely. Changes in aggregate demand and supply would be quite visible. The news of one supplier, say, lowering his price to attract customers would spread quickly and it would be easy for customers to play one supplier against another to obtain the best price.

In markets not so centralized, however, prices need not be as flexible. Suppose for example that there is no centralized market and that cut flowers are sold exclusively by vendors going from door to door. Let us suppose — without going into details — that all vendors initially charge the same price P_0 for flowers every day. Because the demand and supply curves are still represented by Figure 16–1, the market is in equilibrium at this price. To be sure, there is a certain randomness in each vendor's daily sales. Some days he sells all his flowers quickly and is able to quit early, while he must throw flowers away at the end of other days. Although some flowers will almost certainly be thrown away each day, this should not be interpreted as a surplus of flowers representing disequilibrium in the flower market. A flower vendor, even if unacquainted with the very latest techniques in management science, will surely have learned that he can increase his average daily profit by cutting more flowers each day than the number he is absolutely certain of selling. We can incorporate this effect into the demand and supply analysis by interpreting the supply curve to be the quantity of flowers supplied net of the normal daily surplus, S_n.

The size of this normal daily surplus depends on a variety of factors such as the variation in daily demands by individual customers, the size of each vendor's market and the like. We need not go into them here. But note that the continuing daily surplus is not a sign of waste: it is simply another cost of the convenience of having flowers sold on a decentralized basis.

The shift in demand reexamined

Now let us suppose that the demand curve for flowers for the market as a whole suddenly and unexpectedly shifts to D' as in Figure 16-1. How will flower vendors react to this shift? On the first day, vendors may well continue to offer flowers for sale at the old price P_0. Because of the decline in demand, we, as outside observers, know that the quantity of flowers sold must decline from Q_0 to Q_2, so that the daily surplus of flowers will rise from S_n to $Q_0 - Q_2 + S_n$. To the individual vendor, however, it is not so clear what has happened. If he were privy to our information and knew that his misfortunes were due to a decline in market demand, he would certainly cut his price. He might also reduce the number of flowers he cuts each day; indeed, he might even decide to switch occupations. But since he is not and cannot be privy to our knowledge as outside observers, he may be unaware that many other vendors were also unable to sell their flowers. He may therefore conclude that his experience was just a bad day, one of those misfortunes that randomly occur. If so, he will do nothing and confidently expect better sales tomorrow.

Aside from daily fluctuations in the number of flowers he sells, there will be no change in the vendor's fortunes on the second and succeeding days. The decline in demand means that he and other vendors will continue to have an average daily surplus of flowers equal to $Q_0 - Q_2 + S_n$ as long as they continue quoting the old price.

Over time, however, the vendor will come to realize that market conditions have changed. We can only speculate as to how he becomes aware of the decline in demand. Perhaps he becomes aware of it by conversation with some of his fellow vendors or from newspaper accounts of distress in the flower trade. Even if such sources of information fail, all but the most optimistic of vendors will be forced to conclude after several consecutive days of bad sales that the decline in demand is permanent.

As this realization spreads, individual vendors will begin to respond. There will be a decline in the quantity of flowers cut for sale each day and a lowering of the quoted price.[2] This process will continue until the market reaches equilibrium at a new price P_1 with the quantity of flowers sold equal to Q_1. The ultimate adjustment will be the same, but it will not be as rapid in this disorganized, decentralized market as it would be were the flowers sold in a centralized market.[3]

The time-path of price and quantity

Figure 16–2 illustrates how prices might behave in this decentralized flower market as opposed to their behavior in the centralized market. The horizontal axis measures time after the decline in demand and the vertical axis the price at any time. On the first day after the shift in demand, before the quantity cut has

---

[2] To be sure, vendors may cut their prices at different times and in different amounts. Thus we may see flowers being sold by vendors at different prices during this adjustment process. However, it simplifies the story to think of all flowers being sold at a common price. If you like, you may think of this price as the average of the prices charged by different vendors.

[3] But is the flower market in equilibrium *during* this adjustment process? The term equilibrium normally refers to a market in which supply and demand are equal. Clearly the flower market is in equilibrium at the beginning and at the end of this process. It can be argued of course that in between supply and demand are not equal and that the market is in disequilibrium. Alternatively it can be argued that because these large surpluses represent a voluntary decision on the part of suppliers, the quantity supplied and the quantity demanded are equal, the voluntarily accepted surpluses included. The distinction between equilibrium and disequilibrium under these conditions is more semantic than substantive. In what follows we shall have occasion to use both interpretations.

FIGURE 16–2

The price of flowers in a centralized and decentralized market over time after a shift in demand

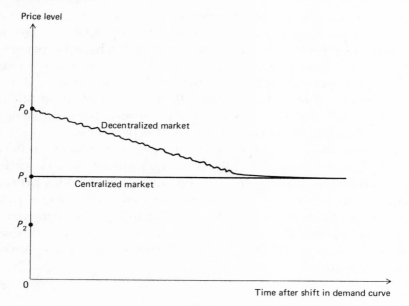

been changed, flowers sell for P_2. Thereafter suppliers can and do reduce the quantity of flowers being cut each day and the price rises to its equilibrium level of P_1 which is, of course, below the old equilibrium level of P_0. The price curve for the centralized market is drawn under the assumption that the market adjusts to its new equilibrium the very next day. If we allow for factors like delays in adjusting supply, the adjustment at the price of flowers to P_1 may take longer. The critical point is that no matter how long it takes supply to adjust, there is *never* any surplus in the centralized market.

In the decentralized market, the price on the first day after the shift is P_0. The adjustment to equilibrium price is much slower than in the centralized market, reflecting the greater time it takes for vendors to realize what has happened.

Figure 16–3 similarly illustrates how the quantity of unsold flowers might behave in this decentralized flower market. The horizontal axis again measures time after the decline in demand; the vertical axis, the quantity of flowers thrown away each day. On the first day after the shift, when flowers are selling for P_0, the unsold quantity of flowers is equal to $Q_0 - Q_2 + S_n$. It declines thereafter to a level of S_n, normal daily fluctuations aside, as the price of flowers declines from P_0 to P_1. In the centralized market, however, there is never any surplus.

Such slow adjustment processes as we have described for the decentralized market are often modeled by equations of the form

$$(1) \qquad\qquad P_t = P_{t-1}(1 - \lambda(S_{t-1} - S_n)),$$

where P_t = price of flowers on the tth day, S_t = surplus of flowers on the tth day, S_n = the "natural" surplus of flowers, which is to say, the quantity thrown away on a typical day, and λ an adjustment coefficient. This equation is certainly consistent with the process we have been describing verbally above. When the surplus on any day S_{t-1} is above the normal level S_n, the vendors will reduce their price P_t on the next day. Prices will continue to fall until the surplus on any day is reduced to the normal level. In the case illustrated in Figure 16–3, that will happen when the price level has fallen to P_1, the new equilibrium price. Precisely how long that will take is reflected in the value of λ, the adjustment coefficient. The larger the value of λ, the faster the adjustment.

FIGURE 16–3

The surplus quantity of flowers in a decentralized market over time after a shift in demand

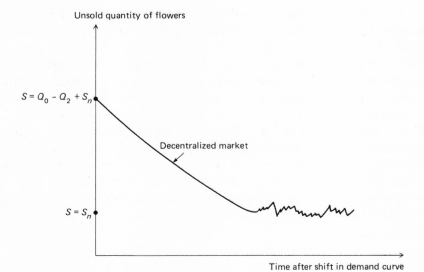

Equation (1) is far too simple to be an accurate description of adjustment in any real-world market. Indeed, it has a variety of weaknesses. It assumes, among other things, that the drop in today's price depends only on whether there was a surplus yesterday, and not on how long such surpluses have persisted. For all its failings, however, this equation does embody the critical property that prices are adjusting over time although no longer immediately to the market-clearing level. In deference to standard usage, we shall use the term "sticky" to describe prices in markets that behave in this manner.

The condition for sticky prices

Equation (1) is similar to the adaptive expectations scheme suggested in Chapter 11 as a model of how inflationary expectations are formed. In that chapter, this equation was criticized and rejected because it runs afoul of Lincoln's Law: if inflationary expectations were really so formed, substantial profits could be made with little or no investment or risk. It is natural, therefore, to ask if the same criticism applies here: were the price of flowers governed by equation (1) or a similar equation which implied substantial lags in price adjustment, could similar above-normal profits be made? In any market where the transactions costs (the costs of buying and selling) are low, the answer would be yes. Profit opportunities would exist if prices took a long time to adjust. The best method of exploiting these opportunities would depend on the commodity involved: a *short sale* would seem the appropriate vehicle here.[4] Carried on in sufficient volume, such activity will quickly alter the price of a commodity so that the time required for the price to adjust to the new equilibrium becomes negligible. The crucial difference between the two versions of the flower market thus lies in differing transactions costs of speculations such as short sales. These costs, as well as the costs of knowing when there is a change in demand, would normally be quite small in the centralized market. They may well be quite high if flowers are vended on a door-to-door basis. Given such costs price adjustment like that described by equation (1) need not imply profit opportunities.

---

[4] A short sale is a sale of borrowed securities or commodities which the seller expects to buy at a lower price before the contracted delivery date.

UNEMPLOYMENT IN THE LABOR MARKET

The example of the flower markets made several critical points about price behavior.

1. A surplus of a commodity can exist if the price of that commodity does not adjust rapidly to changes in demand or supply.
2. When such surpluses occur, however, they are only temporary and will disappear once the price of the commodity reaches its eventual equilibrium.
3. When it is expensive to obtain information or to engage in arbitrage transactions such as short selling (as it might be in a decentralized market), abnormal surpluses can be consistent with rational behavior.
4. The adjustment in such markets can be modeled by a "sticky price" equation like Equation (1).

Although any or all of the prices discussed in earlier chapters — the interest rate, the price level and the wage rate — could be sticky in the short run, we shall, for simplicity, place the main emphasis here on stickiness in the price that governs the labor market, the money wage rate. Indeed, the labor market is analogous in many ways to the decentralized flower market discussed previously. Both potential employers and employees search for each other on a decentralized basis. Because labor is a heterogeneous commodity differing in type and quality from one worker to another, it is hard for unemployed individuals to determine whether their difficulties are general or specific in nature. There can be a shortage of one type of labor while another type of labor has a surplus. Finally, arbitrage transactions such as short sales are almost impossible in the labor market. All in all, the labor market seems to fit all the criteria for sticky prices laid down in the example of the vendor-dominated flower market except for a minor semantic difference: surpluses in the labor market are usually referred to as *unemployment*.

The natural rate of unemployment

Another concept from the flower market which has a direct analog in the labor market is the concept of a normal surplus, though this is referred to as the *natural rate of unemployment* in the case of the labor market. Just as some flowers remain unsold in a decentralized market, so, too, will there always be some unemployment in a decentralized labor market. Workers will always be looking for jobs for a variety of reasons: some will have been fired, some will be looking for better jobs, and some — their days as students having come to an end — will be looking for a first job. Thus, as in the flower market, some unemployment is consistent with equilibrium.

It is unfortunate that this level of unemployment, which we take merely to be the rate consistent with steady-state equilibrium, has been named the *natural* rate of unemployment, suggesting that nothing can change it. To see that this is not the case, consider the effects of the level of support to state employment agencies. If these agencies are well funded and staffed, unemployed workers who avail themselves of their services may require less time to search out a new job; with their assistance, employed workers seeking a better job may be able to avoid quitting their current job to engage in full-time job seeking. Thus, subsidizing the search process can reduce the natural rate of unemployment.

Shocks in an economy with sticky wages

Because the labor market is analogous to the decentralized flower market, our earlier analysis carries over and we can quickly summarize the implications of sticky wages for the labor market. If wages are sticky, anything which "shocks" the demand for or supply of labor can cause unemployment in the short run. However this unemployment is only temporary. Over time, as wages adjust, the impact of any shock on the unemployment rate will be played out though, alas, other shocks may intervene before the full adjustment takes place.[5]

The analogy between the flower and labor markets, though almost exact, is not perfectly exact. Because the labor market is such a large sector of the economy, we cannot rest on a partial equilibrium analysis but must consider the relationship between

---

[5] As in the case of the flower market, one can label an economy with unemployment in the labor market as a *disequilibrium economy* or as an economy with an *umemployment equilibrium*. Some would also distinguish between *voluntary* and *involuntary* unemployment, arguing that unemployment above the natural rate includes people who are involuntarily unemployed.

unemployment and the rest of the economy. Moreover, since workers are more important than a few wilting flowers, we are concerned with what can be done to speed the process of adjustment in the labor market. These questions are the subject of the next chapter.

PROBLEMS FOR CHAPTER 16

1. Suppose the demand curve for flowers shifts to the right. Trace through the consequences for price and quantity adjustment in both the centralized and decentralized markets.

2. If vendors in the decentralized flower market first went from door to door taking orders for flowers before cutting them, there would never be any surpluses of flowers. Would this system be more desirable? Why or why not?

3. What would be the effects of a government-funded dial-a-vendor program for the flower market (i.e., you could telephone for a flower vendor to come to your home) on the normal rate of surplus in the flower market?

4. Suppose an economy has an unemployment rate below the natural rate.
   a. Suggest one way in which the unemployment rate could have fallen below the natural rate.
   b. Assuming that the economy is subjected to no surprises and that it returns to steady-state equilibrium, draw a graph illustrating how the path of the unemployment rate might look over time.
   c. Using this graph, illustrate the effects on the time path of unemployment of
      i.   a liberalization of unemployment compensation,
      ii. an increase in the minimum wage,
      iii. an increase in the level of funding for state employment agencies.

17

The impact of monetary and fiscal policies on unemployment in the short run and the long

IN THE PREVIOUS CHAPTER we saw how unemployment could arise from the failure of the price of labor to adjust immediately to its new equilibrium value after some unexpected shift in the demand or supply of labor. In this chapter we shall extend our basic neoclassical model to allow for sticky wage rates, and hence unemployment, of this kind. The resulting modified neoclassical model turns out to have many of the properties commonly discussed under the heading of "Keynesian economics." In fact, if we look only at how an economy evolves immediately following unexpected shock, the modified neoclassical model and the standard Keynesian model give virtually identical qualitative results. (This is true despite the seemingly substantial differences in the forms of the consumption and investment functions in the two models.) In particular, both models lead to the conclusion that inflation brought about by government policies may be able to reduce the level of unemployment in the short run.

Important differences between the two models begin to arise, however, as soon as attention is directed to longer intervals and to anticipated as opposed to unanticipated inflation. Barring additional shocks, a neoclassical economy eventually returns by itself to a long-run growth path with unemployment reduced to its natural or "frictional minimum" level. That level may or may not be socially optimal, but no amount of inflation can reduce it permanently once that inflation has become fully anticipated. By contrast, some versions of the Keynesian model assume a permanent trade-off between the rate of unemployment and the inflation rate, even if the inflation is fully anticipated.

Before considering these issues about the long-run behavior of the economy, we shall first turn to an analysis of the short-run response to a shock where, as noted above, the two approaches yield much the same results.

SHORT-RUN EQUILIBRIUM WITH STICKY WAGE RATES

Our tool for analyzing the joint price-level and employment effects of government policies in the short run will be a four-panel diagram of the kind pictured in Figure 17–1.[1] (After we have walked through one illustration, we will be able to cut back to a two-panel version.)

The upper left panel (A) in Figure 17–1 shows the combinations of the current price level and of the real interest rate that equilibrate demand and supply for current output and for real balances *for a given expected rate of inflation.*[2] The curves labelled M and Y in the upper left quadrant are essentially the same as the M and Y curves used earlier in Chapters 11 and 14. The only difference is that now we must construct them with due allowance for any unemployment that may be present at the indicated combinations of P and r. Precisely how the allowance is to be made will be somewhat easier to explain if we first put the whole apparatus through its paces and show how an equilibrium for the economy as a whole is established in the presence of a sticky money wage rate.

The upper center panel (B) shows the relation between the current price level and the current real wage rate *for a given value of the current money wage rate* w_0. Since the real wage rate, by defi-

---

[1] The term *short-run equilibrium* is to be taken in its analytical sense, not its calendar-time sense. That is, an analytical short run is the period over which certain variables (such as expectations of future rates of inflation) are taken as given. A long-run equilibrium must show what happens when these variables, too, are allowed to change.

[2] Remember that the demand for real balances depends on the nominal and not on the real rate of interest. Since we are taking next period's expected inflation rate as given, there is a one-for-one correspondence between real and nominal rates in this analysis.

FIGURE 17-1. Equilibrium in the short run with sticky money wage rates

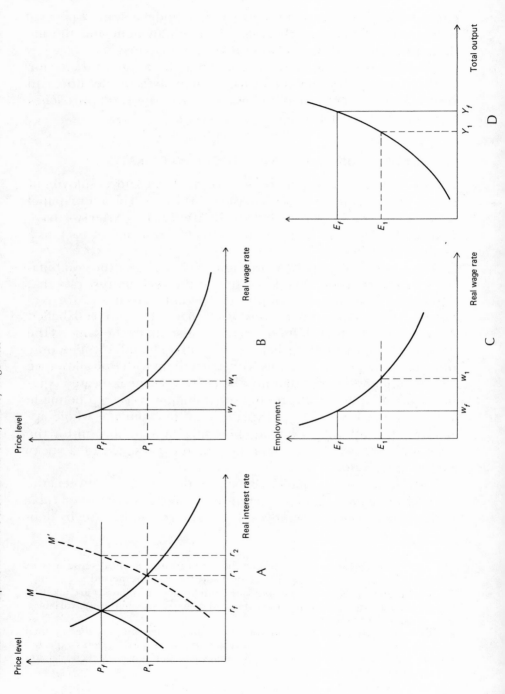

nition, is just the money wage rate divided by the price level, the function pictured in this quadrant is necessarily always a rectangular hyperbola, though its position will shift if the value of the wage rate shifts.

The lower center panel (C) shows the relation between real wage rates and employment *for the given current capital stock.* Although this graph may look new, it is really an old acquaintance. It is just a marginal-productivity-of-labor diagram (with axes reversed) of the kind first encountered back in Chapter 3 when we were exploring the factors governing the demand for capital and labor in the setting of the neoclassical growth model.[3]

The final panel on the lower right (D) shows the relation between output and employment in the short run for the given capital stock. It, too, is an old acquaintance, being just a production function with one fixed factor and one variable factor of the kind first encountered in the opening chapter.

The solid M and Y curves show the full-employment solution that would have been achieved had no unexpected shocks been delivered. The values P_f, r_f, w_f, E_f and Y_f are the corresponding full-employment values for the key variables. The dotted curve labeled M' is intended to represent some unanticipated deflationary disturbance to the supply of or demand for money balances such as a cut in the quantity of outside money. (For simplicity in telling this part of the story, we shall ignore any repercussions on the Y curve.) As before, the auctioneer can reestablish equilibrium in the output and money sectors by appropriate movements in P and r, in this case by a rise in r to r_1 and a fall in P to P_1. If wage rates adjusted instantaneously they would fall in proportion to the decline in P, leaving real wages and employment unchanged at their full-employment levels. But for the reasons described in the previous chapter, money wages may not adjust to this extent immediately. If so, and if the money wage is

---

[3] The proposition that a decline in unemployment requires a fall in the real wage rate — at least relative to trend — was one piece of the neoclassical analysis that Keynes himself wholeheartedly accepted. In fact, he warmly defended it against one of the first critical attacks on his *General Theory* — an attack delivered by a then brash young labor economist named John Dunlop (currently the brash head of the Cost of Living Council and chief price-controller for the U. S. economy). Subsequent research has been able neither to establish the empirical validity of the propostion beyond cavil nor to provide a convincing and accepted explanation of why not.

$w_0 > w_f P_1$, then real wages will rise above the full employment level to w_1 as shown in panel B. Caught between a lower than expected money price for their output and sticky wage rates for their labor inputs, entrepreneurs cut back the volume of labor services they demand to E_1 (panel C), leaving the portion of the labor force represented by the distance $E_f E_1$ unable to find work at the going wage rate. With only E_1 workers employed, output falls to Y_1 (as shown in panel D), leaving a gap between actual and potential output equal to $Y_1 Y_f$.[4]

How the *Y* and *M* curves are affected by the possibility of unemployment

So much, for the moment, for the mechanism connecting the price level and the level of employment in the short run in a world in which wage rates do not fly instantly to their market-clearing equilibrium values. We have traced out that mechanism, it will be recalled, using *Y* and *M* curves of precisely the same kind as in our earlier full-employment cases. What kind of changes in the *Y* and *M* curves must be made when stickiness of wages is introduced and unemployment becomes a possibility that households must take into account? The answer is that the possibility of unemployment will certainly affect the *positions* of the *Y* and *M* curves, but it will not, in general, affect their direction of slope.

To show this, we will again employ the convenient expository fiction of the auctioneer though he is now less powerful: he cannot now change the money wage rate. Suppose that the auctioneer had found one point on the *Y* curve such as the point (P_2, r_2) in Figure 17–2. What change in *P* would he have to make if he were to try a lower interest rate such as r_1? In the full-employment cases considered earlier the answer was clear: he would have to raise *P*. The reason was that the lower interest rate served to raise the demand for current output. By raising the

---

[4] There is no contradiction in having both the higher real wage and the higher interest rate pictured in Figure 17–1 at the same time. Remember that the counterpart to the current real wage is the current rental rate for capital. That rate will definitely fall in the short run as the real wage rate rises. But the interest rate, as we explained in Chapter 6, is based on *next* period's expected real rental rate. For that rate to rise requires only that there be capital shallowing, i.e., that investment be so reduced by the deflationary shock that the capital stock grows more slowly than expected employment.

price level, however, the auctioneer would cut real wealth by cutting the real value of the stock of outside money balances. He would also thereby transfer wealth from creditors (mostly elderly) to debtors (mostly young). Both effects would tend to cut back consumption and to offset the additional demand generated by the lower interest rate. The equilibrating point would thus be one like (P_1, r_1), implying our downward-sloping form for the Y curve.

If the money wage floor were such that unemployment would exist at the initial price level P_2, then the auctioneer would have two additional effects to contend with after cutting the interest rate to r_1. First, by raising the price level he could lower the real wage rate and thereby increase the current output of goods and services. This would clearly help him in balancing off the extra demand created by the lower value of r. But the higher level of output and lower level of unemployment would mean higher income and wealth for the typical household and this would add to the auctioneer's problem by increasing the demand for current consumption.

Under normal circumstances, however, the auctioneer can be reasonably confident that any increase in consumption demand

FIGURE 17–2

Derivation of equilibrium Y curve

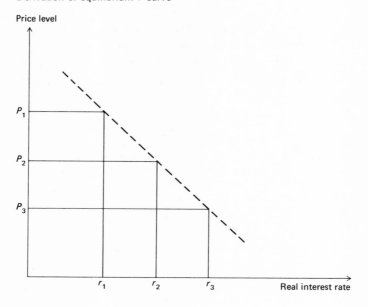

from reduced unemployment will be less than the increase in output. How much less will depend both on the parameters of the consumption function and on the expectations as to future income levels that the current increase in income gives rise to. In the case of our life cycle model of consumption, for example, we know that for an individual of age i, expected to retire at age 65 and to live until age 80, the marginal propensity to consume out of current wealth would be $\frac{1}{81 - i}$. Even if each \$1 increase in current income is expected to be a permanent increase of \$1 for every future year in the labor force, wealth will increase by at most $(66 - i)$ dollars, and normally by substantially less than that because of the discounting of the future payments. Thus consumption for no individual would increase by more than $\frac{66 - i}{81 - i}$ for each \$1 of additional current income. Only in the unlikely event that the increase in current income actually led to a much more than proportional increase in expected future earnings would the auctioneer find that raising the price level after cutting the interest rate would intensify rather than mitigate the market for current output.

In sum, just as in the earlier full-employment case, the auctioneer will find himself trading off lower interest rates for higher price levels and vice versa, though, of course the amount of the trade-off necessary to restore an equilibrium (or, equivalently, the slope of the Y curve), may well be different in the two cases.[5] The demonstration that the M curve, too, retains the same direction of slope despite the presence of unemployment is sufficiently similar that we leave it to you as an exercise for testing your understanding of the model.[6]

---

[5] The steepness of the Y curve will also depend, of course, on how rapidly consumption and investment respond to changes in P and r. These are questions for econometric model builders to wrestle with. Since we are concerned only with the *qualitative* properties of the system, however, we can safely leave to more advanced courses discussion of the problems of estimating the elasticities of the Y and M curves.

[6] As with the Y curve, the M curve can be made to slope in the wrong (i.e., in the destabilizing) direction if expectations are sufficiently perverse. If, for example, any lowering of the price level this period by the auctioneer were to lead to expectations of even more substantial falls in the next period then η_e falls; and if it fell far enough, the auctioneer might have to raise the real interest rate to keep the demand for money from exceeding the supply. In the literature,

A simplified picture of the short-run equilibrium

Having probed in some detail into the mechanisms of short-run adjustment in the presence of sticky wages, we can now safely simplify our graphical portrayal of the process. In particular, we can condense all of the steps in the last three panels of Figure 17–1 into a single panel showing the relation between the price level and the level of total output. The resulting two-panel version of the same events as in Figure 17–1 is shown in Figure 17–3. If, in the course of the subsequent discussion, you should want to make or check a point involving any of the variables now suppressed, just reverse the procedure.[7]

FIGURE 17–3

A simpler representation of short-run equilibrium with sticky wage rates

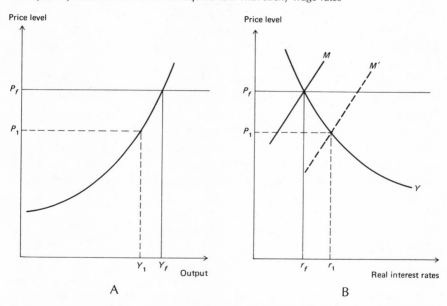

A   B

---

this case is sometimes called the case of greater-than-unitary elasticity of expectations with respect to prices. Our assumption here and earlier that η_e is independent of the current value of P — an assumption equivalent to unitary elasticity of expectations — effectively rules out this perverse case.

[7] For those with some previous exposure to the literature of macroeconomics, we may note that the scenario in Figure 17–3 could be converted into the standard Hicksian *IS-LM* diagram for the case of rigid wages and flexible prices by changing the labels on the axes in the panels and making the corresponding inversions of the functions. That is, the vertical axis of the first and second panels would become the output axis and the horizontal axis in the first panel

Short-run equilibrium with a sticky price level

For reasons discussed in the previous chapter, we have chosen to take the labor market as the one most likely to adjust sluggishly to unanticipated shifts in supply or demand. The apparatus used for analyzing that case, however, can readily be adapted to deal with sluggish response in either of the other two equilibrating variables, P and r. The only difference will be in the location of the resulting excess supply.

Suppose, for example, that the wage level were perfectly flexible but that the price level were sticky.[8] The downward shift in the M curve in Figure 17–1 would now have no effect on the price level; hence real wages, total employment and total output would remain at their full-employment values. To balance the money market at a price level of P_f, the (flexible) interest rate will have to move to r_2. Since that value is higher than r_f, consumption and investment demand will be below their full-employment values. The auctioneer, in short, will now be unable to clear the market for current output.

The disequilibrium is pictured in Figure 17–4. The vertical line at Y_f is the output produced. The curve labeled $D(r_f)$ shows the demand for output as a function of P when the interest rate is r_f. The point of intersection of the two curves thus represents the point (P_f, r_f) in the Y curve of panel A of Figure 17–1. After the unanticipated shift in the M curve, the interest rate rises to r_2 and the demand curve for output in Figure 17–4 falls to $D(r_2)$. With

---

—the P-axis, while the horizontal axis of the second panel would remain the r-axis. The Y curve in the second panel would be replaced by an IS curve which would show the equilibrium combinations of r and Y in the market for current output (with due allowance for the particular value of P that would rule at that value of Y); and the M curve would be replaced by an LM curve showing the corresponding equilibrium pairs in the money market. The ultimate equilibrium values for Y, P, r and all the other variables will be exactly the same, of course, under either representation.

Although the Hicksian version gives the same answer as our version for cases involving unemployment, the fact that P enters only implicitly into the IS and LM curves makes it much less suitable for dealing with problems of inflation and the Quantity Theory under full employment conditions (as in Chapters 11 through 14). Our version permits both kinds of cases to be handled with essentially the same apparatus.

[8] Note that the case to be considered here is not the same as the fixed-price case in standard IS-LM analysis. We are taking the price level as fixed, but wages as completely flexible.

FIGURE 17–4
The supply and demand for output with a sticky price level

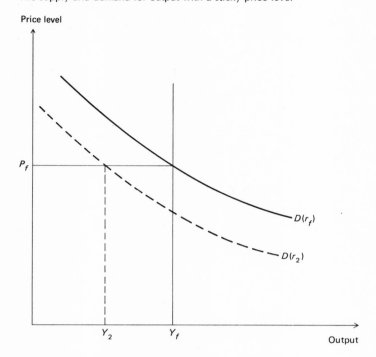

the price level holding at P_f, the amount of output that can be sold falls to Y_2. The distance Y_2Y_f thus represents unplanned inventory accumulation by the producing firms.[9]

Sticky real rates of interest and the liquidity trap

To see what may happen when the real interest rate resists downward pressure, suppose that an unanticipated deflationary shock has been dealt to the economy and that we can represent it as an autonomous downward shift in the Y curve as pictured in Figure 17–5. (The outcome of the story to follow would have been the same if the shock had come through the M curve, but the story itself is somewhat harder to tell. It is perhaps also useful to vary the deflationary scenario a bit at this point to avoid

---

[9] Though output sold is less than output produced, the double-entry national accounts must always remain in balance. The inventory accumulation is recorded as "investment."

FIGURE 17–5
A deflationary shock from the Y curve

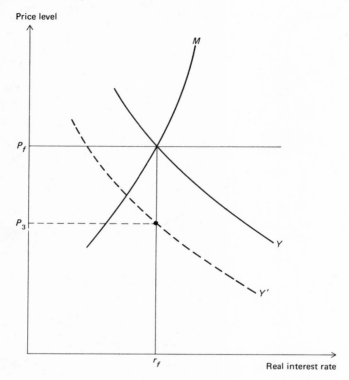

giving the impression that the money sector is the only source of deflationary disturbances. The relative importance of monetary disturbances as opposed to autonomous shifts in the real sector in explaining business fluctuations is still very much in dispute. There is not even yet a concensus among economists as to the role of real and monetary factors in precipitating [and prolonging] the Great Depression of 1929!) If prices are flexible, the auctioneer can maintain equilibrium in the market for current output by moving the price level to P_3. But he can no longer maintain equilibrium in the monetary sector.

The situation he faces is pictured in Figure 17–6. The vertical line at M_0 shows the original supply of real balances and the curve $D(P_0)$ shows the original demand for real balances as a function of r when the price level is P_0. After the auctioneer has moved the

FIGURE 17–6

The supply and demand for real balances with a sticky interest rate

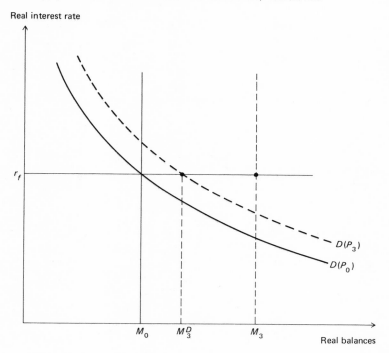

price level down to P_3, the stock of real balances will have increased to M_3. The demand for real balances will also have risen somewhat (because the rise in the real value of money holdings raises wealth) but, for the reasons discussed earlier in Chapter 11, the rise in demand at the given interest rate will be less than the rise in the supply. The public will simply have to hold more real money balances (as measured by the distance M_3^D) and less real earning assets in the short run than indicated by its unconstrained demand curve $D(P_3)$.

You may be wondering why the individuals with the unwanted real balances don't simply rush out and bid for real earning assets (thereby driving real interest rates down). The answer is that under normal circumstances they certainly would. There is, however, one special set of conditions, pictured in Figure 17–7, in which no such straightforward resolution may be possible. Suppose, for example, that r^* the equilibrating value of the real rate

FIGURE 17–7
The Liquidity Trap

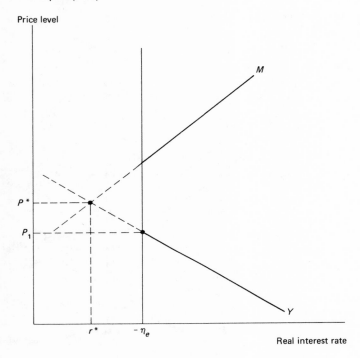

of interest in Figure 17–7, were, say, 2 percent. And suppose further that the public were expecting a rate of price inflation next period η_e of −3 percent. That is, they were expecting prices to *fall* by 3 percent. Then no one would want to hold real assets. An investor could earn the higher real rate of return of 3 percent merely by keeping his assets in cash. The only way the auctioneer can get people to hold real capital is to raise its real return to 3 percent—as indicated by the value $-\eta_e$ in Figure 17–7. The equilibrium combination (P^*, r^*) is thus no longer possible and the price level must fall to P_1. This solution would still leave an imbalance in the money sector of the kind pictured in Figure 17–6 (and by the vertical segment of the M curve in Figure 17–7). But remember that, by Fisher's Law, the nominal rate of interest and hence the cost of holding money must be zero (since $r = -\eta_e$). Hence the auctioneer feels no pressure from the public to rid themselves of the extra real balances created by his adjustment of the price level. They are, after all, losing nothing by holding these extra real money balances rather than other assets, real or nominal. (In this connection, recall the discussion of "excess reserves" in Chapter 15. Here as there, however, the nominal interest rate must virtually be zero before these "corner solutions" can arise.)

A disequilibrium of this sort has come to be called the *Keynesian Liquidity Trap* because Keynes was the first to call attention to it. His awareness of this possibility helps explain, among other things, his much-cited observation that saving and investment were two distinct activities in a money-using economy and could not be adequately represented by the kind of saving/investment function of neoclassical real models. When prices are expected to fall—or as Keynes would have put it, when the public is "bearish"—investment in cash becomes an alternative to investing in real productive capital.[10]

We have now traced through the consequences of stickiness in each of the three equilibrating variables taken separately. We could go on, in principle, to consider cases in which two or more were sticky at the same time and hence in which we had both unemployment and unintended inventory accumulation occurring simultaneously. Fortunately, however, many of the most critical policy issues (and controversies) can be quite adequately explored within the context of the simple model in which wages and only wages are assumed to be sticky.

FISCAL AND MONETARY POLICIES FOR REDUCING UNEMPLOYMENT: THE CONVENTIONAL WISDOM

If an unanticipated deflationary shock can cause unemployment, it would seem natural to suppose that an unanticipated shock in the other direction might alleviate it. But how are such

---

[10] Keynes gave a somewhat different explanation for the emergence of a trap than that given here. His relied more on a presumed speculative demand for money in anticipation of an expected future fall in the price of long-term bonds. The trap pictured in Figure 17–7 could arise, however, even if all bonds have a one period maturity as has been assumed throughout the course of this book.

offsetting shocks to be administered? That problem has been a major preoccupation of macroeconomists since the appearance of Keynes's *General Theory* in 1936.

The effects of an unanticipated increase in the money supply

The analysis in previous chapters suggests a number of possible devices. Suppose, for example, that the government were to print up and distribute newly printed money or, equivalently, that the central bank were to carry out an unexpected open-market purchase of outstanding government bonds.[11] To restore equilibrium in the money market requires either a higher price level (to cut back the real supply of balances) or a lower real interest rate (to expand the demand), or some combination of the two. In terms of Figure 17–8, this means a shift of the M curve up and to the left from M to M'. At the same time, the substitution of non-interest-bearing money for interest-bearing debt has reduced the present value of the public's expected future tax liabilities and thus increased its perceived net wealth. The combined effect of these two shifts must therefore be to raise the equilibrium price level from P_0 to P_1 and hence to raise the equilibrium level of output from Y_0 to Y_1, closer to its full-employment value at Y_f.

Although the scenario just presented is a straightforward enough extension of previous results, it highlights two important points about monetary theory and policy that have been the subject of much misunderstanding. The first point to keep in mind is that the way an economy responds to an unexpected change in its money supply is basically the same, whether or not there happens to be some unemployment. The beginning part of the story in Figure 17–8, involving the Y and M curves, is the same as the story we told earlier in Chapter 11 about the unexpected doubling of the money supply on Christmas Eve. The only difference is that now money wages do not rise quite as fast as prices, and some of the unanticipated inflationary pressure serves to raise employment and output.

The second point to keep in mind is that a change in the money

---

[11] If you have forgotten why these two are equivalent, re-read footnote 6 in Chapter 11 and page 299 in Chapter 15.

supply is *not* to be identified with a shift solely in the M curve. Changes in the stock of outside money also affect the Y curve directly, no matter whether the money is injected by transfer payments (as in our Christmas Eve parable) or by monetizing some government debt and thereby reducing the present value of future taxes. Consequently the sharp distinction that is sometimes made between monetary policy (supposedly affecting only the M curve) and fiscal policy (supposedly working through the Y curve) has no foundation in economic theory.[12]

The effects of unanticipated changes in government spending and taxes

We saw earlier in Chapter 14 that unexpected shocks to the price level can be delivered by changing government spending and revenue policies other than just the money tax. Consider, for

FIGURE 17–8

The effects of an unanticipated increase in the money supply

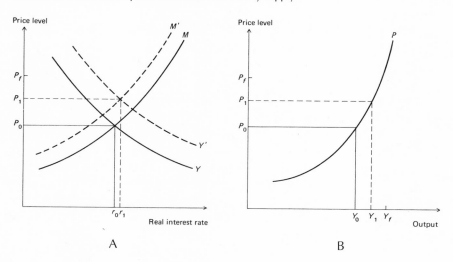

A

B

---

[12] Failure to realize that changes in the money supply must affect the Y curve as well as the M curve is responsible, among other things, for the standard text-book proposition that there are circumstances (notably the Liquidity Trap of Figure 17–7) in which an unanticipated increase in fiat money would exert no upward pressure on the price level.

example, a permanent increase in government spending.[13] Suppose it to be financed either by (*a*) an increase in the wage tax or (*b*) by deficit spending in the year of the increase, with the interest on the debt to be financed in subsequent years by a wage tax. We know from our previous analysis in Chapter 14 that a wage-tax-financed increase in spending will push the *Y* curve to the right to *Y'* and the *M* curve to the left to *M'*, as illustrated in Figure 17–9. Assuming there is no bequest motive, the debt-financed spending increase of case (b) would push the *Y* curve a little bit further to the right to *Y"* and the *M* curve part of the way back to *M"*, lying between the *M* and *M'* curves. In either case, the policies increase output and reduce unemployment in the short run.

The ratio of the increase in output per unit increase in government spending has come to be called a *multiplier*. This term was coined originally by the British economist R. F. Kahn in the 1930s. It was taken up by Keynes and has figured prominently in discussions of government spending ever since.

FIGURE 17–9

Short-run effects of an increase in government spending

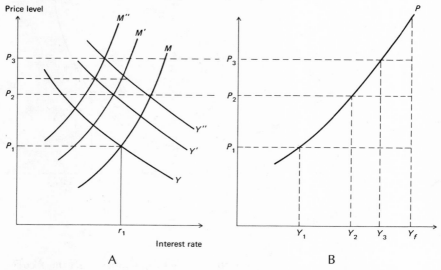

A   B

---

[13] A temporary increase in spending will have much the same effect as a permanent one. Because a permanent increase is the policy considered in Chapter 14, we have chosen to consider it here again to facilitate comparison.

Two types of multiplier can be illustrated with the labels of Figure 17–9. If year 1 government spending increases from G_1 to G_2 and is financed by borrowing, the resultant miltiplier, known as the *expenditure mulitplier,* would be

$$\frac{Y_3 - Y_1}{G_2 - G_1}.$$

If the spending increase is financed by the wage tax, the multiplier, referred to as the *balanced budget multiplier,* would be

$$\frac{Y_2 - Y_1}{G_2 - G_1}.$$

As drawn, the balanced budget multiplier, though smaller than the expenditure multiplier, is positive. But this need not be the case, indeed, we have already seen one scenario in which the balanced budget multiplier may be negative! Suppose the increase in government spending is financed in whole or in part by a tax on interest income. Then, as we saw in Chapter 14, the Y and M curves both shift to the right. And, as Figure 17–10 shows, it is possible that the increased spending so financed will

FIGURE 17–10

A case in which the multiplier is negative

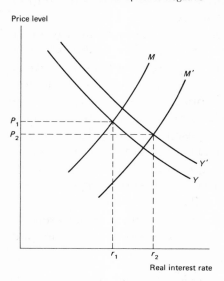

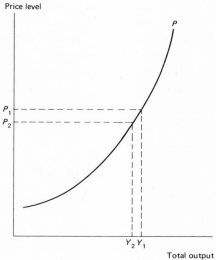

A   B

lower the price level and thereby reduce output and increase unemployment!

THE TROUBLE WITH THE CONVENTIONAL WISDOM

Up to this point our concern has been with the short-run impact of an unanticipated "reflationary" shock delivered after an economy has fallen (or been pushed) into a slump. This focusing on the immediate consequences of a policy action is an expository device with a long history in macroeconomics, but it can give a very misleading picture of the real policy choices unless the subsequent, longer-run consequences are also traced out. Suppose, for example, that the first reflationary shock has not been sufficiently strong and that some unemployment still persists. Can we simply repeat the previous analysis as applied to a second shock? The answer is no. Even if we can legitimately regard the first shock as completely unanticipated, we cannot do so for a second and subsequent shocks. The public must be assumed to learn something, both from what the government says and from what it does.[14]

The anticipation of future reflationary shocks will affect the previous analysis in two ways. First, it will raise the inflation premium component of the nominal interest rate. The higher nominal rate in turn means a higher cost of holding money and hence a smaller demand for real money balances at any given level of P and r. To this extent, therefore, the public's newly-generated inflationary anticipations will create a Friedman surge and thereby reinforce any direct reflationary policies of the government. But the public's inflationary expectations will also affect the money wages that workers demand, and this works in the other direction. Hence any increase in η_e, other things equal, serves to raise the real wage rate and thus to slow down the return to full employment. In terms of Figures 17–8, 17–9, and 17–10, the increase in η_e causes the P curve to shift up and to the left.

The effect of the second-year reflationary policies will therefore depend on the size (and direction) of the gap between the inflation the public expects and the inflation the authorities suc-

---

[14] There will also be changes in the other variables held constant during the short-run analysis, notably the capital stock. The change in expectations of inflation, however, is the crucial one for present purposes.

ceed in producing. If the public has caught on to what the authorities are up to and has anticipated correctly the degree of inflation that the reflationary policies will produce, then there will be no effect on employment whatever. If unemployment goes down under these circumstances, it will be entirely a consequence of the pressure on real wages exerted by the unemployment. The surge in prices caused by the reflationary policies will have been completely negated by the rise in nominal wage demands. If, on the other hand, the public has learned its inflation lesson so well that it actually comes to expect more inflation than the authorities are able or willing to supply, then unemployment may actually increase even in the face of what seem to be expansionary monetary and fiscal policies. The authorities may then face that worst of all nightmares: rising prices and rising unemployment at the same time.

Only in one case, then, would the conventional wisdom about the role of fiscal and monetary policy in reducing unemployment continue to apply. And that, of course, is the case in which the public is somehow fooled into expecting less inflation than actually occurs. The public can sometimes be fooled in this way, as history shows; but, as Lincoln has reminded us, the authorities would be unwise to count on being able to fool the public all the time.

IS THERE A LONG-RUN PHILLIPS CURVE?

The notion that a fully anticipated inflation will have no significant effect on the real variables in the system (including employment) should hardly be surprising. It has been foreshadowed in several earlier contexts where we stressed the distinction between anticipated and unanticipated inflations. As applied to the particular case of unemployment, however, it is by no means the only view that can be found in the literature. Many economists continue to believe that the economy faces a trade-off between the rate of unemployment and the rate of inflation even when that inflation is fully anticipated.

The dynamics of wage adjustment

The difference between their point of view and the one presented above can perhaps best be seen by restating the process of wage adjustment in a more formal way. Recall that in Chapter 16 we represented the process of price adjustment in the case of a decentralized flower market as

(1) $$P_t = P_{t-1}(1 - \lambda(S_{t-1} - S_n))$$

where S_{t-1} was the surplus of unsold flowers on the previous day, S_n·was the "natural" surplus and λ was the speed-of-adjustment coefficient. In the case of the labor market, of course, we speak not of surpluses but of unemployment, and not of prices for labor but of wages for labor. With the appropriate changes in notation, equation (1) as applied to the labor market will thus become

(2) $$w_t = w_{t-1}(1 - \lambda(U_{t-1} - U^n))$$

where U_{t-1} is the fraction of the labor force unemployed in the previous period and U^n the natural rate of unemployment.

Equation (1), and hence its counterpart equation (2), was intended to represent the process of adjustment to a new equilibrium after a once-for-all shock. In a growing economy, however, the equilibrium wage rate will be continually changing over time and equation (2) must be modified accordingly. We know from our earlier analysis, for example, that the equilibrium real wage rate will rise as a result of technological improvement and capital deepening. We have also argued that workers can be expected to mark up their money wage demands to reflect their anticipations of inflation (just as lenders mark up money rates of interest to reflect those same anticipations). Taking these effects into account gives us the following expression as the growth-corrected counterpart to equation (2).

(3) $$w_t = w_{t-1}(1 + \eta_e)(1 + q_e)\left(1 + \left(\frac{\Delta k}{k}\right)_e\right)^\alpha (1 - \lambda(U_{t-1} - U^n))$$

where q_e is the expected rate of technological change, $\left(\frac{\Delta k}{k}\right)_e$ is the expected change in the capital/effective labor ratio, and α is the capital coefficient in our Cobb-Douglas production function.

Equation (3) can also be written in terms of the real wage rate. Dividing both sides by $P_t \equiv (1 + \eta)P_{t-1}$, (3) becomes

(4) $$w_t = w_{t-1}\left(\frac{1 + \eta_e}{1 + \eta}\right)(1 + q_e)\left(1 + \left(\frac{\Delta k}{k}\right)_e\right)^\alpha (1 - \lambda(U_{t-1} - U^n))$$

Note particularly the way in which the inflation terms enter. If actual inflation η is exactly equal to expected inflation η_e, then the term $\left(\dfrac{1 + \eta_e}{1 + \eta}\right)$ becomes unity and the real wage rate reflects only real factors. Only if η differs from η_e does the rate of inflation affect real wages and hence employment.

The Phillips curve

Those holding the view that a trade-off is possible between the rates of unemployment and inflation even when the inflation is fully anticipated are essentially arguing that money wage levels, perhaps aided by official jawboning or wage guidelines, will not rise in full proportion to the expected rise in the price level. They would argue that our money wage adjustment equation (3) should be written as

$$(5) \quad w_t = w_{t-1}(1 + \eta_e)^{\gamma}(1 + q_e)\left(1 + \left(\frac{\Delta k}{k}\right)_e\right)^{\alpha}(1 - \lambda(U_{t-1} - U^n))$$

with $\gamma < 1$ instead of $\gamma = 1$ as in our version. The corresponding equation for the real wage rate would then be

$$(6) \quad w_t = w_{t-1}\left(\frac{1 + \eta_e}{1 + \eta}\right)^{\gamma}(1 + \eta)^{\gamma-1}(1 + q_e)(1 +$$
$$\left(\frac{\Delta k}{k}\right)_e^{\alpha}(1 - \lambda(U_{t-1} - U^n))$$

Note that when inflationary expectations are exactly fulfilled, so that $\eta = \eta_e$, equation (6) becomes

$$(7) \quad w_t = w_{t-1}\left(\frac{1}{1 + \eta}\right)^{1-\gamma}(1 + q_e)\left(1 + \left(\frac{\Delta k}{k}\right)_e\right)^{\alpha}(1 - \lambda(U_{t-1} - U^n))$$

The change in the real wage rate has thus become a function of the actual rate of inflation. More inflation always means lower real wages and more employment.

If equation (7) is valid, and changes in real wages really depend on changes in the price level, even when fully anticipated, then there is no single natural level of unemployment around which actual unemployment fluctuates in the long run. This implies that a society could hope to maintain virtually any long-run target level for unemployment that it chose, provided only that it could maintain the appropriate rate of inflation. That level is implicit in equation (7) but can be made explicit with a little re-arrangement as

(8) $$U^s = U^n + \frac{1}{\lambda}[1 - (1 + \eta)^{1-\gamma}]$$

where U^s is the steady-state level of unemployment.

A graphical representation of equation (8) is shown as the solid line in Figure 17–11. Curves such as this, showing the presumed trade-off between the rates of unemployment and inflation, have come to be called *Phillips curves* after the New Zealand economist A. W. Phillips who was among the first to attempt estimation from historical data. Strictly speaking, the curve pictured should be called a *long-run* Phillips curve since it assumes that the rate of inflation has come to be fully anticipated. By contrast, the P

FIGURE 17–11
Two views of inflation and unemployment in the long run

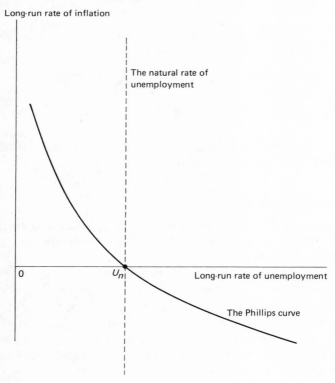

curves in Figures 17–8, 17–9 and 17–10 can be thought of as essentially *short-run* Phillips curves showing the relation between unemployment and unanticipated inflation.[15]

Much of the controversy over fiscal and monetary policy among economists in recent years has, in effect, been over whether a long-run Phillips curve does or does not exist. Those who believe it does exist have been urging the monetary and budgetary authorities not to set so high a premium on avoiding inflation that they saddle the economy with a high level of unemployment and the avoidable waste and distress that such high levels entail. Those who do not believe that a long-run Phillips curve exists have argued that merely agreeing to accept a high-rate of inflation would do nothing to relieve unemployment in the long run. Once any initial surprise had worn off, the economy would drift back to its natural level of unemployment (the dotted line in Figure 17–11). To reduce unemployment below that level over the long pull would require not more budgetary or monetary stimulus but entirely different types of measures. Such measures would be directed to improving the efficiency of the labor market and to removing various man-made and natural obstacles to the matching of buyers and sellers in the market.

After many years of controversy the long-run Phillips curve has achieved a status somewhat like that of the Loch Ness monster. The skeptics, ourselves included, regard it as an entirely mythical beast. Many others, however, believe firmly in its existence. A few even claim to have seen it. But no one has yet come up with a believable photograph!

PROBLEMS FOR CHAPTER 17

1. Show that the M curve in Figure 17–1 is upward sloping.
2. Using the assumptions of problems 3, 4, 5 and 6 of Chapter 11 about

---

[15] Another important distinction between the long-run and short-run curves is that the long-run curve cannot be derived from any "rational behavior" model of economic choice. It violates the fundamental homogeneity property that we earlier called attention to in connection with the cash balances parables of Chapter 9. Another way economists sometimes put it is to say that the long-run Phillips curve assumes a permanent *money illusion,* in the sense of a permanent inability to see that a higher money wage rate is actually a lower real wage if the price level rises faster than the wage rate.

the Y and M curves, show the effects on the price level, the interest rate, and unemployment (if there are sticky money wages) of

   i.   an unanticipated increase in the money supply

  ii.   an increase in government spending financed by borrowing.

3. Using the Y and M curves, show the effect on unemployment of a cut in the tax on wage income, assuming there is no bequest motive. How would your answer change if the economy were populated by Immortal Consumers?

4. Consider an economy in steady-state equilibrium which has sticky money wages. Initially the country's unemployment rate is at the natural rate. A decision is made to halve permanently the annual rate of growth of the money supply.

   a.   Using the Y and M curves, show what effect this will have in year 1, assuming that the change in policy comes as a complete surprise.

   b.   How would your answer to *a* change if the policy is coupled with

      i.   a temporary 25-percent cut in the personal income tax rate?

     ii.   a special one-shot grant to persons over 65? (Remember that old people also hold money.)

5. Using equation (4), show the effects of unemployment of

   i.   an unexpected surge in the size of the labor force,

  ii.   a flood which destroys part of a country's capital stock,

 iii.   a sudden burst of technological innovation.

6. Suppose LOSER (of Chapter 6) had sticky real wages governed by equation (4). What would the wage floor have been in LOSER in year 1? Year 2? What would have been the unemployment rate in year 1? Year 2?

   Hint: Assume throughout that $\eta_e = \eta$, $U^n = 0$, and that $\lambda = .2$. The unemployment rate in any year can be calculated by

$$U_t = (w_t/w_t^f)^{1/a} - 1,$$

where w_t^f = full employment wage rate in year t. Note also that $(.85)^{.3} = .951$, $(.97)^{1/.3} = .904$.

Bibliography for
section five

A bibliography on unemployment naturally starts with

Keynes, J. M. *The General Theory of Employment, Interest, and Money.* New York: Harcourt, Brace, 1936.

The structure of an economy with unemployment is further discussed in

Hicks, J. R. "Mr. Keynes and the 'Classics': A Suggested Interpretation." *Econometrica,* April 1937.

Modigliani, Franco. "Liquidity Preference and the Theory of Interest and Money." *Econometrica,* January 1944.

———. "Liquidity Preference." *International Encyclopedia of the Social Sciences.* New York: Macmillan and Free Press, 1968.

Klein, Lawrence R. *The Keynesian Revolution.* New York: Macmillan, 1947.

A modern reinterpretation of Keynes is

Leijonhufvud, Axel. *On Keynesian Economics and the Economics of Keynes.* Oxford: Oxford University Press, 1968.

The microeconomic foundations of disequilibrium in the labor market are discussed in

Phelps, E. S. et al. *Microeconomic Foundations of Employment and Inflation Theory.* New York: W. W. Norton, 1970.

Stigler, George J. "Information in the Labor Market." *Journal of Political Economy,* October 1962.

Studies in what has become known as the Phillips curve have their source in

Phillips, A. W. "The Relationship Between the Rate of Unemployment and Money Wage Rates, 1861–1957." *Economica,* November 1958.

A clear statement of the position that there is no long-run relationship between inflation and unemployment is found in Milton Friedman's presidential address to the American Economic Association:

Friedman, Milton. "The Role of Monetary Policy." *American Economic Review,* March 1968.

James Tobin's presidential address is intended in part to be a response to Friedman:

Tobin, James. "Inflation and Unemployment." *American Economic Review,* March 1972.

The empirical literature on the Phillips curve is enormous. For a sample, see

Lucas, Robert E., and Rapping, Leonard A. "Real Wages, Employment and Inflation." *Journal of Political Economy,* Sept./Oct. 1969.

Perry, George L. "Inflation and Unemployment." In *Savings and Residential Financing, 1970 Conference Proceedings.* Chicago: U. S. Savings and Loan League, 1970.

Rapping, Leonard A. "The Trade-off Between Employment and Prices" in *Savings and Residential Financing, 1970 Conference Proceedings.* Chicago: U. S. Savings and Loan League, 1970.

index

Index